CYBERSECURITY FOR CONNECTED MEDICAL DEVICES

CYBERSECURITY FOR CONNECTED MEDICAL DEVICES

ARNAB RAY

Academic Press is an imprint of Elsevier
125 London Wall, London EC2Y 5AS, United Kingdom
525 B Street, Suite 1650, San Diego, CA 92101, United States
50 Hampshire Street, 5th Floor, Cambridge, MA 02139, United States
The Boulevard, Langford Lane, Kidlington, Oxford OX5 1GB, United Kingdom

Notices

Knowledge and best practice in this field are constantly changing. As new research and experience broaden our understanding, changes in research methods, professional practices, or medical treatment may become necessary.

Practitioners and researchers must always rely on their own experience and knowledge in evaluating and using any information, methods, compounds, or experiments described herein. In using such information or methods they should be mindful of their own safety and the safety of others, including parties for whom they have a professional responsibility.

To the fullest extent of the law, neither the Publisher nor the authors, contributors, or editors, assume any liability for any injury and/or damage to persons or property as a matter of products liability, negligence or otherwise, or from any use or operation of any methods, products, instructions, or ideas contained in the material herein.

Library of Congress Cataloging-in-Publication Data

A catalog record for this book is available from the Library of Congress

British Library Cataloguing-in-Publication Data

A catalogue record for this book is available from the British Library

ISBN: 978-0-12-818262-8

For information on all Academic Press publications visit our website at https://www.elsevier.com/books-and-journals

Publisher: Mara Conner
Editorial Project Manager: Fernanda A. Oliveira
Production Project Manager: Debasish Ghosh
Cover Designer: Christian J. Bilbow

Typeset by TNQ Technologies

To Anahita

Contents

Preface

When I was contacted by my publisher to explore the possibility of writing a book on medical device cybersecurity, the first question I asked myself was "When was the last time I read a technical book?"

I couldn't remember.

When I have a technical question, I read research papers, look through standards, wade through the net reading StackExchange, Wikipedia, Medium, or anything else a Google search throws up. Usually, I find my answer without needing to open a book. This led me to wonder: in this day and age, why even bother to write a book on a technical topic, that too, on a moving target like cybersecurity, when there are so many great resources online, continually updated, free of cost, available at the click of a mouse?

Then I started doing some online research, putting myself in the shoes of someone new to medical device cybersecurity, trying to find answers to common questions someone in Systems Engineering or Quality or Clinical Engineering might have. Finding these answers online was much more difficult than I thought it would be, sometimes to the point of being virtually impossible. While there were excellent resources for understanding concepts of cryptography, there was very little available in terms of how to apply them for medical devices; the details were all there, but not the context in which to use them. Different regulatory agencies across the world had published well-thought-out guidance for cybersecurity, and they more or less prescribed the same things, except they used different words and different concepts, and there was nothing online that compressed all the best practices into one simple "Here's what you could do." Comprehensive cybersecurity organizational standards have been written by experts at the National Institute of Standards and Technology (NIST), and they had been written for general purpose applicability, but then there was really very little available online that adapted these general frameworks for a typical medical device company. Standards like AAMI TIR 57 and AAMI TIR97 and ISO14971 and documents like "Medical Device and Health IT Joint Security Plan" came the closest in terms of providing tailored answers, but because these were standards and industry guidance, they have to be general enough to accommodate all solutions, whereas sometimes, as a practitioner with a deadline that passed yesterday, you are looking for *one workable solution*, rather than all of them.

The word "workable" in the previous sentence needs some explaining. It has been often said that the great is the enemy of the good. The reason why we chose to work in the healthcare industry is because of its mission: to help people live longer and healthier lives. If the pursuit of the very best cybersecurity solution creates unnecessary delay in the shipping of a life-saving or life-sustaining product, or makes it no longer economically viable to produce, we have lost track of the reason why we get up the morning. This is why the word "workable" is so critical—we need to design solutions that ensure such that (1) patients are reasonably protected from cybersecurity threats, (2) the cybersecurity design of the product will satisfy cybersecurity expectations of regulators and customers, and (3) project timelines and budgets are met.

This book focuses on workability. As an example, let us consider the problem of threat modeling for medical devices. There are multiple ways of doing threat modeling. Each of these threat modeling methodologies is expansive enough to each have a book devoted to it. If I were to present you a survey of all threat modeling approaches and leave the choice of what to use to the reader, then I believe I would have provided very little incremental value over that which already exists. Instead, I describe, only one *integrated way of doing systems and software/hardware threat modeling*. This method, I have found from my experience, scales well to multiple systems—embedded, mobile, app, cloud, and server. It has satisfied regulatory expectations, and has kept projects within time and budget.

Is the approach in the book the only way of doing threat modeling? Absolutely not.

Is this the best way? I am not claiming that either.

It is only "a way," one that I believe meets the criteria of being "workable." Throughout the book, I follow this principle.

In general, this book is opinionated. This is not the dispassionate academic overview of everything in the discipline but a personal roadmap for the modern medical device corporation to do cybersecurity engineering effectively. A roadmap of this sort requires the singular narrative voice possible only in a book. For "HOW TOs" and very deep dives and immediate analysis, there will always be the Internet.

A word about scoping, or rather, what I choose to keep in, and what I choose to keep out. When there are topics where the industry uses the same term to mean many things, I will provide some basic definitions and concepts to level-set the discussion. However, when we encounter mathematical concepts like cryptography, that do not have multiple interpretations but require extensive explanation, I will refer to books and online resources to explain the mathematics, the concepts, the protocols, and the standards. Putting these in scope of the book would provide little benefit—those who do not know the concepts cannot be expected to understand them by reading just one chapter (dedicated books and specialized training is required for that purpose), and those who already know it would just skip over the pages.

So who is this book for?

1. *The medical device expert.* Research and Development (R&D), Regulatory, Quality, and Human Resources leadership across the medical device industry are being challenged to staff up, allocate resources, and develop processes and capabilities for overall organizational cybersecurity risk management. People in this group have a strong foundational background in clinical engineering, regulatory science or systems and software engineering. Many of them though, because of their noncybersecurity background though, may be struggling to understand the following:
   a. why medical device cybersecurity poses such unique challenges to their business (Chapter 1)
   b. basic cybersecurity concepts (Chapter 2) that will allow for more effective communication between them and cybersecurity engineers
   c. what different regulatory authorities are imposing as requirements on their organization and how to fit them into the Quality Management System (Chapter 3)
   d. how to build up a Product Security Organization (Chapter 4)
2. *The cybersecurity engineer.* This section of the book's audience is expected to have a foundation in cryptography, network, and session and application security. For them, the reason to pick up this book is to understand
   a. a method for threat modeling and cybersecurity risk modeling for medical devices (Chapter 5, Chapter 6)
   b. implementing capabilities and processes that allow for secure design, continuous product monitoring and risk assessment, and crafting regulatory submissions for cybersecurity (Chapters 7, 8 and 9).
3. *The medical device expert who wants to become a cybersecurity engineer.* As medical device manufacturers ramp up on cybersecurity, the most practical way of hiring and retaining talent will be to hire medical device experts and train them up in cybersecurity (We go into more

details of this aspect in Chapter 4). For this group, you should read the book from cover to cover, but in a staggered way. First, read from Chapters 1 to 4, then go elsewhere to build foundational knowledge of cybersecurity engineering and cryptography, and then come back to finish the book, to understand how these concepts apply in a medical device context.

Overall, the audience for this book is primarily medical device manufacturers (MDMs). Specifically, by that, I mean those who have to design cybersecurity into medical products and introduce cybersecurity into their existing quality management systems. This book is not written from the perspective of Healthcare Delivery Organizations (HDOs). HDOs procure devices from MDMs, put them on their networks, and are then held responsible for the overall security of their operational environment. Since security is a shared responsibility between MDMs and HDOs, there is significant overlap between the MDM perspective and the HDO perspective. However, they approach the problem from different angles. For MDMs, the primary focus is the design of the device with them having full control of what goes inside it (after all, it is their product). For the HDOs, however, the problem is in getting a number of device endpoints, from different manufacturers, not all of whom are equally secure and over whom they have limited control, to interoperate smoothly in clinical workflows, while ensuring that the overall security of their operations is not compromised by rogue devices. There is much to learn for the HDO security engineer by reading this book, if only so that they understand how the devices they buy are designed. Maybe, there is an idea here for the future, to look at the whole problem of medical device cybersecurity from an HDO perspective, with the focus of the book being on maintaining a secure clinical environment, rather than on secure clinical product design. However, there was no way that both the MDM as well as the HDO perspectives could have been accommodated in one single publication, while doing justice to both.

Finally, medical device cybersecurity isn't a destination, it's a journey. Consider this book as one of your guides on that path, read it from start to finish, or pick and choose chapters, there is no wrong way.

Bon Voyage.

Acknowledgment

It takes a village to raise a child. It takes many more to write a book.

There are many names to who I owe a deep debt of gratitude, to acknowledge all would take a book in itself. So for now, let me thank just a few of them.

First, my parents, and my daughter (to whom this book is dedicated) and my wife, for their support and encouragement. Then, I would like to thank all my teachers at South Point High School, Jadavpur University and Stony Brook for instructing and inspiring, especially Dr. Rance Cleaveland, who was not only my PhD advisor, but also became, over the years, a friend, and a mentor.

One learns as much from colleagues as they do from their professors. That is why I would like to acknowledge Mark Snyder, Ding Ma, Oleg Yusim, Pavel Slavin, Dr. Mikael Lindvall, Dr. Prem Uppuluri, Dr. Pradipta De, Dr. John Jiang, Simon Skup, Mostafa Sadeghi, Greg Bevan, Sean Harrington, and Ashok Iyer for many productive discussions on cybersecurity, medical devices, and computer science in general.

The book owes a huge debt of gratitude to Mark Snyder, who provided voluminous edits to the chapters, and whose inputs have greatly enriched the content and the presentation of what lies ahead. I would also like to thank Greg Bevan for reviewing the chapter on cybersecurity regulations and for his helpful comments.

I would also like to thank my editors at Elsevier for making the book what it is.

Finally, I want to thank, you the reader, for giving me your time and your attention.

CHAPTER ONE

Introduction to medical device cybersecurity

Medical device cybersecurity: a brief history

The year was 2005. Just a year before that, I had graduated with a Ph.D. in Computer Science. As a young academic, I was warned of a trap that ensnares many at the beginning of their research career: of first announcing a solution and then spending a lifetime trying to find the problem. So, I decided to do things the right way, by trying to find out what the "real problems" worth trying to solve were. Toward that end, I conducted a number of structured interviews of industry practitioners to understand what their pain points were. Since my research interests at the time lay in tools and techniques for mathematically proving that software worked as per its specifications (cybersecurity at the time for me was mostly a hobby), the practitioners I chose all came from industries where the failure of software has some of the most serious of consequences: aerospace, automotive, and medical (Fig. 1.1).

As I was going over a set of questions I had crafted, my interviewee, a very senior medical device engineer, who I shall call Jeb from now on, suddenly stopped answering my questions. Then he went totally off-script.

You know all this is well and good, but let me tell you what really bothers me. Really, really bothers me. It's that our management wants medical devices to be connected. They want to take stable systems which have worked reasonably well for decades, and they want to put a wireless card in them. They want these systems to be upgraded remotely, even from the Internet, they want to send data from them to their data centers, and they want continuous monitoring. In essence, they want devices to be like laptops. Yet these devices are not laptops. They were engineered years ago, with the assumption that they will operate alone, and now we are being asked to not just relax but destroy that assumption and make them nodes on a network.

I am not saying connectivity is bad. I am all for it. But if you really want connectivity, you need to fundamentally reengineer these devices. I know that is not going to happen, not given the schedules we have. So now we have higher complexity software running on old hardware, higher complexity because we now have to

Cybersecurity for Connected Medical Devices
ISBN: 978-0-12-818262-8
https://doi.org/10.1016/B978-0-12-818262-8.00004-8

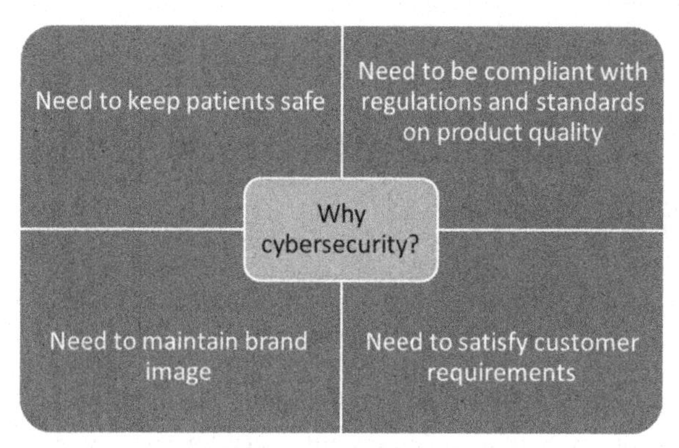

Figure 1.1 Why medical device cybersecurity?

> *support communication too, in addition to therapy. It's all one boiling spaghetti soup bowl. I am afraid, that someday something bad is going to happen, don't ask me what, but it will. Maybe people will break into medical devices, like they do to computers. It was not possible before. Now it will be.*

Years later, I can only marvel at Jeb's prescience.

The cybersecurity of medical devices, or rather the lack of it, is one of the biggest challenges facing healthcare today (Fig. 1.2). In 2002, it was reported that doctors disabled, the Vice President of the United States, Dick Cheney's implanted cardiac device, based on credible intelligence that hackers would try to impact therapy by breaking through its wireless interface [1]. The larger fear of "attack-through-device" was then latched onto by popular culture; a 2012 episode of the very popular political thriller *Homeland* had terrorists hacking a pacemaker [2]. Since then, medical device cybersecurity has consistently kept itself on the public radar. Every year, security researchers expose cybersecurity vulnerabilities in medical devices, often through very dramatic and eye-catching demonstrations of how patients may be impacted [3]. Naturally, almost all of them get wide-spread coverage in the popular press [4,5]. Companies have seen their stock value tumble based on vulnerabilities disclosed to the public [6]. Warning letters have been sent to manufacturers by the Food and Drug Administration (FDA) on the subject of medical device cybersecurity [7]. The FDA has also issued advisories to the general public regarding the cybersecurity risks of use of specific medical devices [8,9]. Manufacturers have had to issue product recalls for cybersecurity reasons [10,11].

Politicians have gotten involved too. In 2016, then-Senator Barbara Boxer sent a letter to five of the major medical device manufacturers (MDMs) enquiring about their plans to deal with cybersecurity [12].

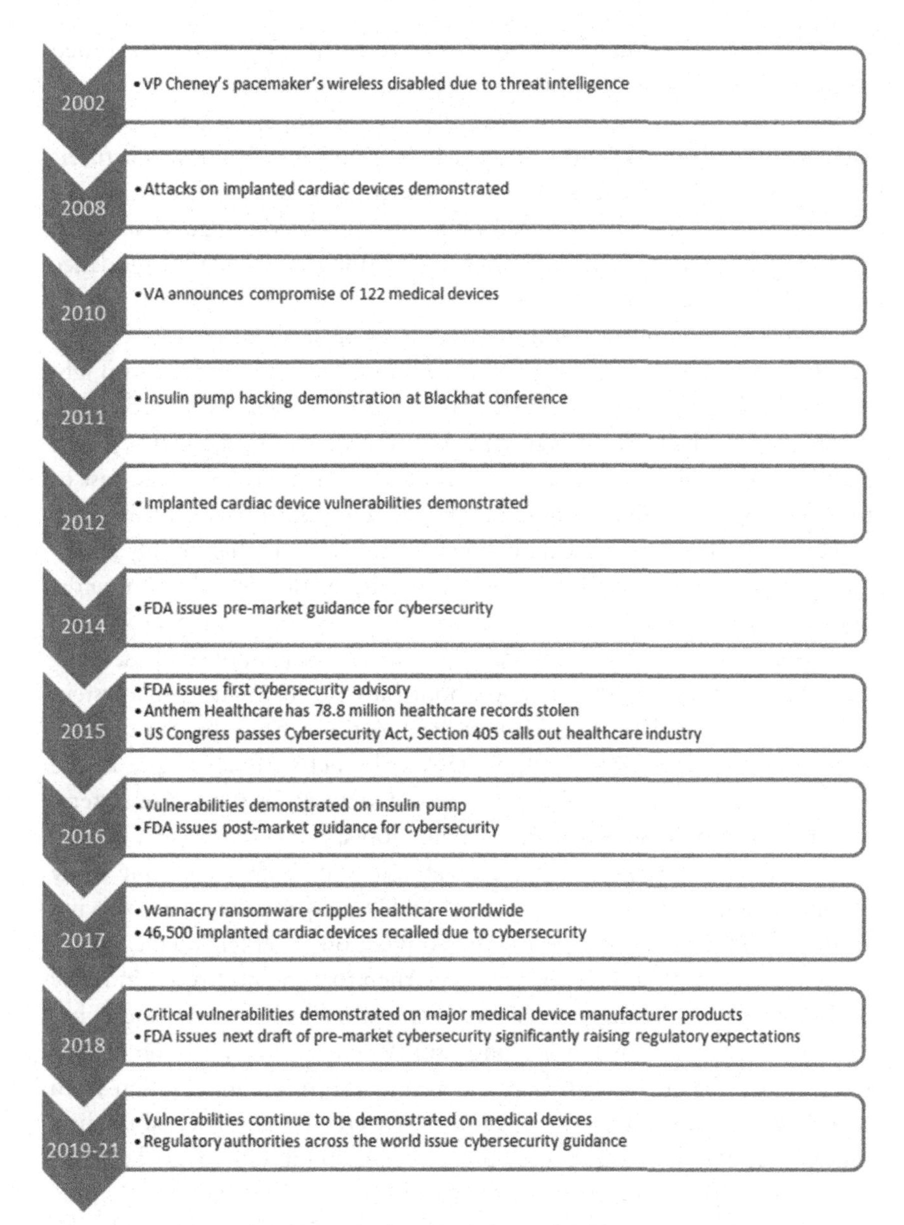

Figure 1.2 A brief history of medical device/healthcare cybersecurity.

There have been attempts to pass US legislation [13] that would mandate specific measures (e.g., a cybersecurity report card) on the medical device industry with respect to cyber security, as well as Congressional mandates on medical device cybersecurity [14]. The FDA has launched several public outreach initiatives on medical device cyber security [15–17] and has issued guidance documents to help the industry understand how to implement cybersecurity risk management [18–21]. The European Union too has made medical device cybersecurity part of regulations for manufacturers [22] and issued their own guidance documents in order to help manufacturers understand specific technical obligations under the regulations [23]. Other countries have followed in terms of issuing cybersecurity guidance to MDMs [24–32].

This pervasive concern about the security of medical devices is not unexpected. Patients are worried that the devices they entrust their lives to might be compromised by the same cybercriminals who now steal their credit cards and appropriate their identities to take out home loans. While identity theft can be fixed, albeit after much effort, and credit cards reissued, a life lost or an injury incurred cannot be rolled back. There is no getting past this truth.

The medical device of today, however, is much more than simply a software system connected to the patient, dispensing therapy, or performing diagnostics. Increasingly, devices are vital cogs of the larger healthcare infrastructure, nodes on a massively interconnected system of systems, spanning organizational and often national boundaries. Cybersecurity of a system is only as strong as that of its weakest link. You can have the most secure network in the world, but if the nodes on the network are fragile in the face of threats, there will be little in terms of security for the entire system.

For a cybercriminal, economics is a big motivator. The price of a healthcare record in the black market is estimated to vary, $250 as per one study [33] and ranging from $1 to $1000 in others [34–36], with the price varying depending on their completeness. In comparison, a stolen credit card is worth a few cents [37]. It is not surprising then that the healthcare industry has found itself increasingly in the crosshairs of malignant actors and cyber criminals. A report from a consulting firm Accenture reported one in four US customers having had their personal medical information stolen from technology systems, and of these, about half were victims of actual medical identity theft and had to pay an approximate $2500 in out-of-pocket costs per incident, on average [38].

In 2015, 78.8 million personal records were stolen from a major health insurer, making it one of the largest data breaches in history [39]. In 2017, the National Health Service in the United Kingdom and several other healthcare systems around the world were crippled by a malware outbreak called WannaCry [40] wherein cybercriminals held patient data to ransom, unless healthcare administrators paid up.

In 2015, the US Congress passed the Cybersecurity Act, and in it (Section 405), the healthcare industry was called out and steps mandated for the improvement of its cybersecurity, among which was the setting up of a Health Care Industry Cybersecurity (HCIC) Task Force [41]. In its report, the HCIC called out MDMs for not prioritizing cybersecurity. To quote: "Providers also report that many device manufacturers treat security as either an afterthought or that the attention is woefully inadequate" [42].

For well over a decade, it has been repeatedly demonstrated that medical devices are susceptible to cyber attacks. As far back as 2008, Halperin et al. had demonstrated that pacemakers could be hacked through software radio-based attacks [43]. In 2010, in a hearing on assessing information security at the US Department of Veterans Affairs before the Subcommittee on Oversight and Investigations of the House Committee on Veterans' Affairs, the Honorable Roger W. Baker said, "*Over 122 medical devices have been compromised by malware over the last 14 months. These infections have the potential to greatly affect the world-class patient care that is expected by our customers*" [44]. The next year, 2011, Jay Radcliffe, a security researcher, demonstrated cybersecurity vulnerabilities on his insulin pump at the Black Hat conference in Las Vegas [45]. In 2012, Barnaby Jack showed how he could remotely provide a deadly 830 V shock remotely to a patient by getting unauthorized remote access to the patient's implanted cardiac defibrillator [46]. In 2015, the FDA issued their first advisory on cybersecurity, based on research done by Billy Rios, asking hospitals to discontinue use of a particular model of an infusion pump [8]. In 2016, Jay Radcliffe demonstrated vulnerabilities on another manufacturer's insulin pump, which led to the company releasing a voluntary disclosure to its patients [47]. In 2017, 46,500 pacemakers were recalled for a critical cybersecurity patch [48]. In 2018, at Black Hat, Billy Rios demonstrated critical vulnerabilities in the software distribution system for implanted devices of a major MDM [49], while other MDMs reported vulnerabilities on their devices [50]. In 2019, several critical vulnerabilities were discovered in programmers, monitors, and implanted devices from an MDM [51], and in 2020, the US Department of Homeland Security issued a cybersecurity advisory [52] on that product line.

Some readers may be thinking, "Almost all of what you just now said about vulnerabilities and exploits seem to be of the "found in lab" type. Where are the real attacks in the field? How many people have actually been harmed by threats?" The disquieting answer is the following: We do not know. Most medical devices are not designed to record cybersecurity incidents, in the way traditional Information Technology systems are, and a successful attack would not typically be even recognized as one, and be passed off as "device malfunction" or "software error." Since this book was originally written during the COVID-19 pandemic, I cannot resist an analogy here with COVID-19 testing. As testing increases, so does the number of COVID-19 cases, stop testing, and there is no more COVID-19 recorded, even though the disease itself may be raging!

Now that the overall problem has been defined, we need to understand what it is that makes cybersecurity of medical devices continue to be a unique challenge (Fig. 1.3).

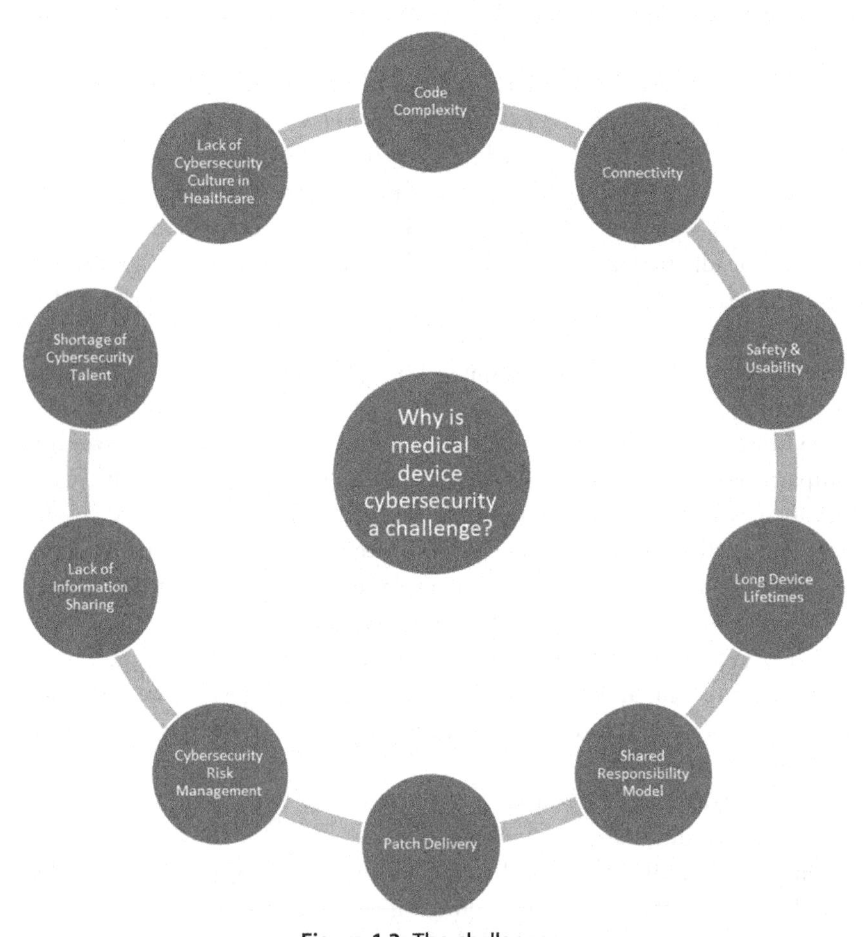

Figure 1.3 The challenges.

Code complexity

According to noted security expert Bruce Schneier, complexity is the worst enemy of security [53]. The connected medical device of today is undoubtedly an extremely complex software system. Software automates clinical workflows, previously only trained caregivers could perform, prevents human errors through implementation of error detection systems, and enables rich user interfaces, empowering patients to take charge of their own treatment, in a way hitherto not possible.

As a result, medical devices have become veritable software behemoths, with codebases running from hundreds of thousands of lines to several millions and complex, often convoluted designs. This naturally leads to software engineering challenges. Third-party code or code inherited from another project is often compiled into the main codebase without a full understanding of the implications of that integration. Customers want new features and functionality, but the device's software architecture is not robust enough to accommodate the request. A new architecture would solve the problem, but there is no time or resources available for a fundamental reengineering. So the old architecture is "adapted" in order to add the new functionality, often with untoward results.

Another contributory factor to the crisis of software is the pressure of approaching deadlines makes developers change the software design in code, without updating the design and requirements documents. While that solves the immediate problem of getting the project manager of one's back, the technical debt accrued as a result has to be paid back, with interest, when the product needs to be maintained or updated, as the design/requirements are no longer consistent with the code. One would hope that software errors would be caught during testing, of both software and system, but conventional requirements-based testing only scratches the surface of the total range of behaviors that the device is capable of. As a result, many bugs escape out into the field, uncaught. Attackers thrive on such inconsistencies between design and code. The mismatch allows them to discover unintentional functional behavior of the system, and then exercise that behavior, behavior that should not be possible, as per the official design, but very much possible given the actual implementation.

The fact that the medical device industry continues to struggle with software is of course great news for the cybercriminal. As it is, the game is fundamentally biased in their favor. The "good guys" have to get it right every time, and the criminal has to get it right just once. The more the lines of code, the greater is the possibility of exploitable errors, of debug interfaces left unintentionally in a shipped product or of buffer overflows or unvalidated input being accepted. The greater the amount of behavior untested in the manufacturer's lab, the more the opportunities available to the hacker to make the device behave in a way it was not intended to.

Connectivity

Connectivity has revolutionized the medical device, improving outcomes, lowering healthcare costs, and enhancing patient safety. Through wireless radio frequency (RF) and now Bluetooth communication, an implanted cardiac pacemaker or defibrillator may be adjusted postimplantation to refine cardiac therapy, something not possible without surgically extracting the device for adjustment and replacement. Connected implanted cardiac devices sense subtle lack of rhythms of the heart, precursors to more serious arrhythmias, and send the data, over the public internet through mobile devices to the cloud, allowing doctors to take preemptive action to prevent damage to the heart. Continuous glucose monitors send their readings to insulin pumps, allowing patients with Type 1 diabetes to more tightly control their blood sugar. Dialysis can now be conducted at home, without the need for regular clinic visits, enabling doctors to remotely monitor the patient's renal health by reviewing data through a cloud interface. Devices send therapy data back to the manufacturer who can then use data analytics at scale to devise new innovative therapies and adjust parameters of existing treatment regimens. Hospital Electronic Medical Records (EMRs) interface with medical devices to coordinate and track therapy, reducing the cost of care and human data entry errors. Surgical robotics allow for remote control of robot arms, allowing surgeons to operate inside the patient's body with the kind of precision not possible for humans alone. The examples are many, varied, and increasing as every year sees more and more innovation in the domain of connected healthcare.

But connectivity has, in the way Jeb had predicted, also brought the cybersecurity monster to the door. Devices that were originally designed for a nonnetworked world struggle to perform without errors when they are pushed into the world of connected digital health. Pathways of control, previously not possible, are exposed through connectivity which can then be exploited by a hacker. Often, therapy and connectivity functionality share common resources, allowing attackers to disrupt therapy by attacking connectivity components. The battery of an implanted device may be depleted by continually sending malformed communication packets to its RF interface, an example of how an attacker can use the connectivity component (the RF interface) to attack the therapy.

The root cause of connectivity problems is often traced to the hardware. Legacy hardware platforms—"legacy" in that the hardware is carried over from a point in time when security was not a consideration for medical device design—simply lack the power to do the kind of mathematical operations (i.e., cryptography) that modern data security requires. Legacy processors often do not have the computational horsepower to perform cryptographic operations without compromising basic functionality. They may also lack available memory space to accommodate cryptographic software libraries. Secret keys used for cryptography require a level of randomness for mathematical properties of cryptographic operations to hold. The hardware of legacy systems cannot natively provide this randomness for key generation, nor can they securely store the keys once they are generated. It's not just a question of providing "more juice" to existing hardware. In order to ensure the isolation of clinical operations from connectivity, a recommended architectural pattern is to have isolated hardware units—a communication chip that handles all communication security and a therapy/diagnostics chip that handles the actual clinical functionality. The dedicated therapy/diagnostics chip would perform the old "nonconnected" operations, while the communication chip would deal with the additional complexity of connectivity, with each execution unit having their independent resources, as far as possible. This hardware-level isolation ensures that attacks through the connectivity interface are less likely to directly "hit" the therapy/diagnostics functions.

So why not just upgrade the hardware for every new release version of a device, taking advantage of advancements in hardware in terms of computation power and secure hardware architecture? Many people, while asking this question, compare the medical device industry with the smartphone industry—if Apple and Samsung can do major upgrades to their hardware every two years, why cannot the medical device industry?

Firstly, medical device software must meet higher standards of verification and validation than software of commodity products like a smartphone. Recertifying software to work with upgraded hardware and obtaining approval from the relevant regulatory agencies is an extremely expensive and time-consuming process. In the smartphone industry, the cost of hardware upgrades is passed onto the customer, and indeed, this is what the customer is willing to pay for: a better camera, better battery life, faster games, and better graphics. However in the medical device industry, Healthcare Delivery Organizations (HDOs) are not willing to spend significantly more for a device if it does not also come with innovative therapies and diagnostics. Just a hardware upgrade for the sake of security is unlikely to be a commercially viable product. To expect medical device companies to follow the hardware upgrade, cadence of the smartphone industry is thus impractical.

This brings us to the next big challenge of securing medical devices: Patient safety.

Patient safety and usability

If you are the security designer of a medical device, you can never lose sight of the fact that availability is paramount. If you cannot log in to your Gmail account because you have forgotten the password, you can contact Google, and after a process which would take days, you may get your account access back. Now imagine you have a medical device protected by a password, and a patient is wheeled into the emergency room, whose life depends on the device, and then you forget the password. We now have a situation where the security design, of a login and a password, has actively compromised safety.

This is absolutely unacceptable.

Would replacing a smart card reader for the password have made things better in the previous example? Well, the caregiver might have misplaced the card, and we are back to the password forgotten problem. Would a biometric fingerprint work? Not in a surgical setting, where everyone has to wear gloves to keep the environment sterile. What about facial recognition? Besides the fact that facial recognition technology does not work all the time, how would it deal with surgical masks? What about the case when the person who needs to use the device comes from outside the hospital, like an external surgeon, surely, we cannot expect the patient to wait while the new doctor gets an "account." Now here comes a vendor with a seemingly great frictionless solution, except that it depends on the availability of wireless connectivity to the cloud throughout. We cannot use that, because that would imply the device would be unavailable when the network goes down. But then why cannot we add a feature, a fail-open of the kind that if the authentication service is unavailable, we just let the user use the system? However, that just means that all that the attacker has to do is to disrupt the network connection to the authentication service, and they get in unimpeded.

Standard security countermeasures from the world of IT systems cannot be transplanted directly to the medical domain, without a deep consideration of their impact on patient safety. Many design decisions that reduce cybersecurity risk end up increasing patient safety risk, and one of the challenges of this domain is in understanding the interplay between the two. This understanding is not easy, because the cybersecurity designer is usually not a clinical expert and the therapy subject matter expert typically does not have a cybersecurity background, and there is always the risk of a security design having unintended consequences during a certain clinical workflow that was not considered during design.

Then, there is the classic tension between cybersecurity and usability. If one forces a patient to have to log in to their remote care management app using a 12-digit alphanumeric password with uppercase and special characters, on a smart phone, the patient, in all likelihood, will just give up on the whole thing. By not participating in remote monitoring of their clinical condition, they may have greatly increased their risk of death or permanent damage. The medical cybersecurity designer has to always remember that the typical users of the device are either caregivers who are chronically short of time or patients, who may have comorbidities, like poor eyesight and arthritic fingers. Expecting people to remember their authentication credentials or remember to carry their USB authentication key or security card with them as a precondition to get access to the device is an assumption, which, if made, may greatly increase patient safety risk. Another problem is that many cybersecurity features end up being perceived as product quality issues ("Your competitor's product is so much easier to use, with your system, I have to reauthenticate every hour, whereas your competitor lets me be logged in for days and months") and many security features generate higher call volumes to service centers, as clinicians struggle with changes to workflows that they are not used to. ("I have forgotten my admin password, what do I do now? Send the device back?").

Decision makers often resist fundamental security design changes that cause workflow changes for clinicians and patients and service technicians, because they are afraid of push-back from users. While frictionless security (security that exists without the user being aware of it) is a good design goal to work toward, sometimes workflow changes become inevitable.

Long device lifetimes

The medical device has unique business drivers and compulsions, which often puzzle outsiders—especially security engineers hired into the organization from other industries. One is the extremely long lifetimes of medical devices, sometimes in the order of decades. Even after a device has been designed as "end of life," i.e., the manufacturer has publicly stopped supporting the device; they are still sold in the secondary market. The main reason is economics: many medical devices are expensive to buy brand new. As an example, consider two fairly standard diagnostic medical devices, a Computerized Tomography (CT) scanner and a Magnetic Resonance Imaging (MRI) machine, found in most hospitals across the world. A CT scanner runs between $500,000 and $1 million [54], and an MRI machine costs between $1 million and $2 million [55]. HDOs naturally do not want to incur the cost of new devices within a few years, often hiring service organizations to continue to replace mechanical and electrical parts for medical devices, long after the manufacturer has stopped support. Needless to say, these service organizations cannot update the software or roll out cybersecurity patches.

With the threat landscape changing so rapidly, the older these devices get, the more a device gets behind the eight ball with respect to cybersecurity. For instance, Windows XP is still present in a significant number of today's devices, an operating system with well-known security issues, years after Microsoft formally stopped providing cybersecurity support for it. Windows 7 entered end of support in January 2020, and if Windows XP is still being used (it entered end of support in 2014), one can only imagine how long it will be before Windows 7—based devices are phased out.

Given the high cost of medical devices, it is unrealistic for manufacturers to expect customers update their fleet for the sake of cybersecurity. "Please buy the new version of my product, because I cannot maintain the security of the old product with the hardware that it has" is not a particularly effective line in device sales. In some cases, manufacturers are willing to absorb the high cost of replacing medical devices, especially when their business model is based on the ongoing sales of device disposables and accessories. Because the real business is in the disposables, these manufacturers can afford to absorb the cost of periodically replacing their devices. This makes the life of their cybersecurity engineers much easier. This is not a luxury available to most MDMs though, since for many, their biggest source of revenue is the sale of the device.

Because devices stay on the market for so long, manufacturers are expected to allow for interoperability of their newest devices with older, legacy devices. Let us consider an example.

There is an MDM by the name of "Ray's Hypothetical Med" (RHM). RHM makes implanted therapy devices that are used at home. The implanted device communicates over a proprietary RF protocol, the protocol being designed by RHM's engineers, to a bedside monitor at the patient's home, sending critical information about the patient's medical condition and the health of the device itself. The bedside monitor then sends the data it receives from the implanted device up to the clinic over the Internet. This device was first released in the mid-2000s. Given the climate of the time, RHM designed the device with little consideration for security. Even though the Internet connection between the bedside monitor and the clinic's servers happens over a secure connection layer (even in the mid-2000s, RHM knew better than to keep that open), the communication between implant and bedside monitor is totally insecure. As long as they receive packets over the proprietary RF interface that conforms to the protocol specifications, each side of the communication accepts the packets as genuine.

Fast forward to the present day, and RHM is going to release a new line of implanted devices and bedside monitors. For their latest generation, RHM implements security on the RF communication such that devices and bedside monitors talk over a secure, authenticated channel. But what happens to clinics that have inventory of the old bedside monitors? Those bedside monitors cannot talk to the new secure implanted devices because the old bedside monitors do not support secure communication. Even if RHM could update the code on the old bedside monitors to support secure communication, the hardware is not robust enough to support modern cryptography. So, RHM has two options: Either replace the old bedside monitors with a new bedside monitor (and absorb the cost of this fleet upgrade of its customers) or design the new implanted devices in a way by which old bedside monitors can still talk to the new implanted devices over a channel that does not require both ends to implement security. Given the long lifetimes of devices, RHM has no idea of how long the old bedside monitors will continue to be used; there very well may be many world markets where they are still being actively sold. Imposing a strict security posture for the new line of implanted devices would "break" connection with old bedside monitors, and there are clinical as well as business risks to RHM of taking that design option. However, allowing the new implanted devices to have an insecure communication channel, just to support talking to the old bedside monitor devices, breaks the whole cybersecurity design of the new line of RHM's devices.

This is the kind of engineering and business dilemma that security engineers and leaders in medical device industry have to deal with on a daily basis, and why medical device cybersecurity continues to be a challenge and will remain so in the conceivable future.

Cybersecurity being a shared responsibility

According to regulators across the world [23,56,57], cybersecurity is a shared responsibility between MDMs and HDOs. In some medical device domains (referred to technically as "medical specialties" by the US FDA [58]), the MDM controls the operational environment of the medical device, e.g., patient remote monitoring of home care medical devices (renal, cardiac, etc.). Here, the MDM is fully responsible for cybersecurity—the design as well as the operation of the system. This is, in many ways, the simpler situation. Only one organization, the MDM, is responsible for cybersecurity, and that organization has total control of the device and its operations.

In most cases though, this is not the case. It is the HDOs that buy and deploy medical devices on their device network, and are responsible, at least in the eyes of the patient, for secure therapy and diagnostics. But then, they do not make the devices, and, traditionally, have had very little insight into the cybersecurity design of the devices they use in their premises. The MDM has no control over the deployment of the device once it has been sold, and the HDOs have no insight into what goes into the device, once it has been bought. And sometimes, as a result of this overall lack of transparency, cybersecurity falls through the cracks.

For example, consider a situation where a medical device in a clinic is accessed by someone who should not have had access to the device and patient data end up being stolen. The MDM would ask how an unauthorized person was even allowed to get near the device in the first place. The root cause of the incident, according to the MDM, would be lax physical security on the HDO premises. The HDO in turn would say that the MDM should have required authentication to access patient data on their device, so it is really the HDO that dropped the ball. Or to take another example, a medical device from MDM A gets hacked because the attacker got the wireless password of the HDO network by hacking into another device from MDM B. One can begin to see how complex the shared responsibility model can become and how challenging it can be to determine who shares what responsibility.

Over the years though, there has been significant progress made in delineating security responsibilities between MDMs and HDOs. Much of the credit for this goes to regulators and industry bodies who have brought MDMs and HDOs together to come to a general consensus. This consensus can be summarized in the following principles [21]:

- The MDM should design their products using principles of "defense in depth." This means that multiple cybersecurity countermeasures should be present, such that if one "falls," the others can compensate for the deficiency. If we go back to the above example of MDM A's device being broken into because someone stole the wireless password from a device manufactured by MDM B, MDM A should have designed in additional levels of security such that even if the wireless network got compromised, there would be still security protections on their data.
- The MDM should be transparent as to what software goes into their devices. For example, if a device has an operating system that has hundreds of open vulnerabilities, with no reasonable expectation of those vulnerabilities being fixed because the operating system in question is no longer being regularly patched by its vendor or supported by the open source community (as happened to Windows XP and certain older versions of Linux), the HDO has the right to know that information. The MDM has to communicate what third-party software components go into their device build, and declare all unremediated vulnerabilities present in their code to the HDOs. All of this is essential for the HDO to manage the cybersecurity risk of their operational environment.
- The MDM should ship their devices in a secure configuration. There should be minimal, any reliance on the HDO to "set up" devices securely. If there is any obligation on the part of HDOs to configure security parameters, it should be clearly communicated in the Instructions for Use.

But of course, this is easier said than done. If a medical device imposes security requirements on other systems (e.g., a medical device only supports secure communication with an EMR system) and the HDO's EMR vendor does not support secure communication, then the HDO's only option is to not connect the two systems. This may lead to disruption in clinical workflows and increase overall safety risk to the patient. To be fair, there is another option available to the HDO, to use a EMR product that supports secure communication, but that migration to such an EMR product may carry a price tag of millions of dollars.

The solution, the careful reader would be thinking, would be to have "configurable" security on the medical device—secure communication for HDOs that want it, and open communication for HDOs that do not. Having this level of configurable security in itself is an engineering challenge, introducing complexity in terms of new menu options, workflows, and security requirements.

Cybersecurity patch delivery

When a product vendor discovers a critical cybersecurity vulnerability in their product, they typically release the fix and announce the vulnerability, both together. However there is always a time lag between when the vulnerability is announced and when the corresponding patch is applied to a vulnerable instance of the product. This provides a window of opportunity for a cybercriminal to launch an attack on a vulnerable product instance by exploiting the unpatched publicly disclosed vulnerability.

This is why it is so important that cybersecurity patch application, especially for critical vulnerabilities, be timely. For your laptop or your phone, with its persistent connection to the internet, the delivery and application of patches is more or less seamless. Once a vendor like Windows or Apple or Adobe or Cisco releases a critical cybersecurity patch, your device is typically made to shut down, the update applied, and then life continues as before.

For medical devices, it is not that simple. For one, most hospital system administrators do not allow, for very good reasons, devices on their healthcare network to accept incoming network connections from the internet. Even if a network path could be created from the MDM to the device network, remote update of code over the Internet is a highly security-sensitive operation, which requires multiple levels of cybersecurity protections. At the very minimum, it requires the device that is being patched to verify that the code is from whom it says it is from, and that no one has altered the code. However, many medical devices currently in the field do not have the ability to perform the relevant cryptographic operations (i.e., digital signature verification), to confirm the authenticity and integrity of code. So, it is actually safer, even though vastly more time consuming, for HDOs to have biomedical engineers make local code upgrades, where they physically go from one device to another with an USB stick, applying updates. Here at least, you have the physical security protection of the devices being on HDO premises and the biomed engineer having a HDO employee badge that they need to swipe at the gate, as opposed to taking unsigned code updates over the Internet, even over a Virtual Private Network.

Even if a device enforces source authentication and cryptographic integrity controls on the code, cybersecurity patches cannot be remotely pushed by the manufacturer. Unlike your laptop or your phone, which can give you an hour to save all work, and then shut down and apply the patch, a medical device, particularly one dispensing therapy, cannot be interrupted, without posing a potential risk to patient safety. As a result, the customers, i.e., the HDOs and the patients, have to be the ultimate adjudicators of when, and sometimes if, they will apply the cybersecurity patch. A doctor may question whether it is worth asking an 80-year-old patient with a cardiac implanted device and reduced mobility to immediately come to the clinic just to apply a cybersecurity patch, and decide that the risk of transporting the patient for the cybersecurity patch is not worth the benefit. Given that the ultimate decisions on the practice of medicine rest with doctors, MDMs have no way enforcing patch adoption. All they can do is to educate and convince users to patch their devices through communication, transparency, and outreach activities.

MDMs do not write all the code that is part of their device image. Some of the code is procured from third-party vendors. These vendors may themselves issue patches for vulnerabilities discovered on their software. In order for the MDM to roll out the third-party patch to its own products, the MDM has to have high confidence that the security update does not alter the functionality of the device. When software vendors get the update process wrong, and they do often as anyone who has encountered a blue screen of death during a Windows update or had battery issues after an iOS update would attest to, they can adjust quickly and reissue a patch. If the MDM gets patch application on their devices wrong, there is the potential for immediate patient harm. Furthermore, as explained before, the patch application process itself is much more time consuming and complex for medical devices than it is for traditional software. This means that the cost of "getting an update wrong" is very high. To reduce the risk of this, the MDM has to perform extensive verification and validation and quality review of a third-party vendor issued patch before approving it for their device. This delay naturally stretches the window of opportunity for an attacker. They have already been notified of the vulnerability the day the original third-party software component vendor announced the patch, and the delay of the MDM in incorporating the patch into their product and in rolling it out to affected products is only going to work to the attacker's advantage.

Cybersecurity risk management

Medical device manufacturers have been doing risk management for patient safety for years, to the stage that mature, robust processes exist for patient safety risk assessments. These are driven by standards and refined through multiple executions. Cybersecurity risk, though, is new to MDMs and the healthcare industry in general. Standards are not mature, and there is not much in the way of organizational experience. This leads to technical decisions being taken that are not properly guided by risk reduction rationale, and managers find their security budgets shooting up, with little to show for how the needle of cybersecurity has moved even with greater investments in security.

What makes cybersecurity risk management so challenging is that it relies on fundamentally different assumptions from traditional safety risk management. In classical safety risk management, the model of the environment is of a benign entity, randomly flipping switches. This is why failures are probabilistically independent; the failures of the primary and that of the secondary are assumed to be independent of each other. In cybersecurity risk management, the model of the environment is of a malignant entity, flipping switches in a goal-directed way. There is now a common cause, the intent of the attacker, and failures are not independent anymore; if a hacker can break through the primary, he will also break through an identical backup. As a result, traditional models of probability calculation no longer work in the cybersecurity domain.

Which brings us to another related problem, how do you even calculate the "probability of occurrence" for a cybersecurity attack? Probability of occurrence is a well-known concept in traditional safety engineering. For mechanical and electrical components, failure rates can be observed in a laboratory or from data collected from the field. For cybersecurity, it is not that easy. A naïve answer, very often put forward, is that the probability is zero, because so far, there have not been any recorded incidents of patient harm due to cybersecurity exploits. We dealt with this question before in the beginning of the chapter. The fact that there have been none recorded does not mean that none have happened. This is something which so far we do not and cannot know, because most medical devices are not set up for logging cybersecurity intrusions. How would you know something has happened, if you cannot even detect it has happened?

More importantly, we have to remember that cybersecurity failures, unlike component failures, are not independent. In the case of component failure, just because device instance A had a sensor failure does not mean an identical but independent device instance B will immediately have the same sensor fail. However, if one instance of a device has been shown to have a vulnerability, we can say for certain that all other instances of the device will have the exact same vulnerability, and can be exploited in the exact same way. It can then be argued that the longer a known vulnerability remains unremediated, the probability of occurrence approaches one.

Then, there is the related problem of threat modeling. In order to model the risk to patient safety and patient privacy from cybersecurity causes, one needs a comprehensive method for identifying all the ways patient safety and privacy can be compromised by an attacker. This is known as threat modeling. There are many methods of threat modeling available, most of them developed from the perspective of generalized information technology systems. The problem is coming up with an approach for MDMs that is scalable, manageable, and would stand up to regulatory scrutiny in terms of assuring adequate coverage of the threat space, as it relates to adversely affecting patient safety and privacy.

Summing up, modeling risk to patient safety from cybersecurity is fundamentally different from modeling risk to patient safety from mechanical, electrical, software, and human factors failure. An alternative risk modeling approach for cybersecurity is needed, with a threat modeling approach driving the identification of risk factors.

Lack of information sharing

Many of the cybersecurity threats faced by the healthcare sector are too big to be handled effectively by one company or entity. In order to mount an effective defense against nation states and organized crime, resources have to be pooled together by MDMs, HDOs, law enforcement, security researchers, and regulators. Information has to be shared, seamlessly and in real time, so that the early signals of impending sector-wide attacks like WannaCry may be detected, experiences and strategies shared, and coordinated responses mounted.

Yet, the medical device sector has suffered from the existence of information silos, especially when it comes to cybersecurity.

There are several reasons for this. For one, there is the understandable reticence in proactively laying out one's dirty laundry in front of the world, what if public disclosures about my organization's and product's vulnerabilities open me up for increased regulatory scrutiny? How do I share actionable information with my competitors, without telling them about the secret sauce that goes into my product design? Even more fundamentally, should I be using cybersecurity as a competitive advantage or should I be collaborating with my rivals on it? Would public disclosures of cybersecurity vulnerabilities adversely affect my brand image, allowing the marketing team of my rivals to beat us down in front of our customers? Faced with the prospect of being asked these questions, most manufacturers choose to err on the side of silence, keeping things close to their chest, sharing information only when they are forced by law or by circumstance. The only people who gain from this are cybercriminals.

Shortage of cybersecurity talent

Cybersecurity is one of the skills for which there is an acute shortage of talent globally, with an estimated 3.5 million unfilled positions by 2021 according to some reports [59] and that cybersecurity demand is twice the supply [60]. A challenge for MDMs is to attract and retain top talent in a job market where supply and demand are so mismatched.

The problem is exacerbated by the fact that the skill sets required for a medical device cybersecurity professional are different from those of that required of a traditional IT security engineer/architect. According to multiple medical device cybersecurity managers I have talked to, most of the resumes they get for open positions are from traditional IT security engineers. The skills found in these applications are largely in network security, router configuration, and traffic monitoring and restriction technologies (firewalls, intrusion detection systems), with experience in the use and deployment of perimeter security and vulnerability management and end-point protection tools. They know what security tools work for what situations, and are skilled in interpreting results from tools and taking appropriate action.

The problem is that one cannot solve the problems of medical device cybersecurity by deploying tools in the conventional IT sense. For one, most IT security tools do not run on embedded real-time operating systems. Even if end-point protections could be engineered for specialized device platforms, and there is some movement in the vendor space in this regard, there are other challenges. For example, traditional malware solutions need malware signatures and virus definitions. Because most devices are not connected to the Internet, medical devices cannot get updates to the malware signature databases in the seamless way a laptop can. Also, a malware signature update is a change in behavior of the software, and would require reverification and validation by the manufacturer to ensure that the update itself does not increase system patient safety risk, and might also require a regulatory approval. This is why malware signature updates cannot just be "applied" to a regulated device, in the way one can do to a laptop.

Because of its unique regulatory and safety drivers, medical devices have to be built security built into the device from ground up. The ideal candidate for such design roles needs a deep knowledge of cryptography, systems engineering, hardware, risk management, and software development. These constitute the toolbox of the product security architect, whereas most of the resumes that are received tend to come from IT infrastructure security architects and engineers. This is not an isolated experience, but uniform, which leads one to believe that there is a fundamental mismatch between the skills required by the medical device industry and those provided by the market.

Cybersecurity culture

The European Union Agency for Network and Information Security in its report "Cybersecurity Culture in Organizations" defines cybersecurity culture in the following way [61]:

> *The concept of Cybersecurity Culture (CSC) refers to the knowledge, beliefs, perceptions, attitudes, assumptions, norms and values of people regarding cybersecurity and how they manifest themselves in people's behavior with information technologies.*

As long as there have been banks, there have been people trying to rob them. That's why security is part of the organizational DNA of banks and financial institutions. Healthcare though has a different kind of history. Here the presumption has always been of trust, of doctors and caregivers doing the very best of what they can do for patients. This perhaps explains why cybersecurity is not part of the institutional memory of many healthcare organizations, in the way it is for those in the banking or defense sector.

This lack of cybersecurity culture is manifested at different levels.

At the product design level, system designs do not start thinking in terms of antagonists and intentional abuse during feasibility, the focus being purely on clinical efficacy and safety. Security is something that is usually left to be bolted on later, based on a risk assessment done after the major decisions regarding the product design have already been locked in. Things like threat modeling are often done after everything has been done, started a few weeks before regulatory submission, purely as an artifact for regulators, and not as something that has guided the actual engineering of the device.

At the senior management level, the lack of cybersecurity culture is often manifested as overall skepticism over the need for cybersecurity for medical devices, and its dismissal as "hype" or "yet another thing the regulators are just asking us to do." Even if cybersecurity is recognized as an issue, the go-to strategy on the part of executive management is to hire an engineer or two or bring in a consultant and hope that it solves the problem (it usually doesn't). There is also the tendency to think of cybersecurity as a collection of one-time costs, a penetration test done by a security firm considered similar, in terms of budgeting, to a certification to an electrical reliability standard. Unfortunately, the real cost of cybersecurity is in its maintenance. Unlike the electrical reliability standard, which one can presume is fairly constant, the threat landscape is changing rapidly, and new vulnerabilities are being continuously discovered and regulatory and customary expectations undergoing continuous recalibration. Continuous monitoring of threat signals, risk management and remediation is essential to maintain cybersecurity posture, and because MDMs are new to this, these expenses are often not planned for.

In conclusion, the absence of an overall cybersecurity strategy and poor organizational risk-management practices, organizations spend more on security than they have to, or spend it in the wrong places, and outcomes cannot justify the costs.

The Product Cybersecurity Organization

So now that I have laid out some of the factors that make medical device cybersecurity challenging, the question that naturally follows is *what can we do, those of us that are in the healthcare community, to meet these challenges?*

One of the opinions of this book is that the best way to reduce organizational risk due to cybersecurity (i.e. the risk that cybersecurity will cause economic harm to the organization, in terms of loss of revenue, recall costs, product delays and overall brand damage) is to create a dedicated Product Cybersecurity Organization. This Product Cybersecurity Organization develops and maintains a set of cybersecurity capabilities. Each capability is characterized by processes, people who execute those processes, and tools that enable the people to execute those processes. The processes are driven by regulatory expectations on cybersecurity, cybersecurity standards, and customer (i.e. HDO) cybersecurity requirements.

Having a dedicated team with a formally defined set of capabilities and a plan of capability development and maintenance is, in my opinion, one of the most concrete structural steps an MDM can due to ensure that an organizational culture of cybersecurity is built and maintained. The alternative, of diffusing cybersecurity responsibilities among different functions, fails to be a sustainable organizational solution. This is because the diffused model fails to create single points of accountability for cybersecurity, provides little in terms of career paths for cybersecurity engineers (making them more likely to leave in a hot cybersecurity market), and does not scale up as more and more products are designed for cybersecurity. Because there is no single team, cybersecurity expenditure is also diffused through multiple functional budgets. This means that on that day that the CEO or the board asks "How much are we spending on the cybersecurity of our products?", and trust me they will, there is not going to be much in terms of an answer forthcoming.

A single "corporate" Product Cybersecurity Organization may be sufficient for smaller MDMs. But with most major MDMs having multiple business units spanning different medical specialties and with different regulatory and business and customer drivers, the recommendation would be to have Product Cybersecurity Organizations at each business unit level, linked to a corporate level Product Cybersecurity Organization.

Before we get ahead, it would not be out of way to have a word about the organization of the chapters moving forward. Chapter 2 will introduce basic cybersecurity concepts, so that we can level-set on definitions and concepts. It will be useful for those who do not have a cybersecurity background (please see the Foreword for more information on how you should read this book) to form a rudimentary idea of some of the fundamental concepts that define the domain. Chapter 3 is an overview of the regulatory landscape for medical device cybersecurity. Because without understanding what they are, how can we build a standards and regulations and regulatory guidance based Product Cybersecurity Organization? In Chapter 4, we introduce the concept of a Product Cybersecurity Organization. The rest of the book then drills down into the details of these capabilities, with threat modeling and cybersecurity risk modeling (Chapters 5 and 6), cybersecurity design and verification (Chapters 7), supply chain, manufacturing and vulnerability management (Chapter 8) and finally regulatory submissions (Chapter 9).

References

[1] A. Peterson, Yes, Terrorists Could Have Hacked Dick Cheney's Heart, Washington Post, October 21, 2013 [Online]. Available: https://www.washingtonpost.com/news/the-switch/wp/2013/10/21/yes-terrorists-could-have-hacked-dick-cheneys-heart/. (Accessed 1 September 2020).

[2] B. Jack, "Broken Hearts": How Plausible Was the Homeland Pacemaker Hack? IoActive, February 26, 2013 [Online]. Available: https://ioactive.com/broken-hearts-how-plausible-was-the-homeland-pacemaker-hack/. (Accessed 1 September 2020).

[3] W. Alexander, Barnaby Jack Could Hack Your Pacemaker and Make Your Heart Explode, Vice, June 25, 2013 [Online]. Available: https://www.vice.com/en_us/article/avnx5j/i-worked-out-how-to-remotely-weaponise-a-pacemaker. (Accessed 1 September 2020).

[4] B.J. Feder, A Heart Device Is Found Vulnerable to Hacker Attacks, New York Times, March 12, 2018 [Online]. Available: https://www.nytimes.com/2008/03/12/business/12heart-web.html. (Accessed 1 September 2020).

[5] Wired, Medical Devices Are the Next Security Nightmare, February 3, 2017 [Online]. Available: https://www.wired.com/2017/03/medical-devices-next-security-nightmare/. (Accessed 1 September 2020).

[6] D.B. Jim Finkle, St. Jude Stock Shorted on Heart Device Hacking Fears; Shares Drop, Reuters, August 25, 2016 [Online]. Available: https://www.reuters.com/article/us-stjude-cyber-idUSKCN1101YV. (Accessed 1 September 2020).

[7] US Food and Drug Administration, MARCS-CMS 519686, April 12, 2017 [Online]. Available: https://www.fda.gov/inspections-compliance-enforcement-and-criminal-investigations/warning-letters/abbott-st-jude-medical-inc-519686-04122017. (Accessed 1 September 2020).

[8] Reuters, FDA Warns of Security Flaw in Hospira Infusion Pumps, July 31, 2015 [Online]. Available: https://www.reuters.com/article/us-hospira-fda-cybersecurity/fda-warns-of-security-flaw-in-hospira-infusion-pumps-idUSKCN0Q52GJ20150731. (Accessed 1 September 2020).

[9] US Food and Drug Administration, Cybersecurity Vulnerabilities Affecting Medtronic Implantable Cardiac Devices, Programmers, and Home Monitors: FDA Safety Communication, March 21, 2019 [Online]. Available: https://www.fda.gov/medical-devices/safety-communications/cybersecurity-vulnerabilities-affecting-medtronic-implantable-cardiac-devices-programmers-and-home. (Accessed 1 September 2020).

[10] US Food and Drug Administration, Medtronic Recalls Remote Controllers for MiniMed Insulin Pumps for Potential Cybersecurity Risks, November 18, 2019 [Online]. Available: https://www.fda.gov/medical-devices/medical-device-recalls/medtronic-recalls-remote-controllers-minimed-insulin-pumps-potential-cybersecurity-risks. (Accessed 1 September 2020).

[11] US Food and Drug Administration, Battery Performance Alert and Cybersecurity Firmware Updates for Certain Abbott (Formerly St. Jude Medical) Implantable Cardiac Devices: FDA Safety Communication, April 17, 2018 [Online]. Available: https://www.fda.gov/medical-devices/safety-communications/battery-performance-alert-and-cybersecurity-firmware-updates-certain-abbott-formerly-st-jude-medical. (Accessed 1 September 2020).

[12] Becker's Health IT, Sen. Barbara Boxer Urges Medical Devices Companies to Detail Cybersecurity Plans, n.d. [Online]. Available: https://www.beckershospitalreview.com/healthcare-information-technology/sen-barbara-boxer-urges-medical-devices-companies-to-detail-cybersecurity-plans.html. (Accessed 1 September 2020).

[13] S.R. Blumenthal, S.1656 - Medical Device Cybersecurity Act of 2017, 2017 [Online]. Available: https://www.congress.gov/bill/115th-congress/senate-bill/1656/text?format=txt. (Accessed 1 September 2020).

[14] U. Congress, Agriculture, Rural Development, Food and Drug Administration, and Related Agencies Appropriations Bill, 2019, 2019 [Online]. Available: https://docs.house.gov/meetings/AP/AP00/20180516/108312/HRPT-115-HR-FY2019-Agriculture.pdf. (Accessed 1 September 2020).

[15] US Food and Drug Administration, Public Workshop - Content of Premarket Submissions for Management of Cybersecurity in Medical Devices January 29–30, 2019, 2019 [Online]. Available: https://www.fda.gov/medical-devices/workshops-conferences-medical-devices/public-workshop-content-premarket-submissions-

management-cybersecurity-medical-devices-january-29-30. (Accessed 1 September 2020).

[16] S.B. Schwartz, Medical Device Cybersecurity: through the FDA Lens, April 17, 2018 [Online]. Available: https://www.usenix.org/sites/default/files/conference/protected-files/security18_slides_schwartz.pdf. (Accessed 1 September 2020).

[17] US Food and Drug Administration, The FDA's Role in Medical Device Cybersecurity: Dispelling Myths and Understanding Facts, 2018 [Online]. Available: https://www.fda.gov/media/123052/download. (Accessed 1 September 2020).

[18] US Food and Drug Administration, Cybersecurity for Networked Medical Devices Containing Off-The-Shelf (OTS) Software, Docket Number FDA-2020-D-0957, January 2005 [Online]. Available: https://www.fda.gov/regulatory-information/search-fda-guidance-documents/cybersecurity-networked-medical-devices-containing-shelf-ots-software. (Accessed 1 September 2020).

[19] US Food and Drug Administration, Content of Premarket Submissions for Management of Cybersecurity in Medical Devices (Final Version), October 2014 [Online]. Available: https://www.fda.gov/regulatory-information/search-fda-guidance-documents/content-premarket-submissions-management-cybersecurity-medical-devices-0. (Accessed 1 September 2020).

[20] US Food and Drug Administration, Postmarket Management of Cybersecurity in Medical Devices (Final Version), December 2016 [Online]. Available: https://www.fda.gov/regulatory-information/search-fda-guidance-documents/postmarket-management-cybersecurity-medical-devices. (Accessed 1 September 2020).

[21] US Food and Drug Administration, Content of Premarket Submissions for Management of Cybersecurity in Medical Devices (Draft Version), November 2018 [Online]. Available: https://www.fda.gov/regulatory-information/search-fda-guidance-documents/content-premarket-submissions-management-cybersecurity-medical-devices. (Accessed 1 September 2020).

[22] Official Journal of the European Union, Regulation (EU) 2017/745 of the European Parliament and of the Council of 5 April 2017 on Medical Devices, Amending Directive 2001/83/EC, Regulation (EC) No 178/2002 and Regulation (EC) No 1223/2009 and Repealing Council Directives 90/385/EEC and 93/42/EE, April 5, 2017 [Online]. Available: https://eur-lex.europa.eu/legal-content/EN/TXT/?uri=CELEX:02017R0745-20200424. (Accessed 1 September 2020).

[23] Medical Device Coordination Group Document, MDCG 2019-16 Guidance on Cybersecurity for Medical Devices, 2019 [Online]. Available: https://ec.europa.eu/docsroom/documents/41863. (Accessed 1 September 2020).

[24] Health Canada, Guidance Document: Pre-market Requirements for Medical Device Cybersecurity, June 17, 2019 [Online]. Available: https://www.canada.ca/en/health-canada/services/drugs-health-products/medical-devices/application-information/guidance-documents/cybersecurity/document.html. (Accessed 1 September 2020).

[25] Australian Government Department of Health, Medical Device Cyber Security Guidance for Industry, July 18, 2019 [Online]. Available: https://www.tga.gov.au/publication/medical-device-cyber-security-guidance-industry. (Accessed 1 September 2020).

[26] F.D.A. China, Medical Device Network Security Registration on Technical Review Guidance Principle, January 2017 [Online].

[27] Agency for the Safety of Health Products, Cybersecurity of Medical Devices Integrating Software during Their Lifecycle, July 2019 [Online]. Available: https://www.ansm.sante.fr/S-informer/Points-d-information-Points-d-information/L-ANSM-lance-une-consultation-publique-sur-un-projet-de-recommandations-pour-la-cybersecurite-des-dispositifs-medicaux-Point-d-information.

[28] German Federal Office for Information Security, Cyber Security Requirements for Network-Connected Medical Devices, November 2018 [Online]. Available: https://www.allianz-fuer-cybersicherheit.de/ACS/DE/_/downloads/BSI-CS/BSI-CS_132E.pdf;jsessionid=9B84D9132CF8A89D659B97765083F5C5A.1_cid502?__blob=publicationFile&v=7. (Accessed 1 September 2020).

[29] Japan Pharmaceutical and Medical Device Agency, Guidance on Ensuring Cybersecurity of Medical Device: PSEHB/MDED-PSD Notification No. 0724-1, July 2018 [Online]. Available: https://www.pmda.go.jp/files/000204891.pdf. (Accessed 2 September 2020).

[30] Saudi Food and Drug Authority, Guidance to Pre-market Cybersecurity of Medical Devices, April 2019 [Online]. Available: https://old.sfda.gov.sa/ar/medicaldevices/regulations/DocLib/MDS-G38.pdf. (Accessed 1 September 2020).

[31] Singapore Health Sciences Authority, Regulatory Guidelines for Software Medical Devices—A Lifecycle Approach, December 2019 [Online]. Available: https://www.hsa.gov.sg/docs/default-source/announcements/regulatory-updates/regulatory-guidelines-for-software-medical-devices--a-lifecycle-approach.pdf. (Accessed 1 September 2020).

[32] South Korean Ministry of Science and ICT, Cyber Security Guide for Smart Medical Service, May 2018 [Online].

[33] Trustwave, Trustwave Global Security Report, 2019 [Online]. Available: https://www.trustwave.com/en-us/resources/library/documents/2019-trustwave-global-security-report/. (Accessed 1 September 2020).

[34] Forbes, Your Electronic Medical Records Could Be Worth $1000 To Hackers, April 7, 2017 [Online]. Available: https://www.forbes.com/sites/mariyayao/2017/04/14/your-electronic-medical-records-can-be-worth-1000-to-hackers/#2444530850cf. (Accessed 1 September 2020).

[35] Becker's Health IT, Patient Medical Records Sell for $1K on Dark Web, February 20, 2019 [Online]. Available: https://www.beckershospitalreview.com/cybersecurity/patient-medical-records-sell-for-1k-on-dark-web.html. (Accessed 1 September 2020).

[36] Experian, Here's How Much Your Personal Information Is Selling for on the Dark Web, December 6, 2017 [Online]. Available: https://www.experian.com/blogs/ask-experian/heres-how-much-your-personal-information-is-selling-for-on-the-dark-web/. (Accessed 1 September 2020).

[37] D. Magazine, Why Medical Data is 50 Times More Valuable Than a Credit Card, October 15, 2019 [Online]. Available: https://www.dmagazine.com/healthcare-business/2019/10/why-medical-data-is-50-times-more-valuable-than-a-credit-card/.

[38] Accenture, One in Four US Consumers Have Had Their Healthcare Data Breached, Accenture Survey Reveals, February 20, 2017 [Online]. Available: https://newsroom.accenture.com/news/one-in-four-us-consumers-have-had-their-healthcare-data-breached-accenture-survey-reveals.htm. (Accessed 1 September 2020).

[39] Wall Street Journal, Anthem: Hacked Database Included 78.8 Million People, February 24, 2015 [Online]. Available: https://www.wsj.com/articles/anthem-hacked-database-included-78-8-million-people-1424807364. (Accessed 1 September 2020).

[40] Infosec Institute, How WannaCry Ransomware Crippled Healthcare, March 29, 2018 [Online]. Available: https://resources.infosecinstitute.com/wannacry-ransomware-crippled-healthcare/#gref. (Accessed 1 September 2020).

[41] 114th Congress, S.754 - To Improve Cybersecurity in the United States Through Enhanced Sharing of Information About Cybersecurity Threats, and for Other Purposes, March 17, 2015 [Online]. Available: https://www.congress.gov/bill/114th-congress/senate-bill/754. (Accessed 1 September 2020).

[42] Healthcare Industry Cybersecurity Task Force, Report on Improving Cybersecurity in the Healthcare Industry, June 2017 [Online]. Available: https://www.phe.gov/Preparedness/planning/CyberTF/Documents/report2017.pdf. (Accessed 1 September 2020).

[43] D. Halperin, T.S. Heydt-Benjamin, K. Fu, T. Kohno, W.H. Maisel, Security and privacy for implantable medical devices, IEEE Perv. Comput. 7 (1) (2008) 30–39.

[44] House Hearing, 111 Congress, Assessing Information Security at the Department of Veteran's Affairs, May 19, 2010 [Online]. Available: https://www.govinfo.gov/content/pkg/CHRG-111hhrg57022/html/CHRG-111hhrg57022.htm. (Accessed 1 September 2020).
[45] Computerworld, Black Hat: Lethal Hack and Wireless Attack on Insulin Pumps to Kill People, August 4, 2011 [Online]. Available: https://www.computerworld.com/article/2470689/black-hat–lethal-hack-and-wireless-attack-on-insulin-pumps-to-kill-people.html. (Accessed 1 September 2020).
[46] Computerworld, Pacemaker Hack Can Deliver Deadly 830-Volt Jolt, October 12, 2012 [Online]. Available: https://www.computerworld.com/article/2492453/pacemaker-hack-can-deliver-deadly-830-volt-jolt.html. (Accessed 1 September 2020).
[47] Reuters, J&J Warns Diabetic Patients: Insulin Pump Vulnerable to Hacking, October 4, 2016 [Online]. Available: https://www.reuters.com/article/us-johnson-johnson-cyber-insulin-pumps-e/jj-warns-diabetic-patients-insulin-pump-vulnerable-to-hacking-idUSKCN12411L. (Accessed 1 September 2020).
[48] The Guardian, Hacking Risk Leads to Recall of 500,000 Pacemakers due to Patient Death Fears, October 21, 2017 [Online]. Available: https://www.theguardian.com/technology/2017/aug/31/hacking-risk-recall-pacemakers-patient-death-fears-fda-firmware-update. (Accessed 1 September 2020).
[49] Wired, A New Pacemaker Hack Puts Malware Directly on the Device, August 9, 2018 [Online]. Available: https://www.wired.com/story/pacemaker-hack-malware-black-hat/. (Accessed 1 September 2020).
[50] Health IT Security, 9 Cybersecurity Vulnerabilities Found in Philips E-Alert Tool, 2019 [Online]. Available: https://healthitsecurity.com/news/9-cybersecurity-vulnerabilities-found-in-philips-e-alert-tool#:~:text=The%20vulnerabilities%20include%20improper%20input,use%20of%20hard%2Dcoded%20credentials.
[51] HIPAA Journal, Critical Vulnerability Affects Medtronic CareLink Monitors, Programmers, and ICDs, 2019 [Online]. Available: https://www.hipaajournal.com/critical-vulnerability-medtronic-carelink-monitors-programmers-icds/.
[52] US Department of Homeland Security, ICS Medical Advisory (ICSMA-20-345-01), n.d. [Online]. Available: https://us-cert.cisa.gov/ics/advisories/icsma-20-345-01.
[53] B. Schneier, Data and Goliath: The Hidden Battles to Collect Your Data and Control Your World, W. W. Norton Company, 2016.
[54] J. Hough, CT Scanner Buying Guide: Slice Counts and Pricing, January 21, 2019 [Online]. Available: https://www.meridianleasing.com/blog/medical-equipment-blog/ct-scanner-buyers-guide. (Accessed 1 September 2020).
[55] J. Hough, MRI Machine Buyer's Guide: Options and Pricing, January 25, 2019 [Online]. Available: https://www.meridianleasing.com/blog/medical-equipment-blog/mri-machine-buyers-guide-options-and-pricing. (Accessed 1 September 2020).
[56] Health Canada, Notice: Medical Device Cybersecurity Reference Number: 18-108099-160, August 15, 2018 [Online]. Available: https://www.canada.ca/en/health-canada/services/drugs-health-products/medical-devices/activities/announcements/notice-cybersecurity.html. (Accessed 1 September 2020).
[57] US Food and Drug Administration, Statement from FDA Commissioner Scott Gottlieb, M.D. on FDA's Efforts to Strengthen the Agency's Medical Device Cybersecurity Program as Part of Its Mission to Protect Patients, October 1, 2018 [Online]. Available: https://www.fda.gov/news-events/press-announcements/statement-fda-commissioner-scott-gottlieb-md-fdas-efforts-strengthen-agencys-medical-device. (Accessed 1 September 2020).
[58] US Food and Drug Administration, Device Classification Panels, n.d. [Online]. Available: https://www.fda.gov/medical-devices/classify-your-medical-device/device-classification-panels. (Accessed 1 September 2020).

[59] Forbes, The Cybersecurity Talent Gap Is An Industry Crisis, August 9, 2018 [Online]. Available: https://www.forbes.com/sites/forbestechcouncil/2018/08/09/the-cybersecurity-talent-gap-is-an-industry-crisis/#2b970940a6b3. (Accessed 1 September 2020).

[60] EcomonicModeling.com, Build (Don't Buy):A Skills-Based Strategy to Solve the Cybersecurity Talent Shortage, July 2020 [Online]. Available: https://www.economicmodeling.com/wp-content/uploads/2020/07/Cybersecurity-BuildDontBuy.pdf. (Accessed 1 September 2020).

[61] European Union Agency for Network and Information Security, Cybersecurity Culture in Organizations, ENISA, 2017.

CHAPTER TWO

Basic cybersecurity concepts

The purpose of this chapter is twofold. First, it provides a gentle introduction, or rather as-gentle-as-possible introduction to some very fundamental security concepts I shall be using in the book. This I believe will be helpful to any reader who is new to cybersecurity, or has a passing familiarity with it. Second, it is necessary to level-set on some of the terms and definitions used throughout the book. Concepts like "threats," "assets," "vulnerabilities," "risk," "authentication," "authorization," and "access control" are often used loosely, and many disagreements in meetings scheduled at 7 a.m. may be resolved if all the participants had a common understanding of the words they were using. This problem of "the same words meaning different things to different people" is due in no small part to a lack of harmony of definitions across the glossary section of standards, internal processes and textbooks, and publications by National Institute of Standards and Technology (NIST). So, in this book, rather than wrangling over which "exact" definition is correct, I define these concepts once, and stay consistent with them throughout the subsequent chapters. I will repeat here, what I said in the Foreword, this is just "a consistent way" of defining things, no claim is being made that this is the "only right way."

This book will not provide an in-depth discussion of concepts in cybersecurity which are rooted in mathematical theory, like Public Key Infrastructure (PKI), asymmetric and symmetric key cryptography, key generation and key transport protocols, keyed secure hashing, digital signatures, and other concepts. Being mathematical, these are precisely defined and standardized. As a result, there is lesser scope of starting with wrong assumptions, as there is with some of the other concepts covered in the chapter. If you are new to cryptography, there are foundational books [1–4] that I encourage you to read. In this chapter, I provide a lightning overview of some of these basic security concepts just for the sake of completeness. So if you have already been exposed to cryptography, but still might need a quick refresher, this might be exactly what you are looking for.

So let's get started.

Cybersecurity for Connected Medical Devices
ISBN: 978-0-12-818262-8
https://doi.org/10.1016/B978-0-12-818262-8.00008-5

A bag full of diamonds

Let's start with a little story. I have just come into possession of a purple velvet bag full of diamonds. How I got this bag is not important, maybe my distant uncle left it to me in his will, or it could be that the bag fell into my lap. What is important though is that this bag of diamonds is the most valuable thing I possess, my principal asset. I know that by having this bag of diamonds, I have now made myself the target of thieves and burglars, and that of course gives me sleepless nights. I intuitively know I can't keep the bag in my house; the risk of it being stolen is too much. Being a security professional, I do a bit of back-of-the-envelope risk analysis to confirm my intuition. Table 2.1 represents an incomplete version of the analysis, incomplete because a full security analysis would be much more extensive, considering many more ways things can go wrong.

I start off my security risk analysis with identifying what it is I am trying to protect. That would be my principal asset, my purple bag of diamonds. Next, I consider who would want to steal my asset. I represent this group of people by the generic threat agent "burglar."

Next I consider the vulnerabilities of my house. Given that my house was never built to protect a bagful of diamonds, there are many "weak spots" where a threat agent may attack. The list of vulnerabilities (column 1) in Table 2.1 explicitly captures some of the design weaknesses of my house. There are of course many more vulnerabilities, only a few are shown. Most of the vulnerabilities, as you will note, are inherent to the way a house is. Every house has a door to enter and exit, as well as windows, which may be opened and broken through. The rest of the house is made up of building materials, in this case, brick. While brick walls are more difficult to drill through than opening a door or breaking a window, it is not impossible for a sufficiently motivated attacker to do this. Not all vulnerabilities in the list are inherent to the structure of house. Some of the vulnerabilities originate from weaknesses inherent in the security controls themselves. For example, a lock is a security control that prevents someone from opening the door unless they have the corresponding key. But the security control itself can be attacked, and the final few threats relate to the possibility of copying or stealing the key. As different security controls are introduced, so too are different threats to those controls. For example, if the locked door had a combination lock rather than a conventional lock, the burglar could learn the combination by watching from afar as I unlocked the door to my house.

Table 2.1 Security assessment of keeping diamonds at home.

Vulnerabilities	Threats	How likely is the diamond to be stolen (without controls)?	Security controls in place	How likely is the diamond to be stolen (with controls)?
The house has a door and a window	The burglar unscrews the iron hinges of the door or the windows and enters	Likely	The house has a wooden fence and the gate is always locked The bag of diamonds is hidden in the shoe cabinet Hinges are on the inside of the house	Likely
	The burglar breaks the plywood door and enters	Likely	The house has a wooden fence and the gate is always locked The bag of diamonds is hidden in the shoe cabinet	Likely
	The burglar cuts through the glass and enters	Likely	The house has a wooden fence and the gate is always locked The bag of diamonds is hidden in the shoe cabinet	Likely
	The burglar opens the door or the window and enters	Very likely	The doors and windows have locks which are kept locked when there is no one at the house The lock of the window is on the inside. The house has a wooden fence and the gate is always locked The bag of diamonds is hidden in the shoe cabinet	Unlikely

Continued

Table 2.1 Security assessment of keeping diamonds at home.—cont'd

Vulnerabilities	Threats	How likely is the diamond to be stolen (without controls)?	Security controls in place	How likely is the diamond to be stolen (with controls)?
The house is made of brick	The burglar drills through the wall or through the roof and enters	Unlikely	The house has a wooden fence and the gate is always locked The bag of diamonds is hidden in the shoe cabinet	Unlikely
The house can be opened with a physical key from the outside	The burglar makes a duplicate key, opens the door and enters	Likely	The house has a wooden fence and the gate is always locked. The bag of diamonds is hidden in the shoe cabinet	Likely
	The burglar steals the original door key and then enters	Likely	The house has a wooden fence and the gate is always locked. The original door key is kept underneath the carpet when there is no one at home The bag of diamonds is hidden in the shoe cabinet	Likely

Now, given the asset (bag of diamonds) and the vulnerabilities (column 1), I consider several threats (column 2) in Table 2.1. Note that in each of these threats, a threat agent exercises/executes a threat by exploiting the corresponding vulnerability in column 1. Once again, this is only a subset of possible threats, and there are understandably many more. For instance, a more sophisticated threat agent may steal the real diamond and replace it by a fake diamond. In that case, I wouldn't even know that I have been robbed if they can otherwise cover their tracks.

Each threat in the table is annotated with a measure of how likely it is for the threat to be successfully executed by a threat agent to steal the diamond. I use a very simple, and highly unscientific, measure of likelihood, with four possible values = {*Very likely, Likely, Unlikely, Very unlikely, Virtually impossible*}. The fact that the house has a wooden fence and has a locked gate is a control for every threat since the fence and the gate reduces access to the doors, windows, and locks of the actual house. The fact that the diamonds are hidden in a shoe cabinet is also a control for every threat because in order to steal the diamonds, the attacker, even if they be inside the house, will still have to figure out where in the house the diamonds are.

Finally, there is column 3 in Table 2.1. This column enumerates the protections I have at my home, for every combination of threat and vulnerability combine. An astute observer will see that the controls I have at my house do not bring down the likelihood of most of the threats. The only exception is the threat "The burglar opens the door or the window and enters" whose likelihood comes down from Very *Likely* to *Unlikely* due to the presence of a lock.

So is it worth the risk to store my bag of diamonds at my house?

Given the number of threats, and the overall weakness of my controls (most of the time it fails to bring down the likelihood of any threat to below *likely*), I make the decision that it is too *risky* for me to store the diamonds at home.

So I walk to the neighboring bank, Acme Bank, and talk to the bank manager to explore the possibility of renting a locker in the vault. It is going to cost me of course, but the bank manager assures me that the cost of the monthly locker rental fee is more than made up for by the protection of my assets a bank vault offers. She guides me through the security protocols and protections in place. Customer lockers are kept in the bank vault. Each customer locker requires two keys to open: the bank manager's and the locker owner's. The vault is always locked with a combination that is known only to bank manager and is monitored 24/7 by security cameras that are connected to a remote monitoring site. The bank manager only allows a locker owner to walk into the vault after checking that the name on the photo ID provided by the person seeking access matches with the name they have registered to the locker, and after the person seeking access provides proper answers to certain security questions that were created (mother's maiden name? model of first vehicle?) during locker set-up.

After listening to all the security controls at the bank, I make a similar table (Table 2.2) to assess the risk of storing the diamonds in the bank vault.

Now that my diamonds would be stored in a bank vault, I am exposed to a different threat agent—bank robbers, who one can assume, at least for the sake of this example, are a more well-equipped, dangerous (likely armed), and sophisticated adversary than the burglar I was trying to protect my diamonds from at my house. In many ways, the threats faced to the vault are similar to the threats faced to my house. Just like a house, a vault is an enclosed space with means of entry (e.g., a door), but it is less vulnerable structurally (e.g., no windows, stronger building materials). Since it has a door, it has hinges, and if there is a hinge, one can detach a door from the hinge. However, the vault door hinges are tamper-resistant with titanium screws that cannot be practically cut through or unscrewed.

The only difference is that the hinge for the vault door, and we can see that from the security controls, is tamper-resistant with titanium screws that cannot be cut through or unscrewed. The vault door has the same vulnerability as my house, in that an attacker can open the door and walk in. However, the security controls (e.g., armed guards, continuous monitoring, always locked with a combo known only to bank manager) that protect against threats that exploit this vulnerability are much stronger. In my house, if someone stole or made a copy of the key, then they could always gain access to where the diamonds were kept. In the bank though, even if my locker key is lost or duplicated, the person who wants to steal my diamonds has to get through an authentication process that will require them to look exactly like me (so that they can pass the photo-id check), and know answers to my secret questions. Now, what if the bank manager is the attacker herself? It is unlikely given that she has gone through a background check and the bank authorities have her personnel data, and this unlikeliness is reflected in the risk assessment (precontrols). However, the possibility of an insider attack has to be evaluated too because she knows the combination to the vault. But even if bank manager is the attacker, she cannot get access to my bag of diamonds because my locker requires both the bank manager's key as well as the locker owner's key to open.

Table 2.2 Security assessment of keeping diamonds in a vault space leased from a bank.

Vulnerabilities	Threats	How likely is the diamond to be stolen (without controls)?	Security controls in place	How likely is the diamond to be stolen (with controls)?
The bank vault has a door	The bank robber unscrews the iron hinges of the vault door and enters	Likely	The vault door is made up of tamper-resistant screws made of titanium The vault is protected by armed guards The vault is monitored 24/7 by security cameras and the feed is streamed in real-time to a remote monitoring station with direct connection to law enforcement Hinges are on the inside of the vault	Virtually impossible
	The bank robber breaks the vault door and enters	Unlikely	The vault door is made of titanium with structural reinforcements The vault is protected by armed guards The vault is monitored 24/7 by security cameras and the feed is streamed in real-time to a remote monitoring station with direct connection to law enforcement	Virtually impossible
	The bank robber opens the door and enters	Very likely	The vault door can be unlocked by a combo known only to manager A locker requires two keys to open: one owned by the locker owner and one owned by bank manager. The vault is monitored 24/7 by security cameras and the feed is streamed in real-time to a remote monitoring station with direct connection to law enforcement	Virtually impossible

Continued

Table 2.2 Security assessment of keeping diamonds in a vault space leased from a bank.—cont'd

Vulnerabilities	Threats	How likely is the diamond to be stolen (without controls)?	Security controls in place	How likely is the diamond to be stolen (with controls)?
The vault is made of reinforced concrete and metal	The bank robber drills through the wall or through the roof and enters	Very unlikely	The vault is monitored 24/7 by security cameras and the feed is streamed in real-time to a remote monitoring station with direct connection to law enforcement	Virtually impossible
The locker can be opened with a key	The bank robber makes a duplicate key of the locker key	Likely	The manager lets the locker owner enter the vault only after the manager authenticates his/her identity by checking that the name on his/her government-issued photo-id matches with the name on the locker and the locker owner answers some security questions, with the answers matching with those in file The vault is monitored 24/7 by security cameras and the feed is streamed in real-time to a remote monitoring station with direct connection to law enforcement	Virtually impossible
	The bank robber steals the locker key	Unlikely	The manager lets the locker owner enter the vault only after the manager authenticates his/her identity by checking that the name on his/her government-issued photo-id matches with the name on the locker and the locker owner answers some security questions, with the answers matching with those in file The vault is monitored 24/7 by security cameras and the feed is streamed in real-time to a remote monitoring station with direct connection to law enforcement	Virtually impossible
The manager knows the vault door combo	The manager accesses the vault space	Unlikely	A locker requires two keys to open: one owned by the locker owner and one owned by bank manager	Virtually impossible

As you can see, the vulnerabilities in the bank are similar, the threats are similar, but after the security controls are tabulated, the likelihood of all the threats goes down to "virtually impossible."

So what do I decide? Based on a cybersecurity risk assessment, the risk of the vault solution is acceptable, since all threats have been evaluated to be "virtually impossible." Not that my diamonds can't be stolen from the bank vault, after all "virtually impossible" isn't the same as "impossible." What we can all agree is that the risk at the bank is much lower than what the risk would be if the bag was in my house.

I put my bag of diamonds in the bank vault, and I sleep soundly.

For now.

Understanding cybersecurity risk

Now that, hopefully, we have an informal idea of how cybersecurity risk assessments work, let us formalize some of the concepts. At the cost of repetition, this is the way I choose to define these concepts in my book. I will reference standard definitions when describing concepts and justify my deviance from standards when necessary.

Asset

The word asset, the way we use it in conversational English, refers to something of value that requires protection. The cornerstone of cybersecurity is the concept of an asset; it stands to reason that if you don't possess anything of value, there is no incentive for anyone to attack it and hence, by extension, there is nothing to secure.

The US Department of Homeland Security Risk Lexicon [5] says that an asset is a person, structure, facility, information, material, or process that has value.

The definition is intentionally very generic because it allows organizations to use the concept to refer to whatever it that makes sense to them. A company board and top-level executive management may consider assets to be organizational crown jewels, things of extreme value that contribute to the success of the organization's mission, like brand reputation, customer trust, intellectual property, and business continuity. An engineer, on the other hand, may consider assets to be the systems themselves. In the traditional IT security threat modeling world, this is perhaps the most common interpretation of what an asset is. Examples of assets, in this interpretation, are compute endpoints like laptops and servers, network infrastructure like routers and load-balancers, software systems like the database and application servers, etc.

In this book, I will avoid mapping assets to nebulous concepts like "brand reputation," and restrict discussions to more technical, engineering properties of a system. The purpose of asset identification in this book is for threat modeling. Hence assets are to be defined in such a way that threats follow immediately from the definition of an asset. An attacker may target your system properties for many reasons, such as tarnishing your brand or to compromise your ability to conduct business. But the threats they execute aren't defined at the level of "brand reputation" or "intellectual property." The attacker is thinking on different lines—how do I get admin access to the database in which patient identifying information is, how do I install code on the server such that I can then transfer the stolen records to a remote website that I control? If the attacker is successful, brand reputation and customer trust will be compromised as a result, but the attack per se is not formulated on such assets, but assets like "passwords" and "code."

One may, of course, loosely say that the "server was compromised" or the "database had data stolen" but the threat, if you drill down to it, is that someone stole the admin account *password* and compromised *code* integrity on the server. Or perhaps, the attacker was able to exploit the fact that the server code did not properly parse input to "overflow" the input space allocated to a legitimate input, and get the ability to execute *code* in the main memory of the server.

This brings me to the definition of system level assets or system assets for short.

System level assets/system assets

System level assets or system assets, for short, are valuable properties of a system that are of interest to anyone who wants unauthorized access to your system. System threats are defined on system properties like code (installing malware), passwords (stealing account credentials), configurations (altering firewall rules to allow threat agents into the network), and critical data (stealing privileged data, altering data so that wrong decisions are taken on the basis of them, destroying data, etc.). This is why I choose to define system assets as properties of the system, because, in my opinion, it makes coming up with realistic threats much easier than if one had defined assets in any other way. Examples of system assets are system code, system configurations, system commands, and personally identifiable patient data. The need to protect these assets introduces secondary assets like secret keys, passwords, etc.

Subsystem level assets/subsystem assets

If assets are the things we need to protect, we aren't done by defining assets just at the system level. At system level, threats are formulated as theoretical "what-ifs." A system is made up of multiple subsystems: electrical, mechanical, software, and hardware. The subsystem level is where the exploitable weaknesses are found, and the actual (as opposed to "what-if") threats are defined.

Let us go back to the diamonds and bank vault example. "The bank robber breaks the vault door and enters" is a generic "what-if" threat applicable for all banks in the world. However, let us presume Acme Bank (which if you recall, was the name of the bank in the example we had used earlier in the chapter) has chosen as the vendor for its vault, a company by the name of "The General Vault Company." Suppose The General Vault Company knows of a structural fault in its vault door. The fault could be abused by a robber with a commercial drill to rupture the door. This is now a weakness in Acme Bank that an attacker can actually exploit (i.e., it is no longer an abstract "what-if"). This weakness exists in Acme Bank because they chose to buy their vault door from The General Vault Company, but this weakness might not be present in vault doors of other banks, banks that had chosen a different vendor for their vault doors. Acme Bank now has an exploitable weakness in the mechanical subsystem of their vault, a weakness that is associated with an asset procured from a vendor, namely The General Vault Company.

In medical devices, subsystem level assets, or subsystem assets for short, are the hardware and software components procured from third parties by the medical device manufacturer (MDM), as well as the custom hardware and software made by the MDM itself. Each such component needs to be tested for weaknesses by the MDM. The MDM also needs to track weaknesses discovered by other entities on the subsystem assets they have; in the example above, the structural weakness in the vault door was not discovered by Acme Bank's own testing, but by the vendor's.

Vulnerability

The word "vulnerability," like the word "asset," means different things to different people.

If we look at the way the US NISTs in its document, Security and Privacy Controls for Information Systems and Organizations (SP 800-53 rev 5), commonly referred to as NIST 800-53 [6], a vulnerability is a *weakness in an information system, system security procedures, internal controls, or implementation that could be exploited or triggered by a threat agent.*

This is a fairly comprehensive definition, in that it covers all the places an exploitable weakness may be located, be it in the product itself or in the processes surrounding the product. These weaknesses may be directly linked to the general design of the product (e.g., the locker can be opened with a key), specific issues of the product (e.g., the structurally defective door bought from the General Vault Company), and specific issues of system processes (e.g., the vault code is not changed every day, or the classic heist movie trope, that there is a window of 2 min when the people at the monitoring station change shifts when the cameras are not being watched).

Now let's contrast this definition above with the definition from the US NISTs again, but this time for its National Vulnerability Database (NVD) [7].

> *A vulnerability is a weakness in the computational logic (e.g., code) found in software and hardware components that, when exploited, results in a negative impact to confidentiality, integrity, or availability. Mitigation of the vulnerabilities in this context typically involves coding changes, but could also include specification changes or even specification deprecations (e.g., removal of affected protocols or functionality in their entirety.*

The careful reader should note the far more limited definition of a vulnerability as a weakness in logic (hardware or software), and not say, in procedures. How shall we reconcile this seeming inconsistency?

By considering that just as there are system level assets and subsystem level assets, there are system level vulnerabilities and subsystem level vulnerabilities. The first definition (from NIST 800-53) is an all-encompassing definition of vulnerabilities, encompassing system level constructs (procedures, controls, etc.) as well as subsystem level constructs (the implementation). The second definition (from NIST NVD) is the more restrictive definition of vulnerabilities, which focuses only on actual issues at the subsystem level. It is thus, not a coincidence, that the place this "subsystem level vulnerability" definition is sourced from (NIST NVD) is a database of all subsystem level vulnerabilities (i.e., software and hardware vulnerabilities) that have been detected in publicly available software and hardware. In the context, their definition of a vulnerability as a weakness in computational logic makes perfect sense.

For the purpose of the book, just like system level assets and subsystem level assets, there will be system level vulnerabilities and subsystem level vulnerabilities, specifically software and hardware vulnerabilities. Why only these two subsystems, one may ask? Why not the mechanical subsystem, surely there may be weaknesses there too? Since hardware and software

are the two subsystems that fall under the purview of cybersecurity, our focus in this book will be on these two subsystems. It is of course recognized that there are vulnerabilities in other subsystems, like mechanical (after all the structural fault of the door of bank vault was an example of a mechanical vulnerability) or electrical (e.g., a product defect that allows someone to intentionally short a circuit) but they are kept out of the scope of the book.

System level vulnerabilities/system vulnerabilities

System level vulnerabilities or system vulnerabilities, for short, are vulnerabilities or weaknesses that are properties of the system as a whole. These may be of the following type.

Design vulnerabilities

Design choices introduce attack surfaces, i.e., interfaces through which the system may be attacked. In the bank example, when you have a room with a door, you will have the vulnerability that someone who is not supposed to will get in through the door. The only way to remove the vulnerability would be to have a room with no doors, but then the absurdity of that is very obvious. There is no way the vulnerability of a door can be removed, but doors can be designed to keep intruders out.

Let us consider a practical medical device example. Let us presume that you have persistent read-write storage in your medical device, like an SSD drive. That storage device is a potential attack surface, and introduces, among others, a system level vulnerability of "Read-write storage can be written to." Now can this vulnerability be removed? The only way to totally remove the vulnerability would be to change the design. In this case, you can replace a read-write storage unit with a read-only persistent storage component (e.g., ROM). Of course that design choice would introduce a lot of system restrictions. For example, you won't be able to easily issue updates to code on the ROM. If there is a need to be able to easily update devices (as opposed to having devices returned to the MDM for every software update), this system design may not be feasible. This means as the system designer, "Read-write storage can be written to" may be a system vulnerability you have to live with. Now of course there are mitigating cybersecurity controls that could make it harder for an unauthorized person to write their code or data to the persistent storage. But that does not mean that the attack is absolutely impossible because the system vulnerability will remain.

Unremediated subsystem vulnerabilities

When it comes to the structural vulnerability in their vault door, Acme Bank has two options: replace the vault door or live with it. The Acme Bank management chooses the latter option. They believe that armed guards being present all the time doesn't make it likely that anyone will even get close to the vault door with a drill without getting intercepted. Not to replace the vault door may be a perfectly valid business decision, but now there is an actual exploitable vulnerability that is present at the system level. The Acme Bank now has an actual vulnerability in their vault door, and any "what if" scenarios now have to consider the very real possibility that this vulnerability may be exploited. As per the definition of a system vulnerability used in this book, this unremediated subsystem vulnerability becomes a vulnerability of the entire system, i.e., becomes a system vulnerability, and needs to be documented as one.

Process vulnerabilities

Process vulnerabilities may be the absence of certain processes, for example, no process for changing the vault code password every day, or weaknesses in existing processes, like the 2 min shift-gap at the monitoring station, alluded to before.

Subsystem level vulnerabilities/subsystem vulnerabilities

Subsystem (hardware and software) level vulnerabilities or subsystem vulnerabilities for short are *actual* issues in the system implementation. Unlike "Read-write storage can be written to," which is a theoretical vulnerability that exists because of a feature of the system design, subsystem vulnerabilities are real, exploitable weaknesses of the subsystem.

Let's assume the operating system of your medical device has a vulnerability that may be exploited remotely by an attacker. You chose not to apply the operating system patch which would close the vulnerability. Now the reason you can afford to leave this software vulnerability unpatched is because your device has a system level control against anyone exploiting the vulnerability. The control is the fact that you have disabled the wireless adapter of the device. Now, because of that control, this attack is not likely to happen. If your control is weak (e.g., the wireless adapters are disabled but could be re-enabled through another known subsystem level vulnerability), then the decision to not patch the operating system may lead to you being attacked.

Threat

Just like the word "vulnerability" the word "threat" is also highly overloaded in the field of cybersecurity. For some, threat refers to a person or group, such as when they talk of "insider-threats" or in the sentence "Nation states are proving to be the biggest threat to the security of this country's digital infrastructure." For others, threat refers to specific techniques and actions, such as phishing (tricking someone to give up their password) and password guessing (trying all combinations of passwords). For some others, threats are very specific sequences of actions that an attacker performs in order to compromise an asset by using a vulnerability.

For the purpose of this book, I shall define threat as specified by the NISTs 800-53 standard [6]. To quote:

> *A threat is any circumstance or event with the potential to adversely impact organizational operations (including mission, functions, image, or reputation), organizational assets, individuals, other organizations, or the Nation through an information system via unauthorized access, destruction, disclosure, modification of information, and/or denial of service.*

A threat should also be distinguished from a threat scenario. A threat scenario is a detailed, step-wise decomposition of a threat. For example, "The bank robber breaks the vault door and enters" is a threat, whereas a threat scenario would contain the exact details of how the bank robber would get to the vault door, what kind of widget they would use to drill through the metal. A threat typically maps to multiple threat scenarios, which are more prescriptive and detailed.

Just like the bilevel stratification of assets and vulnerabilities, there are two kinds of threats: system level threats and subsystem level threats.

System level threats/system threats

A system level threat, or system threat for short, is an event or circumstance that exploits a *system vulnerability* to compromise a *system asset*. For example, "The bank robber breaks the vault door and enters" is a threat that uses the system vulnerability "The bank vault has a door." System threats are theoretical events, what-ifs that the system designer needs to provide protections against. Every system threat is characterized by two measures.

Likelihood

This metric measures how likely it is for a system threat to lead to an adverse event. This likelihood is often split into two factors—the likelihood of a system threat being successfully executed leading to the potential of the adverse event and the likelihood of the adverse event actually happening. To understand this two-level split, consider the threat: "The bank robber unscrews the iron hinges of the vault door and enters." The likelihood of this threat leading to an adverse event (i.e., the stealing of the diamonds) is a function of two likelihoods—one that the bank robber unscrews the iron hinges and enters (at which point of time the threat has been successfully executed), and then the likelihood that the bank robber escapes with the bag of diamonds. There is always the possibility, of the bank robber entering the vault door, i.e., successfully executing the threat but then not being able to leave with the diamonds (e.g., the police or armed guards showing up before they can make an escape). To now use the language used in the domain of medical device risk management world, the successful execution of a threat leads to a hazardous situation, which may then lead to the adverse event (i.e., harm) (Fig. 2.1).

Severity

This metric measures the impact of the adverse event. In the example of the bag of diamonds, the severity of all threats is the same because the impact of all threats is the same, namely the stealing of the bag of diamonds. This is why you do not see severity as a column in Tables 2.1 and 2.2. However, in general, the consequence of the loss of all system assets are not the

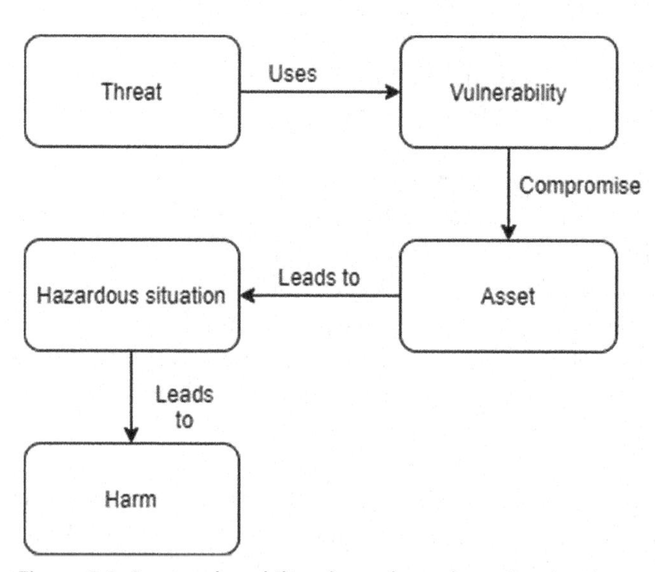

Figure 2.1 Asset, vulnerability, threat, hazardous situation, harm.

same, for example, the severity of a threat that leads to the stealing of a bag of diamonds is not the same as the severity of a threat that leads to the stealing of office furniture because of the differences in their values.

Subsystem level threats/subsystem threats

A subsystem (hardware or software) level threat, or subsystem threat for short, is an event or circumstance that exploits a *subsystem vulnerability* to compromise a *subsystem asset.* Software and hardware-level threats, unlike system threats, are not hypotheticals. They actually exist, either in the form of actual exploit code or as detailed "howtos" which if followed, would allow someone to execute the threat in real-life. Subsystem threats for which there are no patches are often sold in the black market, their price varying from thousands to millions of dollars, and they are sometimes referred to, in popular literature, as zero-day vulnerabilities or zero-day exploits [8].

This blurring of the line between the notion of "vulnerability" and that of a "threat" at the subsystem level is one of the root causes for the confusion in the definition of these terms. The line is blurred because when you have an actual issue, the weakness and the threat are combined together in the specification of the vulnerability. I sometimes prefer to use the word "vulnerability-threat combine" to refer to these issue specifications.

Let us try to understand this further. The NVD [7] maintains a database of all subsystem (software and hardware) vulnerabilities. The NVD pulls its information from the Common Vulnerabilities and Exposures (CVEs) list [9] maintained by MITRE. Each element of this list, characterized by a CVE-id, is a statement of a vulnerability-threat combine. A CVE entry typically has associated with it a Common Weakness Enumeration (CWE), which MITRE defines to be a "nonproduct specific vulnerability type or class" [10], of which a specific CVE entry is an instance of. For example, the actual defect in vault doors manufactured by The General Vault Company would be an example of a CVE entry, whereas the associated CWE would be "structural manufacturing defect." So even though each CVE entry is referred to as a vulnerability (that's the "V"), they are actually threats and vulnerabilities, defined together.

There is a scoring system for every CVE entry in the NVD. Every CVE entry is provided a CVSS score, whose full-form is Common Vulnerability Scoring Scheme [11]. Now if you look at any CVE entry, you will find that each entry is actually a definition of a threat as well as of a vulnerability—in the real world of subsystem level threats, a threat definition cannot exist independently of the vulnerability it exercises. In my opinion, it is not the vulnerability per se that has an impact (and hence can be scored), but a threat that exercises the vulnerability that has an impact. It is the threat, on which a judgment of whether it is easy or difficult can be made, since it is threat which has to be executed, the vulnerability simply exists. This is why, in this book, I associated metrics of likelihood and severity to a threat, both at a system as well as a subsystem level. How exactly we measure likelihood and severity of a subsystem and system threat will be explained in the chapters on Threat Modeling and Risk Modeling.

Cybersecurity risk for patient safety and patient privacy

Risk, as has been introduced previously, is typically expressed as a function of likelihood and severity. In order to model risk, one needs to come up with a risk function, i.e., a functional formulation that when provided the inputs of likelihood and severity, outputs a metric of risk. One common way of facilitating risk decisions is to define risk acceptability zones—acceptable risk (green zone) unacceptable risk (red zone), "acceptable but needs some further analysis" risk (yellow zone).

Let's go back to our example with the bag of diamonds. If one recalls, I had decided then, based on a threat analysis, that the risk of keeping the diamonds at home was just too great. The vulnerabilities at home were highly likely to be exploited; the wooden door could be sawed through, the hinges could be taken apart, and the locks could easily be broken. As long as there were no valuable things at my house, I never really cared for what material my doors were made of, or when I kept the windows open. Now that I have brought home the bag of diamonds though, these all became very important considerations.

My perception of risk thus is borne out of two considerations—how much I would lose if my diamonds were stolen and the likelihood of the threats leading to the diamonds being stolen. As long as the value of my assets was low, I was perfectly fine with the risk of keeping them at home. Now that the value of my assets went up by a lot, I moved them to a place where the likelihood of a threat exploiting a vulnerability were low. I chose to keep them in a bank vault. Only then did I consider my risk as sufficiently lowered. Formalizing this, greater the likelihood of a threat leading to an adverse event, greater is the risk, and greater the impact of a successful realization of a threat, greater is the risk.

In the discipline of medical device risk management, likelihood is nearly always expressed as the probability of occurrence. In the case of cybersecurity, it is very difficult to describe the probability of occurrence of a threat leading to harm. In classic safety and reliability engineering, probability of occurrence can be estimated from field failures and historic trends, the kind of data not currently available for medical device cybersecurity. This is because most fielded products do not have measures to detect a cybersecurity incident, even if it has occurred. As a result, likelihood as characterized by probability of occurrence is not suitable as a measure in the cybersecurity context. Instead, MDMs typically use alternative characterizations of likelihood, usually in terms of a qualitative or a quantitative scale.

Let us now come to the notion of severity. Severity is a measure of impact. But impact where? This is where the notion of a *risk domain* comes in. A risk domain is the context in which the impact of the successful realization of threat is considered. For the bag of diamonds, the risk domain was financial risk. In the medical device world, our primary concern is safety and privacy. In the risk domain of safety, severity is measured as level to harm to the patient. In the risk domain of privacy, severity is measured as the number of patient identifying records that may be compromised. Safety and privacy are system level properties; their severity can be measured only at the system level. Hence, in this book, cybersecurity risk at the system level will be measured in the risk domains of safety and privacy.

Patient safety and patient privacy are, however, not subsystem level properties. At the subsystem level, the best one can do is to evaluate *potential impact to* safety and privacy. If the vulnerability is not remediated at the subsystem level, and it flows up to become a system vulnerability, only at that level can impact to patient safety and privacy be assessed.

Let's go through a hypothetical conversation between a cybersecurity engineer and a firmware engineer to understand what I just said. The formalization of the intuition follows in Chapter 5 and 6.

Cybersecurity engineer (CE): Based on our static code tool analysis, the firmware contains several unsafe C functions, i.e., functions against which a buffer overflow attack can be …

Firmware engineer (FE): I know what a buffer overflow attack is. This code is so deep inside the software architecture that it is just not possible for an attacker to craft a string that can exploit the buffer overflow. It is simply not reachable from the outside world.

CE: But still, these are high severity threats, in that this is therapy code, if anything goes wrong.

FE: I get that, but nothing can go wrong. As I said, how are you going to reach the vulnerable buffer area?

CE: So are you planning not to fix these buffer overflow issues right now?

FE: Not now, maybe in a later version.

CE: Okay, let's do a risk analysis. So at the software level, you have a highly exploitable, well-known vulnerability against which threats can be trivially created. Do you agree, we have a potential impact to safety here? In that if someone was able to, for argument's sake, exploit the buffer overflow, there would be a severe impact to patient safety?

FE: Yes potential. Sure. But that potential is never going to become real.

CE: Bear with me here. Since the software vulnerability is not being patched, it is now becoming a system level vulnerability. Impact at the system level to patient safety is going to be severe, because this is a therapy device, likelihood is high since everyone knows how to exploit a buffer overflow ...

FE: No. Likelihood is not high. That is exactly what I am saying ....

CE: The likelihood is high *without any mitigating control.* What you are saying is that there is a mitigating control that reduces risk by reducing likelihood, namely that the code is not reachable from user input.

FE: Exactly!

CE: In order to use this as a control for a formal risk model, I need to provide evidence of the implementation of the control. Can you please provide me a formal document where, using intra and interprocedural flow analysis techniques, you show that the code is indeed not reachable. Otherwise I will not be able to support this as a valid risk response.

FE (Realizing that formally providing evidence of reachability will take them much more time than fixing the issue): Forget we had this conversation. I will fix the bugs this release.

This provides us the perfect segue to the next section on cybersecurity controls.

Cybersecurity controls

The primary goal of product security architects in an MDM is to bring patient safety and patient privacy risk associated with the use of medical devices to an acceptable. Patient safety and patient privacy risk is reduced through the application of security controls. Security controls are countermeasures that avoid, detect, counteract, or minimize security risks to products (Fig. 2.2).

Security controls may be of the following types:

1. Technical: These are system controls defined on the product, like authentication of users and of code, and authorization checks, and hardening of system interfaces, and secure storage of critical cryptographic parameters.
2. Procedural: These are controls defined on processes surrounding a product, like ensuring that the product development lifecycle has security built into it at various stages, or that cybersecurity or that product maintenance processes have controls built for cybersecurity patch delivery.
3. Legal: These are legal controls defined on the product, like terms and conditions, policies, liability, and contractual obligations.

Returning to our example of the bag of diamonds, the technical controls at the bank vault would be the electronic surveillance and armed guards and special vault doors, the procedural controls would be the criminal

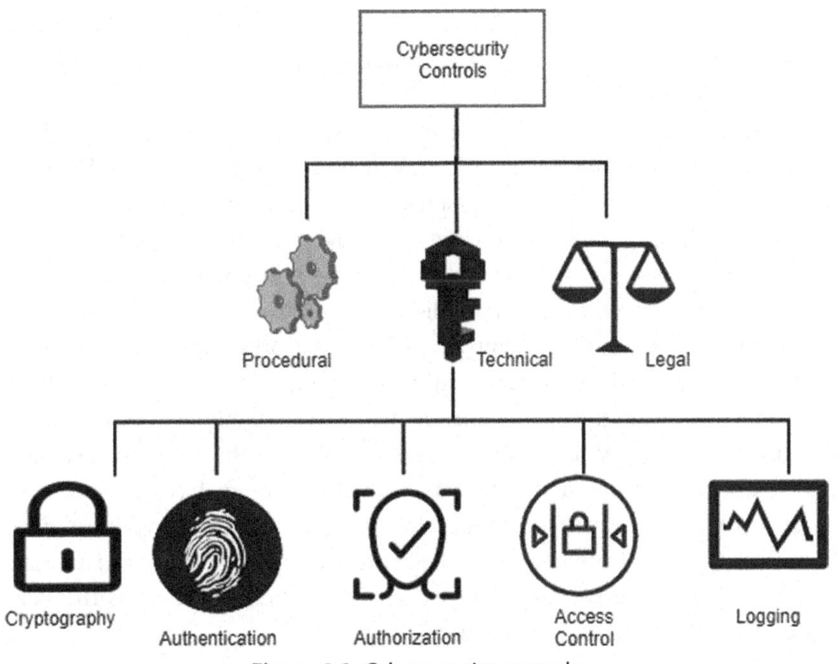

Figure 2.2 Cybersecurity controls.

background checks every employee of the bank has to go through or the process the personnel at the remote monitoring center follow once they suspect a robbery is happening, and the legal controls would be the policies and terms of use that the customer signs when they rent a vault.

Before designing security controls for a product, it is important to define formally what information security is. Let us consider the definition in the US federal regulation: 44 U.S.C. (US Code), Sec. 3542 [12], which is cited by NIST 800-53 [6].

> *The term "information security" means protecting information and information systems from unauthorized access, use, disclosure, disruption, modification, or destruction in order to provide—*
>
> *Integrity, which means guarding against improper information modification or destruction, and includes ensuring information nonrepudiation and authenticity.*
>
> *Confidentiality, which means preserving authorized restrictions on access and disclosure, including means for protecting personal privacy and proprietary information.*
>
> *Availability, which means ensuring timely and reliable access to and use of information.*

In order to ensure information security, a system has to satisfy these three security objectives—Integrity (I), Confidentiality (C), and Availability (A) security objectives.

In traditional IT systems, the order in which system designers prioritize the objectives are C first, then I, then A, often referred to as the CIA triad. That is because the confidentiality of data stored on IT systems trumps pretty much everything else. We need only to look at prominent data breaches over the past few years to convince ourselves how important data confidentiality is, how difficult it is to secure digital data in this day and age, and what devastating impact confidentiality breaches have on people and organizations. The next security objective in order of importance is integrity. If an attacker could change the data inside an IT system, there would not be much faith in any data record it maintains, or for that matter, anything that it does. A customer can buy a product and deny having bought it, because the system cannot ensure the integrity of the transaction data. Last, though as the cliché goes not the least, is availability. If legitimate users of an IT system can be denied access a system, then that defeats the very reason why the system exists in the first place.

However for medical devices, the priority is inverted: Availability (A) is the most important, followed by Integrity (I), and finally Confidentiality (C). This is yet another reason why securing medical devices requires strategies that are often fundamentally different from securing traditional IT systems. Loss of availability means a delay in treatment, which is potentially more harmful than a compromise of confidential patient health information. Having your personal information stolen and sold in the black market will cost you time and money to "make right," but the impact of that is not even remotely as devastating as what would happen if a medical device stops working during an emergency situation. Loss of integrity by altering clinical parameters, like changing the infusion dose, or injecting a false therapy command (e.g., a command to shock the patient through an implanted cardiac device) could potentially be as critical as an attack on availability.

However, what puts availability above integrity as a security objective is that for an attacker, an attack on availability is easier to craft than an attack on integrity. Let us consider a battery-powered, implanted cardiac device that takes therapy commands over wireless. For an attack on availability, an attacker can jam the communication medium (e.g., Bluetooth, Wi-Fi/ 802.11) with fraudulent requests. Those fraudulent packets may be rejected by the device, but the rejection itself would consume resources like memory and CPU cycles, drowning out genuine requests, and draining the battery.

This kind of attack does not require the attacker to gain any knowledge about the underlying protocols used by the device or break any encryption being used to protect the transmission. In comparison, a compromise of integrity would likely prove much more challenging. The attacker may need to know packet format, craft packets in a way that passes input validation, and circumvent cryptographic controls. Because threats that target availability are generally easier than those which target integrity (and hence the likelihood of them being executed), controls that reduce the risk of attacking availability are prioritized over integrity.

Technical cybersecurity controls

Technical cybersecurity controls are security countermeasures incorporated into the product design. Technical controls belong to five categories. These controls reduce the risk of successful attacks by enabling the device to meet the security objectives of availability, integrity, and confidentiality. Technical controls belong to five general classes—cryptography, authentication, authorization, access control, logging; what I like to call the five fingers of security, put them together, and you get a "punch"!

A point to touch upon. In conversations on security and even in security literature, the terms "authentication," "authorization," and "access control" are often conflated and used interchangeably. In this book, the way I will disambiguate the concepts of authentication, authorization, and access control is as follows. Authentication is *establishment of identity*, authorization is the *definition of rights of the authenticated identity*, and access control is the *enforcement of those rights*. Sometimes the implementation of authentication, authorization, and access control happen together in one seemingly atomic operation—you log into a system and start invoking functions, but underneath the hood, there are three distinct domains, each with their own conceptual models, protocols, and attendant technological implementations.

Technical control category: cryptography

Cryptography is defined in NIST SP 800-59 [13] as *the discipline that embodies the principles, means, and methods for the transformation of data in order to hide their semantic content, prevent their unauthorized use, or prevent their undetected modification*. Cryptography cuts across all the other control classes as the underlying mechanism for implementing different kinds of security controls as well as for measuring their strength. Just as walls made of reinforced steel and concrete make it difficult for attackers to breach them through explosives, using cryptography of appropriate strength prevents threat sources from brute-forcing their way through your cryptographic controls.

One thing you should never do with cryptography, no matter how comfortable you might feel about the mathematics behind it, is to write your own cryptographic algorithms or your own implementations of cryptographic algorithms. Standard cryptographic algorithms that are used in the real-world have been developed over years by some of the greatest minds in computer science (the scientists whose initials form the R, S, and A of the RSA cryptographic algorithm went onto win the Turing Prize, the highest award in Computer Science [14]), and these algorithms have withstood mathematical scrutiny by cryptanlysts (i.e., experts in mathematically analyzing weaknesses in cryptographic algorithms) [15,16]. Standard implementations of cryptographic libraries like OpenSSL [17] have been vetted, tested, analyzed, and whatever vulnerabilities have been unearthed, have been patched and fixed. Given the thousands of expert person-hours that have been expended making these algorithms and their implementations as robust and efficient as possible. Because MDMs work in highly resource-constrained environments, the temptation to create a new cryptographic scheme that runs on sparse computational resources, or to change the code of standard cryptographic implementations in order "to make them fit in the available memory space" maybe high, but should be avoided. Even a small change to a standard cryptographic algorithm can vastly weaken it. In case you choose to design your own cryptographic algorithms, you may need to get these algorithms analyzed and certified by recognized cryptanalysts (this is a US FDA requirement [18]). Be warned, this kind of certification can be a very expensive and time-consuming thing to do, even assuming you have the necessary cryptographic skills. The industry consensus is to use standard cryptographic algorithms recommended by an authority like the US NIST. NIST maintains up-to-date standardized lists of cryptographic algorithms that have passed scrutiny and further maintains a list of algorithms to be avoided [19].

Finally, before I provide an overview of cryptography, let me repeat what I said in the foreword. This book does not aim to be a book on cryptography. Hence I shall not formally define cryptographic operations, nor delve into the mathematics behind cryptographic computations. Interested readers are asked to refer to References [1–4] for a full, first principles driven treatment of cryptography. For the duration of the book, we will have to do with intuitive descriptions, which though, understandably imprecise and oversimplified, is sufficient to make this book self-contained.

Confidentiality

To ensure confidentiality of a message, you encrypt the message. Encryption is a function that takes as its input two things—(1) The original representation of the information, referred to as plaintext and (2) an encryption key, and produces as the output, an alternative representation of the information, known as the ciphertext. In an effective encryption system, someone who reads just the ciphertext will not be able to derive any intelligible content. In other words, they would not be able to extract any knowledge of what the content of the plaintext was.

The ciphertext can be passed through the decryption function. Decryption is a function that takes two inputs—the cipher text and a decryption key—and outputs the original plaintext (i.e., the original representation of the information supplied to the encryption function).

In symmetric key encryption, the encryption and decryption key are the exact same. Both sides of a communication have knowledge of this key, and that enables them to encrypt and decrypt messages. If Alice and Bob are communicating, they both share the same key K (Fig. 2.3).

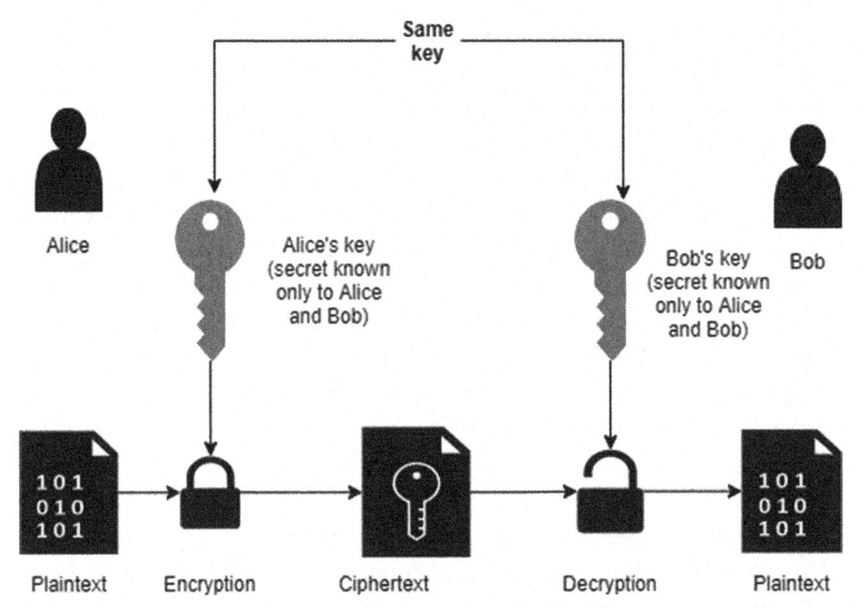

Figure 2.3 Symmetric encryption.

There are other encryption schemes where the keys are not the same. These are known as asymmetric key encryption schemes [20]. In these schemes, each side of the communication has two keys—a private and a public key. The private and public keys are mathematical duals of each other, in that a message encrypted with a public key on one side can be decrypted only with the corresponding private key on the other. The mathematical function that generates the public and private keys has an important property—knowledge of the public key does not provide sufficient information to deduce the value of the corresponding private key.

Each side, Alice and Bob, keeps their private key to themselves and sends the other their public key. Then, when Alice needs to send a message that only Bob can read, she encrypts a message with the public key to Bob. Since only Bob has the private key, only Bob can decrypt the message (Fig. 2.4).

Symmetric key encryption is fast, can be done very efficiently with specialized hardware. It is used for bulk encryption of data, when data are being transferred from the sender to the receiver (data in motion) and for keeping data confidential during storage (data in rest).

There is a problem though that is intrinsic to symmetric encryption. How do you get the two parties, Alice and Bob, to have the same key before

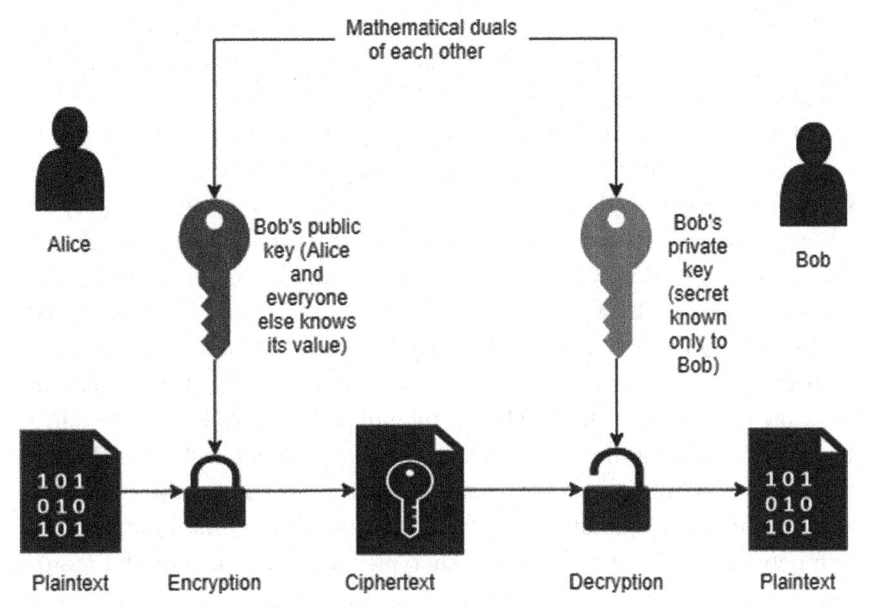

Figure 2.4 Asymmetric encryption.

they start communicating? Alice can't just send the key to Bob over the Internet because Curt listening on the communicating medium between them will just read the key, and decrypt all their future messages. This is known as the *key establishment problem* [21,22], i.e., how to get both parties to securely agree to use the same key, called a session key, for symmetric encryption of communication sessions, where the only way of communication between them is insecure.

One way of doing secure key establishment is by transporting the shared encryption key in plaintext over a trusted communication channel. A communication channel is considered trusted when the system designer has assurance that no attacker is eavesdropping in the channel. In medical device system design, this is sometimes accomplished by doing key transport over communication channels that require near physical contact (either actual physical contact or presence within the range of centimeters) between the sender and the receiver. This closeness, proximity is the assurance that there are no attackers listening during key transport, because if they were, the human participant initiating the key transfer would see the attacker.

Obviously, when two parties communicate over wireless protocols like Bluetooth or 802.11, one cannot trust the communicating medium because of their range. An attacker could be in the next room, or outside the building, listening in to the key being transferred from sender to receiver. They can also use wireless extenders and be in the next building.

This is where asymmetric key encryption schemes that work on integer factorization cryptography [22] come into play. Here is an example of how secure *key transport* works (Fig. 2.5). One side of the communication (let's say Alice) encrypts the symmetric session key (this is called key-wrapping) with the public key of Bob. Curt, who is eavesdropping on this communication, will not be able to decrypt the message, since Curt does not have the private key of Bob. Once Bob decrypts the wrapped symmetric session key with his own private key, Bob acknowledges receipt of the session key by sending the same session key, encrypted with the public key to Alice back to Alice. Once Alice sees that the key she sent and the key she got back from Bob are the same, Alice knows that the session key has been successfully established between her and Bob. All messages in the subsequent communication session between A and B will now be encrypted and decrypted by the session key just established.

Another way of getting both sides to have the same symmetric key is through *key agreement* (Fig. 2.6). In key agreement, which works on the principle of discrete logarithmic cryptography [21], no session key is sent from one party to another over a communicating medium, not even one

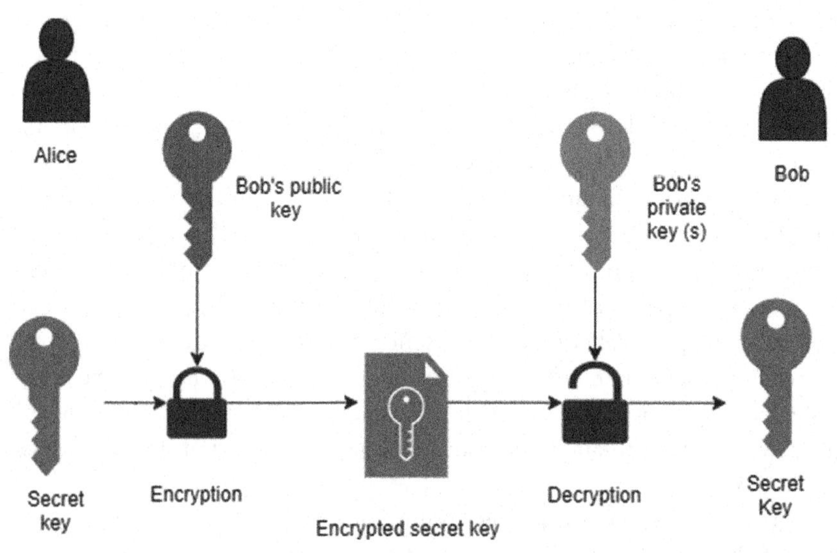

Figure 2.5 Secure key transport.

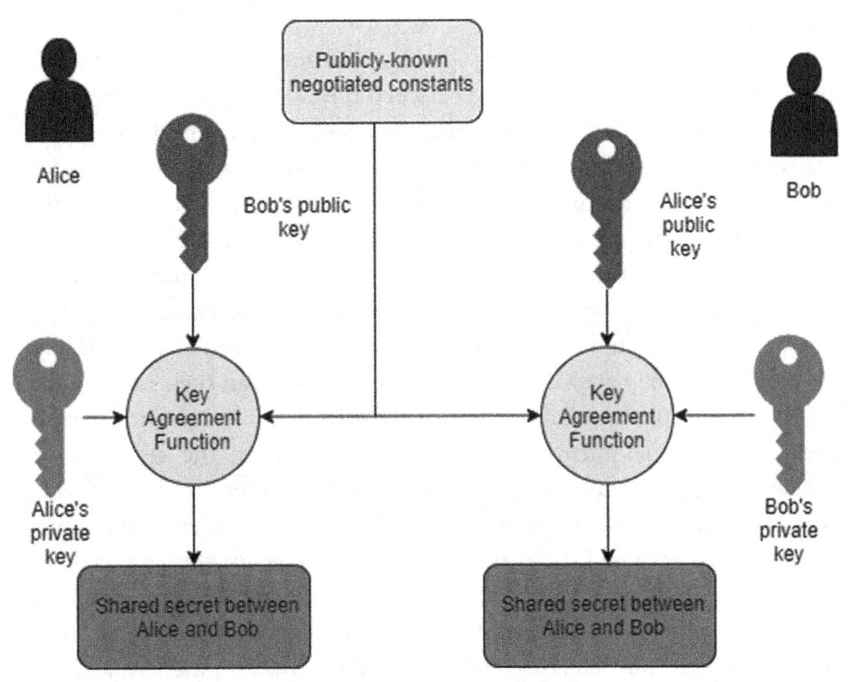

Figure 2.6 Key agreement.

that is encrypted. Instead, both Alice and Bob have a shared key agreement function. At each side of the communication, the key agreement function takes as its input: the public key to the other side, this side's own private key, and some constants that are negotiated and may be publicly known. The mathematical property of the key agreement function is that if both Alice and Bob apply the inputs stated above, the function will output *the same secret value* at both ends. This secret value is then input to certain other functions (details we do not get into here in this high-level discussion but the interested reader may refer here [23]), and these functions output the session key that is going to encrypt messages in the communication henceforth.

Encryption is not to be confused with encoding. Encoding is a data-transformation applied to messages for data usability. For example, an encoding scheme known as Base64 [24] is commonly used when there is a need to encode binary data that needs be stored and transferred over media that expects textual data. This is to ensure that some component does not mistakenly interpret the data as text and apply transformations that change the data itself. In encoding, there is no notion of a secret key, and the algorithm is publicly known, and hence no guarantee of security.

Cryptographic integrity

Note the heading here is "cryptographic integrity." This contrasts with simply "integrity" to disambiguate between the two related, but ultimately, dissimilar concepts. In the world of medical device engineering, integrity of data is ensured by various means I refer to as "integrity measures." Integrity measures work by running data through a publicly known mathematical formula. If the same input is run through the formula multiple times, the formula will produce the same output each time. Some common integrity measures are a parity bit [25] or a cyclic redundancy check (CRC) [26]. A sender can calculate the integrity measure of their data and attach that measure along with the data to a recipient. The recipient can then take the data and recompute the measure on their own. Because the integrity measure produces the same integrity for identical input data, the recipient can compare their calculated measure with what the sender provided them. If the measures match, the recipient is assured of message integrity. If the message had been changed, then the integrity measure on the received data would differ from what the sender provided, and the recipient can reject the data as having been tampered with. While this form of integrity assurance is sufficient for detecting random bit-flips in transmitted data due to interference or connection problems, it cannot protect the integrity of the data from an attacker modifying it in a targeted, nonrandom way. It is trivial for an attacker to craft a malicious message that has the exact same *noncryptographic* integrity measure [27]. In other words, different inputs to the noncryptographic integrity measure formula can produce the same output, and it would be impossible to determine which was the real message by the integrity measure alone.

In order to ensure cryptographic integrity, i.e., protection against an attacker, the standard practice is to compute a cryptographic integrity measure. Usually, a secure hash function is used as a cryptographic measure. A secure hash function is a mathematical function that takes as its input a message and outputs a fixed-size output. The output is called a secure hash. The secure hash is then appended to the message by the sender (Alice). Once Bob receives the message and its secure hash, Bob runs the same secure hash function on the received message. If the secure hash Bob gets by applying the hash function is the same as secure hash appended to the message, then the integrity has been preserved, else not.

So how is a secure hash function different from standard noncryptographic measure, given that they operate in pretty much the same way? A secure hash has the following desirable properties [28].

- It is quick to compute.
- The same message always results in the same secure hash.
- It is infeasible to determine the input to the secure hashing function from the resulting secure hash output.
- A small change to a message (i.e., a bit flip) changes the secure hash so drastically that the new value gives an attacker no inkling as to how small the change has been.
- It is infeasible to find two different messages that have the same secure hash. If you know the secure hash of a message M i.e., H(M), it is computationally infeasible (i.e., very hard using modern computers) to find another message M′ such that H(M) = H(M′). As a matter of fact, for a hash function to be considered a secure hash function, it should be computationally infeasible to find any two messages M and M′ that hash to the same value.

But wait, why should the attacker Curt even have to replace Alice's message M with his own M′ such that they hash to the same value? Why can't Curt just generate his own message M′ and compute H(M′) and send it over to Bob? Since Bob is having a communication session with Alice, he will think M′ came from Alice.

This brings us to the problem of not just ensuring the integrity of the message but also of the message's authenticity. Bob needs to know not just that the message Alice sent was not tampered with, but the fact that the message itself came from Alice. There are two ways of ensuring this.

- Keyed secure hash [29] (Fig. 2.7): Here, the secure hash of the message is encrypted by the shared session key between Alice and Bob. When Bob receives a message purporting to come from Alice, Bob first decrypts the secure hash. Then he calculates the secure hash of the message himself. If the secure hash of the message matches the decrypted secure hash that came with the message, Bob knows that the message came from Alice (who else would have had the shared encryption key to encrypt the hash with?) and the fact that it has not been altered during transit.
- Digital signature [30] (Fig. 2.8): Here, the secure hash of the message is encrypted by the private key of Alice. This is known as *signing* the message. When Bob first receives a message purporting to come from Alice, Bob first decrypts the secure hash using the public key of Alice. Then he calculates the secure hash of the message himself. If the secure hash of the message Bob computes matches the decrypted secure hash that came with the message, Bob knows that the message came from Alice (who else would have had the private key corresponding to Alice's public

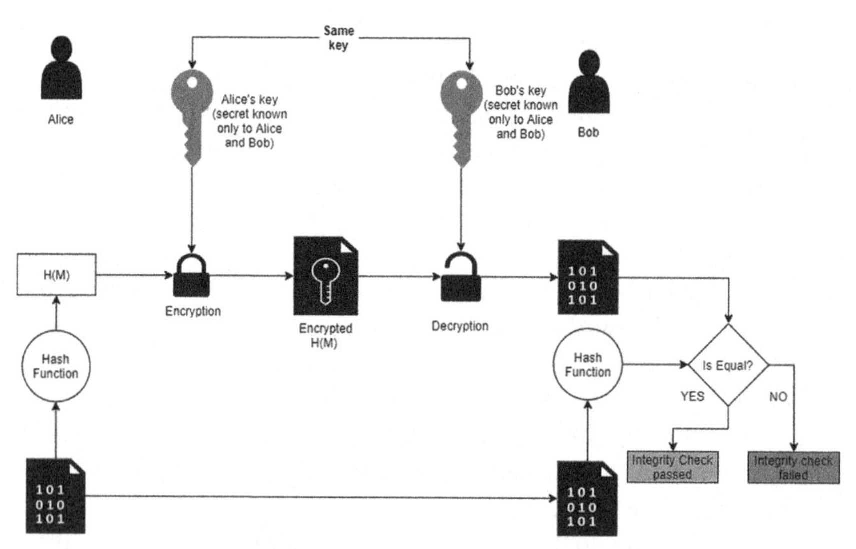

Figure 2.7 Keyed secure hash.

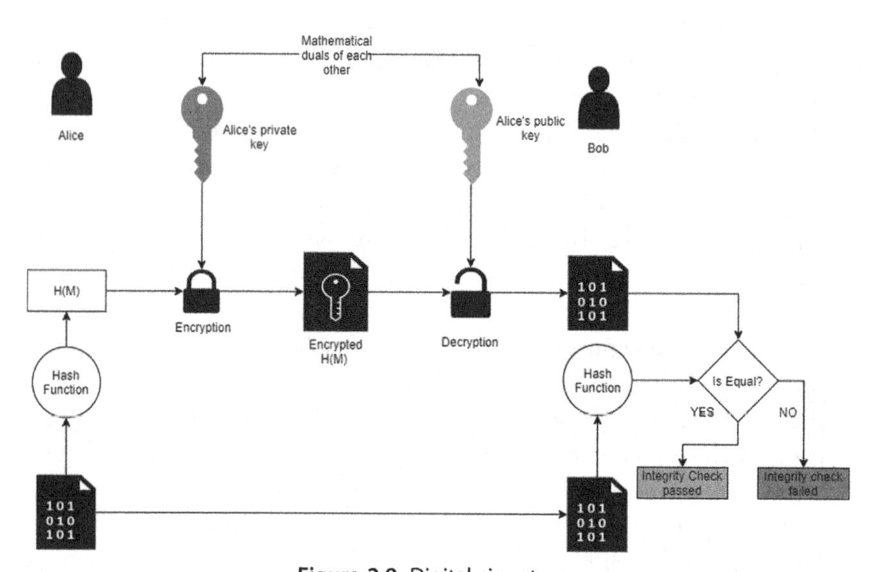

Figure 2.8 Digital signature.

key to encrypt the hash with?) and the fact that it has not been altered during transit. We can now say that the digital signature has been successfully verified.

Because, as mentioned before, symmetric encryption is a computationally much more efficient operation that asymmetric encryption, session integrity for real-time communication is usually ensured through keyed secure hash. Digital signatures though have important applications, in situations that do not require real-time performance, like when you are installing code. When the code passes digital signature verification, the installing party is assured that the code actually came from the vendor, and has not been altered (e.g., no malware has been inserted) during its transit from the vendor to where the software is being installed.

Threats to cryptography

As should be evident, be it asymmetric or symmetric key encryption, the protection afforded by encryption depends on the fact that the attacker does not know the key value. If the attacker knows the shared encryption key during symmetric encryption and the private key during asymmetric, then it is "game over." This follows from one of the fundamental principles of cryptography, articulated by Auguste Kerckhoff in the 19th century: *A crypto-system should be secure if everything about it is known, except the key* [31].

The table below summarizes some common threats to cryptography.

Threats to cryptography	Controls
Brute forcing the key space: Here the attacker tries out all possible values of the key to see which one decrypts the message.	**Choose a recommended key length:** As hardware becomes more and more efficient, key lengths needed to reasonably high in order to protect against exhaustive key-space search keep increasing. The US National Institute of Standards and Technology (NIST) has key length recommendations for each of their recommended cryptographic algorithms, which are periodically increased to account for increasing horsepower of processors [32,33].
Reading the key: The key can be stolen either from the physical location where it is stored or when it is being transported.	**Key wrapping:** Do not send keys over a communication medium without wrapping (i.e., encrypting the key with another key). The only exception can be if the transmission is over a trusted, very close-range communication medium, but here too, one needs to be absolutely sure that there is no way to eavesdrop. **Secure storage:** Encryption keys should be stored in secure storage. This can be in specialized key-storage hardware or on persistent read/write media with the operating system keeping it clear of "prying eyes," but the one place keys should never be stored is in code. If an attacker can get access to your code, even if it be obfuscated, it is not difficult to figure out constant values like keys.

Continued

—cont'd

Threats to cryptography	Controls
Mathematical attacks: Technically called cryptanalysis, these attacks try to deduce some information about the plaintext (if not the plaintext itself) by doing mathematical analysis of a large number of ciphertext-plaintext pairs or by analyzing large amounts of ciphertext.	**Proper generation of the key:** Each time a symmetric key or a key-pair for asymmetric cryptography is generated, the value should be independent of all other keys generated previously. This can be guaranteed through true random number generators (TRNGs)s or cryptographically secure pseudorandom number generator (CSPRNG). When keys are generated from other keys or from passwords, there are myriad other requirements [34–37] which if not met, may lead to weaknesses that may be exploited by cryptanalysis. **Proper usage of cryptographic algorithms:** NIST-recommended cryptographic algorithms, if used properly, provide protection against cryptanalysis attacks. However, using it in the proper way is your responsibility. For example, some algorithms need an initialization vector, i.e., a random or pseudorandom value. If you provide such algorithms a fixed value, the strength of the encryption is vastly reduced, making it susceptible to cryptanalysis.

Since the key is "everything" in cryptography, a best practice is to always change keys. This is known as *key rotation* [38]. As discussed previously, asymmetric key cryptography is used to securely transport symmetric session keys or enable both sides to come up with the same symmetric session key through key agreement protocols. This symmetric key is established new for every session. If an attacker Curt can somehow obtain the session key between Alice and Bob, it is useless for the next session between Alice and Bob. Asymmetric keys have historically had longer life-times, but still they need to be rotated and expired in order to ensure a consistent security posture.

Technical cybersecurity control category: authentication

Authentication is formally defined, by NIST [6], as the "verifying the identity of a user, process, or device, often as a prerequisite to allowing access to resources in an information system."

In the example of the bank vault, the manager lets the owner accompany him into the vault only if the person seeking entrance authenticates their identity by presenting a government-issued photo-id. This is what authentication is—confirming the identity of something or someone before trusting them. In this case, the fact that you possess the card and that your face matches the face on the card is enough for the manager to trust that the person in front of him is indeed you.

The most common form of authentication we encounter in our day-to-day life is that of user authentication using a login-password. For example, if you want to gain access to your emails, your email server must determine whether you are, in fact, you. When you supply a name and password to your email server, the server identifies you as "you" if it received the correct password for your email account.

The login-password is referred to as an authentication "factor." The most common types of authentication factors are something you know (e.g., password), something that you possess (e.g., an access card, a mobile phone), or something that is inherent to your physiology (e.g., face, fingerprint, retina).

The astute reader may recognize that in the previous example, if someone else knows your login and password, then that person will be identified as "you." To address this, some systems require not just a single authentication factor (e.g., a username and password) but instead require multiple factors (e.g., username, password, access card, and facial scanner) to authenticate. This is known as "multifactor authentication" (Fig. 2.9). This raises the bar for successful authentication, in that someone impersonating you will have to pass authentication tests based on proving the possession of multiple factors. For example, not only would they have to know your password but also steal your phone and craft a Mission-Impossible like face-mask.

Figure 2.9 Multifactor authentication.

Authentication is not just about authenticating human users. It also encompasses machines or devices. For example, when an infusion pump is talking wirelessly to a pump server over the hospital network, both the pump and the pump server need to be sure that they are actually communicating with a genuine device. A weak form of mutual device authentication would be the fact that they are connected to the same wireless hospital network, the pump would know it is talking to a genuine server because who else on this network can it be other than the server. The weakness in this scheme is obvious. If the attacker got onto the network because the hospital network password is shared, or because the network is open, or any number of other reasons, then that guarantee of authenticity immediately breaks down.

Another form of authentication that unfortunately is still being used is the simple knowledge of unique device IDs. In this scheme, pumps are configured with the device ID of the pump server and the pump server maintains a list of all pump device IDs. Both parties present their IDs when they wish to communicate and, once the IDs match with what each party knows to be a genuine ID, the communication is considered authenticated. All the attacker has to do in this case is to know the IDs often written on the devices themselves or available in attendant documentation, and it then becomes trivial to impersonate each party in the communication.

Just like devices need to be authenticated, so do data and code. The system engineer at the hospital has to be absolutely sure that the firmware update they are installing on a hospital device is actually from the device manufacturer and not from the attacker or, for that matter, the threat agent did not alter the genuine code somewhere along the way from manufacturer's servers to the device. Similarly one has to be sure about the authenticity of data. For example, the attacker could pretend to be a hospital's electronic medical records system, craft an illegitimate infusion order, and submit it to the infusion pump. A weak form of code and data authenticity is through integrity measures like CRCs, the weakness being that such non-cryptographic measures are sufficient to guard against random bit-errors, but not strong countermeasures against a determined attacker, as discussed previously.

The recommended form of data and code authentication is through keyed secure hash or through digital signatures, which, if you will recall, was described in the section on cryptography. A valid secure hash or digital signature attests to not just the fact that the data and code have not been altered but that they originated from the source that claims to be the originator.

In the discussion on cryptography so far, we had sidestepped one notion, namely that of identity. When Alice sends her public key to Bob, how does Bob know that the public key that he got, that he believes to be Alice's, is actually not Curt's? If he blindly trusts that the public key is actually Alice's, he may end up encrypting his session key with Curt's public key, which would allow Curt to know what the session key is. This is the classic scenario of a Man-in-the-Middle Attack. Alice sends Bob her public key. Curt is sitting between Alice and Bob. He intercepts Alice's message, and replaces her public key with his public key. Bob gets Curt's public key and thinks it is Alice's. When Bob sends Alice his public key, Curt does the exact same thing, replaces Bob's public key with his own. Now, if they were using key-agreement, Alice and Curt establish a shared session key, Bob and Curt establish a shared session key, all data that Curt receives from Alice he passes to Bob, and vise versa, reading every message and altering them too, if he so wishes.

The core problem here is that there is no secure association established between an entity and the public key that entity claims to have. This connection between an entity and a public key is established by what is known as a digital certificate. A digital certificate is an attested digital association between a principal and their public key, with the attestation being made by a trusted third party called a Certificate Authority (CA) [39]. A CA implements what is known as PKI [40,41], which is a set of roles, policies, hardware, software, and procedures needed to create, manage, distribute, use, store, and revoke digital certificates and manage public-key encryption.

The simplest way to understand a certificate is that it is a statement of the sort "The CA attests to the fact that Alice has public key X," and since you trust the CA, you trust the association between Alice and the public key X. This attestation is being done with the association being digitally signed by the CA using their own CA private key. This signature is essential to protect the integrity of the message, else Curt can change it to "Curt has public key X."

CA's help defend against the Man-in-the-Middle attacks. When Bob gets a certificate from Alice, he can be sure that the public key embedded in the certificate is Alice's and Alice's only. How? Bob has a copy of the CA's public key and can use it to verify the digital signature on the certificate.

There are presumptions here though—namely that the CA verified the identity of Alice before issuing her a digital certificate and that it wasn't Curt wearing an Alice mask. This is the trust assumption that both Alice and Bob make, and the security of their communication depends wholly on how much they can trust the CA to "do the right thing."

Root and Chain of Trust (Fig. 2.10): This brings us to a vital concept in authentication—the notion of "root and chain of trust." No matter what authentication scheme is devised, there is always an entity that has to be trusted intrinsically. For example, when Bob verifies the signature of the

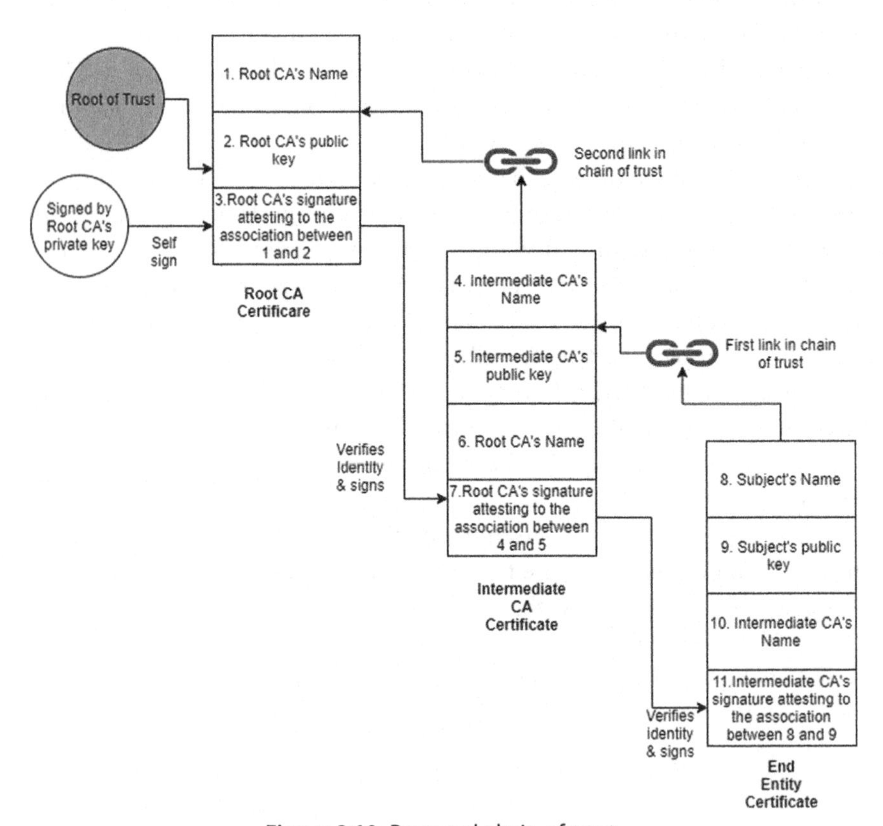

Figure 2.10 Root and chain of trust.

CA using the CA's public key, how does he know that the verification key really is the CA's public key and not Curt's? Well, the association between the CA's identity and CA's public key ("The CA has public key Y") can be digitally signed by someone else, and that's how we know it is the real CA, and not Curt. But then how do we know that "someone else" is not Curt? This leads to a chain of trust that ultimately leads to the root of trust, that public key that one trusts, *without signature verification*. The faith in the root of trust has to be established by means other than signature verification. Usually this is done by storing the public key of the root CA (the CA that is intrinsically trusted without further verification) in special, dedicate areas for sensitive data. Examples of such dedicated areas are programmable read only memory, immutable hardware storage that cannot be written to outside of manufacturing [42], or on locations in persistent read-write storage which requires special elevated privileges, like admin, to write to Reference [43].

If an attacker can overwrite the root of trust with their own public key, then to use the phrase again, "game over." With the root of trust compromised, the entire chain is compromised. With a compromised root of trust, malware may be downloaded or your device may be communicating with threat agents masquerading as trusted devices.

So far, we have talked about how to protect the root of trust on your device from an attack where the attacker replaces the root CA public key with their own public key. But what if the root CA or one of the CAs in the chains of trust established at the root, signs malware without doing due diligence? This is increasingly being seen to happen [44]. The solution to this is for device manufacturers to have their own root CA and own device PKI, so that they do not rely on commercial root CA vendors to provision their root of trust. In situations where this is not possible, certificate pinning, a technique that does not rely on establishing a chain of trust through root CA, should be used [45].

Technical control category: authorization

Authorization is defined as the right or a permission that is granted to a system entity to access a system resource [46]. Often confused with authentication, it is important to understand the distinction. Authentication consists of defining the notion of an identity, be it for a human user, a device, code or data, and then verifying the identity before giving access. Authorization consists of defining policies on what an authenticated entity can then do, and what it cannot once they have been granted access to the system. In short: authentication is determining if someone is who they say they are; authorization is determining what that person is allowed to do.

A layered authorization model is implemented by assigning entities (human users and devices) to groups or roles, and then assigning permissions or privileges (system actions that they are allowed to perform) to these roles (Fig. 2.11).

As an example, let us consider a medical device with three groups or roles, with different sets of privileges.

- A normal clinical user: This user is allowed to perform normal clinical functions.
- An admin user: This user is allowed to add/remove users to device, assign/unassign users to groups, but is not allowed to perform normal clinical functions.
- A service user: This user is allowed to install firmware, change settings on the device that persist across power-offs (e.g., alarm volume), but is not allowed the ability to perform normal clinical functions nor add/remove users.

One of the well-accepted guiding principles in designing an effective authorization scheme is the principle of least privilege. This principle states that an authenticated entity is given only those privileges that are essential to perform its intended function and no other. While this may seem obvious, egregious violations of the principle of least privilege is fairly common in real

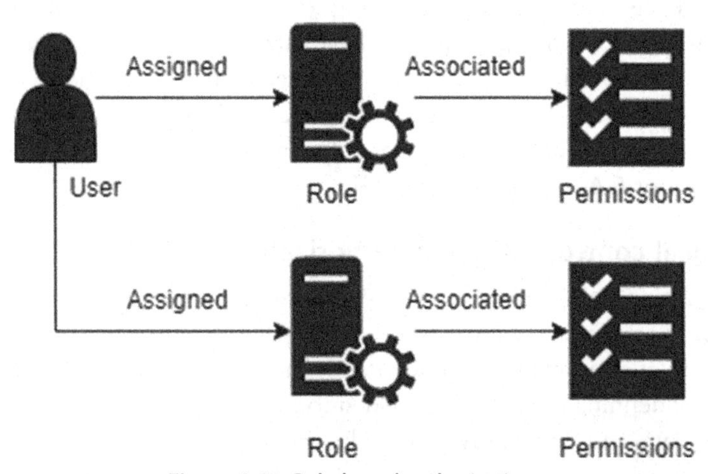

Figure 2.11 Role-based authorization.

world systems. Processes run with higher privileges than they require, and users are put in groups where they are given rights to perform actions that their job requirements do not authorize them to.

Let us consider the example of a role-based authorization model being used in a healthcare delivery organization (HDO). A normal user for a medical device is a clinician, an admin user is hospital IT staff, and a service user is the hospital biomed division. The clinician needs to use the device for clinical use cases and those are the privileges the clinician role gets. The hospital IT user needs to have the ability to maintain user accounts but should not be given the privileges to perform clinical operations. Finally the biomed engineer should be able to perform maintenance operations on the device, but there is no need to give the role the ability to perform therapy or administer user accounts. Every role thus has exactly the privileges it needs to perform its operations, and nothing more.

Technical control category: access control

If authorization is about defining the rights of what a user is allowed or not allowed to do, access control consists in checking whether an authenticated user is allowed access to a particular resource, as per the rights granted to it, and then allowing or refusing access, as the case may be. Authorization defines what can be done by whom, and access control is the enforcement of those rules on a per-resource basis. Hence the definition of access control as *the process of granting access to information system resources only to authorized users, programs, processes, or other systems* [41]. In software systems, access control generally consists of checking the authorization token (typically digitally signed by the authorization authority to prevent someone from forging or generating their own authorization tokens) before allowing a user to perform a system function. Only if the token says that the entity presenting it has the privilege of performing the function is its request to perform said action granted, else not.

There are several models of access control of various degrees of rigidness—the one that I shall discuss in this book because it is the most appropriate model for medical devices will be role-based access control [47], which is based on assigning system users to roles and assigning privileged functions to the roles. You have already been introduced to the concept intuition in the authorization section when we laid out an example involving three roles: a normal clinical user, an admin user, and a service user, the functions authorized for each role.

Extending the principle of least privilege, it is necessary not just to ensure that authenticated users do not have access to privileges that go beyond their function, but also to reduce the attack surface of a system as much as possible. For example, why enable system services that are not being used, or allow network access from addresses that cannot be sources for valid authentication requests. *System hardening* is considered a part of access control as it protects the perimeter, making sure that the access to the system is not uncontrolled. Remember, that even without possessing valid authentication credentials or having broken the security of the communication protocol, an attacker can send an overwhelming number of authentication requests or data packets to a system. The attacker does so knowing very well that they will all be rejected by the device, but also aware that servicing and rejecting malformed packets would exhaust system resources. This is why it is important to close extraneous interfaces, like unused ports and operating systems accounts, and apply restrictions on application traffic, for instance, through techniques like ingress filtering, before spurious traffic starts consuming system resources.

Access control can also be accomplished through physical and mechanical measures. In HDOs, medical devices are usually operated in locations that required someone to swipe a security batch to access. This is an example of a physical security control that enforces access restriction. In some medical devices, interfaces like the USB port are secured with a lock that can be opened only by a special service mechanical appliance. In some other devices, special debug interfaces (e.g., the Joint Test Action Group or JTAG interface [48]) is given a coating of epoxy to restrict anyone from connecting to it. These would be examples of mechanical access controls.

Technical control category: logging

Going back to the example of the bank vault and the bag of diamonds, one of the security controls at the bank was the following: "There is extensive video surveillance of all parts of the bank and inside the vault, and the video feed goes to a remote operating center with direct connection to law enforcement." As a prospective customer evaluating the risks of keeping my diamond bag at the bank versus keeping it at home, this was reassuring. It told me that suspicious activity within the bank vault will be immediately seen and acted upon, and that bank robbers will be dissuaded by this very fact, that if they enter their actions will immediately be discovered and law-enforcement dispatched.

The objective of security logging [49] is similar to that of the surveillance system at the bank—to detect suspicious activity, take a decision when "an attack is imminent or underway," and then respond to a developing bank robbery situation. Any security logging strategy, be it at the bank or for a medical device, has to resolve, at the very minimum, the following technical dilemmas:

What to observe?

There are so many things going on in any complex system that might have significance from a cybersecurity perspective, so what exactly do you monitor and record? The more things you decide to track, the more resources you end up consuming, and more costly monitoring becomes.

For a medical device, one has to choose the specific events (e.g., unsuccessful log-ins, firmware updates) that shall be logged, how much space shall be allocated on the device for storing the logs, and how frequently the logs will be transmitted for analysis.

Loosen the criteria for what constitutes a "recordable event," and you create a lot of logs, in effect generating the proverbial haystack where the needle of the successful indicator of compromise becomes buried. Also the more events you store locally, the faster you will run out of space and be forced to overwrite records of events before they can be analyzed, potentially flushing out valid indicators of compromise. The more aggressive you are in transmitting log events to a central server for analysis, the more real-time traffic you generate and consume scarce bandwidth.

Tighten the criteria for what constitutes a "recordable event," and you swing to the other extreme, running the risk of false negatives, of totally missing indicators of compromise, defeating the very purpose of logging.

When to react?

Just because something appears suspicious, does not mean that an attack is imminent or has happened. Sure, if you see someone in the vault with a mask and a semiautomatic, it is a good time to let law enforcement know. But what about that gentleman who seems to be obsessively interested in studying the locations of the cameras than conducting bank business? Is he doing reconnaissance for a bank robbery or is he just intellectually curious? His behavior may be suspicious, but is it worth calling the cops for?

One of the most challenging problems in cyber security is to determine, based on the mass of events that are recorded by different sensors, which of these events constitute "security incidents" worth reacting to and which are just part of the background noise. Just because someone tried to log-in to an account with the wrong password a number of times does not necessarily mean that a brute force password-guessing attack is underway, the user could genuinely have forgotten his log-in credentials or not realize his caps lock was on. Just because the device rejected a firmware update because it failed cryptographic signature check does not necessarily imply someone tried to change the firmware intentionally, it could have been errors introduced by physical corruption on the USB drive that carried the update.

Cry wolf too often, and your fate becomes as it was for the shepherd in the story, when the actual attack happens, it is ignored as yet another fraudulent signal. Set the bar too low, and you fail to detect attacks.

How to prevent the logging system being attacked?

Another of the tropes of heist movies is that the "hacker" member of the crew breaks into the security system and freezes the cameras or loops a sequence that fools those that are monitoring the cameras to think that there is nothing going on. In cybersecurity, the logging system is a target for attackers. Attacks could range from changing log entries and deleting evidence to generating so many auditable events that the system is overwhelmed by the sheer volume, thereby burying evidence among the mountains of data generated.

Procedural controls

Previously, in this chapter, we had classified security controls into technical, procedural, and legal. So far our discussion has been focused on technical security controls and specifically five distinct control-categories—authentication, authorization, access control, logging, and cryptography. While the technical controls are features/functionalities/capabilities built into products, procedural controls are new processes or enhancements to existing processes that exist to ensure that products are developed, transported, deployed in a secure fashion, and maintained in a way such that product vulnerabilities that pose uncontrolled risk are detected and remediated in a timely fashion. The specific objectives of these procedural cybersecurity controls are to ensure that:

- the appropriate technical cybersecurity controls are designed into the medical device

- software is developed following secure architectural and coding practices
- software is verified and validated using cybersecurity-focused testing technologies
- the identity of third-party components, both hardware and software, are accounted for so that vulnerabilities can effectively be tracked
- the risk of cybersecurity vulnerabilities being present in hardware and software components, sourced from third party suppliers, are controlled to acceptable levels
- cybersecurity risk of the product is continuously assessed from feasibility to end of support
- the risk of introducing cybersecurity vulnerabilities during manufacturing and distributing are controlled to acceptable levels
- secure configurations of the medical device and the customer's obligations in maintaining security of the deployment environment are clearly defined and conveyed, and the risk of degrading product security controls (e.g., turning off authentication, keeping the device on an open wireless network) is formally accepted by the customer
- emerging vulnerabilities and threats are tracked, and impacts to products assessed in a timely manner
- vulnerabilities are tracked and risks of unpatched vulnerabilities assessed
- cybersecurity patches are rolled out in a timely manner as part of product maintenance procedures
- cybersecurity incidents are detected and responded to, third-party disclosures of product-specific vulnerabilities are accepted through a defined process, and existing corrective and preventive actions quality processes properly reflect the intake of cybersecurity signals and impact analysis
- cybersecurity information is shared, in a coordinated fashion, between different regulatory and governmental stakeholders, customers and the general public
- staff undergo adequate cybersecurity training, based on their roles and responsibilities.

It's a point made earlier in the chapter, but deserves repeating. When people refer to "vulnerabilities," they usually refer to product vulnerabilities. But vulnerabilities, and this is a point often missed, exist at the process level also. "Vulnerabilities may exist due to the following procedural deficiencies—(1) Not having appropriate procedural cybersecurity controls or defining them improperly, (2) Procedural controls are not properly followed in practice, and (3) Not updating procedural cybersecurity controls to keep up with changing threat landscape or business imperatives." An organization with a higher cybersecurity maturity is one in which risk from process vulnerabilities is lower than that of an immature organization. The way organizations become more mature from a cybersecurity perspective is by (1) incrementally defining a best-practices-driven, gradually exhaustive set of procedural controls and (2) putting in place a governance and compliance structure to ensure that the controls are followed and appropriately updated.

Legal controls

Legal controls refer to protection provided by the law, the presumption being that the prospect of criminal prosecution and civil penalties would dissuade threat sources from attempting to attack systems. In practice though, this rarely works. Attackers are often in foreign countries and safe havens, especially when they are backed by nation states, and the probability of proving charges with proper cyber evidence, especially in the absence of proper logging controls, and then prosecuting and extraditing cybercriminals is fairly low. The odds unfortunately, on the legal front, are stacked well in the favor of attackers.

One of the situations that organizations find themselves in is when security researchers disclose cybersecurity vulnerabilities in medical devices, either in the popular press or through demonstrations at conferences, but do not attack the device with criminal intent. In the past, some multiple device manufacturers have tried to "lawyer" their way through such situations, threatening legal sanctions against those disclosing cybersecurity vulnerabilities on their products. This doubling down, in my opinion, makes the situation worse. First there is the disclosure of a security vulnerability on your product. In the current environment, that is not big news. If then the response of the MDM is to attempt to muzzle the person who disclosed the vulnerability by taking legal action, then *that* becomes the news. In my view, legal controls can be appropriate secondary controls in certain situations but should not be primarily or solely relied on.

Summary and key takeaways

Now that you have finished this chapter, you should have an intuitive idea of assets, vulnerabilities, threats, likelihood, severity, risk, and controls, as they are used in this book. I will be revisiting these concepts again in the chapter on Threat Modeling and Risk Modeling. You should also have, by this time, a basic idea of what authentication, authorization, access control, logging, and cryptography is; enough to understand and meaningfully contribute to discussions on medical device cybersecurity strategy and design. Once again, if you intend to do cybersecurity design of medical devices yourself and you do not have a formal background in cybersecurity, I strongly recommend other books and online articles (the references section for this chapter would be a good place to start) before you start your journey.

The key takeaways from this chapter are:

1. Assets, vulnerabilities, and threats are defined at the system as well as the subsystem (hardware and software) level.
2. System level assets are system level properties (like code, data, ability to communicate, etc.), system vulnerabilities are theoretical weaknesses that originate from system design choices, and system threats are hypothetical what-if attack possibilities on system assets using system vulnerabilities.
3. Subsystem assets are the hardware and software components, and subsystem vulnerabilities and threats are actual issues in the hardware and software together with actual means of exploiting them.
4. When the risk of a subsystem threat is not controlled at the subsystem level, the subsystem level threat floats up to the system level and the risk of the subsystem threat needs to be assessed at the system level. It is at the system level that properties like patient safety and privacy are defined.
5. Controls serve to bring down risk to levels deemed acceptable.
6. Controls can be technical (defined on the product), procedural (defined around the product), and legal.
7. Technical cybersecurity controls belong to one of five categories: cryptography, authentication, authorization, access control, and logging

References

[1] B. Schneier, Applied Cryptography, 2 ed., Wiley, 1996. ISBN: 0-471-11709-9.

[2] J.-P. Aumasson, Serious Cryptography: A Practical Introduction to Modern Encryption, No Starch Press, 2017.

[3] N. Ferguson, B. Schneier, Practical Cryptography, Wiley, 2003. ISBN: 0-471-22357-3.

[4] J. Katz, Y. Lindell, Introduction to Modern Cryptography, CRC Press, 2014.

[5] US Department of Homeland Security, DHS Risk Lexicon, 2010 [Online]. Available: https://www.cisa.gov/sites/default/files/publications/dhs-risk-lexicon-2010_0.pdf.

[6] US National Institute of Standards and Technologies, Security and Privacy Controls for Information Systems and Organizations SP 800-53, 2020.

[7] US National Institute of Standards and Technologies, National Vulnerability Database, n.d. [Online]. Available: https://nvd.nist.gov/vuln. (Accessed 25 September 2020).

[8] Fireeye, What is a Zero-Day Exploit? n.d. [Online]. Available: https://www.fireeye.com/current-threats/what-is-a-zero-day-exploit.html. (Accessed 25 September 2020).
[9] Mitre, CVE and NVD Relationship, n.d. [Online]. Available: https://cve.mitre.org/about/cve_and_nvd_relationship.html. (Accessed 25 September 2020).
[10] MITRE, Frequently Asked Questions, n.d. [Online]. Available: https://cwe.mitre.org/about/faq.html#what_is_cwe_weakness_meaning. (Accessed 25 September 2020).
[11] FIRST, Common Vulnerability Scoring Scheme Specification Document, n.d. [Online]. Available: https://www.first.org/cvss/specification-document. (Accessed 25 September 2020).
[12] US Federal Government, US Code Title 44: Public Printing and Documents, Chapter 35: Coordination of Federal Information Policy Subchapter III: Information Security Section 3542; 2010, 2010.
[13] US National Institute of Standards and Technology, Guideline for Identifying an Information System as a National Security System SP 800-59, 2003.
[14] American Mathematical Society, Rivest, Shamir, and Adleman Receive 2002 Turing Award, 2002 [Online]. Available, http://www.ams.org/notices/200307/comm-turing.pdf.
[15] D. Aggarwal, U. Maurer, Breaking RSA generically is equivalent to factoring, in: Annual International Conference on the Theory and Applications of Cryptographic Techniques, Eurocrypt 2009, 2009.
[16] V. Stolbikova, Can elliptic curve cryptography be trusted? A brief analysis of the security of a popular cryptosystem, ISACA J. 3 (2016).
[17] Open SSL, n.d. [Online]. Available: https://www.openssl.org/. (Accessed 25 September 2020).
[18] US Food and Drug Administration, Content of Premarket Submissions for Management of Cybersecurity in Medical Devices (Draft Version), November 2018 [Online]. Available, https://www.fda.gov/regulatory-information/search-fda-guidance-documents/content-premarket-submissions-management-cybersecurity-medical-devices.
[19] US National Institute of Standards and Technology, Cryptographic Standards and Guidance, n.d. [Online]. Available: https://csrc.nist.gov/projects/cryptographic-standards-and-guidelines. (Accessed 10 January 2021).
[20] US National Institute of Standards and Technologies, Federal Information Processing Standards Publication 197 FIPS-197, 2001.
[21] US National Institute of Standards and Technologies, Recommendation for Pair-Wise Key-Establishment Schemes Using Discrete Logarithm Cryptography SP 800-56A, April 2018.
[22] US National Institute of Standards and Technologies, Recommendation for Pair-Wise Key-Establishment Using Integer Factorization Cryptography SP 800-56B, March 2019.
[23] US National Institute of Standards and Technologies, Recommendation for Key Derivation Using Pseudorandom Functions SP 800-108, 2009.
[24] The Mozilla Project, MDN Web Docs: Base64, n.d. [Online]. Available: https://developer.mozilla.org/en-US/docs/Glossary/Base64. (Accessed 25 September 2020).
[25] R. Zeimer, W. Tranter, Principles of Communication: Systems, Modulation, and Noise, Wiley, Hoboken, New Jersey, 2014.
[26] US Department of Transportation, FAA, Selection of Cyclic Redundancy Code and Checksum Algorithms to Ensure Critical Data Integrity, March 2015.
[27] M. Stigge, H. Plötz, W. Müller, J.-P. Redlich, Reversing CRC – Theory and Practice, Humboldt University Berlin, 2006.

[28] US National Institute of Standards and Technologies, Secure Hash Standard (SHS) FIPS 180-4, 2015.
[29] US National Institute of Standards and Technologies, The keyed-hash message authentication code (HMAC), FIPS 198−1 (2008).
[30] US National Institute of Standards and Technologies, Digital Signature Standard (DSS) FIPS 186-3, 2013.
[31] Wikipedia, Kerckhoffs's principle, n.d. [Online]. Available: https://en.wikipedia.org/wiki/Kerckhoffs%27s_principle.
[32] US National Institute of Standards and Technologies, Recommendation for Key Management: Part 3: Application-specific Key Management Guidance SP 800-57 Part 3, 2015.
[33] US National Institute of Standards and Technologies, Transitioning the Use of Cryptographic Algorithms and Key Lengths SP 800-131A, 2019.
[34] US National Institute of Standards and Technologies, Recommendation for Cryptographic Key Generation SP 800-133, 2020.
[35] US National Institute of Standards and Technologies, Recommendation for Random Number Generation Using Deterministic Random Bit Generators SP 800-90A, 2015.
[36] US National Institute of Standards and Technologies, Recommendation for the Entropy Sources Used for Random Bit Generation SP 800-90B, 2018.
[37] US National Institute of Standards and Technologies, Recommendation for Random Bit Generator (RBG) Construction SP 800-90C, 2016.
[38] US National Institute of Standards and Technologies, Recommendation for Key Management: Part 2 − Best Practices for Key Management Organizations SP 800-57 Part 2, 2019.
[39] Network Working Group, Internet X.509 Public Key Infrastructure:Certification Path Building, September 2005 [Online]. Available, https://tools.ietf.org/html/rfc4158.
[40] Network Working Group, Internet X.509 Public Key Infrastructure Certificate Policy and Certification Practices Framework, November 2003 [Online]. Available, https://tools.ietf.org/html/rfc3647.
[41] US National Institute of Standards and Technologies, Introduction to Public Key Technology and the Federal PKI Infrastructure SP 800-32, 2001.
[42] Synposis, Scalability, Security and Reliability with One-Time Programmable Non-Volatile Memory, n.d. [Online]. Available: https://www.synopsys.com/designware-ip/technical-bulletin/non-volatile-memory-dwtb-q418.html. (Accessed 25 September 2020).
[43] Microsoft, Trusted Root Certification Authorities Certificate Store, [Online]. Available: https://docs.microsoft.com/en-us/windows-hardware/drivers/install/trusted-root-certification-authorities-certificate-store. (Accessed 25 September 2020).
[44] F. Rashid, Attackers Are Signing Malware with Valid Certificates, May 22, 2019 [Online]. Available, https://duo.com/decipher/attackers-are-signing-malware-with-valid-certificates.
[45] The OWASP Foundation, Certificate and Public Key Pinning, n.d. [Online]. Available: https://owasp.org/www-community/controls/Certificate_and_Public_Key_Pinning.
[46] US National Institute of Standards and Technologies, Guide to Industrial Control Systems (ICS) Security SP 800-82, 2015.
[47] D. Ferraiolo, R. Kuhn, Role-based access controls, in: 15th National Computer Security Conference, Baltimore, Maryland, 1992.
[48] R. Johnson, S. Christie, JTAG 101—IEEE 1149.X and Software Debug, 2009.
[49] US National Institute of Standards and Technologies, Guide to Computer Security Log Management SP 800-92, 2016.

Regulatory overview

Introduction

Medical devices are subject to governmental oversight in most countries of the world [1–14]. Without regulatory approval from a designated authority, it is usually illegal to market and sell medical devices. While specific legal requirements and approved regulatory processes vary across countries, the overall objectives of regulatory requirements remain pretty much the same everywhere: to ensure that medical devices actually provide the clinical benefit they claim to provide (efficacy) and that the risk of patient harm from the operation of the device is kept within acceptable levels (safety). Rather than go over every regulation, guidance and standard, and risk repetition, the focus of the chapter is to go over cybersecurity regulations from a few major jurisdictions, like the European Union, the USA and Canada, and distil the commonalities between them and other global regulations. This approach is consistent with the general approach of the book—given that regulations and guidance and standards are always being updated, the reader is better served by being provided the essence of the regulations and the commonalities, rather than the specifics, for which there is always the source document.

The focus of regulatory oversight has historically been to ensure that medical device manufacturers (MDMs) consider, as part of their risk management processes, failures stemming from previously known or reasonably foreseeable causes (e.g., software bugs, mechanical wear and tear, electromagnetic interference, and accidental user errors). Deliberately hostile user actions, like adding two zeroes to the dosage amount or altering device firmware to deliver a lethal shock, were not an area of focus for MDMs or regulators. After all, mutual trust and the best of intentions have been fundamental to the culture of healthcare.

However, with multiple demonstrations of vulnerabilities and threats in medical devices (details in Chapter 1), the situation has changed dramatically in recent years. Regulators across the world are now pushing MDMs to consider an active adversary with hostile intent as a contributor to the risk a device poses to the user. This regulatory push comes in the form of amendments to existing regulatory frameworks, publishing of guidance documents

Cybersecurity for Connected Medical Devices
ISBN: 978-0-12-818262-8
https://doi.org/10.1016/B978-0-12-818262-8.00010-3

on cybersecurity, and by outreach to the medical device industry through conferences and symposia.

The increasing regulatory focus on medical device cybersecurity has been accompanied by a slew of regulations with regards to electronic data privacy. Many medical devices have personally identifiable information on them in order to associate patients with clinical procedures and therapy data. With data being perceived as the "new oil" in today's world, MDMs are increasingly collecting personal data about their patients, over and above the basic need for the operation of the device. These data can be used to refine therapies or for creating value-added services like remote monitoring. Because of the vast amounts of patient data that MDMs collect, medical devices and their surrounding software ecosystem now fall within the purview of general data privacy laws like the European Union's (EU) General Data Protection Regulation (GDPR) [15] and California Consumer Privacy Act [16] in addition to healthcare-specific data privacy laws like the US's Health Insurance Portability and Accountability Act (HIPAA) [17]. Historically, privacy risk has been mitigated almost exclusively through legal controls, i.e. contracts and through liability clauses. But with the vast amount of data being stored digitally, technical and procedural cybersecurity controls are now considered an important component of privacy risk mitigation.

A subtle point that is often overlooked, especially by those who are new to regulated industries, is that in the regulated world, there are two distinct and yet related challenges: you not only have make your devices secure but also convince independent authorities (regulators and customers) that you have done so. This means not just designing a secure product, but also creating attendant documentation that allows governmental reviewers to quickly understand your product's security posture and the strength of your institutional cybersecurity practices.

If the product is in its premarket stage (i.e., not approved), MDMs need to establish the following high-level objectives before an MDM will approve its use:

1. The device is designed in a way such that all risks to patient safety and privacy are within acceptable levels (the technical term for this, as per FDA, is "no uncontrolled risk") [4] due to cybersecurity causes
2. The cybersecurity risk controls have been adequately designed, and robustly verified and validated.

For postmarket products (i.e., already approved) that are assessed to be in a state of uncontrolled risk [1] due to an actual vulnerability discovered in software or hardware, the MDM would have to do, as per regulatory requirements, a voluntary product recall, which, in this context, would be a correction applied to the device through the application of a cybersecurity patch. If the problem be something that regulators deem cannot be fixed in the field, for example, a device that has no interface for a software update to be applied but still has a vulnerability that exposes a patient to uncontrolled risk, this could lead to product withdrawal or stock recovery [18].

Once fielded products are assessed to be in a state of uncontrolled risk, regulators might have cause to believe that there exist systemic problems within the MDM's product development and quality assurance processes. In the United States of America, this could lead to inspections with regulatory personnel conducting audits of the MDM's quality management process. Such inspections typically entail FDA regulators coming over to the MDM's business premises. They then conduct inspections of the manufacturing and development environments, and conduct document reviews of different aspects of their quality management system (QMS) that the regulator believes might be responsible for their quality problems. Specific noncompliances with regulations, standards, and best practices are then formally communicated by the FDA to the MDM through Form 483 observations [19]. Typical issues found include insufficient monitoring of external signals that would be leading indicators for a noncompliant product (i.e. "you could have known what the problem was if you were paying more attention"), weak corrective and preventive action ("you knew you had a problem, but did not do proper analysis to find the root cause and then fix the systemic problem"), and other general noncompliance to regulations, standards, and one's own quality processes ("you are not following cybersecurity best practices and cybersecurity regulations"). MDMs are given a certain number of days to formulate a response to Form 483 observations which typically include a plan to remediate the deficiencies. Now based on the MDM's responses to the 483s, the seriousness, and severity of the noncompliances, the FDA may choose to issue a warning letter [20]. A warning letter essentially lets the MDM know if that the issues are not fixed promptly, within an MDM-defined timeline that the FDA considers acceptable, the MDM may be subject to an enforcement action without further notice. An enforcement action, as the name suggests, is a legal action the FDA can take which may lead to the MDM's products being mandatorily taken off the market and even criminal and civil prosecution. The warning letter is lifted only after the FDA conducts another assessment and is convinced that the severe systemic issues that led to the warning letter being issued have been rectified. The severity of regulatory action is not just a USA-only phenomenon; virtually, every jurisdiction reserves the right to pursue sanctions against an MDM for quality violations. The cost of violating data privacy regulations as part of GDPR is particularly severe, as per Article 83 of GDPR [21], up to 20 million euros or 4% of the company's annual worldwide revenue for the previous year.

So as should be evident by now, the cost of not complying with regulatory requirements is brand damage, loss of revenue, closure of business, and even civil and criminal prosecution. Just like patient safety and patient privacy risk, MDMs should also formally assess regulatory risk of their premarket and postmarket products. New threats are continuously being discovered, and, in response, regulators across the world are tightening their expectation of MDMs in terms of the maturity of their cybersecurity practice. The bar for what acceptability is for cybersecurity is continuously being raised, and this is as it should be, in terms of bringing the overall healthcare industry to be at the level of maturity of other critical infrastructure domains.

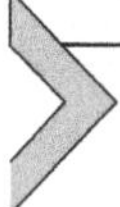

Regulations, quality, and the medical device quality management system

The term "quality" is used loosely in conversations all the time. Something can be considered to be a quality product if it satisfies customer expectations (that is when we leave a 5-star review) or of poor quality when it does not (the 1 star review). Here, the notion of quality is one of conceptual quality—how a new medical device is different from existing therapies/diagnostics in terms of safety, efficacy, cost, and ease of use. Then there is the notion of execution quality, where a product is considered to be a "quality product" if it meets a manufacturer's quality objectives, which are captured in their quality policies.

These quality policies are implemented by quality processes. One can formally say that a product meets execution quality objectives if records can be produced to objectively prove that quality processes have been followed to produce the product. From now on, the word "quality" shall be used to refer to execution quality, because this is typically what regulators refer to when they use the word quality.

In the case of medical devices, the expectation of quality encompasses not just design and manufacture of the device but also postmarket surveillance of their product in the field to ensure that any design defects are quickly detected and remediated. MDMs are also expected to learn from defects in competitive products and evolve their processes based on advancements in the "state of art" as captured through updated guidance documents and industry-recognized standards. It is expected that the lessons learned from design defects on one's own products are used to improve the quality processes themselves. After all, if defective products are being produced, where defective means a noted deviation from what a product should have been as per quality objectives and policies, there is a high likelihood that the process may not have been defined properly, might not have been executed properly, or both.

A QMS is defined as a formal system [22] that documents the structure, processes, roles, responsibilities, and procedures required to achieve effective quality management. A QMS specifies quality objectives and policies and, based on that specification, defines the processes and organizational roles and responsibilities for achieving the quality policies and objectives. Quality objectives are usually driven by customer and regulatory expectations of quality. This, of course, follows from logic—if the customer is not satisfied by the product's quality, they will not use it, and if the regulator is not satisfied by the product's quality, they will not approve it. Regulatory expectations of quality are captured by the regulations themselves as well as by regulatory guidance and standards referred to by the regulatory guidance. When a QMS is constructed as per regulations and standards, it is expected that medical devices that are designed, manufactured, and maintained in compliance with the QMS will satisfy regulatory expectations of quality.

Most regulatory authorities in the world require an MDM to have a formal QMS in place as a prerequisite for approval of products. Regulatory guidance varies from country to country on the structure and the components of an acceptable QMS. Some countries like Canada directly specify the standard (ISO 13485 [23]) that MDMs need to follow for defining their QMSs [24]. Other countries like the United States take a more indirect route where they define specific requirements as part of their regulations and leave the exact implementation details to the MDM. Specifically, the FDA requires that domestic and foreign manufacturers of medical devices intended for commercial distribution within the United States of America formally establish and continuously comply with an organizational QMS. Code of Federal Regulations (CFR) Title 21 Part 820 [25] lays out the parameters of a QMS by defining requirements on medical device design, documentation, purchasing of device components, identification and traceability through the design and production process, device production and manufacturing processes, product testing, process validation, identifying nonconformity, labeling and packaging, and on corrective and preventive actions for fielded medical devices. Since ISO 13485 is the only widely recognized standard for a QMS, implementing a 13485 compliant QMS is considered to be sufficient in all jurisdictions of the world.

QMS implementations of course vary in terms of their depth and rigor, and MDMs making medium-risk (Class II, as per FDA classification system [26]) or high-risk devices (Class III, as per FDA classification system) devices will be expected to have a much more robust and comprehensive QMS implementation than MDMs making low-risk, nonsterile, nonmeasuring, and nonreusable surgical instrument devices (Class I, as per FDA classification system). We will be getting into further details of a QMS in this

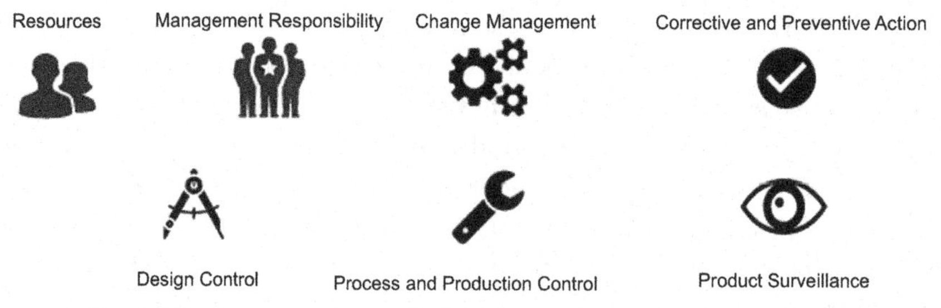

Figure 3.1 Structure of a medical device quality management system.

book because of its scope. It may be worthwhile looking at some of the basic components of a QMS, in order to more fully understand how to build regulatory expectations of cybersecurity into an existing ISO 13485 compliant QMS.

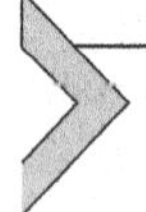

Structure of a medical device quality management system

The components of a QMS (Fig. 3.1) can broadly be described as below.

1. *Management Responsibility*: This component of the QMS defines the supervisory activities (e.g., audit, metric review) that are needed to ensure that the QMS is compliant with quality objectives and policies and that the processes are being executed properly. For those reading the book who come from a traditional IT background, the easiest way to understand Management Responsibility is that this is analogous to the classical IT governance function, responsible for operational excellence, keeping the QMS compliant with all regulatory and customer expectations. To quote from 21 CFR Part 820, "*Management with executive responsibility shall review the suitability and effectiveness of the quality system at defined intervals and with sufficient frequency according to established procedures to ensure that the quality system satisfies the requirements of this part and the manufacturer's established quality policy and objective.*"
2. *Resources*: This component of the QMS is responsible for the "people" aspect of the classic "people—process—tools" troika. It ensures all the activities are properly resourced, personnel have proper technical background and are trained appropriately for their job functions, and that personnel are provided with the proper tools necessary to perform their responsibilities.

3. *Design Control*: This component of the QMS, as the name implies, is responsible for ensuring that all phases of the product design process are properly executed. Specifically, the Design Control component defines processes such that product plans are clearly articulated, design inputs (e.g., requirements) and outputs (e.g., software design, code) are clearly defined, and the entire system as well as subsystems (electrical, mechanical, and software) is verified and validated as per design input, with links being maintained throughout (e.g., linking every design input with design output, ensuring that all requirements have test cases, etc.). A critical aspect of Design Control is defining processes for risk management, to ensure that risks to patient safety and product efficacy are controlled, not just during product design (premarket) but also after the product is released (postmarket)
4. *Process and Production Control:* This component of the QMS serves to ensure that products are being manufactured according to the product design, that manufacturers and suppliers are being assessed for quality, and that the final shipped product meets regulatory and customer requirements as articulated in quality objectives and policies.
5. *Product Surveillance*: This component of the QMS defines processes for postmarket monitoring of signals such that the MDM is aware of operational issues with their product. Operational issues are captured through various means including complaint handling (the customer tells you what is wrong), proactive monitoring (performance logs and metrics are collected from the devices themselves), and vigilance (social media monitoring, proactively querying users, etc.). The operational issues are then analyzed to check if they are resulting from product defects. If defects are identified, the risk of the defect to patient safety and product efficacy is evaluated using the risk management process.
6. *Corrective and Preventive Action (CAPA):* This component of the QMS defines processes for improving product and process quality once an actual or potential product defect is identified. The first step in CAPA is identifying the defect and isolating the defective component(s). Once that is done, interim control measures need to be defined such that more defects are not introduced while the root cause for the defect is being identified. The next phase of a CAPA is root cause analysis, to investigate whether the root cause of the defect was in the process definitions within the QMS itself (a faulty process will produce a faulty product) or whether there were issues with process execution. Example process execution issues include failing to allocate proper resources for the activity or

personnel were not provided proper training. Once the root cause is identified, other defective components may be discovered as stemming from the root cause. The defective items need to be fixed (correction) and the root cause in the QMS needs to be remediated through corrective/preventive actions such that further defective items are not produced. An effectiveness plan needs to be defined, such that the QMS is monitored, for a certain period of time, to ensure that the root cause has actually been remediated by the corrective/preventive actions taken, and that no more defective components are being produced as a result.

7. *Change Management:* This component of the QMS defines the process for managing change. The product design may have to undergo change based on the root cause of defects identified as part of the CAPA process, because of technological enhancements, or due to changing customer and regulatory requirements. Change Management ensures that the product and all related documentation (sometimes called the Design History File) are kept in sync. The QMS itself also might change. This could be because of the root cause of defects was traced to processes within the QMS. Even when there is nothing fundamentally wrong with the QMS, quality objectives and policies undergo changes, driven by new regulations and standards and customer expectations. The changes are usually effected through the definition of a Quality Plan. A Quality Plan contains the rationale for why an update to the QMS is required, the activities and process updates that are required to accomplish the QMS update, and finally, roles, responsibilities, and timelines for effecting the change.

One of the major misconceptions that used to abound in the medical device industry a few years ago was whether regulatory authorities like the FDA even had jurisdiction over the security of a device, given that their remit, as defined in the laws, limit them to safety and efficacy. This misconception had so taken root that the FDA itself had to issue additional clarification to address this under the section "Dispelling Myths" [27].

Myth: Cybersecurity for medical devices is optional.

Understanding the Facts: Medical device manufacturers must comply with federal regulations. Part of those regulations, called quality system regulations (QSRs), requires that medical device manufacturers address all risks, including cybersecurity risk. The pre- and post-market cybersecurity guidances provide recommendations for meeting QSRs.

Cybersecurity threats contribute to system risks, and hence, what the FDA is saying is that any QMS, that is compliant with FDA's quality objectives (which are the law), must address this aspect.

As to the EU jurisdiction, the mandate for cybersecurity is more directly written into law than in the US CFR. For the EU, medical device cybersecurity falls under EU-Regulation (EU) 2017/745 on medical devices (also known as MDR) and EU-Regulation (EU) 2017/746 on in vitro medical devices (also known as IVDR) [12]. The Medical Device Coordination Group has published a Document MDCG 2019-16 titled "*Guidance on Cybersecurity for medical devices*" that extracts out, in Sections 1.3 and 1.4 [13], the exact clauses from the EU-MDR and EU-IMDR regulations that mandate cybersecurity measures. Health Canada also makes explicit the consideration of cybersecurity features of products as part of device regulatory submissions in the following manner, where "these elements" in the extract below refer to the cybersecurity requirements articulated in the guidance document [5]:

> *During the evaluation of Class III and Class IV medical device license and license amendment applications, Health Canada will consider these elements in the assessment of the safety and effectiveness of the device. The elements listed above, and Health Canada's expectations with respect to each element, are outlined in the subsequent sections of this guidance document.*

Now that it has been established that cybersecurity is a definitive regulatory requirement, common to multiple jurisdictions, cybersecurity should be considered to be one of the quality objectives of a medical QMS. This raises two critical questions:

1. What cybersecurity elements need to be incorporated within a medical QMS in order for it to be compliant with global regulatory quality objectives on cybersecurity?
2. How can an MDM integrate these cybersecurity elements into the QMS? Let us look at these two questions in a bit of detail.

Summary of regulatory requirements for cybersecurity

Most countries and jurisdictions have released regulations and/or guidance on cybersecurity for MDMs. Each of them is phrased in its own way, but, given that they all attempt to capture recommended best practices in cybersecurity [27a,27b], they are very similar to each other in terms of what they say and what they want MDMs to do

Shared responsibility

One of the principles shared by jurisdictions is the recognition of cybersecurity as a shared responsibility between stakeholders, including healthcare delivery organizations (HDOs), patients, providers, and MDMs. This means that no single stakeholder is considered solely responsible for the security of a device and regulators recognize that security is about design as well as awareness and use.

The MDM is held responsible for producing what the FDA in its 2018 guidance defined as a "trustworthy" device. The characteristics of a trustworthy device is one that is reasonably secure from cybersecurity intrusion and misuse, provides a reasonable level of availability, reliability, and correct operation, is reasonably suited to performing its intended functions, and adheres to generally accepted security procedures.

The MDM is also expected to be transparent to its stakeholders (i.e., HDOs, clinicians, and patients) as to what they "put in their products." Specifically, it means providing to its user base, on demand, the software and hardware components of cybersecurity significance that are part of their medical device (the "Cybersecurity Bill of Materials"), so that HDOs can make informed purchasing and maintenance decisions. As part of their share of the cybersecurity responsibility, HDOs can take decisions based on the Cyber Bill of Materials (CBOM), for example, a device using an operating system that is no longer being patched by the vendor may be considered to be "high risk" and be either put on its own network or not be used by the HDO at all. The transparency is thus a corollary of the shared responsibility; each stakeholder in the healthcare system is obligated to clearly communicate its cybersecurity requirements and responsibilities to each other, so that the cybersecurity posture of healthcare systems may be maintained.

Secure design principles for safety

The MDM is expected to use secure development processes that are driven by, to use the EU-MDR term, "state of the art." MDCG (the guidance for EU-MDR) defines several practices that capture high-level design objectives. Since these form a good conceptual framework for understanding regulatory expectations on secure design, they are reproduced here:

Security management

This practice ensures that cybersecurity activities are properly planned and managed throughout the product development lifecycle and that components procured from third parties, both hardware and software, are assessed for cybersecurity risk.

Security requirements

This practice ensures that best practices in cybersecurity, i.e., "state of the art," are incorporated as security product requirements. MDCG provides a list of "indicative" security controls (Table 3 in [13]), incorporating authentication, authorization, access control, logging, and cryptography, that MDCG recommends drive product security requirements. The interested reader is requested to refer to MDCG-2019 for the specifics of these best practices [13].

Secure by design

This practice ensures that the product is designed following defense in depth principles. By defense in depth, multiple redundant layers of security controls are designed such that if one control be compromised by a threat agent, the other controls still maintain the cybersecurity posture of the product in a way that the risk of patient harm or privacy compromise due to successful threats is within the zone of acceptability.

Secure implementation

This practice ensures that the device design is implemented following security development best practices.

Security verification and validation testing

This practice ensures the medical device is tested against cybersecurity requirements (verification) and undergoes security validation (e.g., penetration test).

Management of security-related issues

This practice ensures that actual cybersecurity issues (vulnerabilities and threats at the subsystem, i.e., hardware and software level) are identified, the risk evaluated, and their disposition (whether to fix the issue or not) tracked and managed.

1. *Security update management:* This ensures that cybersecurity patches are applied based on an assessment of risk, and if the decision taken to apply a patch, the process of patch development and deployment be managed and tracked.
2. *Security guidelines:* This ensures that proper cybersecurity documentation and labeling instructions are developed to provide users with an understanding of the basic security features and what (if any) cybersecurity features (e.g., firewall rules, admin accounts) they need to configure and maintain.

Secure design principles for privacy

While the FDA is responsible for ensuring that medical devices are safe and effective, its parent organization, the Department of Health and Human Services (HHS), is responsible for the privacy of individual data collected by

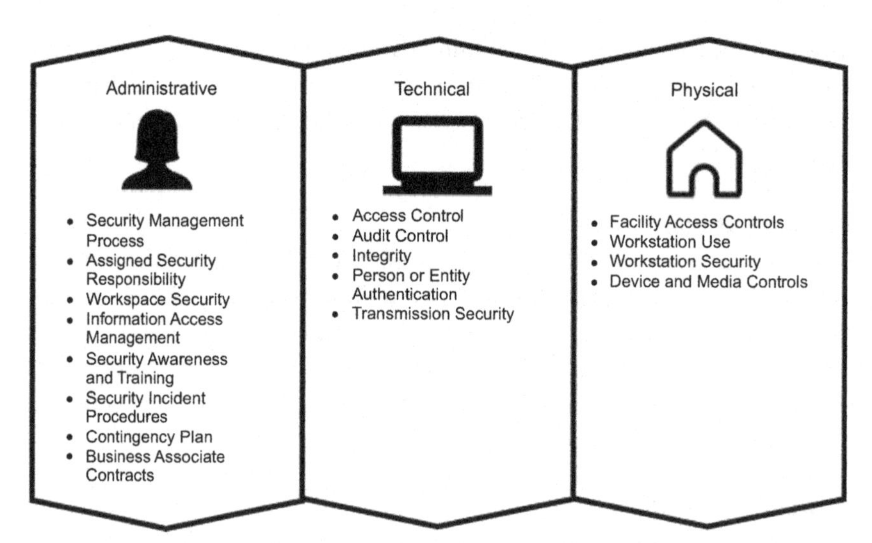

Figure 3.2 HIPAA control classes.

different stakeholders in the healthcare system, hospitals and physician's offices and insurance companies. It is also responsible for the privacy of data that are stored on and transmitted by medical devices. HHS's mandate to protect the private data of individuals originates from Title II of the HIPAA, specifically from two sections—the Privacy Rule and the Security Rule.

The Security Rule defines three classes of security safeguards required for compliance: administrative, physical, and technical (Fig. 3.2).

Technical safeguards are the most germane in the current context, since it defines authentication, authorization, access control, logging, and data security–related privacy controls.

HIPAA-driven controls apply to Electronic Patient Health Information or ePHI. ePHI is considered to be electronic data that can be used to identify a particular individual through data about his/her medical condition, either current or past or future, the kind of medical care provided to the individual, and payment information for past or present or future care. Identification of an individual may happen in two ways:

- Direct identification: This identification happens by retrieving a direct identifier like name or social security number from electronic health data. For example, let us assume a therapy device in a hospital stores the names of patients to whom the therapy was applied to over the past week. Someone walking by pulls up the records screen, finds the name of a celebrity, and reports it to a gossip website

- Indirect identification: This identification happens by retrieving indirect identifiers like date of birth, gender, zip code, and linking that with data from other sources. Let us assume the therapy device in the hospital did not store the name of the patient, but did store their gender, date of birth, and zip code. Given that celebrities dates of birth are public knowledge on Wikipedia, and the gossip magazine knows that the celebrity they suspect of having a condition stays in Beverly Hills, there is a very high probability that if they get the zip code, gender, and the date of birth from the medical record, they can now link the celebrity to their medical condition. This kind of identification is in fact pretty easy; according to a study [28], three indirect identifiers used together (date of birth, zip code, and gender) can uniquely identify 87% of the American population.

ePHI may be deidentified, i.e., attributes that can potentially lead to identification of individuals are removed before they are stored electronically. HIPAA determines two methods by which a manufacturer may determine whether data have been deidentified—either through analysis by an expert or by removing 18 attributes specified by the Privacy Rule. While deidentification leads to an electronic record no longer considered as ePHI and removes the headache of protecting their confidentiality or be liable for breach if it happens, in most cases, deidentification removes many of the reasons why the data were being kept in the first place. If a manufacturer of a home renal therapy device stores patient data so that they can automate the delivery of solutions to the patient's home when patient's supply runs low, not retaining the address or the name of the patient would compromise the whole model of therapy, patients may forget to order supplies and find themselves in situations where they are unable to provide self-care as a result.

The GDPR is an EU data privacy regulation for the protection of personal data of EU citizens. GDPR defines mandatory legal requirements on how personally identifying data of EU citizens is collected, stored, processed, and destroyed, even if the corporation collecting and storing the data is outside the EU, and the rights of those whose data is being collected over their own data.

Besides capturing in legislation the notion of "privacy by design," i.e., recommending the consideration of privacy as a design driver while designing the security of a system and the definition of the information architecture of a system, GDPR introduces a novel concept as a privacy design control: pseudonymization. Recognizing the fact that data that have been totally deidentified are of little business value, GDPR proposes pseudonymization as a compromise between total anonymization and no anonymization and encourages companies to adopt it as an information security design paradigm.

As per GDPR, pseudonymization is defined as follows:

> *Pseudonymization means the processing of personal data in such a manner that the personal data can no longer be attributed to a specific data subject without the use of additional information, provided that such additional information is kept separately and is subject to technical and organizational measures to ensure that the personal data are not attributed to an identified or identifiable natural person.*

What this means, from an implementation point of view, is that data that contain personally identifiable data are split across data stores with independent technical cybersecurity controls. An example of pseudonymized data in the device of medical devices is provided below.

- An infusion pump stores therapy data about a patient on the pump. The data are kept indexed by a patient id and kept encrypted on the device. A separate electronic database managed by the HDO maintains the association with the patient id and direct identifiers of the patient, like name and SSN and address. This database, often implemented as part of an electronic health records system (EHR), is subject to encryption and other cybersecurity controls which are distinct and independent from the controls employed by the MDM on the pump.

Here, the properties of pseudonymization are satisfied in the way GDPR defines them. A data breach wherein the PHI stored on the device is exposed does not immediately lead to the leaking of the association of the medical condition to the individual. The compromise of the EHR also does not lead to the divulgence of this association. Only a compromise of both data sources is required for the association to be made, and the chances of that are low, given that they are maintained by independent organizations (the HDO and the device manufacturer) with independently designed and implemented controls.

Cybersecurity labeling

As part of the shared responsibility model, the MDM is responsible for transparency with respect to cybersecurity. By that, regulators expect that the MDM disclose to HDOs and the users of their products the identity and version information of third-party software and hardware components that are part of their device build. The MDM should also, as part of cybersecurity labeling, clearly articulate their recommendations of how to securely provision their product in the HDO's IT infrastructure and provide specific labeling items defined in guidance documents like the FDA premarket and MDCG that provide an overview of the cybersecurity posture of the device.

Premarket and postmarket cybersecurity risk management

One of the common threads running through every guidance and regulation is the requirement for the MDM to do total life-cycle risk management, cradle to grave, from initial conception to end of life. The objective of cybersecurity risk management is to evaluate the risk that a patient is directly harmed from cybersecurity causes.

Premarket

A properly documented and followed risk management process is recommended uniformly to be the primary guiding factor for cybersecurity design decisions. By following standard cybersecurity risk management approaches (e.g., ISO 14971 [26] and AAMI TIR57 [27]), MDMs are encouraged to come to decisions as to whether to accept a specific kind of cybersecurity risk during product design and development or to remediate it through design controls. In case an unacceptable risk is accepted during product design, a risk—benefit analysis would be required as per ISO 14971.

The set of foreseeable cybersecurity should consider operational threats (i.e., threats to the device when it is performing its clinical function), supply chain threats (i.e., threats to the device from third-party components procured from suppliers), manufacturing threats (i.e., threats to the device during transferring design artifacts from development environment to production environment and threats during manufacturing), and deployment threats (i.e., threats to the device during distribution and set-up in its operational environment). These threat domains are explicitly identified by the FDA [4].

Regulatory authorities caution MDMs from imposing overtly restrictive cybersecurity measures that may have a detrimental safety impact on their products. For instance, mandating authentication before accessing a device being used in an emergency room may lead to increased patient safety risk, because an operator may forget their credentials. Following the principles laid down in AAMI TIR 57 of having two distinct *but interrelated* risk assessments, one for patient safety from noncybersecurity—related causes and another for patient safety from cybersecurity-related causes (i.e., threats), regulators expect MDMs to not only assess safety risk to the patient from threats but also assess the safety risk posed by cybersecurity controls themselves.

Postmarket

For postmarket risk management, regulators from multiple jurisdictions recommend manufacturers have a process for assessing patient safety risk for a vulnerability discovered either in a fielded product or in one of its components or even in a competitor's product that performs similar clinical functions. The result of the risk analysis should be captured in a metric that incorporates exploitability of a vulnerability (how easy it is to craft an attack that uses the vulnerability) and the patient safety impact severity of a vulnerability (what is the worst that can happen to the patient in case of a successful exploitation of the vulnerability). The Common Vulnerability Scoring System is recommended as a reference for creating such a metric by the FDA.

The FDA postmarket guidance goes into some detail regarding risk assessment of fielded products, and it's an approach that aligns with guidance from other jurisdictions. They recommend to create a risk threshold above which the device is in a state of "uncontrolled risk" as part of a risk management framework. A device is in a state of "uncontrolled risk" when the risk of patient harm due to exploitation of a vulnerability is considered significant. This could be because the vulnerability is easily exploitable, or the patient safety impact is high, or, in the worst case, both. When a fielded device is in a state of "uncontrolled risk" the manufacturer is responsible for bringing the device back to a state where it is in a controlled risk, i.e., the residual risk of harm to the patient is lower than the predefined threshold. One way of bringing the device to a state of controlled risk is by recommending users implement compensating controls. A compensating control is a safeguard or countermeasure deployed in lieu of or in the absence of controls designed in by a device manufacturer. These controls are external to the device design, configurable in the field, employed by a user, and provide supplementary or comparable cyber protection for a medical device. Examples of compensating controls are asking users to take a device off a wireless network, disabling remote access, putting the devices on their own protected network, or turning off autonomous therapy. A compensating control usually entails reduced functionality for the device, but even with a compensating control, the essential clinical function of the device must be maintained. In other words, a compensating control cannot be "just do not use the device."

Information sharing

The FDA emphasizes participation in cybersecurity information sharing bodies (ISAO) like NH-ISAC (now known as Health ISAC) as means of being informed of sector-wide threats. Participation in an information sharing organization has to be a two-way commitment—MDMs are also urged to share, in the safe space afforded by an ISAO, vulnerabilities and threats observed on their own products, so that the community can learn from their experience.

Coordinated vulnerability disclosure

Regulators also recommend having a coordinated vulnerability disclosure policy for the organization. A coordinated vulnerability disclosure policy is implemented as a process by which vulnerabilities reported by external sources (e.g., security researchers, customers) are evaluated. Claims are evaluated (just because someone says you have a vulnerability does not necessarily mean it is so), and actual vulnerabilities assessed for risk by following the risk management process. Results from the process are communicated back to the reporting authority.

Proactive vulnerability monitoring

Regulators expect MDMs to proactively look for vulnerabilities that may be relevant to their products. This implies that, besides evaluating vulnerabilities obtained from information-sharing organizations and those reported by external researchers and discovered through internal verification and validation activities (e.g., penetration tests), MDMs continuously monitor open-source vulnerability databases like the National Vulnerability Database for vulnerabilities/threats discovered on third-party components that are part of their product build. Vulnerability information should also be obtained from product monitoring, which is a standard QMS capability.

Patching and communication

Cybersecurity patches are changes to a device that fix known vulnerabilities and increase device security. Patches can of course be applied to a device which is in a state of uncontrolled risk to bring it to a controlled state. But that is not the only reason why they should be applied. Patches should be applied as part of maintaining good cybersecurity posture of a fielded device, such that all known vulnerabilities are remediated, even if the device is in a controlled risk state. This is referred to by the FDA as "routine updates and patches."

The responsibility for remediating a cybersecurity vulnerability that poses uncontrolled risk to the patient is the MDMs, even if the vulnerability occurs in third-party components over which the MDM has no direct control. The MDM may of course rely on the third-party component supplier to develop a patch, but ultimately it is the MDM who is responsible for risk management, compensating controls, patch delivery, CAPA, and all other QMS processes triggered by the presence of the vulnerability in the third-party component.

The FDA considers cybersecurity routine updates and patches as device enhancements. This is why manufacturers are generally not required to report these updates and patches as corrections under 21 CFR part 806 [31]. In general, manufacturers must report to the FDA vulnerabilities that lead to uncontrolled risk, according to 21 CFR part 806, unless reported under 21 CFR parts 803 or 1004 [32]. However the FDA, as part of their postmarket guidance of 2016, has decided not to enforce reporting responsibilities if several conditions are met:

(a) There are no known serious adverse events or deaths associated with the vulnerability

(b) As soon as possible but no later than 30 days after learning of the vulnerability, the MDM communicates with its customers and user community regarding the vulnerability, identifies interim compensating controls, and develops a remediation plan to bring the residual risk to an acceptable level.

(c) As soon as possible but no later than 60 days after learning of the vulnerability, the MDM fixes the vulnerability, validates the change, distributes the deployable fix to its customers and user community such that the residual risk is brought down to an acceptable level, and follows up after 60 days, as required.

(d) The MDM actively participates as a member of an ISAO that shares vulnerabilities and threats that impact medical devices, such as NH-ISAC, and provides the ISAO with any customer communications upon notification of its customers.

Standards

So far, our focus in this chapter has been on government regulations and government-issued guidance documents. In addition to these, there are several industry standards prepared by different standards bodies and communities of practice that provide definitions, objectives, requirements, practices, and broad implementation guidelines for cybersecurity risk management for healthcare IT and medical devices, many of which are also explicitly referred to by regulations and government-issued guidance in footnotes or in the references sections. These standards are typically more detailed than regulatory guidance, providing standard implementations and solution architectures. It is recommended that MDMs track and assess compliance with industry standards/guidance within their QMS. When procedural controls imposed by a QMS are linked to industry standards, it becomes easier to make an argument that the cybersecurity posture of a company and the products they manufacture reflect community-accepted best practice. This is because industry standards result from the consensus of a group of domain experts, undergo an extensive public vetting process in which regulators and public bodies are usually involved, and are subject to ongoing review and continuous revision.

Healthcare delivery organization–specific cybersecurity standards

Most MDMs sell directly to HDOs, with some exceptions like diabetes management businesses which typically sell direct to patient. There are several healthcare standards which capture cybersecurity objectives and best practices for HDO environments. An MDM has to track and comply with these standards because a noncompliant device is likely to cause noncompliance of the HDO environment. HDO's may consider that risk while making purchasing decisions.

Some of the HDO cybersecurity standards that a device manufacturer needs to consider are the following:

- *ANSI/AAMI/IEC 80001*: The ANSI/AAMI/IEC 80001 group of standards is the overarching risk management framework for IT networks which incorporate medical devices as nodes on the network, the kind that is typically found at HDOs. ANSI/AAMI/IEC TIR80001-2-2 [33] provides guidance for implementers of the IEC 80001 standards framework by defining a set of security capabilities (like person authentication, node authentication, and automatic log off of sessions) that are required of medical devices on an IT network in an HDO so that the cybersecurity risk of the overall network can be managed. ANSI/AAMI/IECTIR80001-2-8 [34] provides guidance for implementation of IEC TIR80001-2-2 security capabilities. It addresses each of the security capabilities of 80001-2-2 and takes a deeper dive, identifying specific security controls for consideration during risk management activities.

- HIMSS/NEMA HN 1–2019 (MDS2) Manufacturer Disclosure Statement for Medical Devices: The well-known (MDS2) [35] form is a standard questionnaire that is often requested by HDOs of MDMs to assess the cybersecurity risk the MDM's device poses to the overall cybersecurity posture of the HDO. The MDS2 form is aligned with ANSI/AAMI/IEC TIR80001-2-2 and can intuitively be thought of as a recasting of IEC TIR80001-2-2 in a question–answer format, enabling HDOs to not only quickly evaluate the cybersecurity risk of a device they are considering purchasing, but also compare competing manufacturers of a similar device in the domain of cybersecurity.
- *ISO 27799*: ISO 27799 [36] references the cybersecurity controls framework defined in ISO/IEC 27002 [37], a standard with wide global consensus used for securing IT infrastructure, and adapts it for a healthcare environment. It provides guidelines and best practices to support the interpretation and implementation of ISO/IEC 27002 in a healthcare context, to ensure confidentiality, integrity, and availability of healthcare data.

Medical device manufacturer–specific cybersecurity standards

While HDO cybersecurity standards have existed for a number of years, MDM-specific standards are a much more recent addition to the healthcare landscape. HDO-specific standards are naturally very HDO focused. They lay down broad cybersecurity requirements for devices that are to be deployed on an HDO network and the objective being obviously to minimize cybersecurity risk for HDOs. However, the MDM has concerns other than simply satisfying customer requirements. There are regulatory drivers and business risk considerations driving cybersecurity design decisions. A more focused MDM-specific set of standards have now found acceptance in the medical device community, their content being validated by regulatory authorities recognizing and often pointing to them as part of their guidance process.

- *AAMI TIR 57 and AAMI TIR 97:* AAMI TIR57 [30] takes the safety risk management terminology and methods outlined in ANSI/AAMI/ISO 14971 (Medical devices—Application of risk management to medical devices) [29] and adapts it for cybersecurity risk management for medical devices in the premarket phase. Leveraging classical risk management concepts as much as possible, AAMI TIR57 aligns cybersecurity best practices with risk analysis, risk evaluation, risk control, and risk acceptance. MDMs have extensive experience with the ISO 14971 standard, integrated as it is into their QMSs. This is why approaching cybersecurity from the perspective of safety risk management has several conceptual benefits in the medical device industry as terms and concepts well accepted in the industry can be reused as much as feasible. AAMI TIR97 [38], in contrast, focuses on postmarket cybersecurity activities.

- *UL 2900-2-1*: Underwriter's Lab (UL) 2900 series of standards are targeted toward cybersecurity of industrial control systems and medical devices. UL 2900-1 [39] contains general principles and controls for software cybersecurity, while UL 2900-2-1 extends UL 2900-1 for medical devices and healthcare systems. Aligned with the FDA premarket cybersecurity guidance (2014) and the postmarket cybersecurity guidance, UL 2900-2-1 [40] provides a set of prescriptive technical and procedural controls for controlling cybersecurity risk of devices. One of its greatest strengths is that UL 2900-2-1 lays out a fairly comprehensive set of verification and validation techniques for cybersecurity, many of which subsequently became part of the FDA premarket cybersecurity guidance document of 2018.
- *IMDRF Principles and Practices for Medical Device Cybersecurity:* The International Medical Device Regulators Forum has produced "Principles and Practices for Medical Device Cybersecurity" [41] that harmonizes regulatory expectations from multiple jurisdictions. Though not technically a standard, nor a formal, regulatory guidance, these harmonized documents produced by a body of international regulators are an invaluable resource for understanding the commonalities between regulatory expectations across multiple jurisdictions.

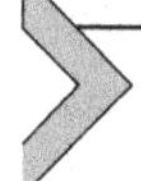

Supporting medical device manufacturer–specific standards

Besides specific cybersecurity standards, there are other supporting standards, in the domain of software development and risk management, which cybersecurity procedural controls have to comply with.

- ANSI/AAMI/IEC62304 IEC 62304 [42] is a standard for medical device software development, and compliance with IEC 62304 is used as an assurance argument of the quality of medical device software. IEC 62304 requires software system inputs to include cybersecurity requirements that encompass authentication, authorization, audit trail, and communication integrity.
- ISO 14971 [29] is the definitive standard for risk management for medical devices, and is referred to by IEC 62304 for the risk management aspect of medical device software development.

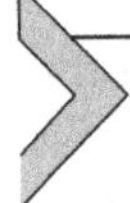

Integrating regulatory requirements into a medical device quality management system

One way of interpreting regulatory mandates is to consider them to be "just some things we have to do to satisfy regulators, because if they are not satisfied, we will not be able to sell our products." MDMs who adopt this line of thinking are typically those creating documentation like a threat model or a risk model right before a product submission. Too often, they discover at a very late stage that the product design is fundamentally noncompliant with regulatory expectations. Disapproval due to major deficiencies is a real possibility. Having to then substantially rework the product ("going back to the drawing board") will not only be time consuming but will also raise questions on QMS rigor and lead to audits and increased scrutiny. Even if the product somehow makes it through regulatory approval, the manufactured product is almost guaranteed to be of poor quality once deployed, because it has not been designed to meet regulatory expectations. This means that it is more likely to develop issues that would require recalls and open the MDM to not just regulatory action, but also to severe financial damage through loss of brand reputation.

The other way, or rather the right way, is to look upon regulatory mandates as fundamentally beneficial to an MDM. When regulatory requirements are precisely formulated, they provide a vital framework for capturing what the state of the art is and what the base expectations of quality for each domain. The strategy then should be to build regulatory requirements into the QMS. Compliance with quality processes then provides MDMs with assurance that cybersecurity quality is being maintained, and that products will be compliant by design.

In order to have a QMS that is compliant to the regulations on cybersecurity which we refer to as a "cyber-QMS," the following steps are recommended (Fig. 3.3).

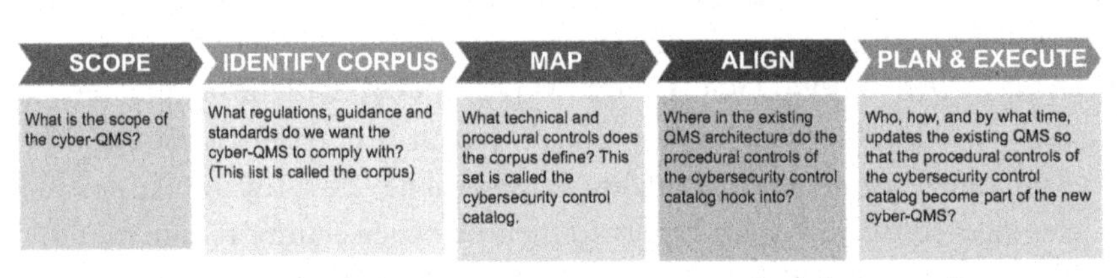

Figure 3.3 Integrating regulatory requirements into a medical device quality management system.

Step 1: scope the cyber-QMS

An initial scoping assessment should be done to understand what elements need to be part of the cyber-QMS. While it is fairly obvious that all products containing software, firmware, or programmable logic should be within the scope of the cyber-QMS, the challenge is in determining the nonproduct systems that should be brought in scope of a cyber-QMS.

Systems that should be considered are as follows:

1. Software design environment, i.e., the development environment software developers use for implementing product software
2. All repositories where product code is stored, i.e., the infrastructure used to store product code while it is in development, while it is in transit to manufacturing, while in the manufacturing environment, and while it is made available for download (e.g., through a portal)
3. Tools used to provision cryptographic secrets or to flash code onto the hardware during manufacture or service
4. Tools that provide security services like *anti*malware software and vulnerability scanners
5. Infrastructure storage of cryptographic secrets (e.g., Hardware Security Module [HSM]) and public key infrastructure (PKI) systems. This is especially critical. If an MDM is digitally signing their code, the private keys used for code signing need to be stored in highly secure storage. If an attacker can read or change the signing keys with their own keys, then the security provided by signed code is lost. According to cybersecurity best practices, private keys used for signing are usually stored in specialized secure hardware called HSMs. Even though the HSMs are not part of the product, given the criticality of the crown jewels of cybersecurity that are being stored within them, the entire HSM infrastructure should be scoped with the cyber-QMS.
6. Systems where patient identifiable data are stored

Step 2: determine regulations, guidance, and standards

The next step is to identify a set of regulations, guidance, and standards the cyber-QMS is to be built and maintained to be compliant with. This consolidated list is what shall be referred to as the *cybersecurity corpus*. This corpus should not only be driven by regulatory requirements but also by specific customer requirements. As an example, some HDO customers require specific standards to be certified against (e.g., some HDOs require their vendor

MDMs to have an FIPS certificate [43] for their products), some ask for annual reporting of open vulnerabilities, product maintenance plan as it relates to cybersecurity (i.e., what is the product's cybersecurity patch cadence?), some require specific communication mechanisms over and above what regulations require in case of uncontrolled risk (e.g., informing the customer before a public disclosure of a vulnerability), while some customers want contractual guarantees of annual patch release.

Customer requirements, and this is increasingly being observed, are sometimes more aggressive than regulatory requirements. It is up to the MDM whether they should incorporate some of the more stringent requirements into the cybersecurity corpus that drives the QMS, or keep these "high bar" requirements outside the ambit of the QMS, till they become an expectation for all customers.

If the first option is chosen, there is the obligation for all products to satisfy the requirements, regardless of whether the specific customers of those products require them or not. However, given the speed at which customers are raising the bar of their cybersecurity expectations, MDMs would be well served by incorporating these "high bar" requirements into the QMS the first time they encounter them. What seems an outlier today will be the standard of tomorrow, so why not get started right away, designing products that are compliant with what your customers will expect in the future?

Step 3: create a set of technical and procedural controls based on the identified regulations, guidance, and standards

In this step, all identified regulations, guidance, and standards identified in Step 3 are distilled down into a set of technical controls and procedural controls, together called the *cybersecurity control catalog*.

Now the technical controls are those controls that need to be built into the medical device (recall from Chapter 2, that technical controls fall into five technical control categories—Cryptography, Authentication, Authorization, Access Control, and Logging). That is why the technical controls that are part of the cybersecurity control catalog should be used to drive medical device design decisions. The procedural controls though are those that "surround" the development, operation, and maintenance of the product. Thus, these need to be integrated cyber-QMS.

Each technical and procedural control in the cybersecurity control catalog should be maintained, along with links to specific clauses and line numbers from documents within the cybersecurity corpus from which they originate. This linkage provides the basis for why a control is present in the control catalog. The linkage can also be used to evaluate the impact of the absence of a technical or procedural control. If it is not possible to implement a technical control on a product or a procedural control in the QMS, by following the traceability of a control to the corpus, one will be able to have a precise identification of the specific customer, regulatory, and standards expectations the product and/or the QMS will not be in a position to satisfy. This is a vital step in evaluating compliance risk.

In subsequent chapters in this book, I provide an exemplar cybersecurity control catalog that is aligned with regulatory guidance at the time of writing.

Step 4: align with existing process architecture

MDMs, based on their size, the classification of the products they manufacture, and their organizational structure, have different implementations of an ISO13485 compliant QMS [44]. Because they are driven by the same standard, the broad structure of a QMS is more or less uniform, across organizations (Fig. 3.4).

At the very top level, there is the quality manual. The quality manual is a very high-level document, usually a statement of very broad policy goals captured as quality objectives. In the case of cybersecurity, a quality policy objective may be to keep the patient safe from cybersecurity threats using state-of-the-art cybersecurity practices. There is of course a lot of subjectivity in what "keeping patient safe" and "state of the art in cybersecurity" is, but that is usually the level of specificity that one requires at the quality manual level.

Procedures in the QMS, often called Standard Operating Procedures (SOPs), are the next level down below the quality manual. They refine quality objectives to more concrete goals, and then define processes for attaining these goals. Procedures typically span multiple departments or

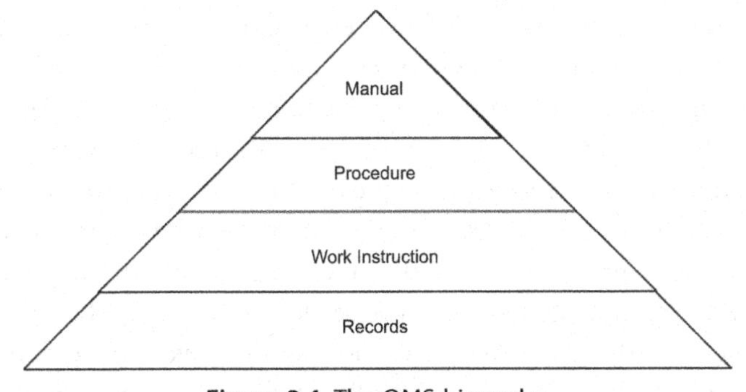

Figure 3.4 The QMS hierarchy.

functions (e.g., Systems, Software, Quality, IT, etc.) within an MDM, define roles and responsibilities as well the specific points of hand-off between different functions, and expectations of input and output. However, the actual step-by-step detailed processes for transforming input to output are defined in a lower-level document called a Work Instruction (WI). These WIs refine the processes outlined in SOPs with concrete implementations. WIs are processes defined at a level that can be ingested and then executed by suitably trained staff. The output of a WI is called a record. One of the responsibilities of the quality function in any MDM is to ensure that the outputs produced by the execution of a WI are as per the WI, i.e., to check that what comes out from executing the process (the actual output) is in accordance with what the WI prescribes. There are other artifacts that are even lower level than WI-like templates. Templates provide a document that captures the different aspects of the WI and producing a compliant record is a matter of filling up the template following the WI.

In passing, here is a question I had myself when I first started studying about medical QMSs. So if you have a procedure and a WI, what is a process in a QMS? A simple intuition to go by is that a process is a specification of how inputs are transformed to outputs for attaining the quality objectives defined in the quality manual, while a procedure and a WI are all implementations of the specification, at progressively lower levels of abstraction, with increasingly greater detail.

Because of the multiple abstractions and the tiers and the sheer complexity of actual implementations of QMSs, the integration strategy of cybersecurity into a QMS will vary from MDM to MDM. Will there be a separate WI for cybersecurity risk assessment for suppliers or will it be integrated into the already existing one for supplier risk assessment, as a separate section? Would all cybersecurity procedural controls used for product design be rolled into one secure design WI or would there be cybersecurity elements baked separately into the already existing WI for design inputs, design outputs, design review, etc.? How would high-level procedures be modified to reflect cybersecurity quality goals, and how much should bubble up into the quality manual? There is no universally correct answer. What usually happens is as follows. An implementation approach is chosen for integration, the processes are piloted on some projects, and execution records collected and analyzed for effectiveness through expert review. If things are found not to be going as expected, the integration strategy for cybersecurity into the QMS is changed.

In Table 3.1, I show an example of this alignment exercise with reference to the US CFR Title 21, Part 820 [25]. This is the US regulation that

Table 3.1 Aligning cybersecurity procedural controls with an existing QMS.

US FDA quality system regulation requirement categories	Strategy for procedural cybersecurity controls
Sec 820.20.a *Quality Policy*: "Management with executive responsibility shall establish its policy and objectives for, and commitment to, quality."	Update quality objectives with objectives that relate specifically to cybersecurity.
Sec 820.20.b *Organization:* "Each manufacturer shall establish and maintain an adequate organizational structure to ensure that devices are designed and produced in accordance with the requirements of this part."	Update relevant QMS element with cybersecurity roles and responsibilities across multiple functions (e.g., Quality, systems, software regulatory, and IT) and also with component suppliers, manufacturing partners, and external service providers.
Sec 820.20.c *Management Review*: "Management with executive responsibility shall review the suitability and effectiveness of the quality system at defined intervals and with sufficient frequency according to established procedures to ensure that the quality system satisfies the requirements of this part and the manufacturer's established quality policy and objectives. The dates and results of quality system reviews shall be documented."	Create a set of cybersecurity metrics to be reviewed through the existing management review QMS element. Examples of such metrics: Number of uncontrolled risks, number of open vulnerabilities in postmarket products, cybersecurity patches adoption rates·by customers, number of cybersecurity issues reported by external researchers or discovered through customer complaints, number of noncompliances with respect to the cybersecurity controls catalog of products in development, in market, and of the QMS itself, number of cybersecurity audit findings, status of cybersecurity quality plans, number of cybersecurity regulations and standards and guidance that have not yet been incorporated into the QMS.
Sec 820.d *Quality Planning*: "Each manufacturer shall establish a quality plan which defines the quality practices, resources, and activities relevant to devices that	In order to keep the QMS compliant with new cybersecurity regulations, guidance, standards, and emerging threats as well as to improve the QMS based on lessons learned from

(*Continued*)

Table 3.1 Aligning cybersecurity procedural controls with an existing QMS.—cont'd

US FDA quality system regulation requirement categories	Strategy for procedural cybersecurity controls
are designed and manufactured. The manufacturer shall establish how the requirements for quality will be met."	executing the QMS, update the quality planning QMS element with a "cyber" trigger. Whenever certain conditions are met (e.g., a new regulation or a significant update or an audit finding or metrics are not considered aligned with quality objectives), a quality plan needs to be created and executed to update the QMS.
Sec 820.*e* *Quality System Procedures*: "Each manufacturer shall establish quality system procedures and instructions."	All cybersecurity procedural controls should be captured in procedures and work instructions. Creating templates can make conformance with work instructions simpler and more consistent.
Sec 820.22 *Quality Audit*: "Each manufacturer shall establish procedures for quality audits and conduct such audits to assure that the quality system is in compliance with the established quality system requirements and to determine the effectiveness of the quality system."	Update the audit QMS element with cybersecurity audit cadence (i.e., how often to do cybersecurity audits) and training requirements of cybersecurity auditors.
Sec 820.25 *Personnel*: "Each manufacturer shall have sufficient personnel with the necessary education, background, training, and experience to assure that all activities required by this part are correctly performed."	Update the training QMS element with training and experience requirements for different cybersecurity roles.
Sec 820.30.b *Design and development planning*: "Each manufacturer shall establish and maintain plans that describe or reference the design and development activities and define responsibility for implementation."	Update the design and development planning QMS element with requirements for an explicit cybersecurity plan that lays out alignment of different cybersecurity deliverables (e.g., requirements, design, test plans) with different phases of the design control process (e.g., design inputs, outputs, etc.).

Table 3.1 Aligning cybersecurity procedural controls with an existing QMS.—cont'd

US FDA quality system regulation requirement categories	Strategy for procedural cybersecurity controls
Sec 820.30.c *Design input*: "Each manufacturer shall establish and maintain procedures to ensure that the design requirements relating to a device are appropriate and address the intended use of the device, including the needs of the user and patient."	Update the design input QMS element with • a procedural control that maps the technical cybersecurity controls of the cybersecurity control catalog (this represents a consolidated list of cybersecurity design features recommended by regulations, guidance, and standards) to system and software requirements (design input) for a particular product. For a particular product, any unmapped/partially mapped technical cybersecurity controls from the cybersecurity control catalog (i.e., technical cybersecurity controls that are not to be implemented in the product design) are considered deviations, and the risk of the deviations assessed and reviewed • a cybersecurity risk management procedural control aligned with ISO 14971 and AAMI TIR57 for comprehensively identifying cybersecurity threats (threat modeling), assessing risks to patient safety and patient privacy from those threats, and then using design input to control those risks to acceptable levels (risk modeling).
Sec 820.30.d *Design output*: "Each manufacturer shall establish and maintain procedures for defining and documenting design output in terms that allow an adequate evaluation of conformance to design input requirements."	Update the design output QMS element with a procedural control that defines secure product development methods, which include secure coding guidelines.
Sec 820.30.e *Design review*: "Each manufacturer shall establish and maintain procedures to ensure that formal documented reviews of the	Update the design review QMS element with procedural controls for cybersecurity review. This should consider specific skill requirements

(*Continued*)

Table 3.1 Aligning cybersecurity procedural controls with an existing QMS.—cont'd

US FDA quality system regulation requirement categories	Strategy for procedural cybersecurity controls
design results are planned and conducted at appropriate stages of the device's design development."	for cybersecurity reviews, requirements (if any) for independent third-party review, and requirements for capturing the risk of deviations of a product from the technical controls prescribed in the cybersecurity control catalog.
Sec 820.30.f design verification: "Each manufacturer shall establish and maintain procedures for verifying the device design."	Update the design verification QMS element with a procedural control for verifying that the design output satisfies cybersecurity design input. This procedural control should provide as an output: • a *cybersecurity test plan* that provides evidence of comprehensive testing of the design input • a *cybersecurity test result* document which is the result of running the test plan on design output.
Sec 820.30.g *Design validation*: "Each manufacturer shall establish and maintain procedures for validating the device design."	Update the design validation QMS element with a procedural control for cybersecurity validation testing, e.g., penetration tests.
Sec 820.30.h *Design transfer*: "Each manufacturer shall establish and maintain procedures to ensure that the device design is correctly translated into production specifications."	Update the design transfer QMS with procedural controls for maintaining the security of the product development environment, in order to ensure, for example, that malware cannot be introduced in code repositories, developers cannot seed backdoors in code, and developers do not have ownership or access to production keys.
Sec. 820.30.i *Design changes*: "Each manufacturer shall establish and maintain procedures for the identification, documentation, validation, or where appropriate verification, review, and approval of design changes before their implementation."	Update the design changes QMS element with a procedural control for assessing whether changes need to be made to the product's cybersecurity design. This procedural control invokes the cybersecurity risk management procedural control (defined as part of design input) to

Table 3.1 Aligning cybersecurity procedural controls with an existing QMS.—cont'd

US FDA quality system regulation requirement categories	Strategy for procedural cybersecurity controls
	assess whether the driver for the design change (e.g., the discovery of a vulnerability) poses uncontrolled risk, and if does, the design change needs to be made.
Sec. 820.50 *Purchasing controls*: "Each manufacturer shall establish and maintain procedures to ensure that all purchased or otherwise received product and services conform to specified requirements."	Update the purchasing QMS element with a procedural control for evaluating the cybersecurity risk of third-party components (hardware and software) and of the component suppliers themselves.
Sec. 820.70 *Production and procedural controls*: "Each manufacturer shall develop, conduct, control, and monitor production processes to ensure that a device conforms to its specifications."	Update the production and procedural controls QMS with a procedural control for maintaining the security of the product manufacturing environment in order to ensure that malware cannot be introduced or backdoors seeded during manufacturing.
Sec. 820.90 *Nonconforming product*: "Each manufacturer shall establish and maintain procedures to control product that does not conform to specified requirements."	Update the nonconforming product QMS element with a procedural control for identifying devices that may have been compromised and hence do not meet system safety or performance requirements. This includes specifying methods of vulnerability monitoring (i.e., monitoring different signal sources for potential product vulnerabilities), and then executing a process for remediation through design change process element, if uncontrolled risk is assessed, and finally communicating the nonconforming product to customers and proper authorities, together with compensating controls and remediation strategies.
Sec. 820.100 *Corrective and preventive action*: "Each manufacturer shall establish and maintain procedures for implementing corrective and preventive action."	Update the corrective and preventive action QMS element with a procedural control that, when a product is assessed as posing uncontrolled risk due to

(*Continued*)

Table 3.1 Aligning cybersecurity procedural controls with an existing QMS.—cont'd

US FDA quality system regulation requirement categories	Strategy for procedural cybersecurity controls
	cybersecurity causes or when the quality audit element discovers nonconformance in the cyber-QMS, requires a cybersecurity-driven assessment to find out the root case of nonconformance to quality objectives, and, based on the finding, requires the execution of remedial actions.
Sec 820.120 *Labeling*: "Each manufacturer shall establish and maintain procedures to control labeling activities."	Update the labeling QMS element with the labeling procedural control that captures specific cybersecurity-specific labeling requirements from different regulatory authorities.
Sec. 820.150 *Storage*: "Each manufacturer shall establish and maintain procedures for the control of storage areas."	Update the storage QMS element with a procedural control to prevent malicious tampering of medical device during storage.
Sec 820.160 *Distribution*: "Each manufacturer shall establish and maintain procedures for control and distribution of finished devices to ensure that only those devices approved for release are distributed."	Update the distribution QMS element with a procedural control to prevent malicious tampering of medical device during distribution.
Sec 820.170 installation: "Each manufacturer of a device requiring installation shall establish and maintain adequate installation and inspection instructions."	Update the installation QMS element with a procedural control to prevent malicious tampering of medical device during installation.
Sec. 820.200 servicing: "Where servicing is a specified requirement, each manufacturer shall establish and maintain instructions and procedures for performing and verifying that the servicing meets the specified requirements."	Update the service QMS element with a procedural control to prevent malicious tampering of medical device or reading of patient data during servicing.

mandates the establishment of a medical QMS and defines the components of a QMS. To quote:

> *Current good manufacturing practice (CGMP) requirements are set forth in this quality system regulation. The requirements in this part govern the methods used in, and the facilities and controls used for, the design, manufacture, packaging, labeling, storage, installation, and servicing of all finished devices intended for human use. The requirements in this part are intended to ensure that finished devices will be safe and effective and otherwise in compliance with the Federal Food, Drug, and Cosmetic Act (the act). This part establishes basic requirements applicable to manufacturers of finished medical devices.*

The left-hand column contains selected clauses from 21 CFR Part 820. An existing medical QMS that is compliant with 21CFR Part 820 will have QMS elements that correspond to each clause. A QMS element, incidentally, could be a procedure, a WI, or a template or a policy, or any other conceptual artifact used by an MDM to implement QMS requirements.

The right-hand column captures a suggested strategy to update these QMS elements with cybersecurity procedural controls, roles and responsibilities, and quality objectives, as appropriate. Informally expressed, this is a simple example of how requirements of cybersecurity quality can be "hooked" throughout an existing, noncybersecurity-aware QMS.

Step 5: create a quality plan

Once the strategy for integrating cybersecurity procedural controls into the QMS has been formulated, a quality plan has to be drawn up. In the world of QMS, a quality plan is the official vehicle for updating elements within a QMS. A quality plan typically consists of tasks, timelines, a list of specific QMS elements to be updated, and roles and responsibilities for the tasks.

The Quality Plan should consider the cybersecurity controls catalog as its reference document. For all the procedural controls in the catalog, one should assess whether these procedural controls are implemented in the QMS as it exists today. If not, one should create a task item in the Quality Plan for each nonmapped procedural control. A table like Table 3.1 helps in understanding where in the QMS the updates need to go. For example, the cybersecurity controls catalog would have as procedural controls vulnerability monitoring and cybersecurity patch management. As one can see from Table 3.1, these would map to FDA requirements Sec 820.90 and to the QMS element responsible for "nonconforming" product, whose implementation in a company's QMS must then be updated then with the above procedural controls. This updating activity would be a task in the QMS. For all procedural controls from the cybersecurity controls catalog that are not mapped/incompletely mapped to the QMS, the deviations should be noted and the compliance risk of the gap should be assessed.

Summary and key takeaways

Now that you have finished this chapter, you should have an intuitive idea of the core requirements laid down by different regulations, guidance, and standards with respect to medical device cybersecurity. This chapter, once again, is not a substitute for reading the relevant documents, but merely a summary of the regulatory drivers for technical and procedural cybersecurity controls. You should also have, by this time, understood where these controls should be institutionalized, namely the QMS, and how a noncybersecurity-aware QMS may be updated to become cyber aware.

The key takeaways from this chapter are as follows:

1. For premarket products, regulatory requirements for all jurisdictions require a secure design process; some even provide a set of technical controls that they recommend as part of guidance.
2. All regulatory authorities require the assessment of patient safety and privacy risk due to cybersecurity threats and the use of technical and procedural controls to bring risk to acceptable (controlled) levels. Verification and validation by suitable staff are essential to demonstrate that controls are effective.
3. For postmarket products, regulations require MDMs to proactively monitor for threats and vulnerabilities, and to have processes for working with external researchers and users who raise security issues observed on the MDM's products.
4. MDMs are expected to be transparent regarding the third-party components they use in their products. If the security of their products is dependent on the operational environment, they are responsible for clearly conveying that information to their customers—users and HDOs.
5. Cybersecurity is a shared responsibility between MDMs, HDOs, and users.
6. Regulatory requirements should be built into the QMS, with different QMS elements being updated with procedural cybersecurity controls.
7. A cybersecurity controls catalog is a list of technical and procedural cybersecurity controls, each mapped to regulatory guidance and standards. The technical controls of the cybersecurity controls catalog drive the cybersecurity design of the medical device. If a certain technical control cannot be implemented as part of the device design (e.g., verification of code

integrity cannot be done by cryptographic verification due to lack of space on the device for cryptographic code) or is only partially implemented (verification of code integrity is done by a noncryptographic check like CRC), the deviation should be noted, and the risk of the deviation should be assessed. If a certain procedural control from the cybersecurity controls catalog cannot be linked to a QMS element, then that too should be noted, and the compliance risk of the deviation assessed.

References

[1] US Food and Drug Administration, Postmarket Management of Cybersecurity in Medical Devices (Final Version), December 2016 [Online]. Available: https://www.fda.gov/regulatory-information/search-fda-guidance-documents/postmarket-management-cybersecurity-medical-devices. (Accessed 1 September 2020).

[2] US Food and Drug Administration, Cybersecurity for Networked Medical Devices Containing Off-The-Shelf (OTS) Software, Docket Number FDA-2020-D-0957, January 2005 [Online]. Available: https://www.fda.gov/regulatory-information/search-fda-guidance-documents/cybersecurity-networked-medical-devices-containing-shelf-ots-software. (Accessed 1 September 2020).

[3] US Food and Drug Administration, Content of Premarket Submissions for Management of Cybersecurity in Medical Devices (Final Version), October 2014 [Online]. Available: https://www.fda.gov/regulatory-information/search-fda-guidance-documents/content-premarket-submissions-management-cybersecurity-medical-devices-0. (Accessed 1 September 2020).

[4] US Food and Drug Administration, Content of Premarket Submissions for Management of Cybersecurity in Medical Devices (Draft Version), November 2018 [Online]. Available: https://www.fda.gov/regulatory-information/search-fda-guidance-documents/content-premarket-submissions-management-cybersecurity-medical-devices. (Accessed 1 September 2020).

[5] Health Canada, Guidance Document: Pre-market Requirements for Medical Device Cybersecurity, June 17, 2019 [Online]. Available: https://www.canada.ca/en/health-canada/services/drugs-health-products/medical-devices/application-information/guidance-documents/cybersecurity/document.html. (Accessed 1 September 2020).

[6] China FDA, Medical Device Network Security Registration on Technical Review Guidance Principle, January 2017 [Online].

[7] Australian Government Department of Health, Medical Device Cyber Security Guidance for Industry, July 18, 2019 [Online]. Available: https://www.tga.gov.au/publication/medical-device-cyber-security-guidance-industry. (Accessed 1 September 2020).

[8] Japan Pharmaceutical and Medical Device Agency, Guidance on Ensuring Cybersecurity of Medical Device: PSEHB/MDED-PSD Notification No. 0724-1, July 2018 [Online]. Available: https://www.pmda.go.jp/files/000204891.pdf. (Accessed 2 September 2020).

[9] Saudi Food and Drug Authority, Guidance to Pre-Market Cybersecurity of Medical Devices, April 2019 [Online]. Available: https://old.sfda.gov.sa/ar/medicaldevices/regulations/DocLib/MDS-G38.pdf. (Accessed 1 September 2020).

[10] Singapore Health Sciences Authority, Regulatory Guidelines for Software Medical Devices—A Lifecycle Approach, December 2019 [Online]. Available: https://www.hsa.gov.sg/docs/default-source/announcements/regulatory-updates/regulatory-guidelines-for-software-medical-devices–a-lifecycle-approach.pdf. (Accessed 1 September 2020).

[11] South Korean Ministry of Science and ICT, Cyber Security Guide for Smart Medical Service, May 2018 [Online].

[12] Official Journal of the European Union, Regulation (EU) 2017/745 Of The European Parliament And Of The Council of 5 April 2017 on medical devices, amending Directive 2001/83/EC, Regulation (EC) No 178/2002 and Regulation (EC) No 2009 and repealing Council Directives 90/385/EEC and 93/42/EE, April 5, 2017 [Online]. Available: https://eur-lex.europa.eu/legal-content/EN/TXT/?uri=CELEX:02017R0745-20200424. (Accessed 1 September 2020).

[13] Medical Device Coordination Group Document, MDCG 2019-16 Guidance on Cybersecurity for medical devices, 2019 [Online]. Available: https://ec.europa.eu/docsroom/documents/41863. (Accessed 1 September 2020).

[14] German Federal Office for Information Security, Cyber Security Requirements for Network-Connected Medical Devices, November 2018 [Online]. Available: https://www.allianz-fuer-cybersicherheit.de/ACS/DE/_/downloads/BSI-CS/BSI-CS_132E.pdf;jsessionid=9B84D9132CF8A89D659B9765083F5C5A.1_cid502?__blob=publicationFile&v=7. (Accessed 1 September 2020).

[15] Eurpoean Union, General Data Protection Regulation (GDPR), May 25, 2018 [Online]. Available: https://gdpr-info.eu/. (Accessed 19 September 2020).

[16] State of California, California Consumer Privacy Act, 2018.

[17] 104th United States Congress, Health Insurance Portability and Accountability Act of 1996, 1996.

[18] US Food and Drug Administration, Recalls, Corrections and Removals, n.d. [Online]. Available: https://www.fda.gov/medical-devices/postmarket-requirements-devices/recalls-corrections-and-removals-devices. (Accessed 19 October 2020).

[19] US Food and Drug Administration, Inspection Observations, November 11, 2020 [Online]. Available: https://www.fda.gov/inspections-compliance-enforcement-and-criminal-investigations/inspection-references/inspection-observations.

[20] US Food and Drug Administration, About Warning and Close-Out Letters, April 29, 2019 [Online]. Available: https://www.fda.gov/inspections-compliance-enforcement-and-criminal-investigations/warning-letters/about-warning-and-close-out-letters.

[21] European Union, Art. 83 GDPR General Conditions for Imposing Administrative Fines, n.d. [Online]. Available: https://gdpr.eu/article-83-conditions-for-imposing-administrative-fines/.

[22] American Society for Quality, What Is A Quality Management System?, n.d. [Online]. Available: https://asq.org/quality-resources/quality-management-system. (Accessed 19 October 2020).

[23] International Standards Organization, ISO 13485:2016 Medical Devices — Quality Management Systems — Requirements for Regulatory Purposes, 2016.

[24] Health Canada, Quality Systems ISO 13485, n.d. [Online]. Available: https://www.canada.ca/en/health-canada/services/drugs-health-products/medical-devices/quality-systems-13485.html.

[25] US Food and Drug Administration, CFR - Code of Federal Regulations Title 21 Subchapter H: Part 820 Quality System Regulations, n.d.

[26] US Food and Drug Administration, Classify Your Medical Device, n.d. [Online]. Available: https://www.fda.gov/medical-devices/overview-device-regulation/classify-your-medical-device. (Accessed 19 October 2020).

[27] US Food and Drug Administration, Dispelling Myths, n.d. [Online]. Available: https://www.fda.gov/downloads/medicaldevices/digitalhealth/ucm544684.pdf. (Accessed 19 October 2020).

[27a] Wirth, A., Gates, C., & Smith, J. Medical Device Cybersecurity for Engineers and Manufacturers. ISBN 978-1630818159, Artech House.

[27b] Healthcare and Public Health Sector Coordinating Councils. Medical Device & Health IT Joint Sector Plan. 2019.

[28] L. Sweeney, Simple Demographics Often Identify People Uniquely, 2000.

[29] International Standards Organization, ISO 14971:2019 Medical Devices — Application of Risk Management to Medical Devices, 2019.
[30] American Association for Medical Instrumentation, TIR57: Principles for Medical Device Security – Risk Management, 2016.
[31] US Food and Drug Adminstration, CFR - Code of Federal Regulations Title 21 Subchapter H: Part 806 Quality System Regulations, n.d. [Online]. Available: https://www.accessdata.fda.gov/scripts/cdrh/cfdocs/cfcfr/CFRSearch.cfm?CFRPart=806.
[32] US Food and Drug Administration, CFR - Code of Federal Regulations Title 21 Subchapter J: Part 1004 Quality System Regulations, n.d. [Online]. Available: https://www.accessdata.fda.gov/scripts/cdrh/cfdocs/cfcfr/CFRSearch.cfm?CFRPart=1004. (Accessed 19 October 2020).
[33] ANSI AAMI IEC, ANSI/AAMI/IEC TIR80001 Application of Risk Management for IT Networks Incorporating Medical Devices - Part 2-2: Guidance for the Disclosure and Communication of Medical Device Security Needs, Risks and Controls, n.d.
[34] ANSI/AAMI/IEC, ANSI/AAMI/IEC TIR80001 Application of Risk Management for IT-Networks Incorporating Medical Devices - Part 2-8: Application Guidance - Guidance on Standards for Establishing the Security Capabilities Identified in IEC TR 80001-2-2, n.d.
[35] ANSI/NEMA, Manufacturer Disclosure Statement for Medical Device Security, 2019 [Online]. Available: https://www.nema.org/standards/view/manufacturer-disclosure-statement-for-medical-device-security.
[36] International Standards Organization, ISO 27799 Health Informatics — Information Security Management in Health Using ISO/IEC 27002, 2016 [Online]. Available: https://www.iso.org/standard/62777.html.
[37] International Standards Organization, ISO/IEC 27002 Information Technology — Security Techniques — Code of Practice for Information Security Controls, 2013 [Online]. Available: https://www.iso.org/standard/54533.html.
[38] American Association for Medical Instrumentation, TIR97: Principles For Medical Device Security - Postmarket Risk Management For Device Manufacturers, 2019.
[39] Underwriter Labs, Standard for Software Cybersecurity for Network-Connectable Products, Part 1: General Requirements, 2020.
[40] Underwriter Labs, Standard for Software Cybersecurity for Network-Connectable Products, Part 2-1: Particular Requirements for Network Connectable Components of Healthcare and Wellness Systems, 2017.
[41] S. Schwartz, M. Lamoureux, IMDRF Principles and Practices for Medical Device Cybersecurity, 2019.
[42] International Standards Organization, IEC 62304 Medical Device Software — Software Life Cycle Processes, 2006.
[43] National Institute of Standards and Technologies, FIPS 140-2 Security Requirements for Cryptographic Modules, May 25, 2001 [Online]. Available: https://csrc.nist.gov/publications/detail/fips/140/2/final. (Accessed 19 October 2020).
[44] The American Society for Quality, Quality Glossary, n.d. [Online]. Available: https://asq.org/quality-resources/quality-glossary/q.

CHAPTER FOUR

The Product Cybersecurity Organization

Introduction

"What cybersecurity risk are we, as a company, exposed to by virtue of the products we sell?"

This is a question that the board or the CEO loves asking the Chief Information Officer, and yet if you ask the CEO, they will say that they never get a single, easily understandable and justifiable metric as an answer.

The problem in a way stems from the ambiguity in the question itself—cybersecurity risk to what? Patient safety? Patient privacy? Going out of compliance with federal mandates? Not meeting customer requirements? Landing up on the front page of the *Washington Post*?

Safety, privacy, compliance, and customer—each of these is an example of a risk domain. Let us recall the definition risk as introduced in Chapter 2. Risk is a function of the likelihood of an adverse event. The way to measure impact as well as severity varies with the risk domain that is chosen. In the case of aforementioned CEO's question, what they are really interested in is the impact to the business, i.e., business risk because of successful cybersecurity threats. The reason why there is never a great answer to this question is because there is no universally acknowledged method or model of calculating the impact to a business of a cybersecurity threat in the medical device domain. For instance, what is the actual cost of a device recall for cybersecurity reasons? Someone would say it is the cost of developing the fix, rolling out the fix, convincing physicians to apply the fix, the corporate communications needed to allay patient fears of adverse effects, responding to headlines in the popular press, the cost of sales lost, the cost of customer confidence lost, and the cost new projects delayed as a result of an unplanned fix to a device already in market. What is the cost for a data breach? All of the above and add to it punitive fines imposed by jurisdictions. What is the cost of not satisfying a regulatory requirement? Obviously, the business lost for

Cybersecurity for Connected Medical Devices
ISBN: 978-0-12-818262-8
https://doi.org/10.1016/B978-0-12-818262-8.00011-5

not being able to put a product out on the market in time, as the manufacturer goes through lengthy submissions, deficiency letters, and resubmissions. What about the cost of not satisfying a customer requirement? That would be the loss of an existing or prospective customer. While qualitatively it is not that difficult to estimate severity, the problem starts when people try to quantify severity. Because remember, that what the CEO is ultimately interested in the potential revenue lost, and only then can they make a cost—benefit analysis of any cybersecurity investment.

Herein is the crux of the problem. While there are models like Factor Analysis of Information Risk [1] for calculating total business impact of a cybersecurity threat, there is no universal consensus or standards regarding their adoption. Estimating the likelihood of a successful realization of a cybersecurity threat is also not easy. Remember, that "successful realization of a threat" does not necessarily mean that someone actually hacks into a medical device and attacks a patient or obtains patient data, but that one merely demonstrates that it can be done, either by showing it via a limited-scope demonstration or merely publicizing a path toward exploitation. This makes estimating likelihood for business risk even more difficult.

Rather than focusing on assessing high-level business risk, measuring it, and then driving a process that mitigates the risks identified to acceptable levels (the classic risk management process), the "workable" solution this book proposes for reducing organizational cybersecurity risk is to straight away adopt a *controls-based* risk reduction framework. A controls-based risk reduction framework captures security best practices that the community believes reduces business risk; adopt these controls and you are guaranteed to reduce your business risk due to cybersecurity. A controls-based approach might lead to higher investments up-front, as opposed to risk driven or threat driven, where you are doing "just enough" to mitigate identified threats. However, this is more than compensated for by potential business loss from the "unknown" threats and risks a risk/threat-based approach would not protect against.

This book has been building up to this controls-based framework. In Chapter 2, I define cybersecurity controls as consisting of technical, procedural, and legal controls. In Chapter 3, I advocate for creating a regulations and standards-driven *cybersecurity controls catalog* that maps to specific regulatory and standards requirements, with this controls catalog consisting of technical and procedural controls. Readers may wonder why the book continuously insists on using the phrase "procedural control" when the much more succinct "process" would suffice. The reason is to not lose sight of the fact that the process exists to control cybersecurity risk for the organization, which makes it a "procedural control for reducing organizational cybersecurity risk." Because saying this each time would be quite a mouthful, it is simply shortened to "procedural control." Also, a procedural control may map to multiple processes, so using the word "process" might cause confusion.

The controls-based risk reduction framework, and this is this book's recommendation, should be implemented by a medical device manufacturer (MDM) through a dedicated Product Cybersecurity Organization (PCO). The characteristics of a PCO are the following:

1. Single point of accountability: Rather than distributing product cybersecurity talent across different functional units (e.g., Regulatory, Systems, Software, Quality), the PCO consolidates resources within an exclusively product cybersecurity focused team. This organization is led by an individual who is accountable for development, maintenance, and execution of cybersecurity capabilities.
2. Ownership of cybersecurity capabilities: Cybersecurity capabilities consist of procedural controls, tools, and the people needed to define, maintain, and execute the procedural controls using the tools as appropriate (Fig. 4.1).

The PCO is responsible for defining, maintaining, and executing capabilities. Some of these capabilities may be delegated to functions outside the PCO. For example, cybersecurity procedural controls for infrastructure (i.e., processes around securing the development and manufacturing environment and cryptographic signing services and the security of the corporate network) are usually maintained by corporate Information Technology (IT) functions or by external service providers. For the capabilities delegated outside of the PCO, the PCO is responsible for execution of service agreements (i.e., a precise specification of what services the PCO obtains from external entities) and quality control of the services and deliverables from the external entities.

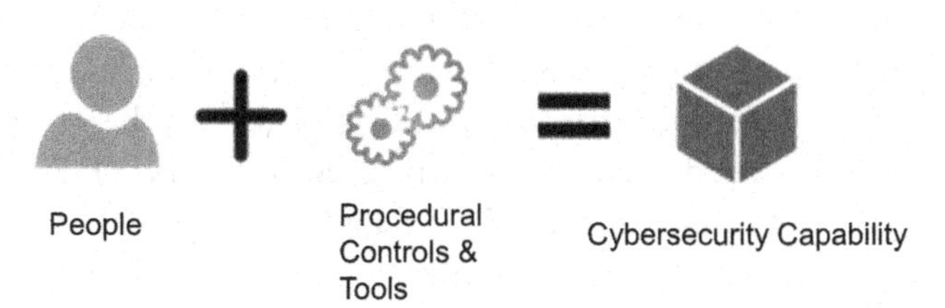

Figure 4.1 Cybersecurity capability.

There are many cybersecurity frameworks (CSFs) available in the community [2,3,8]. Like regulatory guidance, they all require organizations to do similar things but use different language to define those requirements. Each of the frameworks can be used as a reference model for how to construct a PCO, and the capabilities that the PCO should contain. Among the different control frameworks, this book advocates for the NIST Framework for Improving for Critical Infrastructure Cybersecurity, commonly referred to as the NIST CSF [4]. NIST CSF is a US federal document provided by the National Institute of Standards and Technology under the US Department of Commerce. It links to other NIST standards, like Security and Privacy Controls for Federal Information Systems and Organizations (NIST 800-53) [5]. NIST CSF is available for free download and can be used without restrictions. NIST cybersecurity standards are not specific to healthcare or to medical devices, and originated as a security framework for protecting US federal infrastructure. It is voluminous and all-encompassing, often intimidatingly so. However, the NIST framework is still extremely critical to any medical device manufacturer's cybersecurity regulatory strategy. NIST standards are widely adopted across industries inside, and increasingly outside the United States. Using NIST cybersecurity vocabulary enables one to communicate with suppliers and customers and regulators and auditors in a consistent and standardized fashion.

The NIST cybersecurity framework

The NIST CSF recommends that organizations implement a set of capability elements to reduce the overall risk from cybersecurity threats. These capability elements, in the language of NIST CSF, are specified as outcome statements like "Cybersecurity roles and responsibilities are coordinated and aligned with internal roles and external partners" or "Data-at-rest is protected." These outcome statements are then mapped to cybersecurity controls. NIST CSF does not define these cybersecurity controls, but points to other standards and guidance like NIST 800-53 and COBIT (Control Objectives for Information and Related Technologies) [2] for their elaboration. This level of indirection provides flexibility to an organization as to what specific technical strategies the organization adopts to achieve the outcomes.

This outcomes-based paradigm is formalized in the NIST Framework Core through a set of abstractions. At the highest level of the abstraction hierarchy are Functions. Functions can be looked upon as categories into which capabilities belong to. There are five of these broad categories:

- Identify: The capabilities in this category relate to identifying organizational assets that need to be protected, the threats they need to be protected from, and the organization's risk appetite (i.e., when is risk considered uncontrolled).
- Protect: The capabilities in this category relate to identifying specific protection mechanisms that are designed to prevent threats from being successful.
- Detect: The capabilities in this category relate to detecting threats, ideally before they become realized.
- Respond: The capabilities in this category relate to responding to threats.
- Recover: The capabilities in this category relate to recovering from threats that have been successfully realized (Figs. 4.2 and 4.3).

Each of these functions is split into a number of categories and each category is split into a number of subcategories. These subcategories define outcome statements/capability elements which then map to References which have specific technical and procedural controls needed to implement the outcome/capability.

People: building up a Product Cybersecurity Organization

The foundation of a successful Product Security Organization is people. The effectiveness of cybersecurity capabilities reducing organizational cybersecurity risk is a direct function of the skill levels and the motivation of those defining, executing, and maintaining the capabilities.

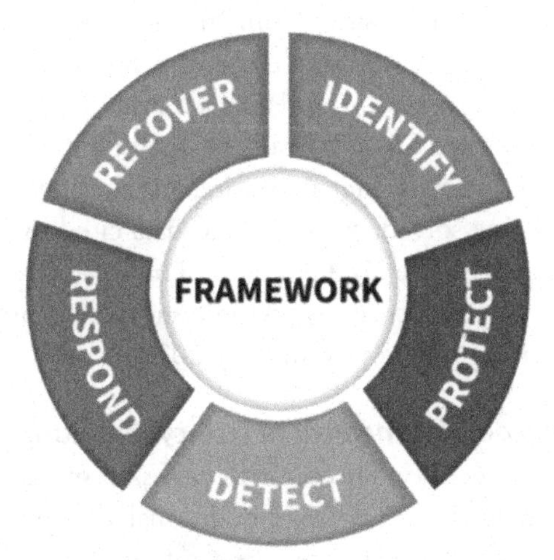

Figure 4.2 The NIST functions. *Reprinted courtesy of the National Institute of Standards and Technology, U.S. Department of Commerce. Not copyrightable in the United States.*

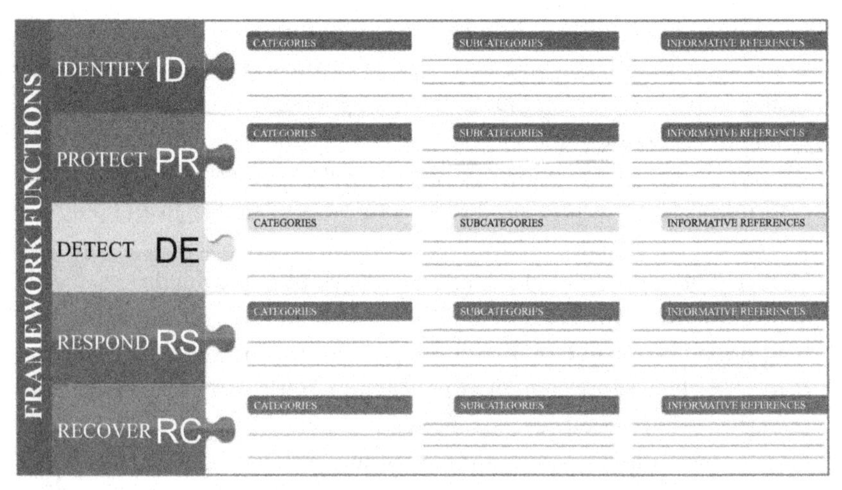

Figure 4.3 NIST CSF functions and categories and subcategories and references. *Reprinted courtesy of the National Institute of Standards and Technology, U.S. Department of Commerce. Not copyrightable in the United States.*

And yet anyone who has ever had open requisitions for cybersecurity knows how difficult it is to get the right candidate to fill the roles. There are a few reasons for that.

Global shortage of cybersecurity professionals

To put it succinctly, there are just not enough trained cybersecurity professionals to meet global demand. The problem is not just for medical device manufacturers, it is across all business domains. A recent international survey done by McAfee reported that 82% of employers report a shortage of cybersecurity skills in their organization, and that as a result of the shortage, cybersecurity jobs in the United States pay an average of $6500 more than other IT professions [6]. Even with higher salaries, the problem of low supply is nowhere close to being solved. According to data cited by Center for Strategic and International Studies in the report "The Cybersecurity Workforce Gap" [7], the global cybersecurity workforce shortage is projected to reach upward of 1.8 million unfilled positions by 2022.

Specializations needed for medical device cybersecurity

Medical device cybersecurity has concerns and skill sets that overlap with, but are fundamentally different, from traditional IT security. Traditional IT security is about operationally securing infrastructure: servers, laptops, and networks. The skill sets needed to fill traditional Security Operational roles focus primarily on expertise in tools, both security and analytics, as well as digital forensics and responding in real time to cyber attacks. While medical device manufacturers would obviously have requirements for operational security roles, the truly critical skill requirements for the PCO are in product development and cybersecurity risk management. It's not enough for engineers to know what security tools to use because, in any case, not too many medical devices are shipped with third-party security tools deployed on them. Instead the skill set needed for product cybersecurity is knowledge of the technologies behind the tools, namely deep knowledge of cryptography and bottom-up security architecture design. Because most roles in the traditional IT security industry are operational, that is where most security professionals gravitate to and consequently develop a background in. Not coincidentally, developing operational cybersecurity skill sets is also where most security certifications concentrate on. All of this creates an acute shortage for cybersecurity professionals with product development skills. Add in other attributes like requirements of systems engineering, regulatory knowledge, and experience in the medical device industry, and we are looking at a highly restricted set of potential candidates.

Culture

It is one thing to attract cybersecurity talent, and it is another to retain it. In a market where demand far outstrips supply, talented cybersecurity professionals know that they have choices. Their next job does not have to be in medical devices, it can be in retail, consumer goods, entertainment, financial services, automotive, aerospace and defense, power and utilities, and also in core tech like Google, Facebook, and Amazon. Since cybersecurity is still a new priority area in healthcare, there is a lack of experienced mentors with an understanding of cybersecurity and its demands. Nor is there a critical mass of cybersecurity professionals within each device manufacturer to form a community of support. Career paths of cybersecurity engineers are also often not defined at medical device organizations because of how new cybersecurity is to the organization. Finally, because they are not part of the core business of developing new therapies, there is often a feeling felt by cybersecurity professionals that their contributions are not properly recognized and appreciated.

Healthcare, being a regulated industry, also has a more conservative work culture than most start-ups and tech companies. Many cybersecurity professionals, used to more agile work environments, become frustrated with the paperwork, the documentation, and the bureaucratic oversight over seemingly mundane activities. For example, cybersecurity professionals from nonregulated industries may not be used to the days of formal reviews and sign-offs triggered by minor changes to an existing design document. Engineers looking to move onto more "fun" things, like system building and threat modeling, may quickly grow frustrated.

So, given the challenges in a high-demand job market with limited supply and the lack of organizational experience for medical device manufacturers in building a PCO, what are some strategies for hiring and keeping the right people?

Here are some of the areas that PCO resourcing strategies should target.

Develop proper organizational structure within business units

Most major MDMs have a similar structure—they are composed of business units, each of which is responsible for one business area, with a thin layer of administration on top, henceforth called "corporate." Corporate defines common policies and objectives across business units. They also provide some services common to all business units, of which cybersecurity governance is often one. There is usually a corporate PCO led by either a Product Cybersecurity VP or a Chief Information Security Officer, providing overall strategic guidance for different business units in terms of defining metrics and general security expectations, and in some cases, some common services, like customer outreach and corporate communications related to cybersecurity. But the heavy lifting for product cybersecurity is the responsibility of the business units: defining and maintaining a cyber Quality Management System (QMS), executing the different procedural cybersecurity controls, ensuring that products have the proper technical cybersecurity controls built into them, vulnerability intake and management, total lifecycle cybersecurity risk management, and generating the metrics for the corporate PCO so that overall organizational policies may be satisfied and objectives met.

At the business unit level, the strategy is usually to have a number of cybersecurity subject matter experts reporting to a Director/VP of Systems or Software or Quality, who is not a cybersecurity subject matter expert. What ends up happening as a result is that there is no one in the business unit's executive management (i.e., the people who take the decisions) with a technical foundation in cybersecurity. Without an executive champion with influence who also is a cybersecurity expert, business decisions often do not align with sound cybersecurity principles, leading to underresourcing for cybersecurity.

It is not that companies always underspend on cybersecurity; the problem is sometimes the opposite. Since cybersecurity is new to healthcare, many in the top echelons of the medical device management, who do not have a strong cybersecurity background, sometimes take decisions based on a presentation they heard somewhere or by virtue of them being on a particularly persuasive sales call. This leads to needless costs and project overruns. The consequence is similar to the story of "the boy that cried wolf." The next time there is a genuine need for cybersecurity investment, the request is not approved, much to the disappointment of the cybersecurity engineers.

The solution to this is to ensure that the leader of the PCO for a business unit has a voice within the executive management of the business unit.

Build or Buy? In a world where supply and demand would be properly calibrated, this question would not perhaps be that important. However, as established before because of the shortfall of trained cybersecurity talent in product engineering, the dilemma that often plagues hiring managers: should I wait for the candidate that is "just right," the one that checks all the boxes required for the role, or should I develop internal candidates to take over cybersecurity roles? While the second option does sound like a long-term option, wherein the role has to be filled right now, the wait for the right candidate itself might be fairly long, sometimes even years in the current situation.

The option to consider is to "build" existing or new talent to take over junior or midlevel cybersecurity roles while trying to "buy" the PCO lead.

There are three broad categories of employees who can be identified to be built into a cybersecurity engineer through proper training, certifications, and mentorship.

- System or Quality or Clinical Engineers: They bring expertise in the total product development lifecycle and deep knowledge of therapies and existing medical system platforms and quality system regulations.
- Software Engineers: They bring expertise in software systems. These systems can be embedded or mobile or cloud or server platforms. They are expected to have some knowledge of application-level security (key management, etc.) and of how to use cybersecurity application programmer interfaces made by third parties (e.g., how to use secure key provisioning for Android).
- Operational Cybersecurity Engineers: They bring expertise in infrastructure security, knowledge of traditional networking, and security tools and data analytics.

Depending on the base skill sets of the engineers, specific training plans need to be developed to fill in the skill gaps. For the System or Quality or Clinical Engineers or Software Engineers, the training would consist of cybersecurity certifications or online or university courses on cybersecurity foundations and cryptography. For Operational Cybersecurity Engineers, the training would consist of a rotation program, wherein they get embedded in existing Systems or Clinical or Quality functions, learn "on the job," and subsequently be assigned tasks of increasing responsibility.

In order to ensure that the engineers in training are progressing toward acquiring the level of expertise that is needed for them to evolve into an independently functioning medical device cybersecurity resource, continuous cybersecurity mentorship is required. This mentor should be responsible for crafting individual development plans based on the engineer's background, providing regular feedback to the engineer, and tracking and reporting progress. While the ideal way of doing this would be to have the leader of the PCO be the designated mentor, it very well might be that the organization does not have someone in executive management with the requisite domain knowledge to provide this level of hands-on oversight. In that case, an acceptable alternative would be to hire external cybersecurity consultants to provide oversight for deliverables being produced by the medical device cybersecurity engineers in training, so that baselines of quality are maintained and positive feedback provided to the engineers and their managers.

As should be obvious, this building-up of engineers to fill in competencies takes time and money, and management should account for the cost of the entire process while budgeting for new roles and where the strategy is to build.

Know what you are looking for

One cannot find the right candidate unless one knows what they are looking for. The generic job description with the word "cybersecurity" thrown in willy-nilly is a recipe for human resources disaster. It is usually advisable to define, at a minimum, three levels of increasing responsibility and clearly specified entry criteria for each role.

- *Analyst:* The analyst should demonstrate competency in one of the following areas: systems/clinical engineering or software engineering or operational cybersecurity. Regardless of their core competencies, an analyst should have coding and code development experience of some sort, ideally in C/C++ (the software engineer is obviously expected to know more of this), an understanding of operating systems (e.g., memory isolation, security kernel, and privileges). The person coming in with operational cybersecurity as their competency is expected to have done hands-on, tool-based threat hunting on networks and/or on cloud deployments of applications and/or on websites, or should have done some level of network security administration. A basic knowledge of cryptography is a plus.

- *Architect:* The architect should have a minimum of 5 years of experience in their area of expertise, one out of systems/clinical or software engineering or operational cybersecurity. If the candidate has systems/clinical as their background, they should have deep knowledge of the medical device and the clinical environment and of regulations and quality systems. If the candidate is coming with software engineering as their background, they need to provide a proven track record of building systems either in the domains of embedded (resource-controlled software systems) or mobile or cloud apps or enterprise. If the candidate is coming with operational cybersecurity as background, they need to provide a proven track record of penetration testing, not just in using automated tools but being able to develop their own customized scripts for security testing, and in being able to do data analytics at scale, using commercial data analytic tools for cybersecurity. An intermediate knowledge of cryptography is a plus.
- *Product Security Organization Lead:* The lead should have a minimum of 10 years of experience in product cybersecurity, with a proven track record of cybersecurity design and architecture. They should have done some level of threat modeling and risk assessments, written product cybersecurity requirements, and designed cybersecurity requirements tests. A strong knowledge of cryptographic primitives and security technology is essential. Having worked previously in a regulated industry is a plus. They should have experience managing programs and projects, and a demonstrated ability to quickly acquire new technical competencies in the medical device cybersecurity space. A significant component of success in the role is technical leadership, of mentoring analysts and architects, and in evangelizing cybersecurity throughout the product development organization.

Be flexible

And finally, in order to retain talent in a competitive market, executive management needs to have some flexibility in their expectations for cybersecurity hires. Unless the role is for the leader of the PCO, which would require a significant face-to-face people management component of their responsibilities, purely technical roles should be given the option of working remotely. With the asymmetry in supply and demand, showing flexibility goes a long way in retaining talent, given that remote work and work from home is considered fairly standard in the tech industry in this day and age, even more so after the Covid-19 pandemic. Another way of retaining talent is support for continuous learning. Beyond the development needed to fill roles discussed previously, resources can be set aside for attending cybersecurity conferences, writing papers and publications, and allocating time to support standards committees and industry body memberships, for those so inclined. Cybersecurity is a rapidly changing and evolving discipline, and staying abreast of the latest trends and threats and regulations and customer expectations is a requirement for effectively discharging the role.

Getting the right people remains perhaps the most critical activity in building up the PCO. The good news is that there is a deep industry-wide interest in healthcare cybersecurity as being an emerging domain where many new fresh graduates want to plant their flag. Rather than waiting for the unicorn candidate, device manufacturers would do well to plug into the prevalent interest in medical device cybersecurity, build talent for cybersecurity through a combination of training and learning on the job, and reward performers with challenging assignments, career advancement, recognition, and flexibility.

Process and tools: building up a Product Cybersecurity Organization

The baseline processes that a PCO needs to maintain should be driven by the procedural controls from the cybersecurity controls catalog. The cybersecurity controls catalog, as defined in Chapter 3, contains a set of cybersecurity technical and procedural controls that are dictated primarily by regulatory requirements. The PCO should be responsible for defining, maintaining, and executing these procedural controls. Table 4.1 contains the procedural controls section of the cybersecurity controls catalog (the technical controls section will be provided later). Since the regulations themselves keep getting updated, I have not included the actual mapping to the base standard; the interested reader is encouraged to take a regulatory guidance (e.g., the FDA 2018 premarket guidance) and construct a mapping of the text in the document to these procedural controls.

Table 4.1 Procedural controls of the cybersecurity controls catalog.

Cybersecurity bill of materials A CBOM (cybersecurity bill of materials) should be maintained. A CBOM consists of a list of commercial, open source, and off-the-shelf software and hardware components of a medical device, as well as components, both hardware and software, that are custom developed by the MDM for the medical device (i.e., their own in-house code and/or hardware).
Threat modeling Threats to the medical device, at the system level, should be captured in a system threat model. A system threat model process should contain a method for identification of system assets, and for evaluating system vulnerabilities and system threats using a structured approach. A system threat model should be made for the product (i.e., the medical device that is being developed) that assesses threats during its operation as well as its deployment (i.e., when it is being set up for operations). Threats, at the subsystem (software and at the hardware level), to confidentiality, integrity, and availability of the medical device should be captured in a software threat model.
Cybersecurity risk modeling System risks to patient safety and privacy from cybersecurity should be continuously identified and evaluated throughout the lifecycle of the product.
Supply chain cybersecurity risk modeling Supply chain cybersecurity risks should be defined and evaluated throughout the lifecycle of the medical device.
Secure requirements The secure requirements procedural control should provide methods for developing cybersecurity system and software requirements for the medical device based on the technical cybersecurity controls from the cybersecurity controls catalog. (The technical cybersecurity controls referred here will be provided in a subsequent chapter)
Secure software specification and implementation The secure software design procedural control should provide methods for performing the following: **1.** Developing product specifications for the medical device, based on security system requirements, using conceptual tools drawn from software engineering like data-flow diagrams, sequence diagrams, and state machines. **2.** Developing secure code for the medical device, using industry best practices for secure code development, and secure coding guidelines. Static and dynamic analysis tools integrated into the development and build process may be used to monitor for security bugs while the code is being developed.

(*Continued*)

Table 4.1 Procedural controls of the cybersecurity controls catalog.—cont'd

Labeling for security

The labeling for security procedural control imposes the following requirements on the labeling process. Specifically, the following items should be captured as part of labeling for the device, if applicable:

1. Device instructions and product specifications related to recommended cybersecurity controls appropriate for the intended use environment (antivirus software, use of a firewall).
2. A description of the device features that protect critical functionality, even when the device's cybersecurity has been compromised.
3. A description of backup and restore features and procedures to regain configurations.
4. Specific guidance to users regarding supporting infrastructure requirements so that the device can operate as intended.
5. A description of how the device is or can be hardened using secure configuration. Secure configurations may include end point protections such as antimalware, firewall/firewall rules, whitelisting, security event parameters, logging parameters, and physical security detection.
6. A list of network ports and other interfaces that are expected to receive and/or send data, and a description of port functionality and whether the ports are incoming or outgoing (note that unused ports should be disabled)
7. A description of systematic procedures for authorized users to download version-identifiable software and firmware from the manufacturer.
8. A description of how the design enables the device to announce when anomalous conditions are detected (i.e., security events). Security event types could be configuration changes, network anomalies, login attempts, and anomalous traffic (e.g., send requests to unknown entities).
9. A description of how forensic evidence is captured, including but not limited to any log files kept for a security event. Log files descriptions should include how and where the log file is located, stored, recycled, archived, and how it could be consumed by automated analysis software (e.g., Intrusion Detection System, IDS).
10. A description of the methods for retention and recovery of device configuration by an authenticated privileged user.
11. Sufficiently detailed system diagrams for end users.
12. Where appropriate, technical instructions to permit secure network (connected) deployment and servicing, and instructions for users on how to respond upon detection of a cybersecurity vulnerability or incident.
13. Information, if known, concerning device cybersecurity end of support. At the end of support, a manufacturer may no longer be able to reasonably provide security patches or software updates. If the device remains in service following the end of support, the cybersecurity risks for end users can be expected to increase over time.

Table 4.1 Procedural controls of the cybersecurity controls catalog.—cont'd

Secure system verification and validation

The secure system verification procedural control imposes the following requirements on the system and subsystem testing process for the medical device:

1. All cybersecurity system and subsystem requirements should undergo comprehensive testing.
2. The system should be tested using a combination of static and dynamic code analysis methods and a test report for cybersecurity should be provided. These test results should provide input to the *vulnerability monitoring* procedural control if security defects are discovered. The static and dynamic methods that may be used are as follows:
   - testing of device performance
   - evidence of security effectiveness of third-party over-the-shelf software in the system (input from *supply chain risk modeling* procedural control for high-risk suppliers)
   - objective-driven testing (e.g., credentials that are "hardcoded," default, easily guessed, and easily compromised)
   - vulnerability scanning
   - robustness testing
   - boundary analysis
   - penetration testing
   - third-party test reports

Secure manufacture

The secure manufacture procedural control should provide methods for the medical device manufacturing environment. It should provide methods for performing the following:

1. Ensuring that manufacturing facilities are secured from cybersecurity threats both from outsiders as well as insiders.

Secure development

The secure development procedural control should provide methods for securing the hardware and software development environment. It should provide methods for performing the following:

1. Ensuring that hardware and software development environments are protected from cybersecurity threats, both from outsiders as well as insiders.
2. Securing the storage where cryptographic signing keys (e.g., Hardware Security Modules) are stored and ensuring that only authorized items are signed.

Vulnerability monitoring

The vulnerability monitoring procedural control should provide methods for intake of vulnerabilities from the external world. Specifically, it should provide methods for performing the following:

1. *Product monitoring*: Interpreting cybersecurity events recorded in cybersecurity

(Continued)

Table 4.1 Procedural controls of the cybersecurity controls catalog.—cont'd

log files, network monitoring systems (e.g., Intrusion Detection Systems), product returns, and customer complaints, to decide which of these events constitute cybersecurity incidents, i.e., successful or failed cybersecurity compromise attempts. Successful compromise attempts should be considered as threats, their root cause should be analyzed and flagged as a product vulnerability.

2. *Threat Intelligence*: Monitoring public sources of vulnerability threat information like the following:
   a. Feeds from Information Sharing and Analysis Organizations (Health-ISAC for medical devices), Department of Homeland Security (DHS), Food and Drug Administration (FDA), and other regulatory authorities
   b. Industry conferences
   c. Vulnerability disclosures made by software component suppliers and contract manufacturers
   d. Vulnerability disclosures made by security researchers either in public or through private channels, on medical devices marketed by the device manufacturer
   e. Vulnerabilities in National Vulnerability Database (NVD) for software assets that are part of the software cybersecurity threat model and then determining which of these signify vulnerabilities actually present on medical devices out in the field or in development.
3. *Penetration testing/vulnerability scanning*: Discovering vulnerabilities and threats on the product through activities that are part of the *Secure System Verification and Validation* procedural control.

Cybersecurity patch management

The cybersecurity patch management procedural control ensures that if a threat poses unacceptable patient safety and/or patient privacy risk, then a security patch is applied to remediate the underlying vulnerability. This procedural control should also define policies for applying cybersecurity patches to medical devices even when the risk to patient safety/privacy risk is acceptable, as per industry best practices and customer expectations. Specifically, it should provide methods for performing the following:

1. Applying (if the vulnerability is on a third-party hardware or software component) or developing (if the patch is on a native hardware or software component) within the time frame stipulated by regulators and agreed to upon in customer agreements
2. Ensuring that the patch is delivered, either through removable media or through online update, to the devices affected
3. Educating clinicians and patients of the need to patch devices
4. Measuring and reporting patch adoption rates

Now that the procedural controls that follow from regulations, guidance, and standards have been defined, it is time to group them under different capabilities. This grouping and the capability definition can be found in Table 4.2. Note that there are some new procedural controls in the extreme right hand column, namely "Cybersecurity Strategy," "Cybersecurity Management Review," "Regulatory Submissions," and "Training for Cybersecurity" that are do not directly follow from regulatory and standards imperatives, but are needed in order for the PCO to align with the existing QMS of the MDM. For example, the Cybersecurity Management Review procedural control defines the operational cybersecurity metrics that have to be collected for the Management Review component of a QMS.

Table 4.2 Cybersecurity capabilities for a Product Cybersecurity Organization.

Capability	Definition	Procedural controls
Product security governance	• Overall oversight of capability definition, maintenance, and execution • Defining and collecting cybersecurity operational metrics	Cybersecurity strategy, cybersecurity management review
Standards and regulatory compliance	• Responsible for putting together regulatory submissions and handling regulatory audits on cybersecurity	Regulatory submissions
Cybersecurity risk management for medical devices	• Threat modeling • Cybersecurity risk modeling	Threat modeling, cybersecurity risk modeling, cybersecurity bill of materials
Product supply chain cybersecurity risk management	• Supply chain risk modeling sourced from third-party suppliers as well of contract manufacturing (third-party manufacturing products on contract from the medical device company)	Supply chain cybersecurity risk modeling

(Continued)

Table 4.2 Cybersecurity capabilities for a Product Cybersecurity Organization.—cont'd

Capability	Definition	Procedural controls
Cybersecurity design engineering for medical devices	• Defining and maintaining a standards and regulations driven set of technical controls • Translating technical controls to cybersecurity system and software requirements • Defining test plans for requirements and executing tests • Developing detailed design for cybersecurity features	Secure requirements, secure system specification and implementation, secure system verification and validation, labeling for security,
Secure product development	• Ensuring that the development environment for device software and hardware is secure • Securing the storage where cryptographic signing keys (e.g., Hardware security Modules) are stored and ensuring that only authorized items are signed	Secure development
Secure manufacture	• Ensuring that the manufacturing facilities are secure	Secure manufacture
Vulnerability management	• Continuous monitoring of external and internal signals for product vulnerabilities • Assessing risk of product vulnerability using *Cybersecurity Risk Management for Medical Devices* capability • Root cause analysis of vulnerabilities discovered on products which includes integration with a manufacturer's complaint handling and CAPA (Corrective and Preventive Action) quality processes • Cybersecurity patching • Communicating with external stakeholders regarding vulnerabilities	Vulnerability monitoring, cybersecurity patch management

Table 4.2 Cybersecurity capabilities for a Product Cybersecurity Organization.—cont'd

Capability	Definition	Procedural controls
Cybersecurity training	• Training entire organization on cybersecurity concepts, as well as for training employees with respect to their roles and responsibilities	Cybersecurity training

Summary and key takeaways

The key takeaways of this chapter are the following:

1. The best way to reducing organizational cybersecurity risk for an MDM is to adopt a controls-based risk reduction framework. A controls-based risk cybersecurity risk reduction framework captures security best practices that the community believes reduces business risk. By adopting these controls, business risk due to cybersecurity is automatically reduced.
2. A controls-based cybersecurity risk reduction framework is defined by defining, maintaining, and executing a set of capabilities. Capabilities are collection of procedural controls and tools with a common objective, and the people needed to define, maintain, and execute the procedural controls, using the tools as appropriate.
3. A dedicated PCO should be made responsible for defining, maintaining, and executing cybersecurity capabilities.
4. Cybersecurity is a domain where market demand for trained professionals far exceeds supply. The cybersecurity skills that are needed for the medical domain and product cybersecurity development experience (as opposed to infrastructure security maintenance) are an even more niche market within the already restricted talent pool. This makes it imperative for MDMs to focus on training their workforce to fill the roles, rather than rely on the proverbial unicorn walking in through the door, and once talent is developed or procured, to retain them by defining cybersecurity-specific career paths within traditionally noncyber-focused medical device development organizations.

References

[1] J. Jones, An Introduction to Factor Analysis of Information Risk, 2006.

[2] Information Systems Audit and Control Association, Control Objectives for Information and Related Technologies, 2016.

[3] ISO/IEC Information Technology Task Force (ITTF), ISO/IEC 27001 Information Technology — Security Techniques — Information Security Management Systems — Requirements, ISO, 2013.

[4] National Institure of Standards and Technologies, Framework for Improving for Critical Infrastructure Cybersecurity, 2018.

[5] US National Institute of Standards and Technologies, Security and Privacy Controls for Information Systems and Organizations SP 800-53, 2020.

[6] MCafee Corporation, Hacking the Skills Shortage [Online]. Available, https://www.mcafee.com/enterprise/en-us/assets/reports/rp-hacking-skills-shortage.pdf. (Accessed 29 October 2020).

[7] Center for Strategic and International Studies, The Cybersecurity Workforce Gap, 2019.

[8] ANSI/AAMI/IEC, ANSI/AAMI/IEC TIR80001 Application of Risk Management for IT Networks Incorporating Medical Devices - Part 2-2: Guidance for the Disclosure and Communication of Medical Device Security Needs, n.d.

CHAPTER FIVE

Cybersecurity risk management-I

Introduction

The purpose of this chapter (Chapter 5) and the next (Chapter 6) is to define a formal approach for cybersecurity risk management for medical devices. Cybersecurity risk management consists of modeling risk of adverse outcomes due to cybersecurity threats, assessing whether the risk of adverse outcomes meet the medical device manufacturer's (MDM) risk acceptability criteria, bringing down risk to acceptable levels using risk responses, and ensuring that these risk responses do not increase the risk of adverse outcomes in other domains. In case risk cannot be brought down to acceptable levels, the cybersecurity risk management activity has to justify why the medical device's benefits outweigh its risk. In this chapter, the focus will be on risk assessment, whereas Chapter 6 shall focus on risk responses.

Table 4.2 of Chapter 4 defines a set of capabilities that a Product Cybersecurity Organization for an MDM should develop and maintain. In this chapter and Chapter 6, the focus will be on "Cybersecurity Risk Management for Medical Devices." In Table 5.1, the relevant row from Table 4.2 of Chapter 4 is replicated, for the sake of completeness.

Managing cybersecurity risk is a regulatory requirement across all jurisdictions. Traditionally, "risk management" for MDMs has concerned itself with managing the risk of adverse outcomes in the patient safety domain. There are well-established models for capturing risk to the patient, driven by decades of safety and reliability engineering best practices. Because of the maturity of this field, MDMs have well-established procedures for assessing safety risk of their medical devices stemming from contributing factors like user errors, software failures, electro-magnetic interference, or failures of mechanical or electrical components. The processes for assessing risk to patient safety from noncybersecurity causes have been codified within their QMS for decades, driven primarily by the industry standard ISO 14971, Medical Devices—Application of Risk Management to Medical Devices [1].

However, extending traditional safety risk management practices to account for cybersecurity threats proved challenging. An early approach

Cybersecurity for Connected Medical Devices
ISBN: 978-0-12-818262-8
https://doi.org/10.1016/B978-0-12-818262-8.00005-X

Table 5.1 Cybersecurity risk management for medical devices.

Capability	Definition	Procedural controls
Cybersecurity risk management for medical devices	Managing risk of adverse outcomes due to cybersecurity threats	Cybersecurity risk management, cybersecurity bill of materials

to bolting cybersecurity on to traditional safety risk management was to treat cybersecurity threats as a type of user-error and software failure. A cybersecurity threat that purposefully causes dosing problems would then be managed exactly the same as a dosage error caused by confusion due to a poorly design user interface, or due to a software bug. The problem with this approach is that cybersecurity just does not lend itself to the kind of mathematical analysis that can be used for other contributors to safety risk. You will never get a probability of occurrence of a threat from the field or laboratory data for cybersecurity threats of the kind that you will get for mechanical or electrical failures. Another subtle point often overlooked is that traditional safety risk management practices involve independent failures. For example, an MDM may find a potential electrical threat in that one in every 1000 of their power supplies malfunctions. To improve the reliability of their devices, they may add a secondary power supply. With two power supplies which fail at a rate of 1 in every 1000, the probability that both power supplies fail would be one in a million.

This is not the case for cybersecurity threats because of the presence of a "common cause," namely the intent of the attacker. If a cybersecurity threat can compromise one subsystem in certain circumstances, then they can always defeat an identical subsystem in those circumstances. Redundancy offers no protection, as it does in conventional safety engineering.

That is why the industry consensus is that there should be a stand-alone process for assessing patient safety risk due to cybersecurity threats, separate from the process for assessing patient safety risk due to other causes. The American Association for Medical Instrumentation (AAMI) TIR-57 [2], a standard referred to by the Food and Drug Administration (FDA) [3], specifically defines a process for assessing patient safety risk in medical devices due to cybersecurity threats. AAMI TIR-57 is closely aligned with ISO 14971 (the traditional process), but still distinct from it. Additionally, AAMI TIR-57 expands the scope of "harm" defined by ISO 14971 to include patient privacy. For example, in AAMI TIR-57, harm is defined to be "physical injury or damage to the health of people, or damage to property, or the environment, or reduction in effectiveness, or breach of data or system security," which encompasses not just classical patient safety harm (the notion of physical injury or damage to patient and/or environment), but also "breach of data."

So, following the principle of having separate stand-alone processes for noncybersecurity risks and cybersecurity risks, there are thus two distinct risk models: The System Risk Model and the System Cybersecurity Risk Model, respectively.

Chapter 2 lays out one of the foundational assumptions of this book when it comes to cybersecurity risk modeling for medical devices, namely the existence of two related yet distinct realms in which risk modeling needs to be done—system and subsystem. There are multiple subsystems (hardware, software, electrical, mechanical), but for this book, the only two subsystems that shall be considered are hardware and software. Hence, we will have two cybersecurity risk models—one at the system level and one at the subsystem level.

Cybersecurity risk management constitutes of the following activities:

1. Identifying the System: This consists of identifying the system for which cybersecurity risk management is to be done.

The output of this activity is the identification of the system, and the consequent subsystems on which cybersecurity risk management activities are to be performed.

2. Subsystem (software and hardware) Cybersecurity Risk Modeling: This consists of the following subactivities:
   a. Subsystem threat modeling: Actual cybersecurity issues present in the device software and hardware are tabulated by identifying subsystem assets, vulnerabilities, and threats.
   b. Subsystem cybersecurity risk assessment: Cybersecurity risk of the vulnerabilities and threats identified in the subsystem threat model is calculated. The adverse outcomes observable at the subsystem level are compromise of integrity, availability, and/or confidentiality.
   c. Defining riskacceptability at subsystem level: The definition of when a risk is acceptable, and when it is not, is defined for the subsystem cybersecurity risk model.
   d. Defining risk response at the subsystem level: The only risk response that can be applied at the subsystem level is patching, i.e., fixing the hardware or software vulnerability that is the root cause of the cybersecurity issue.

The output of this activity is a subsystem Cybersecurity Risk Model.

3. System Cybersecurity Risk Modeling: This consists of the following subactivities:
   a. System threat modeling: Hypothetical "what-if" cybersecurity threats that may be present in the system are tabulated by identifying system assets and vulnerabilities (Fig. 5.5).
   b. System cybersecurity risk assessment: Cybersecurity risk of the vulnerabilities and threats identified in the system threat model is calculated. The adverse outcomes observable at the subsystem level are compromise of patient safety and patient privacy (Fig. 5.8).
   c. Defining risk acceptability at system level: The definition of when a risk is acceptable, and when it is not, is defined for both the system as well as the subsystem cybersecurity risk model.
   d. Defining risk response for system-level threats: Risk responses at the system level are formulated in order to bring down system risk to acceptable levels, and even in case of system threats, where the risk is already acceptable, to bring it down to as low as one can take it. The risk responses should be evaluated to ensure that they do not increase patient safety risk in other domains (e.g., human factors) so that overall patient safety risk increases, even though patient safety risk due to cybersecurity causes goes down.
   e. Defining risk response for subsystem level threats that pose "unacceptable" risk at the subsystem level: It would be ideal to patch all subsystem vulnerabilities, regardless of the risk posed to patients, as soon as possible. However, in the real world, regulators realize the challenges of rolling out cybersecurity patches for all software and hardware vulnerabilities. Instead, they mandate that only vulnerabilities that pose unacceptable risk to patient safety and patient privacy must be patched, while leaving the decision to patch vulnerabilities that do not pose unacceptable risk as a conversation between MDMs and Healthcare Delivery Organizations (HDOs). In order to assess the patient safety/privacy risk posed by a subsystem level threat that is assessed to be "unacceptable" at the subsystem level, it has to be evaluated at the system level. In order to do this evaluation, the subsystem vulnerability is added to the list of system vulnerabilities, and the risk of it is modeled at the system level. System-level risk responses can now be used to reduce the patient safety/privacy risk posed by this subsystem threat. If the residual risk is still "Unacceptable," then a cybersecurity patch would have to be rolled out, else not.

The output of this activity is a System Cybersecurity Risk Model.

4. Risk–Benefit Analysis: If there are still threats whose risk, postresponse, still remains "unacceptable" at the system level, then a risk–benefit analysis (RBA) needs to be performed in order to show that the medical device provides greater benefit than the risk it poses to patient safety/privacy.

The output of this activity is an RBA document. We will explain each stage of the above process in detail.

Threat modeling

The US FDA, as part of its guidance [4–6] as well as in multiple public communications [7] in conferences and symposia, have strongly endorsed threat modeling as a recommended practice for MDMs. There is though, at the time of writing, a lack of uniform consensus in the medical device community as to what constitutes a valid "threat model."

Let us say we have an MDM that is designing a medical device they intend to put on the market in a year. The project manager organizes a day-long workshop where cybersecurity engineers, clinical engineers, system engineers, and software engineers, all brainstorm over copious quantities of coffee and high-carb snacks, to come up with cybersecurity threats to the medical device the team is designing. At the end of the day, the numerous Post-it notes stuck on top of the white board are compiled into a list of threats. While the team is impressed, albeit somewhat overwhelmed, by the sheer number of threats identified, they wonder if they have a valid threat model.

A threat model should be the output of a *systematic* approach. The word "systematic" is very critical here. Unstructured brainstorming may produce a number of threats, and they may turn out to comprehensive. However, because there is no underlying method, there is no expectation that the list of threats is exhaustive. Nor is an unstructured threat modeling exercise predictably repeatable. If the success of a threat modeling exercise depends on the skills of the individual participants and how well they are able to communicate, consistency and completeness of threat models cannot be ensured. If you put into the room another set of engineers and a fresh hot pot of coffee, an unstructured approach will almost certainly yield different results. We should recognize that threat modeling may never be fully automated. Tools, frameworks, programs, and the like can help optimize the threat modeling process, but there will always be an art to threat modeling.

One of the aspects of workability is being able to maintain an engineering artifact. In the absence of a structured approach, a threat model produced by one team, when entrusted to another team to maintain, becomes, over time, a mish-mash of different assumptions and levels of specificity. Some threats are very "high level" and amorphous, some threats are very "low level" and detailed, and they all share the same container, namely the "threat model." There is no unity of voice, nor any level of consistency between the specifications of the different threats. Such threat models increasingly become difficult to maintain. After some time, the organization bites the bullet, has someone redo the threat model, and then once again, after a few years, the exercise is repeated, all because of the lack of a systematic approach.

So what do we mean by a systematic threat modeling approach? Simply that there should be a systematic approach for identifying assets, vulnerabilities, and threats, with standard metrics defined for evaluating the likelihood and severity of each threat. This book also makes a distinction between threat modeling and risk modeling. The threat model defines the space of threats and the likelihood they will be executed by an attacker. A risk model evaluates, given a threat model, how successful our defense strategy has been in terms of reducing risks to levels considered acceptable.

Threat modeling defines the space of the attacks, while risk modeling defines the space of defense. One way of looking at threat modeling is that it is an activity that is part of risk modeling. For those who have written code, a useful visualization is to consider risk modeling as the main function calling the threat modeling function.

There are two threat models

One of the fundamental underpinnings of the threat modeling described in this book is that there are two threat models—one at the system level and the other at the subsystem level. This intuition was first brought forth in Chapter 2, but here let me elaborate it with more examples.

Consider two competing medical devices that serve identical clinical functions, with the only difference being that one is manufactured by MDM Acme and another is manufactured by MDM Brando. They have the same interfaces (let us assume Bluetooth Low Energy), they collect the same kind of patient data, and they perform the same clinical functions. This implies they have identical system assets, system vulnerabilities, and consequently identical system threats. In other words, they have identical system threat models.

But because the devices are produced by different MDMs, we expect them to have very different hardware and software. They will likely have different therapy and BLE chips, and they will definitely have different code, written by different developers, using different libraries. This means they will have very different software/hardware assets, software/hardware vulnerabilities, and different software/hardware threats. That is, they have very different subsystem threat models, even if they have identical system threat models.

Now consider another example by comparing a printer with Acme's medical device. Now in terms of functions, a printer and a medical device are like chalk and cheese. For Acme's device, the worst harm that could happen is death, for the printer, a "paper jam." However, it may be that Acme's device and the printer share the same BLE chip, the same embedded operating system, are using the same libraries, and have very similar subsystem (hardware/software) threat models. Since they use identical, or nearly identical, subsystem components (i.e., have very similar software/hardware assets), they will have identical, or nearly identical, software/hardware vulnerabilities and threats.

These two examples demonstrate that the system threat model and the subsystem threat model are distinct. They are not independent though, after all they both belong to the same medical device. We will explore the relationship between the two later, in this chapter and the next.

Before I get into describing each of the cybersecurity risk management activities for medical devices, let me first describe the running example I will be using to explain the concepts introduced. I shall be using an example of an infusion pump. However, this approach has been used successfully for devices in other therapy areas. As you familiarize yourself with the process, I encourage you to think about how it can be applied to devices in therapy areas you are most familiar with.

Why did I choose an infusion pump out of all medical devices? I was part of the Generic Infusion Pump project [8] in the late 2000s, which was a collaborative effort between multiple universities, research organizations and the US FDA. The other advantage of choosing an infusion pump is that its function is easy to understand.

Running example: the Zeus infusion pump

Ray Devices is a fictional global MDM with multiple business units, of which one is medication delivery. One of the products that Ray Device's medication delivery business unit produces and markets is Zeus: an infusion pump. For those who are not familiar with the concept of an infusion pump, an infusion pump delivers medication or fluids or nutrients to a patient through an intravenous line. Infusion pumps are used because they administer medication to a patient with regularity and precision that would otherwise not be possible.

In order for an infusion pump to deliver medication, the pump needs to be told what is being pumped, how much of that substance to pump, and how long to pump. This is performed by a clinician and is referred to as programming an infusion. A single programming of an infusion pump is called an infusion order. For our example, an infusion order consists of a patient-id (the identifier of the patient), drug-id (the identifier of the medication), concentration (the weight of the drug is present in unit volume), and frequency and period of drug delivery (how often the drug should be delivered and for how long). An infusion order can be programmed locally through a touch screen interface or remotely over Wi-Fi.

Each Zeus infusion pump has a drug library stored in its flash persistent storage. Drug libraries are files with rules for all medications and formularies that the pump can administer. These rules are captured as "soft-limits" and "hard-limits" which limit how much of each medication and formulary a pump can deliver into a patient. The purpose of the drug library is to ensure that any infusion never exceeds the hard and soft limits of the drug. If a clinician attempts to program an infusion that would exceed the soft limit, the pump issues a visual and auditory alarm before prompting the clinician to confirm the infusion. If a clinician attempts to program an infusion that would exceed the hard limit, the infusion is disallowed, visual and auditory alarms sounds, and the event is logged and the log sent to a network server. Soft limits can be exceeded with clinician permission. Hard limits cannot be exceeded.

The Zeus pump is connected to a hospital network over wireless Wi-Fi (i.e., 802.11). The wireless credentials needed by the pump to authenticate to the hospital network are stored on the Zeus flash persistent storage. The credentials are loaded, as a file, onto the Zeus pump through the USB interface. Once connected to the hospital network, the Zeus pump receives infusion orders over the Wi-Fi network from a pump server. The pump-server is trademarked as Titan, and is manufactured by a competitor of Ray Devices. Titan is capable of communicating not just to Zeus pumps, but pumps made by other manufacturers also. Titan is installed on a server in the hospital's server room, while Zeus pumps are distributed throughout the hospital, at the bedsides of patients, emergency rooms, and operating theaters. Other than infusion orders, Titan is also used to broadcast drug libraries to every registered pump (including Zeus pumps) in the hospital. The flow of data from Titan pump server to the Zeus infusion pump is represented by **Flow 1** in Fig. 5.1. (It should be noted that in the Figure, flow numbers are denoted by circles with the flow number inside the circle.)

Titan itself receives infusion orders from the Electronic Medical Record (EMR) System. This is represented by **Flow 2** in Fig. 5.1. The Titan pump server stores the association between patient-id and pump-id. Once it receives an infusion order, the pump server sends, over the hospital Wi-Fi network, the infusion order to the pump-id associated with the patient. This is represented by **Flow 1** in Fig. 5.1. The infusion pump, in turn, sends back up to the pump server, data regarding infusions (i.e., if an infusion was successful or not) as well as log files. This is represented by **Flow 3** in Fig. 5.1.

A Zeus pump has three interfaces:

1. A local touch screen interface: This is used to program/modify infusions locally and to perform local administration activities, like setting pump alarm volumes.
2. A local USB 2.0 interface: This interface is used to perform code updates to the pump, set up Wi-Fi, and upload drug libraries manually.

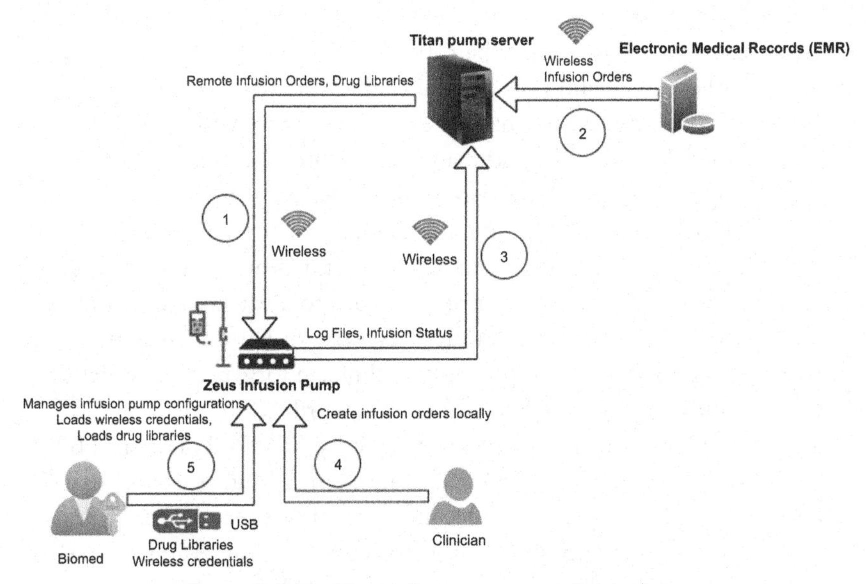

Figure 5.1 The Zeus infusion pump and data flows.

3. A wireless (Wi-Fi) interface: This is used by Zeus pumps to obtain infusion orders and drug libraries as input, and to send log-files and telemetry data up to the Titan pump-server.

The pump has two local interfaces or roles:

1. Clinician: A clinician can program, start, stop, pause, and otherwise change infusions. They can also temporarily silence or lower alarm volumes. This is represented by **Flow 4** in Fig. 5.1.
2. Admin: The admin performs privileged operations on the Zeus pump. Privileged operations include updating the code on Zeus over USB, manually loading a drug library over USB, changing pump configuration settings like alarm volumes that persist over multiple infusions, loading Wi-Fi wireless credentials over USB, connecting/disconnecting the infusion pump to/from the local Active Directory service, and resetting the pump to factory settings. This is represented by **Flow 5** in Fig. 5.1. When a Zeus pump is set to factory settings, all configuration data, patient information, and security configurations are immediately removed and the pump is restored to the condition at unboxing.

In terms of security features, the Zeus pump has the following:

1. Each Zeus pump is provisioned during manufacturing with a private–public key pair. The private key is stored in nonvolatile flash storage, and the public key is embedded in a X.509 certificate that is digitally signed by Ray Devices.
2. In addition to the above key pair, there is a public key that is stored in nonvolatile storage and provisioned during manufacture. The public key is called the public download key and is used to verify code updates. The private download key (the asymmetric key analog of the public download key) is stored securely in Ray Devices' on-premize data center, and is used for signing code updates for the Zeus pump.
3. The clinician interface is intentionally left unauthenticated because of patient safety concerns. Requiring clinicians to authenticate before an infusion could be programmed presents a risk of harm to patients in emergency situations, or in the event a clinician forgets their credentials.
4. The admin interface is protected by a password.
5. Zeus pumps are usually purchased in bulk by HDOs. For every HDO, Zeus pumps are manufactured with a random Admin password that is common to all pumps for a particular order. For every HDO, a Zeus pump is, at manufacturing, provisioned with a random Admin password that is common to all pumps for a particular order.

6. Once the Zeus pumps are delivered to the HDO, the biomedical engineers, also known colloquially as the biomed, use the common password specific to the HDO to access the Admin interface. This is the set-up mode for the Zeus pump. In the set-up mode, the biomed is first prompted to change the default password. Then the biomed loads the HDO Wi-Fi network credentials file using USB. The biomed also uses the USB interface to load the self-signed certificate of the Titan server. The certificate of the Titan server and the Wi-Fi credentials of the HDO network are stored in the nonvolatile flash storage of the Zeus pump. Now that the Zeus pump has the wireless credentials to access the HDO network, and the certificate of the server it should connect to, it connects over wireless to Titan and presents its own device certificate. The Titan pump server verifies that Zeus device certificate is signed by Ray Devices, and if the verification succeeds, registers it in its own database as a Ray Devices pump.
7. The Zeus pump and the Titan pump server are now mutually authenticated. They subsequently use TLS (Transport Layer Security) to communicate. All data in transit from pump server to pump use authenticated encryption algorithms that are part of TLS to ensure that data in transit are protected from unauthorized tampering and reading.
8. During the set-up, after mutual authentication has been established, the Titan pump server generates a unique shared encryption key for every pump, encrypts it with the public key of the pump for whom it is meant, and sends it to that pump over TLS.
9. Every time the Titan pump server sends an infusion order or a drug library over wireless, it does the following:
   - It calculates a SHA2 hash of the infusion order or a drug library and encrypts the hash using AES-256 with the shared encryption key. This is done to prevent anyone from changing an infusion order or drug library in transit.
   - It encrypts the entire infusion order with the shared encryption key using AES-256 algorithm. This encryption is done to prevent anyone from reading an infusion order in transit.
10. The Titan pump server does a key rotation every 2 years, where the certificates are refreshed and the new certificates loaded onto the pumps through the admin interface.
11. When a biomed wants to update code or change drug library or adjust pump settings, they log in to the admin interface using the admin password.

12. If incorrect password is entered three times at the admin interface, a log-file entry is made on the Zeus pump tagged "cybersecurity," and is sent to the Titan pump server.
13. JTAG (Joint Test Action Group) hardware debugging interfaces are disabled after production
14. The persistent storage of the Zeus pump is encrypted by AES-256 at rest with a key derived from the admin password.
15. All code updates to the Zeus pump are signed. Code is allowed to be installed only if the code has been signed by the private analog of the download key that was provisioned on the pump during manufacture.
16. The pump, on boot-up and periodically, computes a SHA256 hash of the current code and compares it with a SHA2 value stored in persistent storage of the code as it was when it was last updated. If they do not match, then code tampering has been detected, and the user is alerted with a message on the pump.
17. Cybersecurity log files are signed by the pump before being sent up to the pump server at a configurable time every day

Now that the motivating example has been laid out, each activity that constitutes cybersecurity risk management for medical devices is defined.

Identifying the system

If you want to secure a system, the first thing you need to figure out is what exactly it is that you are protecting. Should the overall risk modeling be done at a system level or at a system-of-systems level?

Most medical connected devices nowadays are system-of-systems, i.e., a collection of independently developed systems that interoperate to realize a set of clinical use cases. An example of a system-of-systems would be the example of the Zeus pump eco-system. This eco-system is a system of system that consists of four systems: the pump, the server, the hospital Wi-Fi network, and the EMR system. Now the question is should the scope of risk modeling activities, which include threat modeling, be done at the "system of system" level or should it be defined at the system level, i.e., individually at the level of the Zeus pump, the Titan pump server, the hospital wireless network, and the EMR?

An integrated, single system-of-system cybersecurity risk model is likely to be the largest in size, making the model difficult to analyze. In my experience, system-level cybersecurity risk models are usually at the sweet spot of comprehensiveness, maintainability, and amenability to analysis. Some end-to-end threat scenarios may span multiple systems, but these can be broken down into a collection of threats defined at a system scope. As an example, one threat to the Zeus pump could be a compromised wireless (Wi-Fi) password of the HDO network, which then may then be used to gain privileged access to the HDO network, thus establishing a beachhead for the attacker. Once the attacker has access to the hospital Wi-Fi network with the stolen password, they can then try to steal PHI from the HDO EMR. This can be represented as three threats in three different systems—a threat to steal the Wi-Fi password (a threat defined as part of the Zeus infusion pump system threat model), a threat of gaining unauthorized access to the HDO network (a threat that is part of the HDO wireless threat model), and then a threat to steal PHI from the EMR by an attacker controlled device that is connected to the HDO network (a threat defined on the EMR threat model). The way to capture these end-to-end "system-of-system" threats is to have a separate table for them, with traceability being maintained to the specific threats (in this case, the three mentioned above) in the individual system threat models (in this case, in the infusion pump, network and EMR threat models, respectively).

For our running example, the choice for the system will be the Zeus pump. For the Zeus pump, cybersecurity risk modeling shall be done at two levels, with a threat model being defined at each level—one at the system level, and the other defined at the subsystem (software and hardware) level.

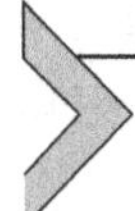

Subsystem (software and hardware) cybersecurity risk modeling

The first subactivity within subsystem cybersecurity risk modeling is subsystem cybersecurity threat modeling.

Subsystem threat modeling

A subsystem cybersecurity threat model captures the *actual* vulnerabilities present in software and hardware, and the threats that can exploit these vulnerabilities to compromise the integrity, availability, and confidentiality of the subsystem.

Subsystem threat modeling consists of first identifying subsystem assets, and then for each subsystem asset, identifying relevant subsystem vulnerabilities and threats (Fig. 5.2).

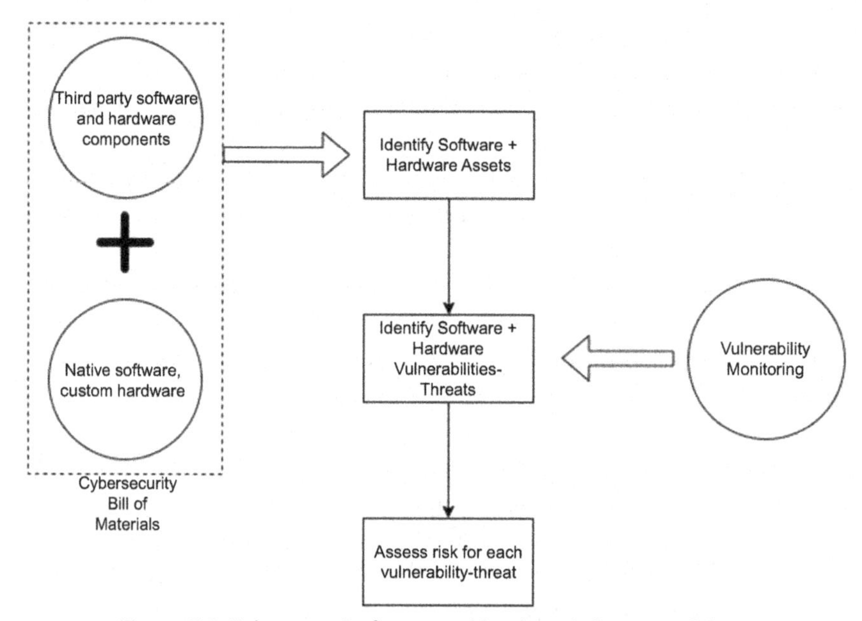

Figure 5.2 Subsystem (software and hardware) threat modeling.

Identify subsystem assets (Cybersecurity Bill of Materials or CBOM)

A subsystem asset (software and hardware) is one, which if compromised, might lead to a compromise of the integrity, availability, and confidentiality of the hardware or software subsystem. The complete list of subsystem assets is called a Cybersecurity Bill of Materials or CBOM for short and it is generated by executing the *Cybersecurity Bill of Materials* procedural control.

For the hardware subsystem, one should include in the CBOM all hardware components that have software running on them. This excludes hardware components like capacitors and batteries, but includes controller hardware that has software executing on them. Specifically, the CBOM should ensure that it has coverage of the following hardware components.

- The therapy hardware (i.e., the hardware components on which the therapy software runs)
- The communication hardware (e.g., Bluetooth, 802.11 chipsets)
- Dedicated security hardware (e.g., Trusted Platform Modules)

For the software subsystem, one should include in the CBOM.

- All software components procured from external sources and that is integrated into the device software build
- All software components that are developed in-house to the MDM

The challenge here is establishing the completeness of the software section of the CBOM, i.e., identifying each and every third-party software component in the device code base. Dependencies are missed often because of the tendency of developers to copy-paste code from other sources, i.e., from third-party libraries or from online code repositories like Github, without recording the provenance of the code. The other complicating factor is that third-party software components may in turn have other third-party software components within them, and they in turn may have others. This is particularly true of operating systems. For example, Red Hat Enterprise Linux contains hundreds of third-party components and libraries. The CBOM should clearly define which of these components and libraries are present in the device build, separating out the kernel version of an operating system from its packaged utilities.

Now that the CBOM procedural control has defined what elements to include in the CBOM, it should also define what metainformation about the element (software or hardware asset) it should record within the CBOM.

If the subsystem asset be a third-party software/hardware component, one should record the following metainformation, at *a minimum*.

a. The vendor

b. The major and minor version number of the software component

c. End-of-support (EOS) for the software component, if applicable. The EOS is the date till which the vendor commits to maintaining the software/hardware component for bug fixes including bugs that have security implications. Many commercial vendors stop providing cybersecurity fixes beyond a certain date. If an MDM uses unsupported software as part of their medical device, the MDM is forced to attempt to maintain the security of something they cannot control. This is an important factor in determining if the device should itself be end-of-supported by the MDM. This is also information that a customer would like to know (e.g., a medical device on a hospital network is built using an operating system the OS vendor no longer supports) and assess as part of their own risk acceptance process.

If the subsystem asset be a native software/hardware component, one should record the following metainformation, at *a minimum*.

a. Names of associated code files and their hashes

Identify subsystem vulnerabilities and threats

When actual issues are identified at a subsystem level, the identification of the vulnerability and threat go hand-in-hand. That is why I refer to subsystem vulnerabilities and threats as a vulnerability—threat combine.

Let me illustrate what I mean with an example of a vulnerability drawn from the NIST National Vulnerability Database (NVD).

CVE-2020-0601:

A spoofing vulnerability exists in the way Windows CryptoAPI (Crypt32.dll) validates Elliptic Curve Cryptography (ECC) certificates. An attacker could exploit the vulnerability by using a spoofed code-signing certificate to sign a malicious executable, making it appear the file was from a trusted, legitimate source, aka Windows CryptoAPI Spoofing Vulnerability.

CVE-2020-0601, for those encountering an NVD entry for the first time, is the identifier of this vulnerability in the database. CVE stands for Common Vulnerability Enumeration, a standard numbering system used by the NVD to uniquely identify vulnerabilities. We can see from the CVE-2020-0601 description that the vulnerability ("the Windows CryptoAPI Spoofing Vulnerability") is intrinsically linked with the threat ("An attacker uses a spoofed code-signing certificate to sign a malicious executable, making it appear the file was from a trusted, legitimate source"). Hence, the CVE here is a vulnerability—threat combine, since it expresses both the vulnerability and the threat.

Subsystem vulnerabilities and threats are input to the subsystem (hardware/software) threat modeling procedural control from the *Vulnerability Monitoring* procedural control. The *Vulnerability Monitoring* procedural control monitors multiple signal sources for cybersecurity issues: supplier disclosures, national databases of vulnerabilities, vulnerabilities discovered by external researchers or uncovered through internal testing, or from customer complaints and product monitoring, or simply through generic threat intelligence. I do not go into details here, but leave the discussion for Chapter 8 where the vulnerability monitoring procedural control is covered in detail.

Subsystem cybersecurity risk assessment

Now that vulnerabilities and threats on software and hardware assets have been identified from the threat model, risk of each threat needs to be assessed at the subsystem level (see Fig. 5.3). Recall, that risk is a function of the likelihood of a threat and the severity of impact of the threat. At the subsystem level, impact can only be ascertained in terms of integrity, confidentiality, and availability. Patient safety and patient privacy are system-level properties. Impact to safety and privacy cannot thus be directly assessed at the subsystem; the best one can do at the subsystem level is assess "potential impact to patient safety/privacy."

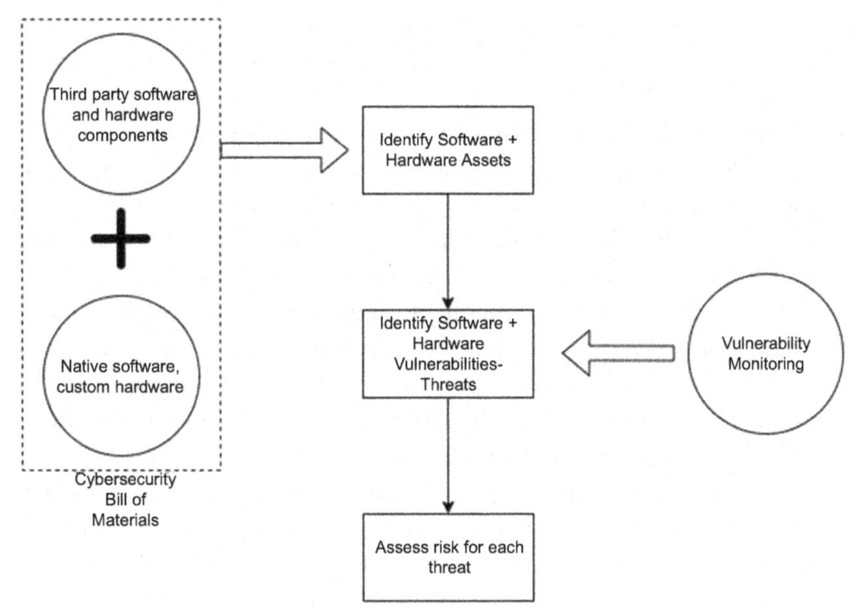

Figure 5.3 Subsystem risk assessment.

For each vulnerability—threat combine, the risk metric the book advocates adopting is CVSS (Common Vulnerability Scoring Scheme). CVSS is an open framework for communicating the characteristics and severity of software vulnerabilities and the threats that may exploit them. In keeping with the philosophy of this book to not explain here in detail that which the reader can find elsewhere, we do not go into detail of the CVSS scoring scheme. For readers who are encountering this term for the first time, I recommend a detour to the CVSS specification to understand what the standard means [9]. For those who are aware of CVSS, a brief description is provided for the sake of completeness.

A CVSS score consists of three metric groups: Base, Temporal, and Environmental. The Base metrics produce a score ranging from 0 to 10, which can then be modified through the Temporal and Environmental metrics. The base metric of CVSS can range from 0 to 10.

According to the NVD, a threat with a CVSS base score of 0.0—3.9 is considered "Low" risk, a base CVSS score of 4.0—6.9 is "Medium" risk, base score of 7.0—8.9 is "High" risk, and base score of 9.0—10.0 is "Critical" risk.

The CVSS base score consists of a likelihood component and a severity component.

The likelihood component of the CVSS base score of a vulnerability–threat combine measures how likely an attacker is to attack your system given a certain vulnerability/threat.

- A part of the likelihood component captures how "close" an attacker has to be to successfully execute an attack (e.g., somewhere far away, on a local network or at the device) (The AV: Attack Vector part)
- A part of the likelihood component captures how easy it is for an attacker to execute the attack (The AC: Attack Complexity part)
- A part of the likelihood component captures if the attacker need some amount of privilege to start the attack (The PR: Privileges Required part)
- A part of the likelihood component captures whether in order for an attacker to be successful, do they have to get the user to do something (The UI: User Interaction part)
- A part of the likelihood component captures whether a successful attack gives the attacker control over a resource just on this system, or can they get more "bang for the buck" by pivoting to other systems? (The S: Scope part)

The severity component of the CVSS base score of a vulnerability–threat combine measures the impact in terms of integrity, confidentiality, and availability of a given certain vulnerability/threat.

The CVSS scoring scheme is referenced by the US FDA in its cybersecurity guidance [6]. It has the advantage of being widely accepted across domains, not just the healthcare or medical device industry, and is likely to be the means by which software and hardware suppliers will convey risks of vulnerabilities on their components. One of the downsides of its wide applicability is that the scoring scheme is highly generalized, which means there different analysts often make different assumptions and come up with widely different CVSS scores. MITRE has created a rubric [10] based on CVSS, which has been endorsed by the US FDA, tailored for the medical device and healthcare industry. The benefit of this specialization is that the rubric may be used to provide a more precise tabulation of a vulnerability–threat combine's CVSS score.

Continuing the example of the Zeus infusion pump, we have a very simplified subsystem threat model in Table 5.2.

Defining risk acceptability at subsystem level

The next activity in cybersecurity risk management at the subsystem level is defining risk acceptability at the subsystem level and then evaluating whether the risk of each vulnerability–threat combine at the subsystem level lies is acceptable or not, given the risk acceptability criteria (see Fig. 5.4).

Table 5.2 Subsystem threat model for Zeus infusion pump.

Subsystems assets	Subsystem vulnerability-threats	Subsystem risk
Pump code developed by ray devices	SW1. Third-party penetration tester identifies a vulnerability in pump code that allows an attacker to send an infusion order that exploits a bug in input validation and crashes the infusion pump	Attack vector = A (attacker has to be on hospital network) Attack complexity = H (the bug can be exploited in the context of a rare corner case) Privileges required = H (attacker needs access to the pump server) User interaction = N (an user at the pump does not need to do anything for this threat to succeed) Scope = U (vulnerable and impacted component are the same) Availability is affected (H), no impact (N) on confidentiality and integrity. Putting it all together, **Risk (CVSS base score) is 4.2 (medium)**
Wireless supplicant from vendor ComSys, v7.8, end-of-support 2022	SW2. CVE 2019–4200 on ComSys wireless 802.11 supplicant version 7.8, a key compromise allows an attacker full knowledge of encryption key used at the wireless network layer	Attack vector = A (attacker has to be on hospital network) Attack complexity = L (the nature of the threat grants the attacker the privilege to get onto the network) Privileges required = N (attacker requires no privileges) User interaction = N (an user at the pump does not need to do anything for this threat to succeed) Scope = U (vulnerable and impacted component are the same) Availability is not affected (N), but confidentiality and integrity are affected, both at H. Putting it all together, **Risk (CVSS base score) is 8.1 (high)**

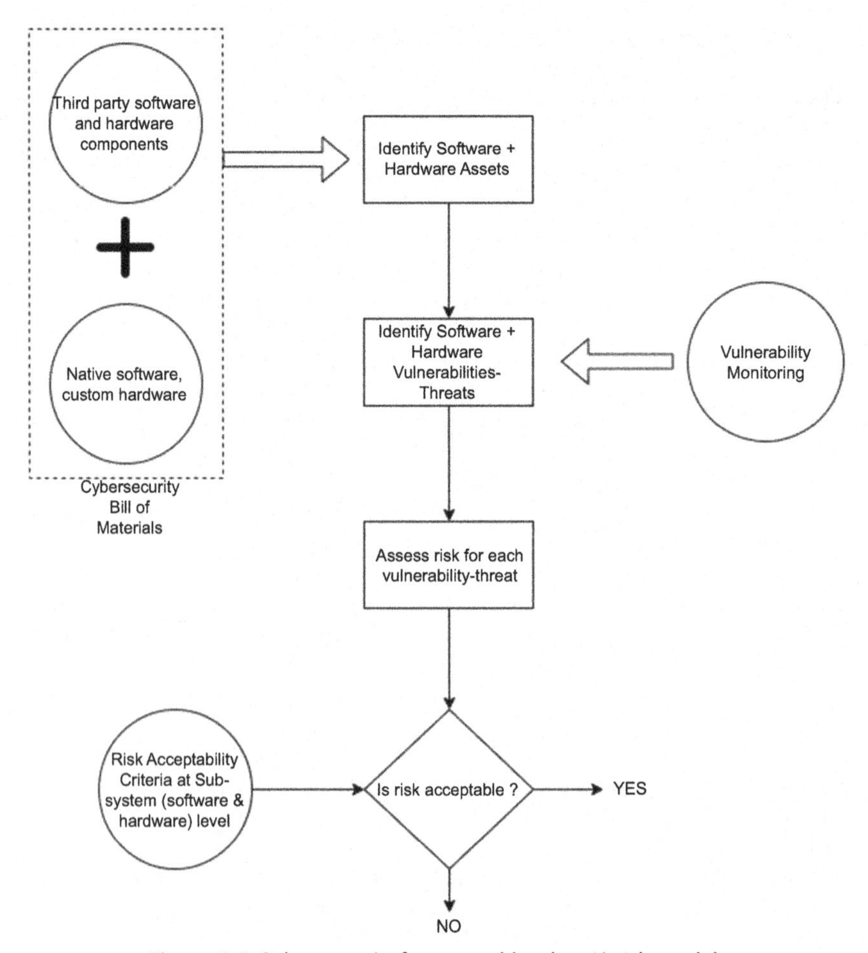

Figure 5.4 Subsystem (software and hardware) risk model.

Is the risk of a subsystem level threat acceptable at the subsystem level? The short answer is, we really cannot say for sure. As discussed before, the impact to safety/privacy cannot be directly assessed at the subsystem level since safety and privacy are system level properties. The only way to assess whether an actual cybersecurity issue in a medical device poses unacceptable patient safety/privacy risk is to assess it at the system level as part of system risk modeling.

One approach, the most conservative approach, would be to consider every subsystem vulnerability—threat combine to be "unacceptable" at the subsystem level, regardless of the risk value. Since we cannot say at the subsystem level what the impact to patient safety is, let us err on the side of caution and just consider every cybersecurity issue to pose "unacceptable" risk at the subsystem level. (This does not imply that the risk at *the system level* of this vulnerability—threat combine will be "unacceptable" as we shall see subsequently.) Other approaches are a bit less conservative, in that they consider every observed vulnerability that has a risk value classified as "Low" (as per the CVSS base score classification) to be "acceptable" at the subsystem level, and everything else (i.e., "Critical," "High," or "Medium") to be "unacceptable."

For this book, we adopt the most conservative approach, while recognizing that MDMs may choose to draw the line of risk acceptability at the subsystem level at any risk value, based on their appetite for risk.

Risk Acceptability Criteria At The SubSystem Level: All identified cybersecurity vulnerabilities in the device hardware and software are considered to be "unacceptable" at the subsystem level, regardless of the value of the risk metric.

Using this definition of risk acceptability at the subsystem level, and going back to the example of the Zeus pump, both the subsystem threats, namely SW1 and SW2, are assessed to be "unacceptable" *at the subsystem level.*

Defining risk response at subsystem level

The only risk response possible purely at the subsystem level is to fix the vulnerability through a patch. Only through a fix, i.e., by the removal of the issue and consequently of the risk itself, can the problem be solved purely at the subsystem level. Increasingly, HDOs and other customers of MDMs are insisting, through contractual obligations or requirements on proposals, on removal of all subsystem vulnerabilities at a regular cadence, typically annually, irrespective of the risk they pose to patient safety/privacy. In other words, patching is becoming the only risk response that customers are willing to accept as a permanent solution.

System cybersecurity risk modeling

Just like it is at the subsystem level, system-level risk modeling starts with the construction of a threat model, in this case a "system threat model." Unlike at the subsystem, where threats are actual issues, system threats are theoretical "what-ifs, like "Attacker installs malware on the device" or "Attacker executes a man-in-the-middle attack during system communication." The purpose of a system threat model is not to claim that these attacks are actual attacks that can be executed on the system, but lay out a hypothetical what-if attack space against which defenses have to be developed as part of the product design process. System threat modeling is a system design activity that is done continuously throughout product development, to formally capture "what is being defended against." Only once we have done this, can we assess how good our defenses are in ensuring the desired outcomes—namely keeping the risk of patient safety and privacy harm within acceptable levels.

System threat modeling

The steps required to create a system threat model (Fig. 5.5) are the following:

1. Identify system assets
2. Identify system vulnerabilities
3. Identify system threats

Let us go through each of these steps in detail, using the running example of the Zeus infusion pump.

Identify system assets

Let us start off by asking the following question.

What does an attacker want to do?

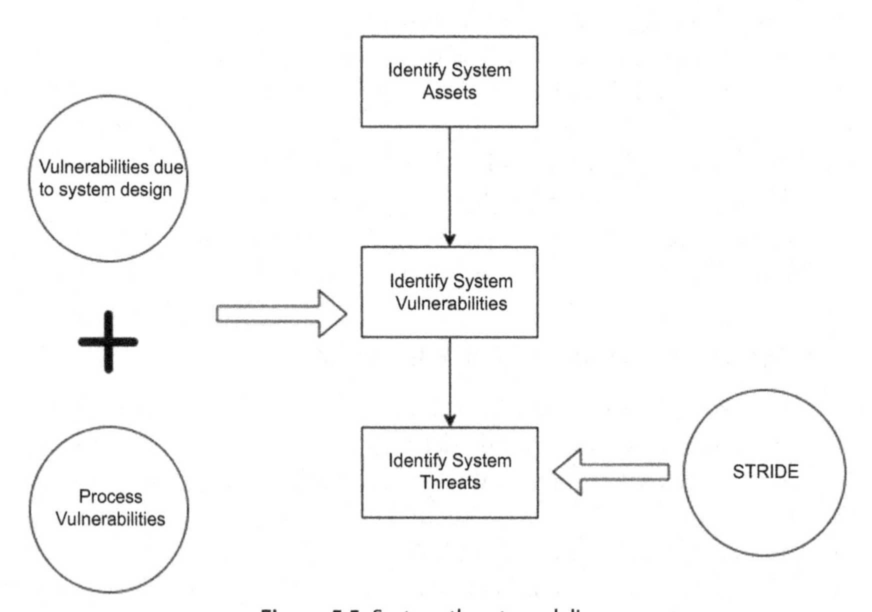

Figure 5.5 System threat modeling.

In order to identify the system components that one wants to defend (i.e., the system assets), it is imperative that we answer this question. In soccer, the opponent wants to score a goal. Because we know that, we then try to secure the asset which if "compromised" would lead to the opponent attaining their objective, namely the goal.

The tree-like structure of Fig. 5.6 breaks down the objectives of the attacker into simpler subobjectives in a hierarchical fashion. At the top most level, the attacker wants to either "disrupt operations" or "obtain confidential information." There is another objective, namely, "compromise the protective mechanism of the system," which we shall come to at the end.

Now, "disrupt operations" can be accomplished by either stopping the operations totally or altering it in a way that is of advantage to the attacker. For example, stopping operations totally for our Zeus pump could be accomplished by providing it malformed input that the pump is not designed to handle.

"Alter operations" can be accomplished in two ways—"alter clinical data" and "alter system behavior."

An attacker can change the clinical data produced by the device such that a clinician takes wrong operational decisions based on the altered data.

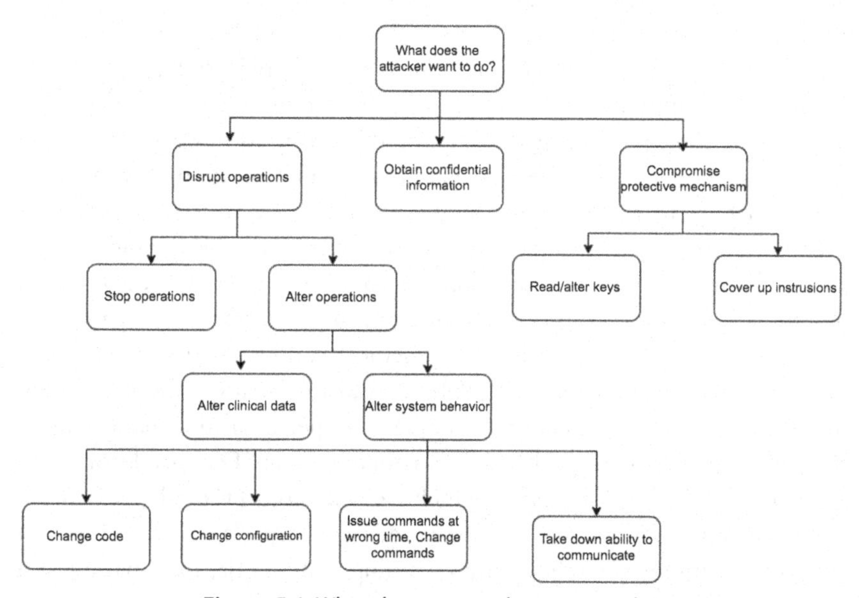

Figure 5.6 What does an attacker want to do?

For example, an attacker could change the infusion status that is sent to the pump server, claiming that the infusion failed when in reality, it succeeded. Seeing a failed infusion, the clinician may issue a duplicate infusion order that is not needed, potentially harming the patient.

System behavior can be altered in the following ways:

Change code. By changing system code, the attacker can change the system behavior. In our example, this could be the attacker loading malware onto the Zeus pump.

Change configuration. By changing system configurations, the attacker can change the system behavior. In our example, this could be the attacker tampering with different pump hardware and software settings (e.g., alarm volume or the drug library).

Issue commands at the wrong time. Here, the attacker does not change the commands provided by a genuine user, but merely makes the system behave in a way it should not. For example, an attacker could capture and replay a command at the "wrong" time. For Zeus, this would be an attacker capturing an infusion order over Wi-Fi and replaying it later when the patient has no clinical need of that infusion.

Change command. By changing the commands issued to the system by a user, an attacker can make the system do something the attacker intends. In our example, this could be the attacker tampering with a remote infusion order sent by the Titan pump server to the Zeus pumps. over the wireless Wi-Fi communication

"*Take down ability to communicate.* The attacker here is trying to make the pump go in-communicado, i.e., take down its remote wireless interface. It's not that the therapy is stopped (that would be covered under "stop operations"), just the ability of the Zeus pump to communicate over wireless."

This brings us to the second high-level objective of the attacker, i.e., "obtain confidential information." In our example, this would be the attacker being able to read information about a patient that they should not be able to. This could be personal information about the patient or information that links a patient to a medical condition. In our example, this would be the attacker being able to read information about a patient that they should not be able to, whether it is personal information about the patient or information that links a patient to a medical condition.

The last high-level objective, which we had kept to the side, now needs to be looked at. When we introduce security controls to protect against attackers disrupting operations and obtaining confidential information, our job is not done yet.

We must recognize that an attacker could target Zeus' security controls themselves to achieve their objectives. To hark back to our example from Chapter 2, in order to steal the diamond, the attacker has to first attack successfully the defenses of the bank. In Fig. 5.6, the objective is expressed as "compromise protective mechanism." This can be broken into two subobjectives: "Read/alter key material" so that cryptographic security mechanisms may be subverted, and "Cover up intrusions" so that any logging and monitoring mechanisms may be suppressed.

Now that we have created a tree of attacker intent, we have a structured method for identifying system assets. In Fig. 5.7 we replicate Fig. 5.6 and annotate each of the bottom-most nodes of the tree (called a leaf) with the system component that the attacker has to compromise in order to

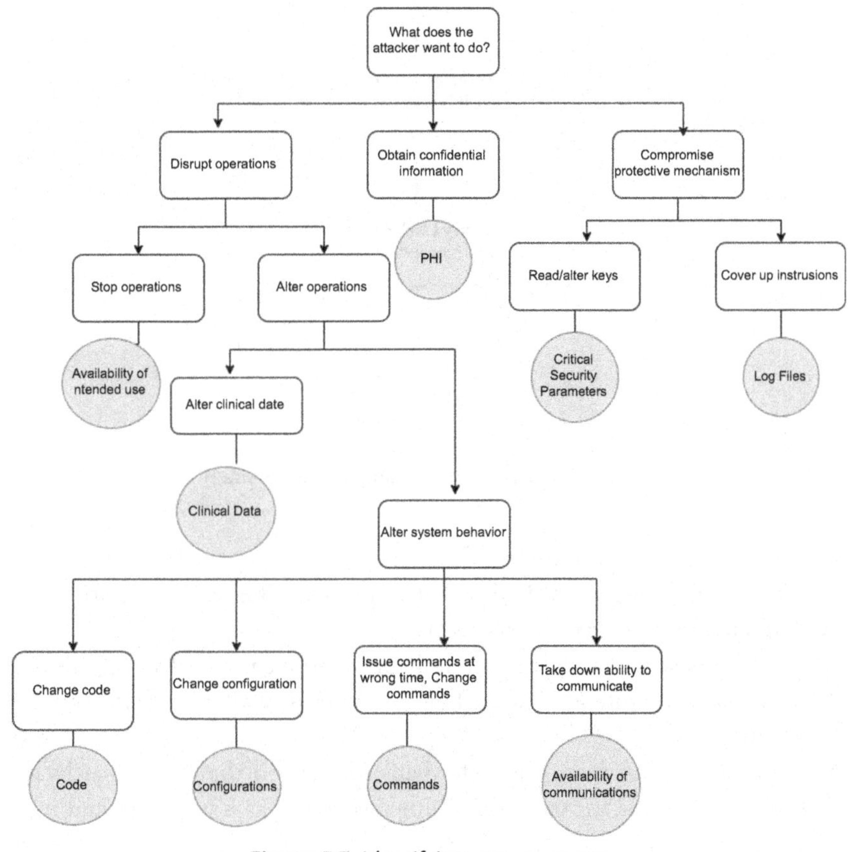

Figure 5.7 Identifying system assets.

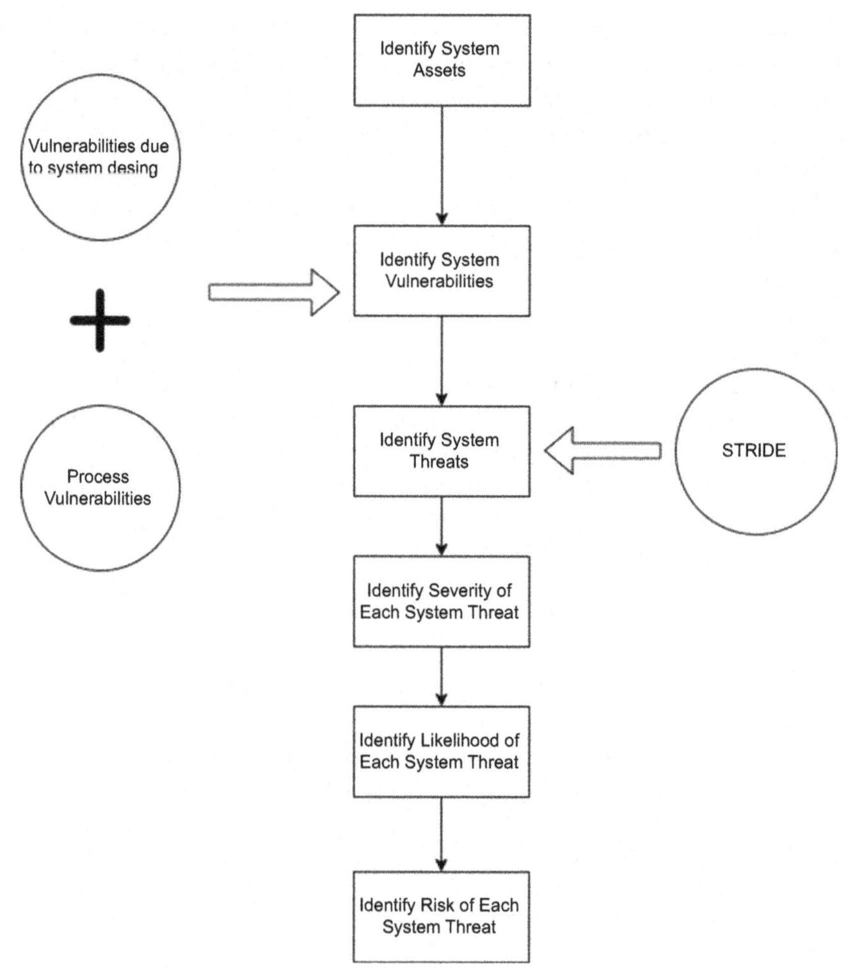

Figure 5.8 System cybersecurity risk assessment.

realize the objective captured in the leaf node. These system components (denoted by the blue-shaded circles) that annotate the leaf nodes are what are defined as the generic system assets.

So, the *system assets* that are output from the above method are as follows:

- Availability of intended use: This is the ability of the device to be operational.
- Code: This constitutes the code that executes on the device hardware and is responsible for the clinical functionality that is implemented in software.

- Configurations: This constitutes data parameters that configure the operation of the device.
- Commands: This constitutes the commands that are issued to the device.
- Availability of communications: This constitutes the ability of the device to engage in communication. It should be noted that just because a device is not being able to communicate, does not mean that it is not operational. For example, an infusion pump can lose the ability to communicate but still can be fully functional at the local interface. Of course, by taking down its ability to communicate, the attacker has reduced its functionality (e.g., its ability to take infusions wirelessly), and that is why "availability of communication" is an asset an attacker may want to target.
- Clinical Data: This constitutes clinical data that the device produces or consumes.
- PHI: This constitutes the data that associate an individual with their clinical data. While PHI and Clinical data are often found together, the nature of attacks on them is different—while an attacker wants to read PHI, the attacker wants to change clinical data. That is why it makes sense to have them as separate system assets.
- Critical Security Parameters: This constitutes different cryptographic materials like private and public keys, and shared symmetric keys.
- Log Files: This constitutes records of cybersecurity events collected by the device.

The next step is to ascertain the specific assets of a system the system assets identified by the procedure maps to. For the infusion pump example, the mapping is shown in Table 5.3. The mapping would of course vary from system to system, even though system assets are expected to stay more or less uniform, given the attacker model formulated in Fig. 5.7. For example, if the system whose threat model was being constructed was a medical app on a smart phone, the generic system asset "code," would map to the app code. If the system whose threat model was being constructed was a cloud medical app, the system asset "configurations" would map to, among other things, network and application firewall settings, network security group definitions, virtual machine configurations, etc.

Identify system vulnerabilities

System vulnerabilities may be of two types:

1. Design vulnerabilities
2. Process vulnerabilities

Table 5.3 Identifying specific system assets.

System assets	Specific system assets for the Zeus pump
Availability of intended use	The availability of the Zeus pump to conduct therapy
Code	Zeus pump code including the pump drivers, therapy code and communication code
Configurations	Configuration files for the Zeus pump software, user settings like pump alarm volume, and device configurations like drug library for defining safe limits of infused drugs
Commands	Commands given at clinician interface and admin interface, remote infusion orders over Wi-Fi from pump server
Availability of communications	Availability of Zeus pump to communicate over the network
Clinical data	Infusion status
PHI	Patient hospital id, patient height, patient weight
Critical security parameters	Pump private key, pump public key, shared encryption key between pump and pump server, wireless password for hospital network
Log files	Lines in the event log tagged as "cybersecurity"

Design vulnerabilities are weaknesses in the product that stem from choices made during product design. Process vulnerabilities, on the other hand, exist because of processes that are absent or that are imperfectly implemented.

As an example, the Zeus infusion pump has a USB port. Since it has a USB port, there is nothing one can do, short of removing the USB port from the system design, to prevent an attacker from inserting a USB drive with malware. Of course, you can have strong protections that can prevent attacker-controlled code from being installed on the Zeus pump, but that does not mean that an attacker cannot insert a USB drive and be "connected" to the system, just that code cannot be installed from the USB drive.

Similarly, the Zeus pump uses a wireless communication medium, Wi-Fi or 802.11. There is nothing one can do to prevent an attacker from observing the data transmitted through over the air, from introducing their own traffic into the communication channel, or flooding the wireless spectrum to jam communication. Whenever a system communicates with a remote system, an attacker can always pretend to be a legitimate remote system. Once again, there may be strong countermeasures that prevent an attacker from reading or writing packets in a communication medium or spoofing someone's identity, but, once again, that does not mean that the vulnerability does not exist at a system level.

Now, consider the use of read-write persistent flash storage. The moment you decide to use read-write persistent memory you open yourself to the possibility that someone can write their own code and data to the read-write persistent storage. There might be protections that make it practically impossible for someone to write code and data onto persistent storage, but that does not mean that the risk is zero.

Some system vulnerabilities exist because of deliberate design choices to "not have security." For example, for the Zeus infusion pump, the clinician interface is kept unauthenticated in order for the device to be "always available." Since infusion pumps are used in emergency room situations, locking out the local interface is considered to pose a much higher safety risk than an attacker using an unauthenticated local interface.

Besides vulnerabilities that are introduced as consequences of design choices, some system vulnerabilities exist because of processes. Consider, for example, the downloading of signed code. Once you have code already installed on a medical device, the code that is on the device can verify the cryptographic signature of the code update. But what about the first time, when the code is being installed on the raw hardware during manufacturing? What if an attacker, who has managed to infiltrate the manufacturing floor, and installs malware on the hardware even before it is even put in a box and shipped? Similarly, what if the attacker happens to be one of the code developers, and they seed in a backdoor that allows them to circumvent security protections and access the device, once it is operational in the field? These vulnerabilities are all examples of processes vulnerabilities, inherent in the very process of code development and manufacturing.

A systematic process to identify system vulnerabilities is to first enumerate all interfaces and design choices that would have cybersecurity implications. Once this is done, one should associate system vulnerabilities that follow from these choices, as we have done for the Zeus pump, in Table 5.4. Then one should analyze system processes surrounding the device, as has been done for the Zeus pump in Table 5.5. Both these lists are nonexhaustive, and serve to illustrate how the process works.

Table 5.4 System vulnerabilities introduced by system design.

System design elements	Vulnerabilities introduced by system design
Wireless (802.11) communication to remote entities	The Zeus pump communicates wirelessly and packets flowing over a wireless communication medium can be read The Zeus pump communicates wirelessly and packets can be written to a wireless communication medium. The Zeus pump communicates remotely and an attacker can spoof a remote communicating entity
Local touchscreen for input/output	The Zeus pump accepts input from a local interface The Zeus pump displays output at a local interface
USB interface for data input	The Zeus pump accepts input over USB
Persistent read-write flash memory	The Zeus pump uses a read-write flash drive and persistent read-write storage can be written. The Zeus pump uses a read-write flash drive and persistent storage can be read.
The Zeus pump allows installation of updates	The Zeus pump is field upgradable (i.e., software can be updated)
The Zeus pump has user-configurable pump parameters	The Zeus pump is field configurable (i.e., system configurations like alarm volume can be changed)
The Zeus pump uses a drug library to set hard and soft limits for infusions of drugs	The Zeus pump uses a drug library to set the safe limits for an infusion
Because of patient safety reasons, the clinician interface on the Zeus pump cannot be authenticated.	The Zeus pump does not authenticate clinician users at the pump physical interface
The Zeus pump is configured with a default password for the admin account	The admin password is initially the same in all Zeus pumps at a particular HDO Passwords can be guessed or brute-forced through exhaustive enumeration
The Zeus pump uses cryptographic algorithms and symmetric and asymmetric keys	Cryptographic algorithms may be broken Secret key material may be guessed or brute-force through exhaustive enumeration

Table 5.5 System vulnerabilities introduced by processes.

Processes	Vulnerabilities introduced by the processes
Manufacturing of pump	During manufacturing, some of the cybersecurity controls available during normal operations are still not active
Development of pump code	During code development, the developers are trusted to code as per system design
Procurement of third-party hardware and software components	Components, procured from third-party vendors, are trusted to be free of intentionally seeded vulnerabilities

Identify system threats

So far, a systemic approach for identifying system assets and system vulnerabilities has been presented. The last piece of the puzzle is coming up with a systematic approach for identifying threats. Here, we are helped by the existence of multiple system threat modeling approaches in literature. Out of the many that are available, I recommend Microsoft's STRIDE [11]. The reason for that is that I find it to be one of the simplest and most intuitive methodologies out there in the community.

The simplest way to think of Microsoft's STRIDE is that it is a methodology for structured thinking about threats. There are a great number of resources to learn about STRIDE [12,13]; I provide only a brief overview here.

STRIDE approach consists of six threat categories:

1. *Spoofing*: Here, the attacker imitates a trusted system element, either a machine or a human user. As an example, an attacker spoofing the Titan pump server to send spurious infusion orders to the Zeus infusion pump would be an example of a threat that belongs to this category. Similarly, an attacker who steals the default password would be launching a spoofing threat by pretending to be a genuine admin by providing the password.
2. *Tampering*: Here, the attacker alters system assets at rest (i.e., when it is on persistent storage or in memory) or in motion (i.e., when it is being moving from system component to another, for example, from the pump server to the pump itself). As an example, an attacker changing the code on the infusion pump by detaching the persistent flash storage and writing to it, would be tampering a system asset (code) at rest. For data in

transit, an example of a tampering threat would be an attacker modifying an infusion order or drug library while it is being transmitted over Wi-Fi from the pump server to the pump.

3. *Repudiation*: Here, the attacker uses a service or performs an action and then denies having done so. As an example, the operator of the pump server Titan may later, after an incident involving a patient injury, deny having sent an infusion order, one that may have caused an unsafe dose of a drug having been administered. Ray Devices would then have to prove that there is no way anyone could have tampered with an infusion order that originated from Titan pump server. If an infusion order for an unsafe dose of a drug came from the Titan pump server, then the operator at the pump server would be held responsible.
4. *Information Disclosure*: Here, the attacker tries to obtain information that they are not authorized to access. In our example of the Zeus pump, this could be trying to read the wireless credentials of the hospital network, or the private key that represents the cryptographic identity of the Zeus pump, or PHI stored on the pump or in-motion.
5. *Denial of Service*: Here, the attacker depletes system resources such that the system cannot service legitimate requests or perform normal operations. Such threats could be where the attacker floods the wireless medium with spurious packets, taking down connectivity, or "bricks" the Zeus pump by being able to overwrite a critical data section by sending a specially crafted infusion order that the pump cannot parse properly.
6. *Elevation of Privilege*: Here, the attacker is a legitimate user of the system but exercises a threat to access functionality that the user is not authorized to. If the Zeus infusion pump had authenticated clinician users (which it does not), an elevation of privilege would be a clinician user executing a threat that gives them admin privileges, e.g., the ability to install code.

Many times those using STRIDE for threat modeling get too stuck with the "STRIDE" aspect of it. It should be remembered that the six threat categories of STRIDE are not mutually exclusive. A system threat may belong to more than one category, and it really does not matter which category contributed a threat, as long as it is there in the threat model.

For example, a repudiation threat can also be classified as a tampering threat. Tampering with log files can be seen as a threat that belongs to the tampering category (obviously!) but can also be thought to belong to the repudiation threat category. If log files can indeed be tampered, a user cannot be held accountable for actions that happened when that user was logged in, as the user can always claim someone else tampered with the logs later. Similarly, one may argue that elevation of privilege can mean an unprivileged user getting the "elevated" admin privilege, and hence, this belongs to the "Elevation of Privilege" category, while someone else, like I have, may consider this an example of "Spoofing," where someone is spoofing the identity of the admin, and restrict "elevation of privilege" to scenarios where the user already has some privilege (as opposed to none) and is raising their level of privilege. Which one is the right interpretation? It does not matter, as long as the system threat is captured in the model.

So putting it together, following is the process for system threat modeling:

1. Consider a system asset from the set of system assets
2. For each STRIDE category, come up with system threats that compromise the system asset using one or more system vulnerabilities
3. Do this for all system assets

If we are constructing a system threat model for the Zeus infusion pump, we will take each system asset from the set of {Availability of intended use, Code, Configurations, Commands, Availability of communications, Clinical Data, PHI, Critical Security Parameters, Log Files}. For every system asset, we will take a threat category from STRIDE, and see if we may construct a threat that belongs to the threat category, and can compromise the system asset using one or more system vulnerabilities identified in Table 5.4: system vulnerabilities introduced by system design and Table 5.5: system vulnerabilities introduced by processes.

In Table 5.6, we take each of the system assets "Availability of Intended Use," "Code," "Configurations," and "Commands." We then define, for each STRIDE category, a threat which can, using one or more system vulnerabilities enumerated for the Zeus infusion pump, compromise the system asset. In the interests of space, the entire system threat model is not presented (i.e., we do not consider the system assets) "Availability of communications," "Clinical Data," "PHI," "Critical Security Parameters," and "Log Files," but the interested reader may want to complete the system threat model, as an exercise, taking the remaining system assets from Table 5.3: identifying specific system assets, and running the system threat modeling process.

Table 5.6 Partial system threat model for Zeus infusion pump.

System asset	System vulnerabilities	System threat
Availability of intended use	The Zeus pump accepts input over USB The Zeus pump communicates wirelessly and packets can be written to a wireless communication medium The Zeus pump communicates remotely and an attacker can spoof a remote communicating entity	[Denial of service] attacker crafts input that triggers a bug in the Zeus software to cause the Zeus pump to crash
Code	The Zeus pump is field-upgradable (i.e., software can be updated)	[Spoofing] attacker installs malware on the pump
Code	The Zeus pump accepts input over USB The Zeus pump communicates wirelessly and packets can be written to a wireless communication medium The Zeus pump communicates remotely and an attacker can spoof a remote communicating entity	[Tampering] attacker gets malware running in memory through a remote code exploit
Code	The Zeus pump uses a read-write flash drive and persistent read-write storage can be written to during manufacturing, some of the cybersecurity controls available during normal operations are still not active	[Tampering] attacker loads malware onto the infusion pump during manufacturing
Code	The Zeus pump uses a read-write flash drive and persistent read-write storage can be written to during code development, the developers are trusted to code as per system design	[Tampering] attacker loads pump code with backdoor or intentionally seeds other off-specification code elements
Code	The Zeus pump uses a read-write flash drive and persistent read-write storage can be written to	[Tampering] attacker disassembles pump, extracts flash persistent storage, modifies code, and loads it back into the pump
Configuration	The Zeus pump accepts input from a local interface	[Spoofing] attacker changes pump alarm volumes or alters other pump configurable items using touch screen

Configuration	The Zeus pump communicates remotely and an attacker can spoof a remote communicating entity The Zeus pump uses a drug library to set the safe limits for an infusion	[Spoofing] attacker pretends to be the pump server and sends spurious drug library over wireless
Configuration	The Zeus pump accepts input over USB The Zeus pump uses a drug library to set the safe limits for an infusion	[Spoofing] attacker loads a spurious drug library over USB
Configuration	The Zeus pump communicates wirelessly and packets can be written to a wireless communication medium The Zeus pump uses a drug library to set the safe limits for an infusion	[Tampering] attacker tampers with a drug library while it is in transit from pump server to pump
Configuration	The Zeus pump uses a read-write flash drive and persistent read-write storage can be written to the Zeus pump uses a drug library to set the safe limits for an infusion	[Tampering] attacker disassembles pump, extracts flash persistent storage, modifies drug library, and loads it back into pump
Commands	The Zeus pump accepts input from a local interface	[Spoofing] attacker pretends to be a clinician and programs an infusion at the touch screen local interface
Commands	The Zeus pump communicates remotely and an attacker can spoof a remote communicating entity	[Spoofing] attacker pretends to be the pump server and sends an infusion order over the wireless 802.11 interface
Commands	The Zeus pump communicates wirelessly and packets can be written to a wireless communication medium.	[Spoofing] attacker stores genuine infusion orders and replays them later
Commands	The Zeus pump communicates wirelessly and packets can be written to a wireless communication medium.	[Tampering] attacker tampers with an infusion order while it is in-transit over the wireless 802.11 medium from pump server to the Zeus infusion pump

System cybersecurity risk assessment

Risk from cybersecurity threats, be they at the system or at the subsystem level, is a function that takes as its input two parameters:

1. Severity of a threat
2. Likelihood of a threat

At the subsystem level, if you recall, the base score of CVSS was used as a metric that captured both severity and likelihood together. CVSS captures the impact of a threat in terms of compromise of integrity, confidentiality, and availability. At the system level though, impact, and consequently the severity of the impact, is "clinical" in nature, specifically in patient safety and patient privacy. As a result, a new system-level characterization of severity and likelihood thus has to be defined, different from what it was at the subsystem level.

Severity, one should note, is not a function only of the threat but also the risk domain (patient safety or privacy) in which the threat is being assessed. A threat, for instance, may have high severity for patient safety and negligible severity for patient privacy.

Severity of a system threat

For the risk domain of patient safety and patient privacy, the impact of a threat, at the system level, is measured in terms of severity of the harm it causes. Harm is the physical manifestation of an adverse outcome. Harm can be severe consequences like death or injury to the patient and delay of treatment, down to consequences that are less serious, like an extra visit to the doctor's or loss of data. Harm, as per ISO 14971, is formally defined as "physical injury or damage to the health of people, or damage to property or the environment." AAMI TIR57 extends the ISO 14971 definition of harm to explicitly address patient privacy as well as the intentional degradation of the operations of a medical device even when it does not cause "physical injury or damage."

A hazard, as per ISO 14971, is a potential source of harm. An example of a hazard, in the context of our infusion pump example, is overinfusion (i.e., too much drug delivered). Note the word "potential." It is not as if every overinfusion of a drug would lead to death or injury. Some infused drugs might not cause harm, even if there is a large overdose. In some cases, the effect of the overdose may be observed by a clinician and action taken before it evolves into an adverse consequence for a patient. One patient may have an adverse reaction to an overdose, whereas another patient might not. Just because a hazard has happened, does not necessarily mean there will be harm, merely that there exists a sequence of events from the introduction of the hazard to the realization of the harm. This sequence of events is called a hazardous situation.

When we are assessing risk to the patient from cybersecurity causes, the existence of a threat is a hazard, and the exploitation of the threat is a hazardous situation, because once the hazardous situation has come to pass, there exists a sequence of events which then can lead to harm.

In Table 5.7, a candidate scale for severity for the risk domains of patient safety and privacy is provided. In real life, the Patient Safety scale should be directly taken from the harms analysis and/or risk management plan from the MDMs quality system, while the Patient Privacy scale should be obtained from the MDM's Privacy Office.

Likelihood of a system threat

In classical safety engineering, likelihood is measured by probability of occurrence of harm. The probability of the occurrence of harm, in turn, is the product of two probabilities, probability of occurrence of a hazardous situation (referred to as P1) and the probability of that hazardous situation leading to harm (P2) [1]. As discussed earlier, we cannot use probability as a means of capturing likelihood of a hazardous situation in the domain of cybersecurity in the same way we can for, say, mechanical and electrical failures.

Instead, we have a metric called "exploitability" for P1 and "timely observability" for P2 and characterize likelihood of a threat as a function of exploitability and timely observability.

Likelihood of a threat is directly proportional to exploitability, i.e., greater the exploitability, greater the likelihood of a threat. Likelihood of a threat is inversely proportional to timely observability, i.e., lesser the timely observability of a threat, greater the likelihood of the threat leading to harm. Timely observability measures the likelihood that the successful execution of a threat will lead to harm, while exploitability simply measures the likelihood that the threat will be successfully executed.

Table 5.7 A scale for severity of system threats.

Severity (at system level)	Patient safety	Patient privacy
1-Negligible	A successful threat leads to inconvenience, of the kind that can be remediated instantly by the patient themselves or by some other nonclinical person	A successful threat leads to no release of PHIs (PHI as defined by HIPAA regulations), but other informational aspects of a patient, like their location for a *limited period of time* may be visible (e.g., during a clinic visit, a patient's location may be temporarily tracked but no information that enables the patient to be identified)
2-Minor	A successful threat could lead to manifestation of minor symptoms and/or interruption of therapy, and may require clinical intervention (e.g., for home care clinical scenarios, a successful threat may lead to a clinic visit)	A successful threat leads to no release of PHIs (PHI as defined by HIPAA regulations), but other informational aspects of a patient, like their location, may be available *for a time that is controlled by the attacker* (e.g., a patient's device may be transmitting an identifier that can be tracked indefinitely, but the identity of the patient cannot be associated with the device)
3-Serious	A successful threat could lead to major symptoms and/or interruption of therapy, requiring clinical intervention, but no injury or death	A successful threat leads to a release of PHI but only of one individual. Executing the threat again on the same medical device would not lead to any new PHI being extracted
4-Critical	A successful threat could lead to reversible or healable injury	A successful threat leads to the release of the PHI of multiple individuals with number of individuals less than a predefined limit (e.g., 500)
5-Catastrophic	A successful threat could lead to death or irreversible injury	A successful threat leads to the release of the PHI of multiple individuals with the number of individuals more than the limit for "critical."

At the system level, since we are dealing with what-if threats, some amount of subjectivity in assessment is inevitable. Hence, with each exploitability level, there is some guidance provided for assessing if a threat belongs to that category or not. In case a threat meets criteria in multiple categories, the higher exploitability should be chosen. For example, if a threat may be assessed as both "Low" as well as "Medium" Exploitability, the higher exploitability (in this case "Medium") is chosen.

In Table 5.8 a candidate scale for exploitability of threats, at the system level, is presented.

Table 5.8 A scale for exploitability of system threats.

Exploitability	Attackers with the capability to execute the threat
Incredibly low	A system threat assessed to have "incredibly low" exploitability is a threat that is mathematically improbable for any attacker to execute, given current hardware and computation power, within an amount of time that would make it worth the effort for the attacker (e.g., if it takes thousands of years for an attacker to try all possible combinations of a secret and obtain its value, is it worth their while to even attempt to do so?).
Low	A system threat assessed to have "low" exploitability is a threat that is very difficult to execute, i.e., it has low likelihood. Guidance: Factors to consider in order to classify a threat as "low": • successful execution of the threat would require the attacker to be in permanent, close physical proximity of the target (which means high chance of being discovered) • successful execution of the threat would require the attacker to have acquired knowledge of the product design and knowledge of proprietary data formats • successful execution of the threat would require physical disassembly of unit
Medium	A system threat assessed to have "medium" exploitability is a threat that is moderately difficult to execute, i.e., it has medium likelihood. Guidance: If the threat is a hypothetical system-level threat, then factors to consider in order to classify a threat as "medium":

(Continued)

Table 5.8 A scale for exploitability of system threats.—cont'd

Exploitability	Attackers with the capability to execute the threat
	• successful exploitation of the threat requires the attacker to have some knowledge of the product design or the resources/skill to reverse engineer proprietary functionality and proprietary data formats in order to execute the threat. • successful exploitation of the threat requires the attacker to have some level of access to the target system (e.g., having an account on the system or be on the same wireless network as the system or be in physical proximity to the system).
High	A system threat assessed to have "high" exploitability is a threat that is easy to execute, i.e., these threats have high likelihood. These threats can be executed by attackers with very little or no knowledge of the system. Guidance: If the threat is a hypothetical system-level threat, then factors to consider in order to classify a threat as "high" are as follows: • the threat can be executed remotely over wireless and the attacker does not require an account on the system or access to the same wireless network the target is on or physical access. • the vulnerability does not require the attacker to reverse engineer or otherwise procure any product-specific design details to execute the threat (e.g., scripts that execute the threat or detailed how-to-s are available or the threat is so self-evident to any lay person that little intellectual effort is needed to execute the threat). • the threat cannot be categorized in any of the other exploitability categories (i.e., is not "incredibly low" or "low" or "medium").

Timely observability

The word "timely" implies that early indications of a hazardous situation, i.e., the successful realization of a threat are observed within a time window in which action can be taken such that no harm happens. Timely observability (Table 5.9) is a clinical parameter which depends on the clinical use case and the environment in which a medical device is being used. For instance, in exclusively home-care settings, one may presume that

Table 5.9 Timely observability.

Timely observability	**Clinical use cases**
Low	Home care where a clinician is not expected to be present
High	Emergency room, surgical environments, clinically supervised environments where a clinician is expected to be present

timely observability will have a low value, because there will be no clinician at hand if symptoms of harm start manifesting themselves. Alternatively, for clinical use cases that require a caregiver to be present, for instance, during implantation of a cardiac device in an operating room environment, timely observability will have a high value, because the clinician is continuously observing the patient as well as device operations for anything that seems "not normal."

For Ray Device's infusion pumps, the notion of timely observability requires some thought. In an emergency room, the pumps are under constant medical supervision. When they are being used at bedside in a hospital, the pumps are technically under medical supervision too, but then response times to observed adverse events may vary from hospital to hospital, depending on the staffing and training of the caregivers and hospital protocols. In almost all HDOs, the number of pumps far outnumbers the number of clinicians. So even though the therapies are technically under supervision, the chance of a caregiver missing symptoms of something going wrong is high. This, in the case of the Zeus pump, taking a more conservative approach of assuming Timely Observability = Low for all clinical use cases might be the safer option.

Now putting it all together, each of the system threats identified in Table 5.6: Partial system threat model for Zeus infusion pump is taken, and its severity in the domain of patient safety and privacy, together with its exploitability is assessed using the scales defined in Table 5.7: a scale for severity of system threats and Table 5.8: a scale for exploitability of system threats. Timely observability is "Low" for all system threats, as per the decision taken to be conservative. The result can be found in Table 5.10.

Table 5.10 System cybersecurity risk model for Zeus pump (prerisk response).

System threat	Severity (system level) for patient safety	Severity (system level) for patient privacy	Exploitability (system level)
[Denial of service] attacker crafts input that triggers a bug in the Zeus software to cause the Zeus pump to crash	3-Serious (In the worst case, a fleet-wide attack on all pumps at an HDO over wireless could lead to all pumps connected to the HDO Wi-Fi network crashing and interrupting therapy. However, the pump can be rebooted, and disconnected from the Wi-Fi network subsequently, and all infusions programmed locally)	None	Medium (attacker needs local or remote access and also requires significant knowledge of pump design to know what kind of input to craft in order to "brick" the pump)
[Spoofing] attacker installs malware on the pump	5-Catastrophic (malware can lead to administration of fatal overdoses or too little, when the patient needs the medication)	5-Catastrophic (malware can steal all PHI that passes through the device)	Medium (attacker needs local access since code installs can be done only over USB and also requires significant knowledge of pump design and code structure to load code that runs on target hardware)
[Tampering] attacker gets malware running in memory through a remote code exploit	5-Catastrophic (malware can lead to administration of fatal overdoses or too little, when the patient needs the medication)	5-Catastrophic (malware can steal all PHI that passes through the device)	Medium (attacker needs local or remote access and also requires significant knowledge of pump design and code to discover an exploitable vulnerability in input processing that leads to remote code execution)
[Tampering] attacker loads malware onto	5-Catastrophic (malware can lead to administration of fatal	5-Catastrophic (malware can steal all	Medium (attacker requires privileged access to the target

the infusion pump during manufacturing	overdoses or too little, when the patient needs the medication)	PHI that passes through the device)	system, specifically has to be on the manufacturing line, in order to execute the threat)
[Tampering] attacker loads pump code with backdoor or intentionally seeds other off-specification code elements	5-Catastrophic (malware can lead to administration of fatal overdoses or too little, when the patient needs the medication)	5-Catastrophic (malware can steal all PHI that passes through the device)	Medium (attacker requires privileged access to the target system, specifically has to be in the system development team, in order to execute the threat)
[Tampering] attacker disassembles pump, extracts flash persistent storage, modifies code, and loads it back into the pump	5-Catastrophic (malware can lead to administration of fatal overdoses or too little, when the patient needs the medication)	5-Catastrophic (malware can steal all PHI that passes through the device)	Low (attacker needs to disassemble pump and reassemble it, besides significant knowledge of pump design and code)
[Spoofing] attacker changes pump alarm volumes or alters other pump configurable items using touch screen	1-Negligible (an inconvenience)	None	Medium (attacker needs to be in physical proximity of the pump to access touch screen)
[Spoofing] attacker pretends to be the pump server and sends spurious drug library over wireless	5-Catastrophic (removing drug library limits may lead to administration of fatal overdoses or too little when the patient needs the medication)	None	Medium (attacker needs to be on same network as the pump and pump server, and also requires knowledge of drug library format and function to execute the threat)

(*Continued*)

Table 5.10 System cybersecurity risk model for Zeus pump (prerisk response).—cont'd

System threat	Severity (system level) for patient safety	Severity (system level) for patient privacy	Exploitability (system level)
[Spoofing] attacker loads a spurious drug library over USB	5-Catastrophic (removing drug library limits may lead to administration of fatal overdoses or too little when the patient needs the medication)	None	Medium (attacker needs local USB access and also requires knowledge of drug library format and function to execute the threat)
[Tampering] attacker tampers with a drug library while it is in transit from pump server to pump	5-Catastrophic (removing drug library limits may lead to administration of fatal overdoses or too little when the patient needs the medication)	None	Medium (attacker needs to be on the same network as the pump and the pump server, and also requires knowledge of drug library format and function to execute the threat)
[Tampering] attacker disassembles pump, extracts flash persistent storage, modifies drug library, and loads it back into pump	5-Catastrophic (removing drug library limits may lead to administration of fatal overdoses or too little when the patient needs the medication)	None	Low (attacker needs to disassemble pump and reassemble it, besides having knowledge of drug library and its format)
[Spoofing] attacker pretends to be a clinician and programs an infusion at the touch screen local interface	5-Catastrophic (malignant infusion orders may lead to administration of fatal overdoses or too little when the patient needs the medication)	None	Medium (Attacker needs to be in physical proximity of the pump to access touch screen)

[Spoofing] attacker pretends to be the pump server and sends an infusion order over the wireless 802.11 interface	5-Catastrophic (malignant infusion orders may lead to administration of fatal overdoses or too little when the patient needs the medication)	None	Medium (attacker needs to be on the same network as the pump and requires knowledge of the pump design to know how the pump server authenticates itself to the pump)
[Spoofing] attacker stores genuine infusion orders and replays them later	5-Catastrophic (malignant infusion orders may lead to administration of fatal overdoses or too little when the patient needs the medication)	None	Medium (attacker needs to be on the same network as the pump)
[Tampering] attacker tampers with an infusion order while it is in-transit over the wireless 802.11 medium from pump server to the Zeus infusion pump	5-Catastrophic (malignant infusion orders may lead to administration of fatal overdoses or too little when the patient needs the medication)	None	Medium (attacker needs to be on the same network as the pump and requires knowledge of the pump design to know the format of infusion orders)

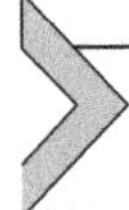

Summary and key takeaways

The key takeaways of this chapter are as follows:

1. A systematic threat modeling approach is needed in ensure that threat models are maintainable, understandable, and replicable.
2. There are two levels at which threat models should be constructed—the system level and the subsystem level. We consider two subsystems, the software and hardware, as the subsystems on which vulnerabilities and threats will be defined.
3. A threat model should define assets, vulnerabilities, threats, and the exploitability of each threat.
4. Subsystem (software and hardware) threat modeling first consists of identifying subsystem assets. This is achieved by execution of the *Cybersecurity Bill of Materials* procedural control. For each subsystem asset, *the Vulnerability Monitoring* procedural control provides the subsystem vulnerabilities and threats. The risk of each subsystem threat is captured using Base Metrics of the CVSS framework. For risks deemed "unacceptable" at the subsystem level, patching is the only valid risk response.
5. System threat modeling first consists of identifying system assets using a process that is driven by attacker intent. System vulnerabilities are introduced by system design decisions and system design processes. For each system asset and for sets of associated vulnerabilities, threats are then identified using Microsoft's STRIDE framework to complete the system threat model. The system cybersecurity risk model is then constructed by evaluating the exploitability, severity, and timely observability of each threat.

References

[1] International Standards Organization, ISO 14971:2019 Medical Devices — Application of Risk Management to Medical Devices, 2019.

[2] American Association for Medical Instrumentation, TIR57: Principles for Medical Device Security – Risk Management, 2016.

[3] US Food and Drug Administration, Recognized Consensus Standards: AAMI TIR57, n.d. [Online]. Available: https://www.accessdata.fda.gov/scripts/cdrh/cfdocs/cfStandards/detail.cfm?standard__identification_no=34082. (Accessed 12 December 2020).

[4] US Food and Drug Administration, Content of Premarket Submissions for Management of Cybersecurity in Medical Devices (Final Version), October 2014 [Online]. Available: https://www.fda.gov/regulatory-information/search-fda-guidance-documents/content-premarket-submissions-management-cybersecurity-medical-devices-0.

[5] US Food and Drug Administration, Content of Premarket Submissions for Management of Cybersecurity in Medical Devices (Draft Version), November 2018 [Online]. Available: https://www.fda.gov/regulatory-information/search-fda-guidance-documents/content-premarket-submissions-management-cybersecurity-medical-devices.
[6] US Food and Drug Administration, Postmarket Management of Cybersecurity in Medical Devices (Final Version), December 2016 [Online]. Available: https://www.fda.gov/regulatory-information/search-fda-guidance-documents/postmarket-management-cybersecurity-medical-devices.
[7] US Food and Drug Administration, Public Workshop - Content of Premarket Submissions for Management of Cybersecurity in Medical Devices January 29–30, 2019, 2019 [Online]. Available, https://www.fda.gov/medical-devices/workshops-conferences-medical-devices/public-workshop-content-premarket-submissions-management-cybersecurity-medical-devices-january-29-30.
[8] A. Ray, R. Jetley, P. Jones, Y. Zhang, Model based engineering for medical device software, Biomed. Instrum. Technol. 44 (6) (2010) 507–518.
[9] FIRST, Common Vulnerability Scoring System version 3.1: Specification Document, n.d. [Online]. Available: https://www.first.org/cvss/specification-document. (Accessed 20 December 2020).
[10] M. Chase, S. Christey Coley, Rubric for Applying CVSS to Medical Devices, MITRE, 2020.
[11] S. Hernan, S. Lambert, T. Ostwald, A. Shostack, Uncover Security Design Flaws Using the STRIDE Approach, MSDN Magazine, November 2006.
[12] A. Shostack, Threat Modeling: Designing for Security, Wiley, 2014.
[13] A. Shostack, STRIDE Chart, Microsoft, September 11, 2007 [Online]. Available: https://www.microsoft.com/security/blog/2007/09/11/stride-chart/.

CHAPTER SIX

Cybersecurity risk management-II

Introduction

The purpose of the previous chapter (Chapter 5) and this (Chapter 6) is to define a formal approach for cybersecurity risk management for medical devices. To recall, cybersecurity risk management consists of modeling risk of adverse outcomes due to cybersecurity threats, assessing whether the risk of adverse outcomes meet the medical device manufacturer (MDM)'s risk-acceptability criteria, bringing down risk to acceptable levels using risk responses, while ensuring that these risk responses do not increase the risk of adverse outcomes in other domains. In case risk cannot be brought down to acceptable levels, the cybersecurity risk management activity has to justify why the medical device's benefits outweigh its risk. In this chapter, the focus will be on risk response, whereas in Chapter 5 focuses on risk assessment. Recapping from the previous chapter

1. Identifying the system: This consists of identifying the system for which cybersecurity risk management is to be done.

   The output of this activity is the identification of the system and the consequent subsystems on which cybersecurity risk management activities are to be performed.

2. Subsystem (software and hardware) Cybersecurity Risk Modeling: This consists of the following subactivities:
   a. Subsystem threat modeling: Actual cybersecurity issues present in the device software and hardware are tabulated by identifying subsystem assets, vulnerabilities, and threats.
   b. Subsystem cybersecurity risk assessment: Cybersecurity risk of the vulnerabilities and threats identified in the subsystem threat model is calculated. The adverse outcomes observable at the subsystem level are compromise of integrity, availability, and/or confidentiality.
   c. Defining risk acceptability at subsystem level: The definition of when a risk is acceptable, and when it is not, is defined for the subsystem cybersecurity risk model.
   d. Defining risk response at the subsystem level: The only risk response that can be applied at the subsystem level is patching, i.e., fixing the

Cybersecurity for Connected Medical Devices
ISBN: 978-0-12-818262-8
https://doi.org/10.1016/B978-0-12-818262-8.00003-6

hardware or software vulnerability that is the root cause of the cybersecurity issue.

The output of this activity is a subsystem Cybersecurity Risk Model.

3. System Cybersecurity Risk Modeling: This consists of the following subactivities:
   a. System threat modeling: Hypothetical "what-if" cybersecurity threats that may be present in the system are tabulated by identifying system assets and vulnerabilities.
   b. System cybersecurity risk assessment: Cybersecurity risk of the vulnerabilities and threats identified in the system threat model is calculated. The adverse outcomes observable at the subsystem level are compromise of patient safety and patient privacy.
   c. Defining risk acceptability at system level: The definition of when a risk is acceptable, and when it is not, is defined for both the system as well as the subsystem cybersecurity risk model.
   d. Defining risk response for system-level threats: Risk responses at the system level are formulated in order to bring down system risk to acceptable levels, and even in case of system threats, where the risk is already acceptable, to bring it down to as low as one can take it. The risk responses should be evaluated to ensure that they do not increase patient safety risk in other domains (e.g., human factors) so that overall patient safety risk increases, even though patient safety risk due to cybersecurity causes goes down.
   e. Defining risk response for subsystem—level threats that pose "unacceptable" risk at the subsystem level: It would be ideal to patch all subsystem vulnerabilities, regardless of the risk posed to patients, as soon as possible. However, in the real world, regulators realize the challenges of rolling out cybersecurity patches for all software and hardware vulnerabilities. Instead they mandate that only vulnerabilities that pose unacceptable risk to patient safety and patient privacy should be patched. In order to assess the patient safety/privacy risk posed by a subsystem—level threat that is assessed to be "unacceptable" at the subsystem level, it has to be evaluated at the system level. In order to do this evaluation, the subsystem vulnerability is added to the list of system vulnerabilities, and the risk of it is modeled at the system level. System-level risk responses can now be used to reduce the patient safety/privacy risk posed by this subsystem threat. If the residual risk is still "Unacceptable," then a cybersecurity patch would have to be rolled out, else not.

The output of this activity is a System Cybersecurity Risk Model.

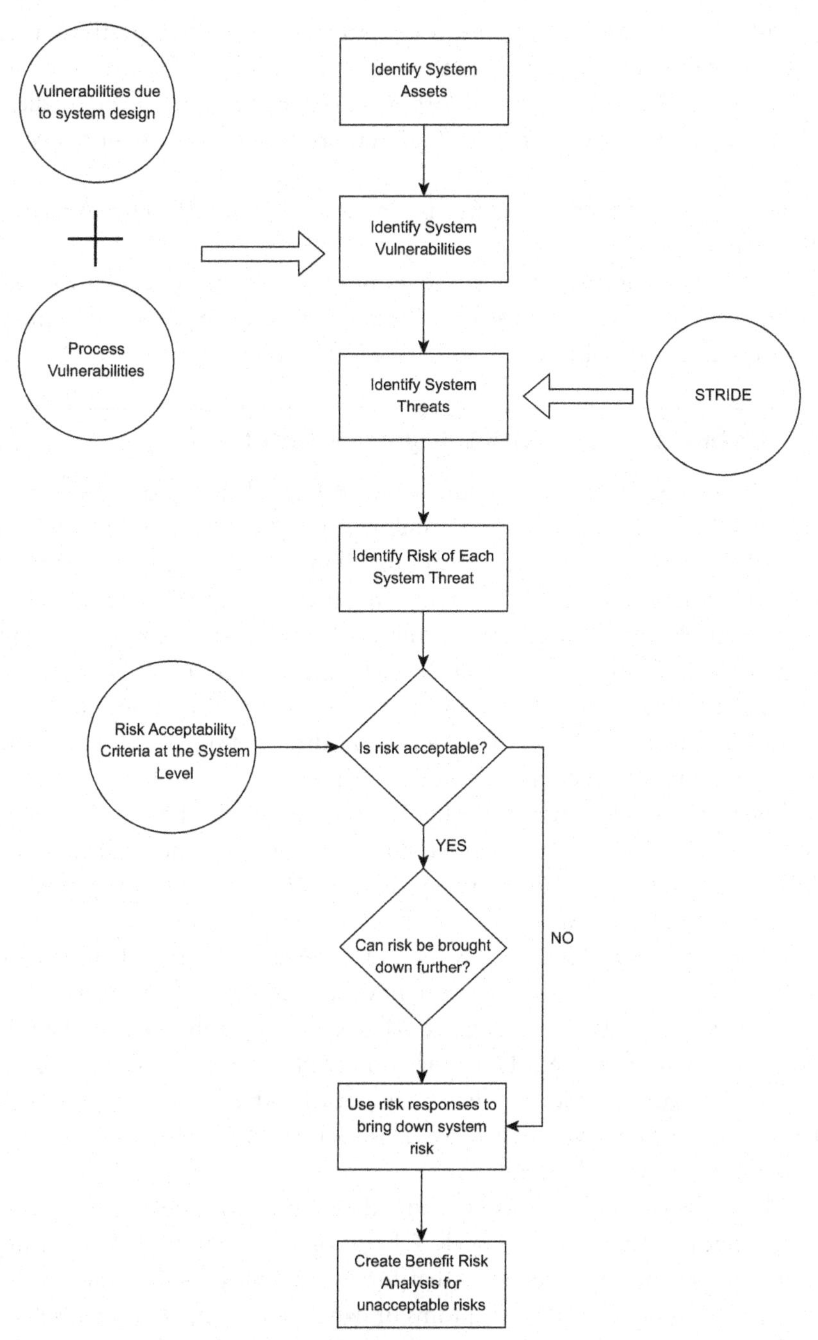

Figure 6.1 System cybersecurity risk model.

4. Risk—Benefit Analysis: If there are still threats whose risk, postresponse, still remains "unacceptable" at the system level, then a risk—benefit analysis (RBA) needs to be performed in order to show that the medical device provides greater benefit than the risk it poses to patient safety/ privacy.

The output of this activity is an RBA (Risk—Benefit Analysis) document.

In the previous chapter, we had stopped at system cybersecurity risk assessment. Here, we pick up from the next stage of the process, namely "defining risk acceptability at system level" (Fig. 6.1).

Defining risk acceptability at system level

As discussed previously [1,2], system risk is calculated from Severity, Exploitability, and Timely Observability variables. The resulting system risk is determined by the organization to fall in one of three zones: acceptable risk, unacceptable risk, or requiring further analysis referred to as "Acceptable.*" For "Acceptable,*" the final verdict of whether to accept the risk depends on further analysis, including an assessment of whether risk can be further reduced or if further risk reduction is not possible. Analysis of "Acceptable*" risk is expanded on in the "Defining Risk Response for System Threats" section later in this chapter.

Given this simplification, whether the risk lies within the organizational risk acceptability zone can be captured in tables like the ones in Tables 6.1 and 6.2, where the columns represent Severity of Harm and rows represent Exploitability of a threat.

If Timely Observability is Low (i.e., the expectation is that there will be no caregiver within a reasonable amount of time to react to an adverse clinical outcome), the Risk Acceptance Matrix is as in Table 6.1. If Timely Observability is High (i.e., the expectation is that there will be a caregiver within a reasonable amount of time to react to an adverse clinical outcome), the Risk Acceptance Matrix is relaxed, as in Table 6.2, because of the presumed presence of a clinician.

The strategy described above captures the intuition that devices that operate in clinical settings where Timely Observability = Low (e.g., home care) have a stricter, more conservative, bar for Acceptability, since there will be no clinician to be at hand if symptoms of harm start manifesting themselves.

A medical device manufacturer (MDM) may choose to use both the Risk Acceptance Matrices, because some of their clinical use cases are at-home and some of their clinical use cases are in-hospital. For example, for MDMs that manufacture implanted devices, some of their clinical use cases

Table 6.1 System risk acceptability matrix (timely observability = low).

Exploitability					
High	Acceptable*	Unacceptable	Unacceptable	Unacceptable	Unacceptable
Medium	Acceptable	Acceptable*	Acceptable*	Unacceptable	Unacceptable
Low	Acceptable	Acceptable	Acceptable	Acceptable*	Acceptable*
Incredibly low	Acceptable	Acceptable	Acceptable	Acceptable	Acceptable
	1-Negligible	2-Minor	3-Serious	4-Critical	5-Catastrophic
Severity					

Table 6.2 System risk acceptability matrix (timely observability = high).

Exploitability						
	High	Acceptable*	Acceptable*	Acceptable*	Unacceptable	Unacceptable
	Medium	Acceptable	Acceptable*	Acceptable*	Acceptable*	Unacceptable
	Low	Acceptable	Acceptable	Acceptable	Acceptable*	Acceptable*
	Incredibly low	Acceptable	Acceptable	Acceptable	Acceptable	Acceptable
		1-Negligible	2-Minor	3-Serious	4-Critical	5-Catastrophic
	Severity					

Table 6.3 System cybersecurity risk model for Zeus infusion pump (premitigation).

System threat	Patient safety risk	Patient privacy risk
Attacker crafts input that triggers a bug in the Zeus software to cause the Zeus pump to crash	Exploitability: Medium Severity: 3-Serious Risk: Acceptable*	None
Attacker installs malware on the pump	Exploitability: Medium Severity: 5-Catastrophic Risk: Unacceptable	Exploitability: Medium Severity: 5-Catastrophic Risk: Unacceptable
Attacker gets malware running in memory through a remote code exploit	Exploitability: Medium Severity: 5-Catastrophic Risk: Unacceptable	Exploitability: Medium Severity: 5-Catastrophic Risk: Unacceptable
Attacker loads malware onto the infusion pump during manufacturing	Exploitability: Medium Severity: 5-Catastrophic Risk: Unacceptable	Exploitability: Medium Severity: 5-Catastrophic Risk: Unacceptable
Attacker loads pump code with backdoor or intentionally seeds other off-specification code elements	Exploitability: Medium Severity: 5-Catastrophic Risk: Unacceptable	
Attacker disassembles pump, extracts flash persistent storage, modifies code, and loads it back into the pump	Exploitability: Low Severity: 5-Catastrophic Risk: Acceptable*	Exploitability: Low Severity: 5-Catastrophic Risk: Acceptable*
Attacker changes pump alarm volumes or alters other pump configurable items using touch screen	Exploitability: Medium Severity: 1-Negligible Risk: Acceptable	None
Attacker pretends to be the pump server and sends spurious drug library over wireless	Exploitability: Medium Severity: 5-Catastrophic Risk: Unacceptable	None

(Continued)

Table 6.3 System cybersecurity risk model for Zeus infusion pump (premitigation).—cont'd

System threat	Patient safety risk	Patient privacy risk
Attacker loads a spurious drug library over USB	Exploitability: Medium Severity: 5-Catastrophic Risk: Unacceptable	None
Attacker tampers with a drug library while it is in transit from pump server to pump	Exploitability: Medium Severity: 5-Catastrophic Risk: Unacceptable	None
Attacker disassembles pump, extracts flash persistent storage, modifies drug library, and loads it back into pump	Exploitability: Low Severity:5-Catastrophic Risk: Acceptable*	None
Attacker pretends to be a clinician and programs an infusion at the touch screen local interface	Exploitability: Medium Severity: 5-Catastrophic Risk: Unacceptable	None
Attacker pretends to be the pump server and sends an infusion order over the wireless 802.11 interface	Exploitability: Medium Severity: 5-Catastrophic Risk: Unacceptable	None
Attacker stores genuine infusion orders and replays them later	Exploitability: Medium Severity: 5-Catastrophic Risk: Unacceptable	None
Attacker tampers with an infusion order while it is in transit over the wireless 802.11 medium from pump server to the Zeus infusion pump	Exploitability: Medium Severity: 5-Catastrophic Risk: Unacceptable	None

are during implantation and follow-up both of which happen under expert supervision, while some of their clinical use cases happen at home when the patient is unsupervised. For such devices, engineers would have to annotate each threat with whether the underlying clinical use case is at-home or in-clinic in order to assess which Risk Acceptability Matrix is applicable for assessing the risk of the threat. Ray Devices adopted the more restrictive Risk Acceptability Matrix (Table 6.1) for all products in the infusion pump business unit, and thus do not need to do this level of analysis.

Table 6.3 captures whether the risk of each system threat of the Zeus pump is "Acceptable," "Acceptable,*" or "Unacceptable" using the risk acceptability matrix (Table 6.1) of A term to note in the table level is "premitigation." This is the patient safety risk due to cybersecurity threats without any migratory countermeasures, hence "premitigation." In the next subsection, system-level mitigations, or as they are sometimes called risk responses, will be used to bring the risk of each threat down to as low as possible.

Defining risk response for system threats

Now that the risk for each threat at the system level has been identified, the next step is to formulate risk responses for each threat.

Technical and procedural controls are used to bring down the risk of a specific threat to patient safety and privacy. Technical controls usually bring down exploitability of the threat, by making the threat much more difficult to exploit. For instance, encrypting critical data makes it much more difficult for an attacker to read the contents, unless they have the key. Encryption, therefore, lowers the exploitability of threat of the "Information Disclosure" class for critical data.

Sometimes, though less often, technical controls also bring down severity. For instance, consider an attack on the wireless communication of an implanted, low-power device that causes the communication stack to "crash," and through the crash, not just take down the ability of the device to communicate, but to consume power, thus bringing down its effective useful life. A design feature that reboots the communication stack every minute, and brings the stack up after 5 min, ensures that the impact of a successful threat never goes beyond a minute. This reduces the severity of the threat, by limiting the power drain to a maximum of a minute per attack. The exploitability though is not reduced by this design feature.

Not all technical and procedural controls are equally effective as risk responses. Based on the strength of the controls and the amount of confidence one has in their efficacy, controls need to be classified into "primary" and "secondary."

Primary controls

A primary control is a control to which a high degree of confidence may be attached.

A control is deemed "primary" when both the properties below are satisfied by it.

- A primary control should either be a product feature (e.g., low physical distance of communication making remote attacks physically infeasible, removal of debug interface during manufacturing) or a standard cryptographic feature, with the cryptographic scheme using only algorithms, key sizes, key transport, and key negotiation schemes, approved by an international standards authority like NIST
- A primary control should be traced to system or software requirements, and should be tested using positive and negative test cases

If a control does not satisfy any of the above properties, it can be considered, at best, a secondary control.

Secondary controls

A secondary control is a control to which a lesser degree of confidence, when compared to primary controls, may be attached.

A control is deemed "secondary" when one or more properties are satisfied by it:

- The control is a procedural control, which means that while adherence to the process is presumed, but cannot be enforced all the time
- The control is a labeling control, which means that one cannot be sure that the concerned parties have read the labels or are following the labeling instructions
- The control relates to detecting and responding to cybersecurity threats, rather than preventing them from happening in the first place
- The control is a cybersecurity control that does not follow best practices of algorithm selection, key length, key transport, and key negotiation. For example, the integrity of a certain data element is enforced through hashing, but the algorithm used is one that has been deprecated by NIST like MD5 or the data are encrypted using AES-256, but the key is packaged along with the data in an obfuscated form, which means the confidentiality of the data is not as easily compromised as it would be if it was unencrypted (which is why this is a secondary control). However, a sufficiently motivated attacker can break the obfuscation algorithm. And once the obfuscation algorithm has been broken (the "secret sauce") and the details suitably publicized within the hacking underground, the data are almost as good as if unencrypted.

- The control cannot be traced to a product system or software requirement or has not been tested with positive and negative test cases.

If the system risk of a threat is evaluated as "Unacceptable" in the domains of patient safety and/or privacy, the risk can be brought down to "Acceptable" or "Acceptable*" only by the use of a primary control.

In general, one should use a combination of primary and secondary controls as risk responses, following the principle of "defense in depth." "Defense in depth" ensures that if one control is found to be broken, due to manifestation of subsystem (software and hardware) vulnerabilities later on, the risk can still be kept in the "Acceptable" region.

Take, as an example, the following threat on the Zeus infusion pump:

"Attacker tampers with a drug library while it is in transit from pump server to pump."

As per Table 6.3, the risk of this threat is "Unacceptable" in the patient safety domain. Now there are certain cybersecurity design elements of the Zeus infusion pump that can be considered to be primary controls that mitigate this risk.

1. All data in transit from pump server to pump use authenticated encryption algorithms that are part of transport level security (TLS) to ensure that data in transit are protected from unauthorized tampering and reading
2. Every time the pump server sends an infusion order or a drug library over wireless, it calculates a SHA2 hash of the infusion order or a drug library and encrypts the hash using AES-256 with the shared encryption key that was established during pump set-up.

By the principle of "defense in depth," if one of these two controls is "broken" by an attacker, the risk of the threat will still remain "Acceptable." If the security provided by TLS is broken, the integrity of the drug library in transit will be maintained by the independently keyed hash of the drug library. If the keyed hash scheme is broken, but not TLS, then TLS will ensure that the data cannot be tampered with. If both break, then, there are no valid primary controls, and the risk swings back to "Unacceptable."

If the premitigation risk is "Acceptable,*" one does not require a primary control to bring risk to "Acceptable", secondary controls would suffice. This is where, in the amber zone, there is some subjectivity—how many secondary controls do we need to bring the risk to "Acceptable"? There is no hard and fast answer; it depends on the secondary control, and the perceived strength of the control, which is evaluated on a case-by-case basis.

Take, as an example, the following threat on the Zeus infusion pump:

Attacker crafts input that triggers a bug in the Zeus software to cause the Zeus pump to crash.

As per Table 6.3, the risk of this threat is Acceptable* in the patient safety domain. There is a cybersecurity design element of the Zeus infusion pump that may be considered as a primary control, and a procedural control that can be considered as a secondary control, in order to bring the risk down to Acceptable.

1. Primary: The pump and pump server mutually authenticate each other using digital certificates before communication
2. Secondary: The pump code is crash tested as part of dynamic testing procedures for malformed input.

The first is a primary, because it is a cryptographic control. It cryptographically ensures that no unauthenticated attacker can communicate with the Zeus pump. Because this control is primary, there is a linkage of the control to system and software requirements. There are positive and negative test cases for the requirements that can be pointed to, as proof that the control holds true.

The second control, however, is a secondary. It is a procedural control. Confidence in it is less than one would have in the first control, because, for the second, there is no linkage to a product requirement. As a result, there is no formal guarantee of coverage of testing behavior, or in other words, no guarantee that the crash testing was comprehensive and that some exploitable input processing did not sneak in between the cracks of the testing protocols. We may have evidence that crash testing was done, but how good was it?

As another example of a threat that is "Acceptable*" premitigation, let us consider the following: "Attacker disassembles pump, extracts flash persistent storage, modifies code, and loads it back into the pump." The Zeus infusion pump encrypts the flash nonpersistent storage using AES-256, and that is a mitigatory control that brings the risk down to "Acceptable." However, it is not a primary control. Even though it is a cryptographic control, it is a control for confidentiality, and not integrity (which is what we are trying to ensure). Of course, having the persistent storage encrypted makes it very difficult for an attacker to meaningfully change the encrypted code, such that the decrypted version does what they want it to do, without knowing the encryption key. The problem is that the encrypted key is also stored on the persistent storage, and so when the attacker detaches the storage, the key becomes available to them. What would have made this "primary" was if the data encryption key used for the persistent storage was stored in secure, tamper-proof hardware (e.g., a Trusted Platform

Module). In that case, the attacker would not have access to the key even if the persistent storage was detached and read. Be as it does not make the bar for being considered a "primary," this is still a strong secondary control and should be considered to be adequate to bring the risk down to "Acceptable."

But what if the designers of the Zeus pump choose not to implement the above encryption scheme? Let us assume that instead of encrypting the persistent storage, they had put a sticker at the place where the pump could be disassembled, and then just written a line in the pump's Instructions for Use (IFU) that said "If the sticker is removed, then consider the fact that the pump has been tampered with, and discontinue use." This would be a secondary control, but a much weaker secondary control than the encryption. What is the guarantee that anyone will read the IFU, or consider what is written there seriously? How easy would it be for an attacker to replace the sticker exactly as it was before or put on a new sticker after tampering with the pump? This is where the subjectivity comes into place: can we consider the risk to be "Acceptable," given the weakness of the secondary control? One way of strengthening the secondary control, in this specific case, would be to use special tamper-resistant screws and stickers. Then there would be greater confidence in tamper evidence, though one can still argue that a clinician could just ignore visible signs of tampering and use the pump.

Now, what should be the risk response if system threat is already "Acceptable" *even without a risk response*? On the face of it, it seems our job is done; if without any controls a risk is "Acceptable," what more do we need to do? The modern approach to risk management, and this is particularly true for cybersecurity risk management where defense in depth is a guiding principle all the time, is that we should try to reduce risk to as far as possible (often called AFAP). This means, that even if a risk is "Acceptable" premitigation, we should still use primary and secondary controls to bring the risk down to as low as possible.

Take, as an example, the following threat on the Zeus infusion pump:

> *Attacker changes pump alarm volumes or alters other pump configurable items using touch screen.*

As per Table 6.3, the risk of this threat is "Acceptable" in the patient safety domain. However, even then, there is a cybersecurity design element of the Zeus infusion pump, a technical control, which can be used to bring the risk down even further, namely that "Privileged operations require admin access (login—password)."

Table 6.4 lists every system threat from the partial threat model so far constructed. It maps risk responses that lower system risk and shows the residual system risk for each system threat after the application of the risk responses.

Table 6.4 System cybersecurity risk model for Zeus infusion pump (postmitigation).

System threat	Risk response and postmitigation safety risk	Risk response and postmitigation privacy risk
Attacker crafts input that triggers a bug in the Zeus software to cause the Zeus pump to crash	Controls: **1.** The pump and pump server mutually authenticate each other using digital certificates before communication [primary] (this control ensures that only cryptographically authenticated components can send input to the pump, which means that an attacker will not be able to send input that is accepted by the Zeus pump over wireless) **2.** The pump code is crash tested as part of dynamic testing procedures for malformed input [secondary] Postmitigation: Exploitability: Incredibly low Severity: 3-Serious Risk: Acceptable	None

Attacker installs malware on the pump	Controls: **1.** Code can be installed to the pump only through admin role [primary] **2.** The admin role requires a password [primary] **3.** The pump is shipped with a default password specific to the HDO, and the password has to be modified during set-up [primary] **4.** All code updates to the Zeus pump are signed. Before allowing a code update, code on the pump checks if the certificate with the code update is signed by the download key that was provisioned on the pump during manufacture [primary] **5.** If incorrect password is entered thrice, a log-file entry is made on the Zeus pump tagged "cybersecurity," and is sent to the Titan pump server, together with all other log entries [secondary] Postmitigation: Exploitability: Incredibly low Severity: 5-Catastrophic Risk: Acceptable	Controls: Same as the cell to the left (i.e., same as the controls for mitigating patient safety risk) Postmitigation: Exploitability: Incredibly low Severity: 5-Catastrophic Risk: Acceptable

(Continued)

Table 6.4 System cybersecurity risk model for Zeus infusion pump (postmitigation).—cont'd

System threat	Risk response and postmitigation safety risk	Risk response and postmitigation privacy risk
Attacker gets malware running in memory through a remote code exploit	Controls: **1.** The pump and pump server mutually authenticate each other using digital certificates before communication [primary] (this control ensures that only cryptographically authenticated components can send input to the pump, which means that an attacker will not be able to send input that is accepted by the Zeus pump over wireless) **2.** The pump code undergoes static and dynamic testing that provided coverage for publicly known patterns for remote code execution [secondary] Postmitigation: Exploitability: Incredibly low Severity: 5-Catastrophic Risk: Acceptable	Same as the cell to the left (i.e., same as the controls for mitigating patient safety risk) Postmitigation: Exploitability: Incredibly low Severity: 5-Catastrophic Risk: Acceptable

Attacker loads malware onto the infusion pump during manufacturing	Controls: **1.** Manufacturing stations that are responsible for loading code onto the pump can be accessed through login–password authentication by authorized operators [primary] **2.** Only signed updates can be installed on manufacturing stations and any code update requires logging into admin role which requires two-factor authentication [primary] **3.** The manufacturing stations are on their own isolated subnet that is not accessible from the internet [primary] **4.** Underlying OS access to monitoring stations is locked for operator accounts [primary] **5.** Manufacturing stations are in a secure location, monitored by camera, and all actions by operators on manufacturing stations, logged and continuously monitored [secondary] Postmitigation: Exploitability: Incredibly low Severity: 5-Catastrophic Risk: Acceptable	Same as the cell to the left (i.e., same as the controls for mitigating patient safety risk) Postmitigation: Exploitability: Incredibly low Severity: 5-Catastrophic Risk: Acceptable

(*Continued*)

Table 6.4 System cybersecurity risk model for Zeus infusion pump (postmitigation).—cont'd

System threat	Risk response and postmitigation safety risk	Risk response and postmitigation privacy risk
Attacker loads pump code with backdoor or intentionally seeds other off-specification code elements	Controls: **1.** Access to code repository is controlled and provided only to authorized developers of X-Con who access the repository using their employee credentials [primary] **2.** Development code is periodically analyzed for malware and known backdoors using static and dynamic analysis [secondary] **3.** All third-party software and hardware components used in the device are assessed for cybersecurity risk using the supply chain risk assessment process [secondary] Postmitigation: Exploitability: Incredibly low Severity: 5-Catastrophic Risk: Acceptable	Same as the cell to the left (i.e., same as the controls for mitigating patient safety risk) Postmitigation: Exploitability: Incredibly low Severity: 5-Catastrophic Risk: Acceptable

Attacker disassembles pump, extracts flash persistent storage, modifies code, and loads it back into the pump	Controls: **1.** The persistent storage of the Zeus pump is encrypted at rest using AES-256 with a key derived from the admin password [secondary] Postmitigation: Exploitability: Low Severity: 5-Catastrophic Risk: Acceptable (secondary control brings down the risk from Acceptable* to Acceptable)	Same as the cell to the left (i.e., same as the controls for mitigating patient safety risk) Postmitigation: Exploitability: Low Severity: 5-Catastrophic Risk: Acceptable
Attacker changes pump alarm volumes or alters other pump configurable items using touch screen	Controls: **1.** any persistent change to the pump configuration can be done only through admin role [primary] **2.** The admin role requires a password [primary] **3.** The pump is shipped with a default password specific to the HDO, and the password has to be modified during set-up [primary] Postmitigation: Exploitability: Incredibly low Severity: 1-Negligible Risk: Acceptable	None

(*Continued*)

Table 6.4 System cybersecurity risk model for Zeus infusion pump (postmitigation).—cont'd

System threat	Risk response and postmitigation safety risk	Risk response and postmitigation privacy risk
Attacker pretends to be the pump server and sends spurious drug library over wireless	Controls: **1.** The pump and pump server mutually authenticate each other using digital certificates before communication [primary] **2.** All data in transit from pump server to pump use authenticated encryption algorithms that are part of TLS to ensure that data in transit are protected from unauthorized tampering and reading [primary] **3.** Every time the pump server sends an infusion order or a drug library over wireless, it calculates a SHA2 hash of the infusion order or a drug library and encrypts the hash using AES-256 with the shared encryption key that is established during pump set-up [primary] Postmitigation: Exploitability: Incredibly low Severity: 5-Catastrophic Risk: Acceptable	None

Attacker loads a spurious drug library over USB	Controls: **1.** Any uploading of a drug library over USB can be done only through admin role [primary] **2.** The admin role requires a password [primary] **3.** The pump is shipped with a default password specific to the HDO, and the password has to be modified during set-up [primary] Postmitigation: Exploitability: Incredibly low Severity: 5-Catastrophic Risk: Acceptable	None
Attacker tampers with a drug library while it is in transit from pump server to pump	Controls: **1.** All data in transit from pump server to pump use authenticated encryption algorithms that are part of TLS to ensure that data in transit are protected from unauthorized tampering and reading [primary] **2.** Every time the pump server sends an infusion order or a drug library over wireless, it calculates a SHA2 hash of the infusion order or a drug library and encrypts the hash using AES-256 with the shared encryption key that was established during pump set-up [primary] Postmitigation: Exploitability: Incredibly low Severity: 5-Catastrophic Risk: Acceptable	None

(Continued)

Table 6.4 System cybersecurity risk model for Zeus infusion pump (postmitigation).—cont'd

System threat	Risk response and postmitigation safety risk	Risk response and postmitigation privacy risk
Attacker disassembles pump, extracts flash persistent storage, modifies drug library, and loads it back into pump	Same controls as for the system threat "attacker disassembles pump, extracts flash persistent storage, modifies code, and loads it back into the pump" Postmitigation: Exploitability: Low Severity: 5-Catastrophic Risk: Acceptable (secondary control brings down the risk from Acceptable* to acceptable)	None
Attacker pretends to be a clinician and programs an infusion at the touch screen local interface	No primary controls Exploitability: Medium Severity: 5-Catastrophic Risk: Unacceptable	None
Attacker pretends to be the pump server and sends an infusion order over the wireless 802.11 interface	Same controls as for the system threat "attacker pretends to be the pump server and sends spurious drug library over wireless" Postmitigation: Exploitability: Incredibly low Severity: 5-Catastrophic Risk: Acceptable	None

Attacker stores genuine infusion orders and replays them later	Controls: **1.** All messages going over wireless 802.11 have sequence numbers, and the integrity of sequence numbers is protected by the authenticated encryption of TLS Postmitigation: Exploitability: Incredibly low Severity: 5-Catastrophic Risk: Acceptable	None
Attacker tampers with an infusion order while it is in transit over the wireless 802.11 medium from pump server to the Zeus infusion pump	Same controls as for the system threat "attacker tampers with a drug library, while it is in transit from pump server to pump" Postmitigation: Exploitability: Incredibly low Severity: 5-Catastrophic Risk: Acceptable	None

Defining risk response for subsystem—level threats that pose "unacceptable" risk at the subsystem level

At the subsystem level, when a subsystem threat poses "Unacceptable" risk, the threat has to be evaluated at the system level in order to assess whether it poses "Unacceptable" risk at the system level also. If that be the case, the subsystem threat poses uncontrolled risk to the medical device and the MDM is obliged to roll out a patch (recall, the only risk response that can remedy a subsystem threat vulnerability combine at the subsystem level), as per regulatory guidance from multiple global jurisdictions.

When a subsystem—level threat has to be assessed at the system level, the following have to be done:

1. Add the subsystem vulnerability to the list of system vulnerabilities
2. Add the subsystem threat to the list of system threats
3. Assess the severity of the new system threat
4. Assess the exploitability of the new system threat

In order to assess the exploitability of the new system threat, the Exploitability scale for system threats from Chapter 5 needs to be adapted for subsystem threats "floating" up to the system level. Recall, that the scale applied to theoretical "what-if" threats. Subsystem threats, on the other hand, are actual issues observed in the software and hardware system. Table 6.5 has such a candidate scheme for evaluating the exploitability of subsystem threats at the system level.

Table 6.5 System exploitability for subsystem threats being assessed at the system level.

Exploitability	Subsystem threats being assessed at the system level
Incredibly low	Premitigation, no subsystem—level threat can have "incredibly low" exploitability. This is because the vulnerability exists and the threat has actually been observed.
Low	Premitigation, a subsystem threat can have "low" exploitability if the risk of the subsystem threat at the subsystem level is assessed to be "low" (i.e., base metrics of CVSS for the threat is between 0 and 3.9)
Medium	Premitigation, a subsystem threat can have "medium" exploitability if the risk of the subsystem threat at the subsystem level is assessed to be "medium" (i.e., base metrics of CVSS for the threat is between 4 and 6.9)
High	Premitigation, a subsystem threat can have "high" exploitability if the risk of the subsystem threat at the subsystem level is assessed to be "high" or "critical" (i.e., base metrics of CVSS for the threat is between 7 and 10)

Now, let us see how all of this comes together, by falling back to our running example of the Zeus infusion pump, specifically the subsystem—level risk model from the previous chapter.

Now let us take SW1, the first subsystem vulnerability threat combination. This kind of issue was covered in our system risk model as part of the generic "what-if" system threat: "Attacker crafts input that triggers a bug in the Zeus software to cause the Zeus pump to crash," the only difference being that what was considered a hypothetical what-if is now an actual issue. If one looks at the corresponding entry for this system threat in Table 6.3, the premitigation Exploitability value was "Medium." Now that the threat has been realized in real life, the Exploitability value should be revisited, in the light of that fact. The reevaluation of risk based on new information obtained from the *Vulnerability Monitoring* procedural control is a vital activity in risk modeling. Now since the risk value for SW1 is 4.2 which is a Medium, the Exploitability at the system level remains "Medium."

Hence, the row in the system risk model remains unchanged and this subsystem threat is subsumed by the system threat that already exists in the System Cybersecurity Model.

Now, let us consider SW2: "On ComSys wireless 802.11 supplicant version 7.8, a key compromise allows an attacker full knowledge of encryption key used at the wireless network layer." The Exploitability of this vulnerability at the subsystem level is High since its CVSS base score is 8.1.

Following this scheme, the Exploitability of SW2 at the system level is "High."

Let us look at the second row of Table 6.6 where the risk of SW2 is assessed at the system level. As we can see, there are a number of primary controls that bring down the system risk, postmitigation, into the Acceptable zone. As a matter of fact, the system designers of the Zeus infusion pump never really considered the wireless security protections provided by 802.11 (Wi-Fi) to be worth considering as a risk response in their system risk assessment, and that is why there was never a control related to Wi-Fi security. This is a valid design presumption, given that the Wi-Fi network maintained by the HDO cannot be trusted—the wireless password may be compromised, either by clinicians keeping it on a Post-It note on the ER bulletin board or by another manufacturer's device on the device network. Then there is also the possibility of vulnerabilities like CVE 2019—4200 being found in the 802.11 protocol or in vender-specific implementations, which is why it makes sense to take a layered defense

Table 6.6 Subsystem vulnerability threat assessed at system level.

System vulnerability	System threat	Pre-mitigation risk	Controls	Postmitigation risk
A bug has been identified in input handling through penetration testing by an external security firm	Attacker crafts input that causes the Zeus pump to crash	Exploitability: Medium Severity: 3-Serious Risk: Acceptable*	**1.** The pump and pump server mutually authenticate each other using digital certificates before communication [primary] **2.** The pump code is crash tested as part of dynamic testing procedures for malformed input [secondary]	Postmitigation: Exploitability: Incredibly low Severity: 3-Serious Risk: Acceptable
A vulnerability has been identified (CVE 2019—4200) that may lead to compromise of 802.11 wireless security protections	Attacker uses exploit code that utilizes CVE 2019—4200 to compromise message integrity and confidentiality	Exploitability: High Severity: 5-Catastrophic Risk: Unacceptable (for both patient safety and patient privacy)	**1.** All data in transit from pump server to pump use authenticated encryption algorithms that are part of TLS to ensure that data in transit are protected from unauthorized tampering and reading [primary] **2.** Every time the pump server sends an infusion order or a drug library over wireless, it calculates a SHA2 hash of the infusion order or a drug library and encrypts the hash using AES-256 with the shared encryption key that was established during pump set-up [primary] **3.** Every time the pump server sends an infusion order or a drug library over wireless, it encrypts the entire infusion order with the shared encryption key using AES-256. [primary]	Exploitability: Incredibly low Severity: 5-Catastrophic Risk: Acceptable

approach, as the designers of Zeus infusion pump have done, using TLS and application-level security to provide at least two layers of independent cryptographic protection of data while it is in transit over the wireless.

Risk—benefit analysis

Table 6.4 contains one system threat that has no primary controls, and whose risk to patient safety, postmitigation, remains "Unacceptable." That threat is the following:

Attacker pretends to be a clinician and programs an infusion at the touch screen local interface.

For this threat, an RBA would have to be attached with the risk model, in order to demonstrate, that the unacceptable risk is more than compensated by the benefits provided by the device.

Formally, an RBA is a document that assesses hazardous situations whose impact to patient safety is deemed unacceptable, even after all possible risk mitigations have been put in place. It is now a call to be taken by a medical device executive authority which includes clinical experts in the Medical Review Board and representatives of the business whether the risk posed by the hazardous situation is compensated by the benefit or the feature or of the device.

As another example, many ultralow-power implanted devices would just not be able to support the memory space requirements of cryptographic code and the computational overhead of cryptographic operations, without significantly affecting battery life. The decision then has to be made as to what is better for the patient community: more frequent surgical implantations due to the battery running out or having a device that cannot cryptographically verify its code.

A method for assessing system risk of risk responses

Design dimensions are often at conflict each other. For example, usability is typically in conflict with cybersecurity—the more usable you want to make a system, the more open it has to be and the less secure it typically becomes. An example of this kind of "design tension" may be found while considering the patient safety risk of the threat: "Attacker pretends to be a clinician and programs an infusion at the touch screen local interface." Now, authentication of the clinical operator would reduce the risk of an unauthorized operator programming an infusion. This authentication can happen through a login password, or through touching a card to a reader, or through finger print or facial recognition. Each of these solutions though introduces a risk of availability of therapy—for example, what would happen if the clinician forgets their password or misplaces their access card when a patient is being wheeled into the emergency room with a gunshot wound and immediate therapy is needed? What would be the safety risk introduced if the clinician has to remove their gloves in a sterile environment to authenticate using their finger print or remove their surgical mask to authenticate through facial recognition?

A system designer has to consider all these scenarios and take the decision that reduces the overall risk.

In this case, the chances of a clinician forgetting their passwords or misplacing their authentication card are much higher than an actual cyber attack, which, in this case, would require the attacker to physically access the pump. Hence, the patient safety risk posed by the infusion pump being inoperable at a time when a patient needs it the most is much higher than the risk from an attacker programming a malignant infusion. Because risk in one dimension is much higher than risk in another, and there is no way to reduce both, the designers go for the choice that brings down the overall patient safety risk more. This is why the local interface is left unauthenticated for the Zeus pump.

Each primary and secondary control, used a risk response, needs to be assessed to check that they do not increase the overall patient safety risk of the system.

As an example, let us consider cryptographic verification of code that is being done by the Zeus pump. Consider a previous version of the Zeus pump which did not do such checking of code before an install. While the new version of the pump is more secure in terms of malware protection, the cryptographic verification of code introduces several ways in which the system may fail that were not present in the older version. What if you have a genuine code update, but the signature verification fails because of some bug in the code that is responsible for implementing the cryptographic operations, either at the signing or the verification end? What if nobody actually tampered with code, but because of a random bit flip, the public root key (the download key in the Zeus infusion pump) has somehow been changed unintentionally? Now as a result, a genuine code update is not allowed.

The point here is that each risk response (primary and secondary control) introduces a certain system risk, and an evaluation has to be provided that the risk introduced at the system level is controlled. A candidate method for this is as follows:

Step 1: Take each risk response (i.e., primary and secondary control) used for reducing patient safety and privacy risk.

Step 2: Consider multiple failure modes of the risk response (e.g., software failure, hardware failure, noise in the environment).

Step 3: Take the System Risk Model (i.e., the risk model for the medical device in which all noncybersecurity hazards and hazardous situations are assessed for risk of harm) and ensure that hazardous situations resulting from each failure mode from Step 2 are covered in the System Risk Model. This is typically done by tracing every primary and secondary control to a hazardous situation in the System Risk Model. If no such hazardous situation exists in the System Risk Assessment from a failure mode of a risk response, then that should be added and evaluated for system risk following the risk modeling approach for the System Risk Assessment.

A process for continually evaluating risk throughout the product lifecycle

The *Vulnerability Management* capability (from Table 4.2 from Chapter 4) of an MDM continuously executes the *Vulnerability Monitoring* procedural control to ingest sources of vulnerability information from multiple sources, in order to ascertain the presence of actual vulnerabilities at the subsystem level on medical devices that are out in the field. The *Vulnerability Monitoring* procedural control also tracks vulnerabilities being discovered in third-party software and hardware components they are part of the CBOM of devices under development. When a vulnerability is detected, the *Cybersecurity Risk Management* procedural control is executed to assess the risk posed to patient safety and privacy by threats that exercise the discovered vulnerabilities.

Risk modeling activities, at the system level, may need to be reexecuted in the face of new and emerging threats. For example, in 2016, when a wave of ransomware threats first hit the healthcare industry, a suitably vigilant and proactive MDM would have run a system risk modeling exercise on their medical devices to assess their exposure if a ransomware attack on their system were to happen. They would do this, even if no actual ransomware vulnerability had been discovered in their devices at that time.

If the risk was found to be unacceptable or very close to being unacceptable, this proactive MDM could then take preemptory mitigatory steps (like telling their customers to take their devices off the network) before an actual incident happened on their medical device in the field.

Summary and key takeaways

The key takeaways of this chapter are the following:

1. A systematic risk modeling approach, periodically executed, is needed to ensure that patient safety risk and patient privacy risk are continuously controlled for a medical device.
2. There are two levels at which risk modeling should be performed—the system level and the subsystem (software and hardware) level. Risk acceptability has to be defined at both the system as well as the subsystem level. At the subsystem level, when a subsystem threat poses "Unacceptable" risk, the threat needs to be assessed at the system level to see if it poses "Unacceptable" risk at the system level.
3. Primary and secondary controls are risk responses for mitigating patient safety and patient privacy risk due to cybersecurity threats. The concept of primary versus secondary is to capture the intuition that not all controls are equally strong—design elements and cryptographic controls that can be traced to design input (system and software requirements) and are exhaustively tested and validated meet the bar of primary. Expectation of compliance (e.g., expecting users to follow best practices or labeling instructions), cryptographic controls that do not meet best practice (e.g., a deprecated cryptographic algorithm or improper key generation), or design elements that are not verified with positive/negative test cases and independently validated are considered secondary. A primary control is needed to bring risk down from "Unacceptable" to "Acceptable" or "Acceptable*"
4. Risk modeling needs to be done whenever a vulnerability is output by the *Vulnerability Monitoring* procedural control or when there is a change in the threat landscape, with hitherto new and novel threats and vulnerabilities being discovered.
5. Primary and secondary controls, introduced as risk responses to cybersecurity threats, should be assessed for the system risk they introduce. The overall objective of a medical device designer is to reduce patient safety to the patient as far as possible from all causes. If while reducing patient

safety risk due to cybersecurity causes, one increases the risk from other causes (e.g., usability) above acceptable levels, the design decision needs to be revisited.

References

[1] American Association for Medical Instrumentation, TIR57: Principles for Medical Device Security – Risk Management, 2016.
[2] International Standards Organization, ISO 14971:2019 Medical Devices — Application of Risk Management to Medical Devices, 2019.

CHAPTER SEVEN

Cybersecurity design engineering

Introduction

Table 4.2 of Chapter 4 defines a set of capabilities that a Product Cybersecurity Organization for a Medical Device Manufacturer (MDM) should develop and maintain. In this chapter and the next, the focus will be on one of those capabilities, namely "Cybersecurity Design Engineering for Medical Devices." In Table 7.1, the relevant row from Table 4.2 of Chapter 4 is replicated, for the sake of completeness.

Secure requirements

Secure requirements is a procedural control developed and maintained by the Cybersecurity Design Engineering capability, in which a master set of product-agnostic technical controls mapped to regulatory guidance, laws, standards, and organizational experience is developed and maintained. For every product, these master controls are then converted to product-specific design input (i.e., system and subsystem requirements). Technical controls from the master set may not be fully mapped to system and subsystem requirements due to underlying platform restrictions or device limitations in some circumstances (Fig. 7.1). For instance, device hardware may not support cryptographic operations, a device may need to interoperate with older systems, older platform design restrictions may be carried forward in the new system, or there may be a lack of supporting infrastructure like cybersecurity monitoring services. In these cases, the deviances should be noted and assessed for regulatory risk.

Master set of technical controls

The master set of technical cybersecurity controls capture general cybersecurity design imperatives that are agnostic of medical devices and map to regulatory guidance and best practices. In this section of the chapter, a candidate list of technical controls is presented. The exact mapping to regulatory requirements is not included because of the ever-changing language of guidance and standards. However, the set of technical controls themselves are

Cybersecurity for Connected Medical Devices
ISBN: 978-0-12-818262-8
https://doi.org/10.1016/B978-0-12-818262-8.00007-3

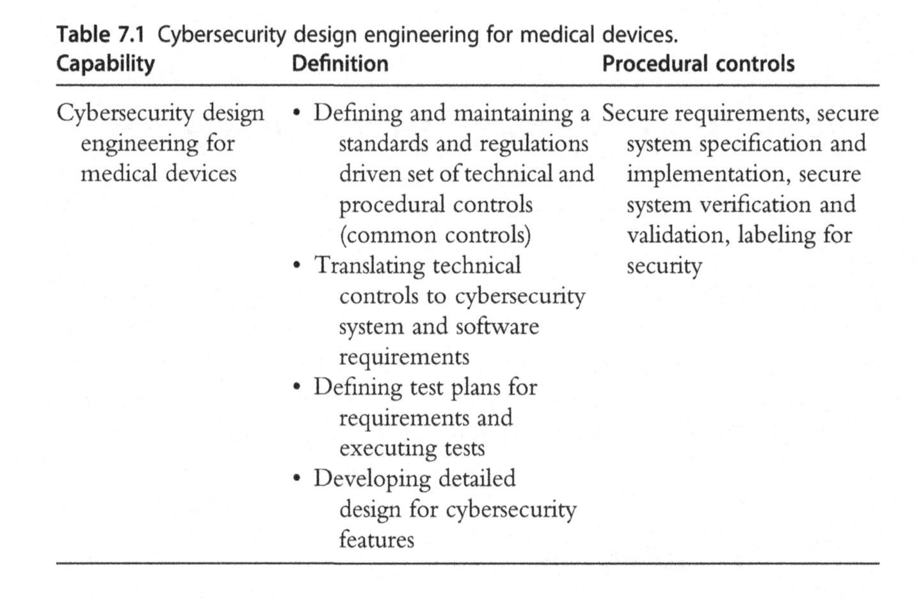

Table 7.1 Cybersecurity design engineering for medical devices.

Capability	Definition	Procedural controls
Cybersecurity design engineering for medical devices	• Defining and maintaining a standards and regulations driven set of technical and procedural controls (common controls) • Translating technical controls to cybersecurity system and software requirements • Defining test plans for requirements and executing tests • Developing detailed design for cybersecurity features	Secure requirements, secure system specification and implementation, secure system verification and validation, labeling for security

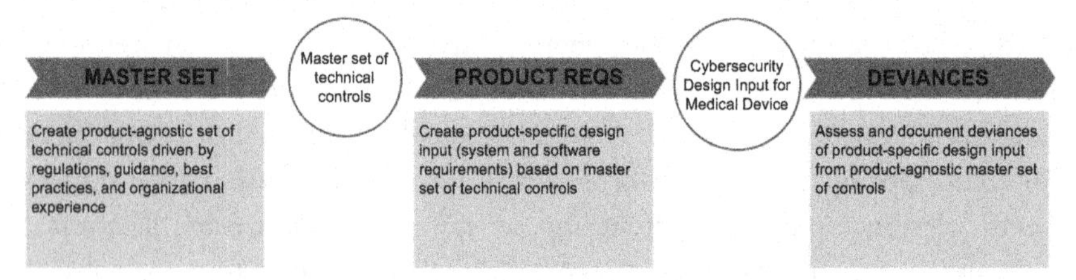

Figure 7.1 Secure requirements procedural control.

not expected to change drastically, unless new and revolutionary industry wide threats and technological advancements significantly alter the cybersecurity.

System authentication

Before establishing a connection, the system shall authenticate the unique cryptographic identity of the other party in a communication and shall not allow an establishment of a connection if the cryptographic identity cannot be verified.

Unique cryptographic identity can be established in the following ways:

1. Providing a third-party signed digital certificate [1] as proof of identity: As described in Chapter 2, a digital certificate is the secure association of a system node with its public key. The security of the association is cryptographically attested to by a digital signature performed by a trusted

third party, i.e., a Certificate Authority (CA). By presenting a digital certificate, a party seeking to communicate with the system is endeavoring to cryptographically establish its identity as a trusted system.

2. Claiming the possession of a shared symmetric key: The party seeking authentication can claim to have, in its possession, a shared symmetric secret key that was previously established through some other means. The fact that it possesses this shared secret is proof that it has already established its identity as a trusted system. Otherwise, how could it have that shared secret?

In both these cases, the system has to verify the identity being claimed by other party.

In the scenario where a digital certificate is being provided as proof of identity, the system has to verify that there is a chain of trust from the digital certificate that has been offered as proof of identity to the root of trust (refer to Chapter 2 for the concepts of "root of trust" and "chain of trust").

In the scenario where the possession of a shared symmetric key is being claimed as a proof of identity by the other party, the system has to verify this claim through a challenge response mechanism. This is typically done by sending a random number to the other party, with the random number being encrypted by the shared secret which the other party claims to possess. The other party is supposed to apply some fixed transformation (e.g., add 1 to the random number) and send it back, encrypted by the shared secret. The system then decrypts the message using the shared key. If it finds that the value is exactly the response to the challenge it was expecting (in this example, one plus the random number it sent), the identity of the other party is cryptographically established. After all, if the other party did not have the shared secret, how would it have known what random number (the challenge) that was sent to it?

The shared secret key used for authenticating a party as a trusted system can be established through exchange of key material over a trusted channel. For example, an implanted cardiac device may be provisioned with a shared secret key during implantation by the programmer sending the shared secret key over close proximity inductive (i.e., magnetic) communication. Since the range of the communication is in inches, it can be visually confirmed that there is no other attacker eavesdropping on the medium when the secret is being transmitted. That shared secret can then be used to authenticate subsequent connections between the programmer and the implanted cardiac device over long range wireless communication.

Even when digital certificate—based authentication is used, requiring every session to use digital certificate—based identity verification to establish the identity of the communicating system nodes is computationally expensive. The solution is to do digital certificate—based authentication the first time a communication is established between two system nodes, and then do the faster shared secret key—based authentication (the shared secret key is generated through key transport or key agreement during the first session) for every successive session. This is how Transport Layer Security (TLS) implementations do secure session management.

Example requirements:

- During manufacturing, the private/public key pair is generated on the device. The public key together with the device serial number is sent securely to the device CA, where it is wrapped in a digital certificate and sent back to the device.
- The shared symmetric key shall be provisioned to the device using close proximity inductive communication.
- Once authentication is accomplished using verification of the digital certificate of the requesting node, a National Institute of Standards and Technology (NIST)—approved [2,3] key agreement protocol shall be used to establish a shared secret between the two, to be used for authenticating subsequent connections between the nodes
- ECDSA (Elliptic Curve Digital Signature Algorithm) [4] certificates in the X.509 [1,5] format shall be used to establish cryptographic identity.

User authentication

Before allowing access, each system shall verify the credentials of all human users, and deny access in case the credentials provided are not valid.

The credentials of human users can be established in the following ways (each of which is called a factor of authentication) [6—9]:

- Something the user knows (e.g., password)
- Something the user has (e.g., sending a One-Time Password to their phone)
- Something the user is (e.g., fingerprint, facial scan)

Product-specific design input (system and subsystem requirements) needs to be written to capture design choices related to the implementation of the parent control. Specifically, you may want to consider the following:

Requirements for exact mechanism used for establishing user identity

The designer has a wide number of choices when it comes to devising an authentication mechanism for users. Should you authenticate using a single factor or multiple factors? If you go with a single factor, should the user be allowed to choose the factor (e.g., you either unlock the screen with a numerical code or through finger print scan) or is the factor fixed (i.e., you can only authenticate using a login password and nothing else)? Within a factor, which authentication mechanism should one choose—if you decide to go with something the user is, for example, should you do a fingerprint scan or facial recognition? Should you maintain your own authentication credentials using one's directory service or should one use a third-party identity provider? Should you use session-based authentication or token-based authentication? The choices for authentication are many, with multiple frameworks available. Since there is a topic that lies within the realm of general IT security, and is not specific to healthcare or medical devices, we do not delve further here.

Example requirements:

- The user shall authenticate to the device either using a unique login and password or through fingerprint recognition using the fingerprint scanner.
- The user's second factor of authentication is a one-time password (OTP) which can be delivered either to the user's phone or to their email, depending on which option the user chooses.

Requirements for provisioning/restoring user credentials

The process by which a user is granted credentials to a system for the first time, and the process by which a user has their credentials restored (in the case an account is locked out or the user has forgotten their credentials), needs to be captured as design input (system and subsystem requirements).

Example requirements:

- A password set/reset link, valid for 10 min, shall be sent to the email registered during account sign-up, on first sign-up/reset request.

Secure updates

Before installing any code update, the system shall verify the authenticity of the code using cryptographic signature verification.

Code authentication [10] has to ensure that the code that is being installed on the device originated from the manufacturer, and that the code has not been altered in any way. In order to ensure this, the system has to verify that there is a chain of trust from the digital certificate that has been offered as the code-signing certificate to the root of trust.

The signature used to ensure the authenticity of the code should not cover just the binaries, but also metadata associated with the code update. This metadata should include version number of the update, any data that the installer requires, and any date after which the update cannot be applied.

Time limiting a software update is a security best practice that limits the risk of downgrade attacks. Let us presume that version 1 of the device code has a critical vulnerability for which exploit code exists. The vendor rolls out a cybersecurity patch to version 1.1 in order to fix the issue. Now in a downgrade attack, the attacker takes the vulnerable version 1 device code (remember that too was signed by the MDM) and installs it over version 1.1, effectively downgrading the device to the vulnerable code version. The risk of this kind of attack can be reduced by having a timed upper limit for an update, after which even a validly signed code update will not be installed by the device.

Example requirements:

- The system shall verify all code updates using the download key provisioned during manufacture.
- The system shall not install any code update that has its "date of deployment" field that is 90 days before the current date.

Session integrity and confidentiality

After a communication session is established between two systems, all data that are exchanged shall be protected from tampering and unauthorized disclosure through cryptographic means of integrity and confidentiality protection.

After session authentication establishes the authenticity of the parties in a communication, the data that flow within a communication session have to be protected from unauthorized tampering and from being read by an attacker.

The cryptographic primitives being used to ensure integrity and confidentiality need to be specified. If the responsibility of session integrity is being delegated to a standard implementation (e.g., TLS [11] or Bluetooth [12] security modes), then that too needs to be captured.

Example requirements:

- The device uses TLS 1.3 to ensure data integrity and confidentiality for all sessions.
- The device uses a keyed hash to ensure data integrity and encrypts session packets to ensure data confidentiality, with both the key used for hashing and the key used for encryption being established per session.

Session management

Each session should time-out after a period of no activity or on an explicit session termination action.

Product-specific design input (system and software requirements) needs to be written to capture design choices related to the implementation of the parent control. Terminate a session too soon because of inactivity and run the risk of a bad user experience, extensive reconnection delays, and a general perception that "security on the device makes it too restrictive." Terminate a session on inactivity too late the very purpose of reducing your exposure in case of a session key compromise has been undermined.

Other factors that need to be considered relate to the data retained between sessions. On one hand, the data that are operated on in one session need to be protected in another session for cybersecurity reasons because a different user may be using the device. On the other hand, the designer has to ensure that this does not compromise user experience by making users/system do the same things in every session (e.g., regenerate data from the last session that could have just been reused without any impact in terms of cybersecurity). So what kind of data is retained during sessions? Do you remove all protected health information (PHI) from persistent storage once a session is over? What about temporary files? How long do you keep the shared secret negotiated during session authentication for faster reconnects before you purge it and force a reverification of digital certificates?

Example requirements:

- The device terminates a session on an explicit log-off action of the user or if no packets have been exchanged for 30 min.
- All PHI is removed from the device once a session is terminated by the user.
- All user session data for a user session is stored encrypted on persistent storage using a key derived from the user's credentials.

Data integrity and confidentiality in motion

Critical data shall be cryptographically protected end to end from unauthorized tampering. PHI shall be cryptographically protected from end to end from unauthorized disclosure.

Session integrity and confidentiality only protects data while it is in an active session, not when it is stored on a system. For example, consider a device ecosystem where a device obtains configuration files from a mobile app, which in turn gets it from a central server on the cloud. Now, session security protects the data while it is in transit from cloud to mobile app and from mobile app to the device. But these protections are not there when the data are being stored on the phone. It is true that a modern smart phone has built-in operating system protections for data that are being stored on the hardware, but what if the attacker has jail broken or rooted the phone, i.e., compromised the operating system. This is why it is good security practice, consistent with the defense-in-depth principle, to have additional cryptographic protections on the data that are "end to end" (i.e., the protections are enabled at the time of creation and checked at the time of consumption).

Example requirements:

- Critical data used by the device shall be signed by the server
- All therapy data that contain PHI shall be encrypted with a data encryption key that is known to both ends of the communication through a key agreement protocol.
- During export using USB, the system shall encrypt data files using a symmetric encryption key with the encryption key being encrypted with the public key of the server where the data are to be read.
- Data received should be validated by range checks and checked for compliance to data format, protocol specifications.

Data integrity at rest

The integrity of all critical data stored on persistent storage (code, data files that influence code execution, and clinical data) shall be protected by cryptographic means.

Code is protected during installation by cryptographic verification. But what prevents an attacker changing the code while it is stored on persistent storage? After all, it is nothing but a data file for the operating system. In general, what are the protections for files on a persistent storage, what mechanisms exist to protect them from fraudulent modification?

The system should only allow code execution after cryptographic signature verification and should verify code integrity after every reboot [13]. This process is colloquially known as secure boot. In secure boot, every stage of the booting process of the node's hardware verifies the cryptographic integrity of the next stage—starting with the integrity of the firmware of the motherboard which verifies the integrity of the bootloader, which then verifies the integrity of the operating system and the executables. A secure boot process allows a user to have the confidence that every time they boot up, only authentic code is executed.

The system should verify code before allowing for execution. This is done by allow list technologies (also called application whitelisting [14]), where the system only allows execution of executables that meet certain criteria. This can be as rudimentary as allowing execution from certain directories, or having signatures for each executable, and execution allowed only if the cryptographically verification of the executable is successful. Antimalware technologies are typically default-allow technologies, in that they only deny execution when some property of the executable matches their internal database of malware patterns or behavior patterns.

Example requirements:

- The system shall ensure the integrity of the boot process through cryptographic verification of each stage of the boot process.
- The system shall implement a default deny policy for code execution, where code, that is launched, can only be executed on successful cryptographic signature verification.

Data confidentiality at rest

Data at rest, i.e., data when stored on persistent storage, should be protected from unauthorized disclosure by cryptographic means.

It is security best practice, where feasible, to have confidentiality protection on all data following the principle of least privilege rather than defining confidentiality controls for each system asset individually.

Data at rest should be encrypted at multiple levels, to provide defense-in-depth protection.

Disk-level encryption [15] provides encryption at the physical storage level with the symmetric encryption key either being derived from a password provided by the user during boot-up or with the symmetric encryption key being stored off the disc in secure crypto-processor hardware like a

Trusted Platform Module [16]. This protection ensures that if an attacker detaches the persistent storage, they will not be able to read the data, as they will not have the key required to decrypt it.

Filesystem encryption [15] provides encryption at the operating system level with individual files and directories being encrypted, rather than the physical storage medium itself (which is what disk-level encryption is). Unlike the protection provided by disk-level encryption which is for attacks that detach the persistent storage but which provide no protection once the device is booted up, filesystem encryption provides protection when the system is operational, as files are decrypted only when required.

Application-level encryption [17] is when data are encrypted and key management done by the application itself.

The more layers of independent encryption (e.g., disc level, filesystem, and application level) one designs, the more secure the confidentiality posture for data protection becomes, since each layer of encryption provides protection against a different class of attack.

Example requirements:

- The system shall encrypt the flash storage with the symmetric encryption key being stored in secure hardware.
- The system shall encrypt files using encryption facilities provided by the operating system.

Code and data authenticity during execution

Code and data integrity in memory should be maintained.

The easiest way of ensuring integrity maintenance is to make sure that the system has an operating system that enforces execution sandboxing, i.e., address space isolation and resource capping, such that executing processes cannot write into each other's memory space.

Example requirements:

- The system shall ensure that running processes are isolated from each other

Key and credentials management

Credentials (user secrets like passwords) and keys (private keys, associated public keys, shared secret keys) should be changed periodically, or on credentials compromise.

Digital certificates which establish identity have an expiry date in order to reduce exposure in case of compromise of the corresponding private key. Any signature verification procedure should check the expiry of the digital certificate. If the certificate has expired, then depending on whether there is an user interaction, the user should be warned about the fact that the signing certificate is expired, or if no user interaction is needed during verification, the signature verification should fail on account of the expired certificate. Similarly, user credentials like passwords should expire, and the user be prompted to renew their credentials.

In the situation where a key or user credentials are compromised (there are several publicly available databases of compromised passwords and credentials), procedures should exist to force the user to disallow access unless they have changed their password, or to blacklist compromised certificates or, in case of a disaster, change the public key in the root of trust.

Example requirements:

- The system shall renew digital certificates every two years.
- The user shall be prompted to change every three months.
- A shared secret key established for quicker connection reauthentication should expire every seven days.
- In case the system detects a user using a password that has been part of a publicly-known compromise, the system shall force the user to change the password.

Key and credentials strength

Keys (private keys, shared secret keys), credentials (passwords), and other cryptographic material (e.g., initialization vector for certain cryptographic algorithms) should meet length/security strength recommendations of NIST or equivalent standards body. Deprecated encryption schemes and key lengths, where deprecation is defined by standards bodies like NIST, should not be used. Any default device password, if used, must be changed before the device is deployed.

Security strength of cryptographic algorithms [2,3], calculated in bits, measures the amount of work (i.e., the number of operations) that is required to break a cryptographic algorithm or system. Security strength of a cryptographic scheme depends on the algorithm and the key length. While security strength and key length are same for symmetric encryption schemes (e.g., AES with key length of 128 bits has 128 bits of security strength; AES with key length of 192 bits has 192 bits of security strength), it is not so simple for asymmetric schemes like RSA, where a 1024 bit key has a security strength of only 80 bits and a 2048 key length has a security strength of only 112 bits.

Another thing that is often overlooked in favor of pure key length is the randomness of the key. A key may be 256 bits of length, but if the value can be predicted, the key has zero randomness and the resultant encryption, regardless of the algorithm security strength, is trivially broken.

Example requirements:

- The system shall use cryptographic algorithms of security strength of 128 or greater.

Keys and credentials secure storage

Keys and credentials shall be stored securely in a way such that private/shared symmetric keys are protected from unauthorized reading and public keys are protected from unauthorized modification.

Requirements for securing private/shared symmetric keys

If the attacker can read a shared secret key or the private key or user credentials, they can masquerade as the system whose key material they stole or the user whose credentials they stole. They then can engage in communication or sign data/code, masquerading as the entity whose keys/credentials they stole.

Hence, it is imperative to store private keys and shared secrets in storage such that they are protected from illicit reading. There are many "wrong" ways of doing this. For example, if the private key is hardcoded in the code itself, then an attacker merely needs to disassemble the code and extract the private key. Similarly, if the private key is stored in plain text on the persistent flash memory, then the attacker can now read the key off the storage medium. A slightly better, but not by much, method of storing a private key is through obfuscation. Rather than storing the key in contiguous locations on the persistent storage on the disc or in a program variable, the private key is split up into blocks and "hidden" by storing them in different locations of the persistent storage or in the program. This ostensibly makes it slightly more difficult to find the private key. While this is definitely a better solution than keeping the key in one place, the logic to reconstruct the key from the secret locations is present in the code, and all that the attacker has to do is decipher the "secret sauce" within the code. The "secret sauce" can be made more difficult to understand by code obfuscation, but none of these are best-in-class solutions. Unfortunately, in many cases, this may be the best option due to device hardware constraints.

Depending on the specific product (whether it is a resource-constrained embedded system) or an app on a smart phone or a cloud/on-premise deployment, secret key material can be stored in various ways. This includes special "secure hardware" like a Trusted Platform Modules, or storage under operating system control in a location readable only through admin access Private keys that are especially critical (i.e., whose compromise can lead to fleet-wide compromise like root CA private keys or code signing keys) should be stored in a specialized, stand-along hardware unit called Hardware Security Module [18] (HSM). If the medical device is deployed on a cloud, most public cloud vendors provide HSM-backed secure key management using a platform-as-a-service [19] model. User credentials should always be stored as salted hashes, and the master file containing all salted and hashed passwords should be encrypted on persistent storage.

Example requirements:

- All private/shared symmetric keys shall be stored encrypted on persistent storage of the device, with the encryption keys being stored in secure hardware.
- All private/shared symmetric keys shall be kept confidential using cloud vendor provided secure key storage services.

Requirements for securing public keys

The device trusts the public key of the root CA intrinsically as the "root of trust" (refer to root of trust and chain of trust in Chapter 2). If an attacker can get a device to intrinsically trust an attacker controlled public key, the attacker can poison the entire chain of trust. That is why the MDM has to protect the public key of the root CA, stored on the device, from illicit modification. This can be accomplished by storing the public key of the root CA in a protected operating system account (sometimes called the trust store) which can be written only with admin privileges.

Another alternative is certificate pinning [20]. Certificate pinning is the process of associating an external entity with their expected certificate. Certificate pinning has many flavors, of which a popular one used by device manufacturers is to embed the hash of the certificate in code where it is protected from tampering by the digital signature of the code. The device only trusts an external entity if the hash of the offered public key of the CA matches the hash pinned in its code. Yet another way of certificate pinning is to trust the certificate offered by an external entity the first time it is visited (this first-time visit is intrinsically trusted in this approach) and store that certificate. Every subsequent time, the external entity is authenticated by comparing the certificate offered by the external node with the certificate stored from the first time that external node was visited. Only if they match, is the external node trusted.

All of the above (trust store, certificate pinning) protections for root of trust presume operating system protections. But how does one protect the root of trust during the first phase of secure boot, before the system control has passed to the operating system? If the attacker is able to get the device to intrinsically trust attacker controlled root CA public key at the very start of the boot process, they can compromise the entire boot chain, leading them to load their own operating system and application code. This kind of attack is prevented by burning device root CAs (or rather their hashes) onto one-time programmable fuses [21]. These fuses are part of the device hardware. The boot process proceeds only if the first phase of the boot process can be verified using the same public key whose hash is stored in the one-time programmable fuse. The trick here is the "one-time programmable" nature of the fuses; once these fuses are "burnt" during manufacture with the manufacturer's root CA public keys, it is extremely difficult for an attacker to overwrite these fuses with their own root CA public keys.

Example requirements:

- The device shall be provisioned with the public key of the root CA during manufacturing and the public key will be stored on an OTP fuse.
- The root certificate will be provisioned during device set-up, with the root certificate being stored in the operating system "Trust Store," writable only through admin credentials.

Role-based authorization and access control

A documented role-based authorization model should specify (1) how users are mapped to roles and (2) mapping of roles to privileges. The principle of least privilege should be followed while determining these mappings. Once authentication is successfully performed, access to privileged operations, as defined in the role-based authorization model, should be enforced through cryptographic means. No authenticated entity should be allowed to perform an action they are not authorized to perform.

Requirements should be written that capture the specific privileges, e.g., in terms of read/write/execute to specific functions that membership to the roles provide to users. Specifically, the privilege to update the code of a device or change critical persistent parameters should require admin privilege. Roles that have higher privilege like admin may require specific authentication requirements. For example, users that belong to the admin role would require multiple factors of authentication to establish their identity.

The mechanism of checking whether a system has the proper authorization to perform a privileged action may be implemented through operating system capabilities (e.g., using the Unix [22] or Windows implementation [23] of Role-Based Access Control [24]) or through distributed standard solutions (e.g., OAuth [25] implementations) or through custom implementations.

Example requirements:

- On cryptographic authentication of the external system, the device shall allow write access to privileged clinical functions only on cryptographically verifying that the external system has a signed "clinician" authorization token.
- Users who belong to the admin role shall provide two distinct factors of authentication.
- Code updates or any change to the device configuration shall require the admin role.

Emergency access

Device interfaces where loss of immediate access is associated with patient safety risk should provide for an emergency access mechanism that allows for user authentication to be bypassed in emergency scenarios.

An emergency access mechanism is a mechanism by which requirements of user authentication can be bypassed for a limited period of time, by invoking the mechanism. Any such mechanism should ideally satisfy the following properties:

- Only essential clinical functions should be allowed to be accessed during emergency access
- The emergency access mechanism can only be triggered locally (i.e., emergency access cannot be used for remote interfaces)
- Each emergency access session must be bound by time or terminated by user inactivity

- The number of emergency accesses must be capped at a predefined upper limit, to prevent continuous use of a feature that is designed to be used infrequently. Once the limit is reached, the emergency access feature should be disabled (all accesses mandatorily require user authentication), unless emergency access is reset by a role that is authorized to perform privileged system functions (e.g., the admin role).
- Triggering the emergency access mechanism should raise an alarm and be logged.

Example requirements:

- The emergency access feature can be used for five clinical sessions before the feature is disabled and can be reenabled only through access through admin role.

Restrict access

The system should follow the principle of least privilege by shutting down ports and services not being used, removing user accounts at the operating system (i.e., accounts that can be logged into), and removing/restricting access to hardware debug interfaces like JTAG (Joint Test Action Group). The use of physical locks and tamper evident seals should be considered.

The purpose of this control is to restrict attack surfaces as much as possible. This is done by exposing the minimal amount of network interfaces (hence the shutting down of ports and services) and operating system interfaces (hence the removing of user accounts). Physical locks and tamper-evident seals provide some limited protection against an attacker physically taking apart the device, tampering with its internals, and putting it together again. Hardware interfaces like JTAG [26] allow for hardware level access for system debugging, and are useful for root cause analysis/system recovery in case of system failures. They also allow attackers to directly access hardware subverting software-level controls. JTAG interfaces can be perennially removed, by either depopulating the JTAG or by the use of epoxy or by setting a JTAG password and then not retaining the value. Of course, the cost of doing this has to be balanced with the benefit of debugging and restoring returned units. One compromise is to lock JTAG with a per-unit unique password and retain these passwords in case the JTAG has to be unlocked again. This of course implies that the MDM securely store all these passwords at their manufacturing/service center, and that the JTAG password itself is stored in secure storage on the device, like any symmetric shared key.

Example requirements:

- All operating system user accounts (i.e., require a user id and password to access) shall be removed from the system.
- The chassis opening of the device shall be protected by a tamper-evident seal.
- The system shall have its JTAG interface rendered inaccessible using an epoxy coating.

Denial-of-service protection

The system should be designed to defend against malicious attempts to use up system resources like battery life, network bandwidth, and computational and storage responses. Anomalous consumption of system resources should be detected, followed by the throttling of further attempts to take up system resources.

Denial-of-service (DoS) attacks are based on the attacker bombarding system interfaces with fraudulent traffic to deny services to legitimate users and consume system resources.

These fraudulent requests can be network connection attempts or requests for system services or attempts to authenticate [27].When a DoS attack is underway, the effect is not just limited to legitimate entities being unable to gain service while the attack is on. Sometimes, by exhausting resources that cannot be replenished (like battery life), DoS attacks may be successful in running down the useful lifetime of a medical device, severely impacting its clinical function.

The system should be designed to detect anomalous usage. When service requests are coming in too fast or too many data packets are being received that fail the input format expected or fail data integrity checks, that is a sign that an attacker is trying to either initiate fraudulent connections or jam existing sessions. Once such anomalous usage is detected, the system can react in multiple ways: by shutting down the interface totally (e.g., shut down the Bluetooth Low Energy (BLE) communication stack or refuse to accept connections on a certain protocol or on a certain port number), or by decreasing the frequency of servicing of requests by introducing a deliberate time delay between successive request grants, or by asking the entity requesting the service for proof of work, i.e., by asking them to successfully pass a CAPTCHA [28] or some other challenge.

Example requirements:

- The system shall shut down BLE communication after a predetermined limit, which can only be turned back on by a user belonging to the admin role.
- The system shall implement a CAPTCHA after five unsuccessful authentication attempts within 120 s.

Code updateability

The system should be designed to allow secure code updates.

This on the face of it seems to be almost trivial, but anyone who has been in the medical device industry for a long time would know that it is not. In an age where vulnerabilities and threats are being discovered continuously, one of the most critical aspects of keeping a medical device secure at all times is the ability to roll out cybersecurity patches and apply them quickly and securely. If the medical app is running on a public cloud or on-premise servers or is on a commercial smart phone, the MDM is not on the hook to design the update delivery mechanism: they are dealt with at the platform level as a service, in that App Store [29] or Google Play [30] will securely deliver an app update, and server updates, be it cloud or on-premise, will also be delivered securely using standard update mechanisms.

The challenge for MDMs is to develop secure update mechanisms for devices where no such standard application update platform service is available. For decades, an unplanned in-field update (which is what a cybersecurity patch for an uncontrolled risk is) was a rare occurrence, and the design culture in MDMs did not focus on efficient and quick patch application.

There are several factors that make designing secure update mechanisms for such devices particularly challenging:

1. *Update delivery*: There is often no direct connection between a medical device in the field and the MDM's own servers. This can either be because the device itself does not have the capability to be connected to the Internet (e.g., no Wi-Fi or 4G) or it does, but the Healthcare Delivery Organization (HDO) keeps it on isolated networks, with no ingoing or outgoing connections to the Internet being allowed. This means that updates can be delivered only over local interfaces like USB or over close proximity wireless communication like inductive or conductive or infrared. For devices with wireless interfaces like BLE, the patch may be delivered to an intermediate device that does have Internet connectivity, like a transmitter or a mobile phone, and from there the

update can be rolled over to the device. The sheer variation in update delivery mechanisms across devices makes it difficult to develop update delivery as a platform service, as it exists for smart phones, for example.

2. *In-service software updates*: For devices which provide continuous therapy, the update process has to happen *without interrupting therapy*. In order to do that, during a code update, the device needs to go into a backup state where critical life-sustaining therapy functions can be done without software.
3. *User involvement in the update process*: Should the user (patient or clinician) be provided the final authority to decide when to apply a device update or if at all? Or should an update, especially a cybersecurity patch that is not a functionality enhancement, be pushed by the MDM without the ability of the user to intervene? When a device is not accessible over the public Internet, the decision of when and if to apply a patch has to rest with the clinician or the user, since there is no way for the manufacturer to force an update. The clinician may decide that the risk of not applying a cybersecurity update is negligible, compared to the trouble of applying the patch, where the patient needs to be notified, brought into the clinic, exclusively for the purpose of a cybersecurity patch. Even if the update is done during a regular scheduled clinic visit, the time of consultation may be extended in order to apply the patch. The hands of the MDM are tied in such situations, for devices that may be accessed over the public internet directly or through an intermediary, MDMs must consider whether to involve the user in the update process (e.g., through a notification where the user may choose to not apply the patch) or just force a critical update regulatory authorities are concerned about timely patch adoption for fixing cybersecurity vulnerabilities because users and clinicians do not have the full information or the training to determine the risk of keeping their devices unpatched. Given regulatory concerns, and the demand for frequent cybersecurity patching by HDOs, the trend will be to force critical cybersecurity patches for devices that may be accessed directly by the MDM.

Example requirements:

- The device shall continue to deliver critical therapy functions using a fail-safe mode implemented in hardware while a software update is being applied
- The device code shall be split into a core and noncore section. Any code update that impacts only the noncore section shall be applied while the core code section is running.

Secure configuration

If the system allows users to configure security parameters, the system should be shipped in a secure configuration (i.e., all configurable parameters set to secure settings) and the user should be educated through labeling and documentation about the need to maintain a secure configuration.

Devices may require users to configure specific aspects of the device, for example, setting an admin password or setting network security configurations. The device should be shipped in a mode where security is enabled by default. For example, let us consider a device that has user authentication as an optional feature, one which an admin may choose to deactivate. Design option 1 is to ship the device with authentication turned off. The user, once they unbox the unit, activates authentication. Then, they set their admin password. Design option 2 is to ship with authentication turned on and the admin account protected by a default password. Once the unit is unboxed, the user is forced to change the default password to a unique admin password, after which if the admin wants, they can turn off authentication. The control asks designers to favor option 2 over option 1. The reason why option 2 is preferred is that the act of making the device less secure (in this case turning off authentication) is an explicit action being taken by a privileged user, i.e., admin, whereas in option 1, the admin might not even know that there is an option to turn on user authentication.

Example requirements:

- The device shall ship with "default deny" for all inbound network connections, which can be modified by the admin.

Cybersecurity logging and monitoring

The system shall record cybersecurity events. The event shall be captured using a standard schema, with an associated timestamp, so that it can be automatically analyzed. The system should monitor cybersecurity logs and other operational signals (e.g., crashes, connection drops) in order to detect cybersecurity incidents.

An event [31] is any observable occurrence in an information system. A security-relevant event or a *cybersecurity event* is any event that attempts to change the security state of the system (e.g., change access controls, change the security level of a user, change a user password) [32]. Examples of cybersecurity events are the following:

- A failed log-in attempt
- A successful log-in

- A connection request, denied or granted
- A code download that is denied because of signature verification failure, and a code download that is allowed to be applied

A question that may arise here is the following: "I understand why a failed log-in attempt might be a sign of an attempted compromise, but why should a successful log-in be a cybersecurity event?" The thing is that one never knows for sure whether a seemingly valid log-in happened because of a stolen password. One also never knows whether a legitimate user of the system with valid credentials will not then try to elevate their privileges or perform unauthorized actions, and that is why it is important to audit their actions throughout. Similarly, we do not know in advance whether a valid connection request is the start of an attack. This is why many perfectly legitimate events should all be recorded, so that monitoring services can analyze and correlate them together, to detect or prevent compromise or provide forensics once a breach has happened.

The success of an attack on a medical device is usually manifested as a negative system consequence that realizes the final goal of the attacker. Examples of this are system crashes, unauthorized use of system privileges, unauthorized access to sensitive data, and execution of attacker controlled code. Sometimes, the attacker may have been successful in violating some security policy or procedure or system expectation but may not have been able to attain their objectives yet. But if the system does not take any action based on the violation detected, the attacker will likely be able to attain their final goal.

A *cybersecurity incident* [31] is an occurrence that actually or potentially jeopardizes the confidentiality, integrity, or availability of an information system or the information the system processes, stores, or transmits or that constitutes a violation or imminent threat of violation of security policies, security procedures, or acceptable use policies. In other words, a cybersecurity incident is a cybersecurity event with a negative system consequence. Thus, all cybersecurity incidents are cybersecurity events, but all cybersecurity events are hopefully not cybersecurity incidents.

Some cybersecurity incidents may be caught by log file monitoring. For instance, a cybersecurity log entry indicates that the integrity of a data store failed cryptographic verification, implying that someone has tampered with the data. Or, one may suspect a data breach if a user logs in from an IP address not usually associated with the user's country and is currently downloading large quantities of data which is well above what the user usually does. Some cybersecurity incidents will not be initially identified by log monitoring services because of limitations in the log files or of the monitoring service itself. However, once the adverse outcome is noted, log files can be more deeply inspected during root cause analysis. This would lead to identification of specific cybersecurity events traced to the adverse outcome, thus fully defining the full causal chain of events forming the cybersecurity incident. From this, new vulnerabilities and threats may be discovered.

An example would help illustrate this point. An MDM is contacted by law enforcement to inform them that a number of their patient records have landed up on the dark web, where a criminal is selling them to the highest bidder. The negative system consequence observed here is that data have been stolen from their clinic portal, and one can conclude a cybersecurity incident has taken place. After the investigation, a correlated set of cybersecurity events pulled from log files are presented as cybersecurity events that led to the cybersecurity incident.

- An attacker sends a malicious connection request with an attack payload. The connection request with the payload and source IP address is captured as a cybersecurity event in a log file.
- The attacker first exploits a vulnerability in an application running on the server. By doing so, the attacker is able to get their own code running with the privileges of the application code. This obviously is not captured as a log file event. Had it been a detectable event, then the system administrators would have been able to take action. The executing malware then downloads the attacker's own executable files onto the web server. This downloading, however, is captured as a cybersecurity event in the operating system logs of the server.
- The attacker's malware then tries to initiate connections to other computers on the network in order to check if they are running applications with known vulnerabilities. If it can detect that they are running vulnerable applications, the first two steps are repeated. These connection attempts are captured as cybersecurity events in the logs of the individual target machines.
- The attacker zips all files on the servers to which it gets access to and sends them to a server in a foreign country. The destination IP address is captured as part of a cybersecurity event recorded in the log as well as the total amount of data transferred during the connections.

Each of these log file entries, properly correlated, defines the full trace of the cybersecurity incident. Note how initially the cybersecurity incident was just the observed negative consequence, namely patient data being exfiltrated. However, on investigation, the definition of the cybersecurity incident is expanded to capture the "fingerprints" on the attack on the system, as captured in as cybersecurity events in various logs.

The following considerations should be addressed while writing down system and subsystem requirements for cybersecurity logging and monitoring [33,34].

1. What to capture as cybersecurity events: One of the challenges of designing cybersecurity logging is defining what cybersecurity events to record. Collect too much data as part of cybersecurity logging and you risk being overwhelmed with irrelevant information. Collect too little and you may miss critical cybersecurity events that constitute a cybersecurity incident. Every cybersecurity event should be captured with its timestamp and in a specified format. Here are some other things to consider while recording cybersecurity events as logs for any medical device.
   a. Any connection request accepted or denied: For all successful and denied connections, record the value of the source and destination identifiers (e.g., IP address or a wireless protocol identifier, ports of connection endpoints, or public keys or certificates provided to establish identity). For successful connections, record the duration of the connection and the amount of data transferred in a connection. For connections that are denied, record the reason for denial (e.g., an endpoint identifier is on a deny list of IP addresses, the endpoint identifier is making requests at too high a rate, the endpoint is presenting certificate signed with untrusted key or the provided certificate has expired or that the certificate provided was on a denied list)
   b. Authentication attempts: For all successful and denied application authentication attempts, record the login identifier provided, with a special annotation if the password provided was part of a leaked list (i.e., passwords that are known to have been compromised in credential breaches elsewhere—this happens when people use the same passwords across multiple sites). For denied authentication attempts, record reason for denial (wrong account password, wrong one-time password), etc. If a user wants their password reset, these requests should be recorded too. If account credentials are being provided at a rate that signifies use of automated methods, implying someone is trying to use a dictionary to cycle through passwords, then not only should the account be locked-out, but the event should be logged.
   c. Code downloads and loading and execution: Successful downloads of code should be recorded, as well as failed downloads of code with reasons of failure (e.g., cryptographic integrity check failed, either because the code was signed by an untrusted key or the key had expired, attempt to roll back the software version to a previous

one). Failure at boot time to verify cryptographically each stage of the boot process (i.e. secure boot failure), and attempt to execute code outside application "allow list" (also known as whitelist) should also be recorded.

2. How to package cybersecurity events: Another design concern is how to package cybersecurity events. Usually cybersecurity events are captured as entries in a log file. In some cases where monitoring is happening real time, log entries can be streamed to the monitoring server as they are generated. If cybersecurity events are to be captured in a file, one of the design decisions that need to be taken is specifying the size of the log files in terms of the maximum number of entries it can accommodate, before new cybersecurity events start overwriting the old. Given that many medical devices are nonconnected, the maximum sizes of log files have to be coordinated with the cadence at which the device is serviced by a service technician. If the log file sizes are too small compared to the cadence, there is a reasonable chance that many events would have been overwritten by the time a service technician reviewed the files.
3. How to transmit cybersecurity events: This part of the cybersecurity logging design specifies how cybersecurity events, captured as log entries, are transmitted to a central server. For nonconnected medical devices, this transmission protocol should be part of the service process, where the service technician physically extracts the log files, either through USB storage or through local wireless, to a laptop or phone connected to the public internet from where it is sent to the device manufacturer's servers. For connected devices, this transmission should be part of the device design, including the specification of the cadence in which log files are sent to the monitoring service—whether near real time, hourly, daily, or monthly.
4. How to protect cybersecurity events from attackers: An attacker would want to erase traces of their activities on a medical device, and this is why records of cybersecurity events as log files need to be protected from tampering. It is recommended practice that log files are signed by the private key of the system node that is generating the log file. Cybersecurity log files should always be transmitted over a secure, mutually authenticated session. Sometimes a cybersecurity event may have, within its data elements, confidential information, such as a patient identifier, and in such cases, the log files should be encrypted.
5. How to identity cybersecurity incidents from cybersecurity events (log monitoring): Cybersecurity log monitoring detects whether a cybersecurity compromise of the medical device has already happened or is imminent unless further actions are taken. Any cybersecurity log

monitoring workflow correlates cybersecurity events from multiple signal sources (network, OS, application, authentication, access control logs) and domain-specific knowledge of current threat landscape (e.g., known malicious IP addresses, compromised passwords, attack patterns, and signatures), passes them to their proprietary analytic algorithms, and presents the results in the form of warnings and alerts. It is then left to the human analyst in the monitoring function to take a call on whether they are looking at an actual cybersecurity incident or false alarms.

If this sounds difficult, it is. MDMs are not advised to develop their own cybersecurity monitoring solutions, as they are enterprise-level monitoring solutions, technically called Security Information and Event Management (SIEM) [35] tools that automate significant elements of this analysis. MDMs should focus their attention on ensuring that the cybersecurity logs from their devices contain the data these SIEM solutions require to take decisions, and are in a format that can be ingested by these tools.

Example requirements:

- The system shall record cybersecurity log events with a time-stamp
- The system shall protect the integrity of the cybersecurity log file by signing every log file entry
- The system shall ensure that once the cybersecurity log file maximum capacity has been reached, the cybersecurity log file should be sent to the monitoring server, and the cybersecurity log file cleared
- All cybersecurity log files shall be streamed to a cybersecurity monitoring service

Cybersecurity alerting

The system should notify system users in case of suspected cybersecurity incidents or cybersecurity-related events.

While cybersecurity log file monitoring is the definitive method for detecting cybersecurity incidents, some of the more egregious indicators of compromise can be immediately relayed to the user so that they may take immediate action. Examples of such egregious indicators of compromise may be failure of integrity check of the device during boot-up or a detected attempt to launch an executable that is not on the application allow list (also known as application whitelist). Other examples of cybersecurity alerts are notifications to users of system actions taken on the basis of suspected attacks: for example, shutting down a Bluetooth interface because of too many packets that failed integrity checks, or a code update being disallowed on the basis of a cryptographic signature verification failure.

Example requirements:
- The device shall alert the user in case of a boot-time integrity failure
- The device shall alert the user in case of an application failing cryptographic verification during launch
- The device shall alert the user if a code update failed cryptographic verification

Secure system specification and implementation

This process control is to ensure that cybersecurity features for medical devices are designed following cybersecurity best practices and taking into consideration constraints imposed on the system like battery life, memory space, clinical workflows, communication throughput, need to interoperate with third-party components, etc. The medical device of today can be any of a large number of system archetypes: an embedded device (e.g., infusion pump, implanted device, glucose monitoring device) with no operating system, an FPGA (Field Programmable Gate Array) a Linux or windows "box" (e.g., capital equipment like programmer, MRI machine, etc.), mobile apps running on commodity smartphones, applications running on a public cloud, or on on-premise data centers (e.g., clinical data analytics and reporting). Given this heterodoxy of platforms that constitute the typical device ecosystem of today, process objectives and guidelines for secure design of all of them are beyond this book.

However, one specific design aspect is called out for special attention in this section, because too often, the root cause of why medical devices have inadequate cybersecurity protections is because of the limitations of the underlying hardware. Hardware platform changes are expensive for MDMs because of device software reverification and revalidation costs. Unlike in the smart phone business, the hardware is not a selling feature for medical devices, clinical features are, and that is why hardware platform changes are rare. This makes it even more important that cybersecurity engineers communicate hardware platform requirements early in the project development phase when hardware changes are typically deliberated upon.

Hardware limitations for cybersecurity typically stem from the following:
- *Lack of Processor Power*: Here, the system hardware platform does not have the horsepower to do modern cryptographic operations or the memory space to store cryptographic code or both. While in many cases, a hardware upgrade to a modern platform would solve the problem, sometimes, the nature of the device makes hardware update simply not

possible. For example, ultralow-power implanted devices that have small form factors and have long battery lives, the risk reduction from cybersecurity threats due to a hardware upgrade cannot justify the overall risk increase due to more frequent explants/implants caused by the battery running out sooner, because of cryptographic operations.

- *Lack of a True Random Number Generator*:
  US NIST defines a random number in the following way [36]:

> *A value in a set of numbers that has an equal probability of being selected from the total population of possibilities and, in that sense, is unpredictable. A random number is an instance of an unbiased random variable, that is, the output produced by a uniformly distributed random process. Random numbers may, e.g., be obtained by converting suitable stings of random bits.*

The need for random numbers arises in many cryptographic applications. As an example, many cryptographic protocols require keys, nonces, and other algorithmic parameters to be generated in a random fashion.

Random numbers [37–39] can be generated in two different ways. One way of generating a random number is to produce a sequence of bits nondeterministically, where every bit is the output of a physical process that is unpredictable. Examples of such physical processes, technically called entropy sources, may be electrical circuit noise, mouse movement, or key strokes (i.e., their exact timing cannot be predicted a priori) or quantum effects in a semiconductor. True random numbers, in order to meet mathematical tests of "randomness," are often sourced from combinations of multiple sources of entropy. This kind of random bit generator is called RNG (Random Number Generator) or TRNG (True Random Number Generator).

The other way of generating random numbers is to compute bits deterministically using a software algorithm, called PRNG (Pseudo Random Number Generator). A PRNG produces a pseudorandom sequence of bits from an initial value that, in turn, is determined by a seed that is determined from the output of a RNG/TRNG. If the random seed is kept secret, and the algorithm is well designed, the bits output by the PRNG will be unpredictable enough for cryptographic applications. The catch here is that if an attacker gets to know the secret seed value or is able to guess it, then if they input this seed to the PRNG, they will get the exact same sequence of pseudo random numbers. In other words, they will always be able to guess the next key that will be generated.

- *Lack of Secure and Immutable Storage* In the absence of hardware secure storage (e.g., Trusted Platform Modules) or hardware immutable storage (e.g., One-Time Programmable fuses), private/secret shared keys/secret seed, and public keys/certificates have to be stored on persistent storage. While operating system controls provide some level of protection on persistent storage, the best practice is to keep these cryptographic key materials stored in specialized hardware.

Based on this, cybersecurity designers should ensure that hardware platforms chosen have sufficient CPU and memory to perform cryptographic operations, sufficient persistent storage space to store cryptographic code, have a mechanism for generating true random numbers, ideally by a certified on-board TRNG, and also have secure hardware elements for storing device secrets and immutable hardware elements for storing public keys/certificates that form the root of trust.

Secure coding guideline defines a set of general software security coding practices, in a checklist format, that can be integrated into the software development lifecycle. Following secure coding guidelines allows for code to be "secure by construction" by eliminating security "antipatterns," i.e., known mistakes that make implementations insecure. There are excellent secure coding guidelines available from OWASP [40,41] (these are language agnostic) and for different languages (C [42], C++ [43], Java [44]). The content of these secure coding guidelines should be integrated into an MDM's QMS, as appropriate.

Secure system verification and validation

Verification seeks to answer the following question: has the system been built right? Requirements-based testing is an example of verification. If a system satisfies its requirements, it has been built right, where what is "right" is defined by the requirements. Validation, though, asks a different question: has the right system been built? In the context of cybersecurity, validation is convincing oneself that the system is "secure." At the validation stage, we are not concerned so much with the requirements, the security design, or the secure process followed to design the system as we are to whether the system is free from vulnerabilities that may be exploited by an attacker.

Secure system verification

In order for secure system verification [45] or requirements-based testing [46], it follows that requirements have to be testable. A requirement is testable when tests can be developed that can exhibit success or failure, in an unambiguous manner (Fig. 7.2).

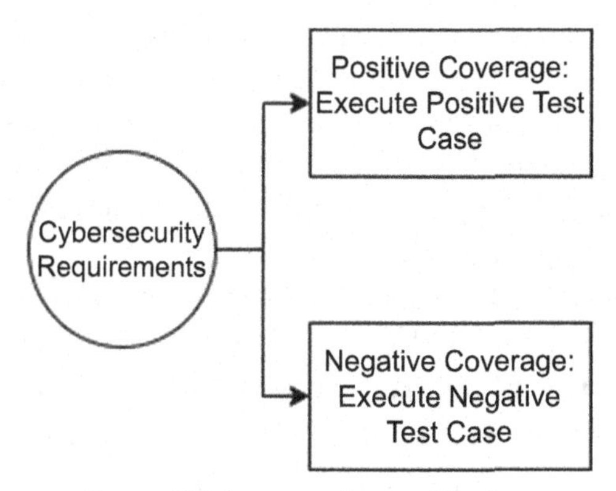

Figure 7.2 Secure system verification.

Testability for cybersecurity system and software requirements is determined by the abstraction level of the requirement: A system requirement of the sort "Data integrity at session layer is protected through cryptographic means," is not directly testable, because the requirement is not specified at the level of abstraction needed to directly test. This is not a problem in itself with regards to testability, as long as it is linked to lower level software requirements that have sufficient detail which allows testing, for example, "Data integrity at session layer is protected through AES GCM encryption mode" and "All cryptographic keys used should be 256 bit or above." These requirements, unlike its parent, can be tested, and have very clear definitions of passing and failing, evident from the statement of the requirements themselves. The parent system requirement "Data integrity at session layer is protected through cryptographic means" would be considered tested, when all requirements at a software level that link to it are tested.

Any comprehensive testing strategy for cybersecurity requirements needs to consider the following:

Positive coverage

The system requirement or software requirement being tested should be completely covered by the test cases that are associated with it. This means that all the behaviors that are covered by the requirement have to be tested. For example, if a requirement is deemed satisfied when a number of conditions linked by logical "OR" are satisfied. Tests should be planned to ensure that, at the very minimum, the behavior of the system is tested for each condition being individually true, while the rest are false.

Consider the requirement: "The system shall allow programming of parameters only if the user has a signed "clinician" or "administrator" role or if the emergency access mode is enabled." The presumption here is that a user can have either of these roles, but in the case of emergency access, the user does not have any role. In this case, test cases should be defined that cover the following behavior:

1. User has a signed "clinician" role but not "administrator" and no emergency access mode is enabled
2. User has a signed "administrator" role but not "clinician" and no emergency access mode is enabled
3. User has no signed "clinician" or "administrator" role but emergency access is enabled.

Negative coverage

Cybersecurity system and software requirements should each have negative test cases. In other words, we need to test behavior not just for when the requirement "passes" but for when it "fails," Using the example "The system shall allow programming of parameters only if the user has a signed "clinician" or "administrator" role or if the emergency access mode is enabled," negative test cases should cover the cases:

1. User has no signed "clinician" or "administrator" role and no emergency access is enabled.

In the above test case, the system is expected to disallow programming of parameters. As another example, if one is testing mutual authentication between two systems using third-party signed certificates, one has to test not only that the system accepts a valid signed certificate, but also that it rejects all other attempts to communicate. Negative test cases should cover the situations:

1. No certificate provided in request to connect
2. Certificate signed by an untrusted third party
3. Valid certificate that has expired

The goal of any good testing strategy would be to ensure that most test cases are executable, i.e., the requirements are tested using tests that exercise the operation of the system under test. Examples of nonexecutable test cases are tests that are exercised through code review or system inspection. While sometimes tests cannot be executable, for example, if the requirement is of the JTAG being sealed through epoxy, a visual inspection would be the best that can be done. However, far more requirements are often dispensed through "code review" than should be, and the reason for that is not technical, but managerial, too little time given for testing. For example, many cryptographic requirements like the use of a 256 bit key or specific algorithms are often tested through code inspection and the evidence provided to demonstrate that a certain key length is being used or that an API is being invoked using a specific algorithm is a screenshot of a line number in the code base. Ideally, these critical security behaviors should be tested by the use of a test oracle. A test oracle is an alternative implementation of the cryptographic algorithms being used in the system under test. The test oracle is provided inputs (e.g., same message or encrypted message) identical to those provided to the system under test. In order for the test to pass, the outputs of the test oracle should then match with those from the system under test. This strategy may seem like an overkill if one is using standard open-source cryptographic libraries like OpenSSL [47] or WolfSSL [48] without any modification. However, this strategy is advised when either one writes their own cryptographic implementations (a design decision that should be avoided except in extreme circumstances like when no cryptographic library has a port to the hardware platform of your device), or when functions are copy-pasted from standard cryptographic libraries like OpenSSL and integrated into the code base, usually to avoid carrying the "full weight" of cryptographic libraries in resource-constrained environments.

Secure system validation

In system verification, all testing is driven by the requirements with the objective being to prove that the system satisfies the requirements. Secure system validations [45] (Fig. 7.3), in contrast, are requirements agnostic practices and procedures that are performed in order to discover vulnerabilities and threats in code developed in-house and acquired from third parties.

Static analysis

In static analysis [49], the software subsystem is analyzed for vulnerabilities without executing the code. Static analysis takes files (source code or executables) as input and outputs potential issues. Static analysis results must be assessed by an analyst to determine whether the potential issues identified are actual vulnerabilities.

Under the hood, static analysis spans various methods [50] from sophisticated pattern matching (comparing code to patterns which indicate vulnerabilities [51]) to mathematical analysis [52] (i.e., creating control and data flow models and then mathematically simulating their run-time behavior). Static analysis essentially provides an expert programmer looking over your shoulder to identify potential issues, except there is a tool instead of a human.

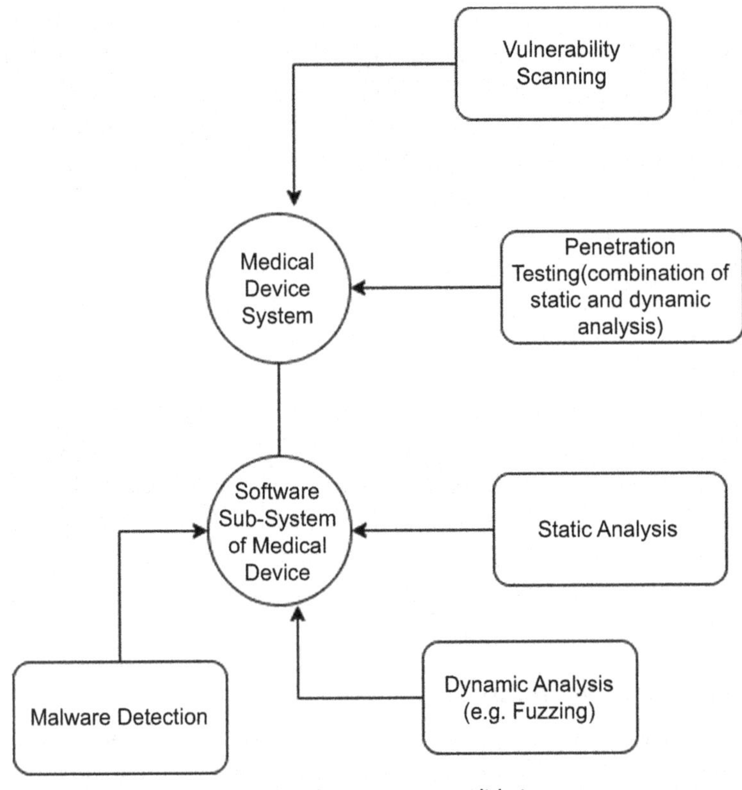

Figure 7.3 Secure system validation.

The biggest advantage of static analysis [53] is that it is highly scalable, capable of handling millions of lines of code efficiently. This is because of the very nature of the process, in that the software does not have to execute in order to do the analysis, so the size and complexity of the code base is not an issue when it comes to scalability. Because static analysis does not require the code to run, this technique finds weaknesses or issues even in code that is not yet complete or with undefined dependencies, i.e., a call to a function that has not been yet implemented. Static analysis tools integrated into the development environment are typically easy to use and detect flaws as they are introduced, providing instant feedback to developers. In addition, static analysis tools are generally very effective for detecting common vulnerabilities such as buffer overflows, SQL injection flaws, and hard-coded passwords [54].

Static analysis is not a silver bullet solution to vulnerability hunting though. There are many things it misses, like dependencies between systems created during run time, or configuration parameters set for systems outside code, in text files, for instance. There are many classes of weaknesses (e.g., authentication problems, insecurities in the program logic) that static analysis tools typically do not do a great job in finding because of the way they work. Aside from not being able to catch some vulnerabilities, static analysis is known to flag as "issues" those that in reality are not (false positives). This stems from some of the underlying analysis routines, which end up constructing an over approximation of the number of actual traces that are possible, leading to identification of issues on infeasible paths. Most of the frustration with static analysis tools stems from the profusion of false positives, requiring analysts to manually sift through thousands of "potential" vulnerabilities to find a few actual one. To this complaint, tool vendors respond that many of these false positives are contextual false positives, issues a general purpose static analysis tool can never find, because they are dependent on factors outside the domain of analysis (e.g., values of environment variables) [55]. The takeaway is that static analysis tools, no matter what the marketing material may say, never "point to the code base and outcome the vulnerabilities." There are multiple stages of configuration, tuning, and postanalysis manual triaging that need to be performed before actual vulnerabilities are identified. Despite this, static analysis remains one of the most comprehensive and scalable methods for vulnerability hunting, and is a must for any MDM developing systems using a secure development lifecycle. Since different static analysis tools work on different underlying theories and algorithms [56], it makes sense to run several static analysis tools and to focus first on issues identified by most of them.

In terms of cadence, static analysis tools should be run while code is being written, ideally within the development environment, then during nightly builds, and at the end of every software development phase [57]. The earlier vulnerabilities are caught, the easier they are to fix, which is why static analysis should be run as often as possible.

Dynamic analysis

Dynamic analysis, in contrast to static analysis, finds software vulnerabilities by executing the software under test [45]. Since issues identified by dynamic analysis result from actual system traces, what they identify is most likely to be an actual vulnerability. What dynamic analysis gains over static analysis in terms of precision though, it loses in terms of coverage. Just because no further vulnerabilities have been found after doing, say a week of dynamic testing, one cannot automatically conclude there are no vulnerabilities remaining; it could just as well be that the dynamic analysis conducted so far has not exercised all "insecure" behavior. While static analysis results from analysis of all possible paths, dynamic analysis exercises only certain paths through the code, and what those paths are, are determined by the inputs and the behavior of the system.

Fuzz testing [58–60] is a dynamic analysis technique where the system under test is subject to intentionally invalid input. The behavior of the system is then observed with respect to this malformed input—if the system crashes, or allows for privilege escalation (i.e., allows a principal a set of privileges they are normally not authorized to have), then these effects may be considered to be symptomatic of vulnerabilities. Fuzz testing simulates the modus operandi of an attacker, who is going to try all forms of input, providing values a developer would normally not consider normal (e.g., special characters like "~" or "!" in a text field that expects names), with the hope of triggering behavior that an attacker expects has not been observed during requirements-based product testing.

If one just randomly changes the input value between runs of fuzz testing, most of these values will likely be rejected by the input parser of the system under test before these inputs have had a chance to exercise potentially untested paths. For example, if the input logic for system under test requires data to be in a certain format (e.g., a network packet parser would expect a certain structure of the header, then payload, then the checksum computing a CRC, an integrity measure, on the header and payload), then a sophisticated fuzz testing tool would change the input between successive rounds of fuzzing while ensuring that the packet format was being satisfied every time. This includes the CRC being properly computed on the header and payload, such that the fuzzed data would be guaranteed to be accepted by the input parsing process after which it can then go and trigger executions within the system under test.

Vulnerability scanning [61] is another dynamic testing technique, but this focuses on network-level testing. A vulnerability scanning tool looks for insecure ports and services being advertised that have known vulnerabilities, providing a report of vulnerabilities it finds, together with remediation information. Vulnerability scanning is often confused with penetration testing (described later). While vulnerability scanning searches for known vulnerabilities and security policy violations, penetration tests are focused toward finding new vulnerabilities and threats.

Fuzz testing and vulnerability scanning should be executed as part of validation activities during system development. The earlier vulnerabilities are caught, the cheaper and easier they are to fix.

Both static and dynamic analysis are used by two specialized cybersecurity validation procedures that are well known in the cybersecurity community (and outside it too)—malware analysis and penetration testing.

Malware detection and analysis tools

Malware, or malicious software [31], are programs that are created by threat agents with the specific intent to compromise systems. Unlike developer-introduced unintentional errors in software that lead to vulnerabilities, malware is deliberately seeded by attackers with malignant intent, usually packaged together with genuine executables, variously manifested as viruses, worms, surveillance software (spyware) and ransomware (where the threat agent takes control of your data and demands money to be able to get access back to your data). Some malware have very targeted objectives. For instance Stuxnet [62] was designed to compromise very specific models of Supervisory Control and Data Acquisition systems. Many other malware are much more general purpose, to be used as part of a multistage attack strategy: first to establish a beachhead in the target's network, then download further malware, establish a remote command and control of resources in the victim's network, and go on to compromise other assets. General-purpose malware is now being packaged as tools and are sold being to cyber criminals using the model of "software-as-a-service," except now it is "malware-as-a-service," the Colonial Pipeline security breach [63] being an example of cyber criminals using "ransomware-as-a-service" to hold businesses to ransom by encrypting and exfiltrating their data.

Malware analysis tools take as their input, not source code, but executables, often obfuscated and encrypted by malware developers to escape detection [64]. Some malware tools focus exclusively on malware hunting. Provided an executable file as an input, these tools flag whether there is malware present in the file or not. Traditionally, malware detection tools have worked on the basis of comparing continuous sequences of bytes (called the signature) of a suspected malware file with the signatures of known malware files in their database. Signature-based malware detection works well on known malware, i.e., malware whose signatures are in the database, and fail mostly on totally novel, unknown malware or existing malware which has intentionally changed its sequence of bytes to prevent detection. The more modern approach to malware detection is signatureless algorithms, which use machine learning techniques in conjunction with execution of the file within a sandboxed environment to study behavior [65] and see if the behavior of the file falls within the known space of what is considered to be malignant behavior.

Some malware tools [66] focus more on analysis rather than detection, with the tool providing means of disassembling an executable (i.e., converting machine language back into a human-readable form), and facilities for stepping through the execution of the malware in order to observe its control and data flow.

Malware detection tools should be used by an MDM to prevent malware from being packaged within executables (e.g., to check that the USB stick with firmware update sent to their hospital customer does not also have ransomware on it) or from malware being installed on operating equipment they maintain (e.g., the server on which their patient portal runs or a manufacturing station). Malware analysis tools should be used to analyze executables sourced from high-risk suppliers to check that they do not contain malware and backdoors. Malware detection tools should also be run at a regular cadence on code repositories, on development and deployment endpoints (laptops, servers, etc.) and must be mandatorily run on the software before it is released to the public.

Penetration testing

A penetration test [67,68] is an authorized, simulated attack on a software system (in the context of this book, a medical device), with the tester using all methods a sophisticated attacker would be expected to have at their disposal to find vulnerabilities within the system.

The notion of what a "penetration test" is amorphous and ill defined, and just because there are no serious issues identified in a penetration test, does not necessarily mean there are no exploitable vulnerabilities. In order to have confidence in the results of a penetration test, one has to trust the basic hypothesis of a penetration test, namely that the penetration tester subjected the system to the kind of analysis that a sophisticated attacker would subject it to. A sophisticated attacker has a high level of skill, access to sophisticated software and hardware equipment, and, given that a successful attack will give them something of value, sufficient time and resources at hand. What, a skeptic may ask, is the guarantee that an internal or external penetration tester has the same level of skill, the same set of tools, the same time available, and the same level of dogged persistence?

In order to increase confidence in the comprehensiveness and coverage of a penetration test, the provider of the penetration test should supply as part of the report:

1. *The amount of time expended for the actual penetration testing:* A penetration test where the pen tester spent a day is likely (though of course not guaranteed) to be much more perfunctory analysis than one where the penetration tester spent two weeks.

2. *The certifications or qualifications of the penetration tester:* While much of penetration testing is based on automated tools and scripts, one cannot deny the "art" behind a good "pen test." An expert penetration tester, based on extensive experience and the intuition and insight this leads to, is more likely to hone in faster on to weak areas of the design than one who does not have that level of insight.
3. *Compliance to threat rubrics*: There are several threat rubrics available in the security community that capture vulnerability patterns and threat archetypes observed in the real world. Following one or more of these threat rubrics provide an assurance that the penetration tester is, to quote Isaac Newton, "standing on the shoulder of giants." If a penetration test report claims compliance to (and provides evidence if asked) a standard threat rubric, then one may be reasonably assured that standard vulnerabilities and threats have been covered as part of the penetration testing. Examples of publicly available threat rubrics include OWASP Top 10 [69], MITRE's ATT&CK framework [70], and OWASP Application Security Verification Standard [71]. The Application Security Verification Standards is specifically focused on penetration testing, clearly delineating the kinds of vulnerabilities that can be found using only dynamic testing, those that require static analysis, and those that require interviews with development teams and document review.
4. *A full enumeration of all dynamic and static analysis tools used*: The penetration test report should provide a list of all tools used and also mention whether the penetration tester developed their own scripts. It should also mention whether only malware detection tools were used or whether the penetration tester also used malware analysis tools, as a method to dive deep into the way the executables were structured.
5. *A full enumeration of penetration testing strategies and tactics*: For example, did the penetration tester try to breach the manufacturer's organization, targeting its employees through spear phishing, in order to get access to the kind of "low hanging fruit" that a sophisticated attacker would definitely try to get a hold of? Did the penetration tester physically disassemble the device under test and try breaking in through internal ports and interfaces? Or did they just confine the scope of the testing only to external software interfaces?
6. *The rules of engagement for a penetration test*: There is a school of thought that says a penetration test should be a perfect black box test, the penetration tester should be provided the system, just as it would appear to any nonprivileged user, with no additional information provided, no source code, no design documents, and no privileged access provided

(for instance, the tester is not provided an account on the system or access to an internal network as a staging ground for attacks). Those who belong to this school of thought justify this very limited set of information being provided, as the only way one can ensure the validity of the hypothesis of a pen test, namely that the penetration tester is a surrogate for an actual attacker.

Others disagree.

From OWASP Application Security Verification Standard 4.0 [71]:

Malicious attackers have a great deal of time, most penetration tests are over within a couple of weeks. Defenders need to build in security controls, protect, find and resolve all weaknesses, and detect and respond to malicious actors in a reasonable time. Malicious actors have essentially infinite time and only require a single porous defense, a single weakness, or missing detection to succeed. Black box testing, often performed at the end of development, quickly, or not at all, is completely unable to cope with that asymmetry.

Over the last 30+ years, black box testing has proven over and over again to miss critical security issues that led directly to ever more massive breaches.

This is a valid criticism of the full black box approach. While in an ideal world one would provide a black box to the penetration tester in order to be true to the hypothesis, given that a penetration tester is unlikely to have the same amount of time and resources and skill as a highly sophisticated attacker, perhaps sponsored by the resources of a nation state, it is essential to level the field somewhat by providing the penetration tester a higher level of access to the system under test. An actual attacker can be a disgruntled insider, so it makes sense to provide the penetration tester with all product documentation, requirements, design and code, so that they may acquire the knowledge of an insider. An actual attacker may obtain credentials of a nonprivileged account through various means, or get access to an internal network, and this is precisely why nonprivileged accounts and corporate network access should be provided to the penetration tester, so that their testing may more closely simulate that of a sophisticated attacker.

Whatever school of thought one belongs to, it is imperative that the scope of a penetration test is clearly defined in a penetration test report, based on which the reviewer can properly calibrate the confidence they want to place in the results of the test.

As to cadence, a penetration test should be done before every major product release (i.e., a release with a major version change) and ideally, every year, and each time, by a different penetration testing vendor. This makes it more likely that different penetration testing techniques, different tools, and different scripts are used from year to year, raising confidence in the coverage of the penetration tests.

Labeling for security

The objective of the procedural control of cybersecurity labeling is to inform device users, be patients and caregivers, or those who provision devices, like HDO Information Technology engineers, about steps they need to do to ensure secure operation of the device. Security of a medical device is a joint responsibility of MDMs, users, and HDOs. The design of the device is however the exclusive responsibility of the MDM. As the owner of the design, it is imperative for an MDM to clearly and unambiguously explain to its user community their responsibilities in keeping the device secure—be it in configuring certain features (e.g., setting up Wi-Fi in a secure way) or general security hygiene (e.g., keep the operating system of the smart phone on which this medical app is installed updated to the latest version, securely store the device in a locked cabinet when not in use).

It should be remembered that, during cybersecurity risk management, the MDM should always consider that responsibilities conveyed through labeling are likely not to be followed. Devices are likely to lie around unattended in physically insecure locations, operating systems are not likely to be patched quickly, Wi-Fi networks at the HDO may not require authentication, or even if they do, the Wi-Fi password may be widely known. That is why technical controls that are communicated to the user using through labeling and cannot be enforced through design should not be treated as primary risk mitigations. For example, recommending the user change the default password the device is shipped with before use is a secondary control, at best. However, in a device where the design enforces a password change before use, this can now be used as a primary control. "Forcing" the user to *do the right thing*, in terms of cybersecurity, should be evaluated for overall system risk. For example, consider that you have a medical app running on a smart phone. You take a design decision to check the version of the smart phone OS installed and restrict service until the user updates their phone's OS. You may be reducing risk due to cybersecurity causes, but increasing risk of the patient simply not availing of the medical device. The better (i.e., less overall risky) option in this case might be to convey to the user, through labeling, the need to keep their operating system to the latest version, and flashing an alert to the user if an update of the smart phone OS is essential without actually stopping the app from working on older phone OS versions.

Besides the "here is what you need to do in order to keep the device secure" component of labeling, MDMs should provide in the Instructions for Use, essential information about the cybersecurity design of the design. As cybersecurity of medical devices stays in the headlines, users are rightfully concerned about the cybersecurity posture of the medical device they are entrusting their lives or the lives of their loved ones to. In this context, the cybersecurity "Instructions for Use" should contain some basic information, at a level of detail appropriate for the general user, about how the device is kept secure.

For HDOs, a greater level of detail needs to be provided in comparison to what is there in the IFU, as the details feed the HDO risk management decisions, and by extension their purchasing and maintenance decisions.

Two items that are typically asked for by HDOs are the following:

- The CBOM (Cybersecurity Bill of Materials). By knowing the third-party software and hardware assets on the medical device, the HDO can perform their own vulnerability management activities on the medical device.
- The Manufacture Disclosure Statement for Medical Device Security [72], also known as the MDS2 form. Consisting of a series of questions that are driven by IEC TR 80001-2-2:2012, NIST SP 800-53 Rev. 4, and ISO 27002:2013, the MDS2 form is a standard way of eliciting the overall cybersecurity posture of a medical device, to a level of detail required by HDOs for their own risk management activities.

Several regulatory authorities, like the Food and Drug Administration [73] and the European Union [74], now provide detailed guidance on what information needs to be provided by an MDM as part of cybersecurity labeling. These specific requirements should be made part of the cybersecurity procedural control. Since this is a part of the Quality Management System, evidence of compliance to the procedural control must be maintained. This is typically done by linking each labeling requirement to specific page and line numbers in the IFU where the text/diagrams that comply with those regulatory requirements reside.

Summary and key takeaways

1. An MDM should maintain, as part of its product design capabilities, a product-agnostic set of technical cybersecurity controls, with each control traced to regulatory and standards requirements (Table 7.2). These should be used to drive early product design decisions (e.g., choice of hardware and overall system architecture) and should be used to derive product-specific design input (system and subsystem requirements).

Table 7.2 Master set of technical cybersecurity controls.

System authentication: Before establishing a connection, the system shall authenticate the unique cryptographic identity of the other party in a communication and shall not allow an establishment of a connection if the cryptographic identity cannot be verified.

User authentication: Before allowing access, each system shall verify the credentials of all human users and deny access in case the credentials provided are not valid

Secure updates: Before installing any code update, the system shall verify the authenticity of the code using cryptographic signature verification.

Session integrity and confidentiality: After a communication session is established between two systems, all data that are exchanged shall be protected from tampering and unauthorized disclosure through cryptographic means of integrity and confidentiality protection.

Session management: Each session should time-out after a period of no activity or on an explicit session termination action

Data integrity and confidentiality in motion: Critical data shall be cryptographically protected end to end from unauthorized tampering. PHI shall be cryptographically protected from end to end from unauthorized disclosure

Data integrity at rest: The integrity of all critical data stored on persistent storage (code, data files that influence code execution, and clinical data) shall be protected by cryptographic means.

Data confidentiality at rest: Data at rest, i.e., data when stored on persistent storage, should be protected from unauthorized disclosure by cryptographic means.

Code and data authenticity during execution: Code and data integrity in memory should be maintained.

Key and credentials management: Credentials (user secrets like passwords) and keys (private keys, associated public keys, shared secret keys) should be changed periodically, or on credentials compromise.

Key and credentials strength: Keys (private keys, shared secret keys), credentials (passwords), and other cryptographic material (e.g., initialization vector for certain cryptographic algorithms) should meet length/security strength recommendations of the National Institute of standards and Technology (NIST) or equivalent standards body. Deprecated encryption schemes and key lengths, where deprecation is defined by standards bodies like NIST, should not be used. Any default device password, if used, must be changed before the device is deployed

Keys and credentials secure storage: Keys and credentials shall be stored securely in a way such that private/shared symmetric keys are protected from unauthorized reading and public keys are protected from unauthorized modification.

(Continued)

Table 7.2 Master set of technical cybersecurity controls.—cont'd

Role-based authorization and access control: A documented role-based authorization model should specify (1) how users are mapped to roles and (2) mapping of roles to privileges. The principle of least privilege should be followed while determining these mappings. Once authentication is successfully performed, access to privileged operations, as defined in the role-based authorization model, should be enforced through cryptographic means. No authenticated entity should be allowed to perform an action they are not authorized to perform.

Emergency access: Devices interfaces where loss of immediate access is associated with patient safety risk should provide for an emergency access mechanism that allows for user authentication to be bypassed in emergency scenarios.

Restrict access: The system should follow principle of least privilege by shutting down ports and services not being used, removing user accounts at the operating system (i.e., accounts that can be logged into), and removing/restricting access to hardware debug interfaces like JTAG (joint test action Group). The use of physical locks and tamper evident seals should be considered.

Denial of service protection: The system should be designed to defend against malicious attempts to use up system resources like battery life, network bandwidth, and computational and storage responses. Anomalous consumption of system resources should be detected, followed by the throttling of further attempts to take up system resources.

Code updatability: The system should be designed to allow secure code updates.

Secure configuration: If the system allows users to configure security parameters, the system should be shipped in a secure configuration (i.e., all configurable parameters set to secure settings) and the user should be educated through labeling and documentation about the need to maintain a secure configuration.

Cybersecurity logging and monitoring: The system shall record cybersecurity events. The event shall be captured using a standard schema, with an associated timestamp, so that it can be automatically analyzed. The system should monitor cybersecurity logs and other operational signals (e.g., crashes, connection drops) in order to detect cybersecurity incidents.

Cybersecurity alerting: The system should notify system users in case of suspected cybersecurity incidents or cybersecurity-related events.

---

2. Cybersecurity requirements at system and subsystem level should be written to make them testable. The system should be subject to requirements-based (verification) and requirements-agnostic (validation) testing. Requirements-based testing should ensure coverage of positive (i.e., the condition of the requirements is met and the requirement passes) and negative (i.e., one or more conditions of the requirement are not met and the requirement fails) tests. Requirements-agnostic testing consists of vulnerability scanning and penetration testing, all of which are

conducted using a combination of static (where the analysis works by parsing source code or executable code) and executable (where the analysis works by executing the code) analysis techniques.

3. Cybersecurity is a shared responsibility between the MDM, the HDO, patient, and clinicians. Cybersecurity labeling clearly lays out specific "action items" that users, be they HDO IT engineers or clinicians or patients, must do to ensure the device is operated securely. Cybersecurity labeling is also used to convey general security information to the concerned user and more detailed information to HDOs for their own cybersecurity risk management activities.

References

[1] S. Wu, R. Sabett, S. Chokhani, W. Ford, C. Merrill, Internet X.509 Public Key Infrastructure Certificate Policy and Certification Practices Framework, 2003.

[2] US National Institute of Standards and Technologies, NIST Special Publication 800-131A: Transitioning the Use of Cryptographic Algorithms and Key Lengths, 2019.

[3] US National Institute of Standards and Technologies, NIST Special Publication 800-57 Part 1 Recommendation for Key Management, 2020.

[4] D. Johnson, A. Menezes, The Elliptic Curve Digital Signature Algorithm, ECDSA), 1999.

[5] S. Boeyen, S. Santesson, T. Polk, R. Housley, S. Farrell, D. Cooper, RFC 5280: Internet X.509 Public Key Infrastructure Certificate and Certificate Revocation List (CRL) Profile, 2008.

[6] US National Institute of Standards and Technologies, NIST Special Publication 800-63-3: Digital Identity Guidelines, 2020.

[7] US National Institute of Standards and Technologies, NIST Special Publication 800-63A Digital Identity Guidelines: Enrollment and Identity Proofing, 2020.

[8] US National Institute of Standards and Technologies, NIST Special Publication 800-63B: Digital Identity Guidelines Authentication and Lifecycle Management, 2020.

[9] US National Institute of Standards and Technologies, NIST Special Publication 800-63C Digital Identity Guidelines: Federation and Assertions, 2020.

[10] US National Instiute of Standards and Technologies, White Paper: Security Considerations for Code Signing, 2018.

[11] E. Rescorla, RFC 8446: The Transport Layer Security (TLS) Protocol Version 1.3, 2018.

[12] Bluetooth Special Interest Group (SIG), Bluetooth Specifications, n.d. [Online]. Available: https://www.bluetooth.com/specifications/specs/. (Accessed 22 May 2021).

[13] US National Institute of Standards and Technologies, NIST Special Publication 800-193 Platform Firmware Resiliency, 2018.

[14] US National Institute of Standards and Technologies, NIST Special Publication 800-167 Guide to Application Whitelisting, 2015.

[15] US National Institute of Standards and Technologies, NIST Special Publication 800-111 Guide to Storage Encryption Technologies for End User Devices, 2007.

[16] International Organization for Standardization, ISO/IEC 11889-1:2015 Information Technology — Trusted Platform Module Library — Part 1: Architecture, 2015.

[17] E. Pilyankevich, Application Level Encryption for Software Architects, December 18, 2020 [Online]. Available: https://www.infoq.com/articles/ale-software-architects/. (Accessed 5 May 2021).
[18] J. Attridge, An Overview of Hardware Security Modules, 2002 [Online]. Available: https://www.sans.org/reading-room/whitepapers/vpns/overview-hardware-security-modules-757. (Accessed 22 May 2021).
[19] US National Institute of Standards and Technologies, NIST Special Publication 800-145 the NIST Definition of Cloud Computing, 2011.
[20] The Open Web Application Security Project (OWASP), Pinning Cheat Sheet, n.d. [Online]. Available: https://cheatsheetseries.owasp.org/cheatsheets/Pinning_Cheat_Sheet.html.
[21] H.-W. Huang, Embedded System Design with C805, Cengage Learning, 2008.
[22] G. Farden, RBAC in Unix Administration, 1999.
[23] Microsoft, Role-based Access Control, June 8, 2020 [Online]. Available: https://docs.microsoft.com/en-us/windows-server/networking/technologies/ipam/role-based-access-control. (Accessed 22 May 2021).
[24] D. Ferriaolo, D. Kuhn, Role based access control, in: 15th National Computer Security Conference, 1992.
[25] D. Hardt, RFC 6749 the OAuth 2.0 Authorization Framework, 2012.
[26] IEEE Standards Association, IEEE 1149.1-2013 - IEEE Standard for Test Access Port and Boundary-Scan Architecture, 2013.
[27] US National Institute of Standards and Technologies, NIST Special Publication 800-189 Resilient Interdomain Traffic Exchange: BGP Security and DDoS Mitigation, 2019.
[28] v.L. Ahn, M. Blum, N. Hopper, J. Langford, CAPTCHA: using hard AI problems for security, in: International Conference on the Theory and Applications of Cryptographic Techniques, 2003.
[29] Apple, Apple App Store, n.d. [Online]. Available: https://www.apple.com/app-store/. (Accessed 22 May 2021).
[30] Google, Google Play Store, n.d. [Online]. Available: https://play.google.com/store. (Accessed 22 May 2021).
[31] US National Institute of Standards and Technologies, Security and Privacy Controls for Information Systems and Organizations SP 800-53, 2020.
[32] US National Institute of Standards and Technologies, NISTIR 5153 Minimum Security Requirements for Multi-User Operating Systems, 1993.
[33] US National Institute of Standards and Technologies, NIST Special Publication 800-92 Guide to Computer Security Log Management, 2006.
[34] US National Institute of Standards and Technologies, NIST Special Publication 800-94 Guide to Intrusion Detection and Prevention Systems, 2012.
[35] US National Institute of Standards and Technologies, NIST Special Publication 800-128 Guide for Security-Focused Configuration Management of Information Systems, 2011.
[36] US National Institute of Standards and Technologies, NIST Special Publication 800-107 Recommendation for Applications Using Approved Hash Algorithms, 2012.
[37] US National Institute of Standards and Technologies, NIST Special Publication 800-90A Recommendation for Random Number Generation Using Deterministic Random Bit Generators, 2015.
[38] US National Institute of Standards and Technologies, NIST Special Publication 800-90B Recommendation for the Entropy Sources Used for Random Bit Generation, 2018.
[39] US National Institute of Standards and Technologies, NIST Special Publication 800-90C Recommendation for Random Bit Generator (RBG) Constructions, 2016.

[40] The Open Web Application Security Project, OWASP Secure Coding Practices Quick Reference Guide, 2010.
[41] The Open Web Application Security Project, Code Review Guide, 2017.
[42] Software Engineering Institute, SEI CERT C Coding Standard: Rules for Developing Safe, Reliable, and Secure Systems, 2016.
[43] Software Engineering Institute, SEI CERT C++ Coding Standard: Rules for Developing Safe, Reliable, and Secure Systems, 2017.
[44] F. Long, D. Mohindra, R. Seacord, D. Sutherland, D. Svobobda, The CERT Oracle Secure Coding Standard for Java, Addison-Wesley Professional, 2011.
[45] The Open Web Application Security Project, OWASP Testing Guide, 2008.
[46] G. Mogyorodi, Requirements-based testing: an overview, in: 39th International Conference and Exhibition on Technology of Object-Oriented Languages and Systems.TOOLS, 2001.
[47] Open SSL, n.d. [Online]. Available: https://www.openssl.org/.
[48] Wolf SSL, n.d. [Online]. Available: https://www.wolfssl.com/.
[49] US National Institute of Standards and Technologies, NIST Special Publication 500-326 SATE V Report: Ten Years of Static Analysis Tool Expositions, 2018.
[50] S. Johnson, Lint: A C Program Checker, 1978.
[51] N. Ayewah, W. Pugh, D. Hovemeyer, J.D. Morgenthaler, J. Penix, Using static analysis to find bugs, IEEE Software 25 (5) (2008) 22–29.
[52] D. Beyer, T. Henzinger, R. Jhala, R. Majumdar, The software model checker BLAST, Int. J. Software Tool. Technol. Tran. 9 (2007) 505–525.
[53] Synopsys, Coverity Static Analysis Data Sheet, n.d.
[54] D. Baca, K. Petersen, B. Carlsson, L. Lundberg, Static code analysis to detect software security vulnerabilities - does experience matter?, in: International Conference on Availability, Reliability and Security, 2009.
[55] J. Späth, The Myth of False Positives in Static Application Security Testing, October 20, 2020 [Online]. Available: https://dev.to/johspaeth/the-myth-of-false-positives-in-static-application-security-testing-146g. (Accessed 23 May 2021).
[56] US National Institute of Standards and Technologies, Source Code Security Analyzers, n.d. [Online]. Available: https://www.nist.gov/itl/ssd/software-quality-group/source-code-security-analyzers. (Accessed 23 May 2021).
[57] The Open Web Application Security Project, Source Code Analysis Tools, n.d. [Online]. Available: https://owasp.org/www-community/Source_Code_Analysis_Tools.
[58] The Open Web Application Security Project, Fuzzing, n.d. [Online]. Available: https://owasp.org/www-community/Fuzzing.
[59] B. Miller, M. Zhang, E. Heymann, The relevance of classic fuzz testing:have we solved this one? IEEE Trans. Software Eng. (2021).
[60] M. Felderer, M. Büchler, M. Johns, A.D. Brucker, R. Breau, A. Pretschner, Chapter one - security testing: a survey, Adv. Comput. 101 (2016) 1–51.
[61] US National Institute of Standards and Technologies, NIST Special Publication 800-115 Technical Guide to Information Security Testing and Assessment, 2008.
[62] K. Zetter, An Unprecedented Look at Stuxnet, the World's First Digital Weapon, 2014 [Online]. Available: https://www.wired.com/2014/11/countdown-to-zero-day-stuxnet/.
[63] ZDNet, Colonial Pipeline Attack: Everything You Need to Know, May 13, 2021 [Online]. Available: https://www.zdnet.com/article/colonial-pipeline-ransomware-attack-everything-you-need-to-know/.
[64] N. Idika, A. Mathur, A Survey of Malware Detection Techniques, 2007.
[65] M. Christodorescu, Dissertation: Behavior-Based Malware Detection, 2007.
[66] C. Eagle, The IDA PRO Book, 2011.

[67] W. Allsopp, Advanced Penetration Testing: Hacking the World's Most Secure Networks, Wiley, 2017.
[68] P. Engebretson, The Basics of Hacking and Penetration Testing: Ethical Hacking and Penetration Testing Made Easy, Syngress, 2015.
[69] The Open Web Application Security Project, OWASP Top 10, 2021 [Online]. Available: https://owasp.org/www-project-top-ten/.
[70] MITRE, ATT&CK, n.d. [Online]. Available: https://attack.mitre.org/. (Accessed 23 May 2021).
[71] The Open Web Application Security Project, Application Security Verification Standard, 2020.
[72] ANSI/NEMA, Manufacturer Disclosure Statement for Medical Device Security, 2019 [Online]. Available: https://www.nema.org/standards/view/manufacturer-disclosure-statement-for-medical-device-security.
[73] US Food and Drug Administration, Content of Premarket Submissions for Management of Cybersecurity in Medical Devices (Draft Version), November 2018 [Online]. Available: https://www.fda.gov/regulatory-information/search-fda-guidance-documents/content-premarket-submissions-management-cybersecurity-medical-devices. (Accessed 1 September 2020).
[74] Medical Device Coordination Group Document, MDCG 2019-16 Guidance on Cybersecurity for Medical Devices, 2019 [Online]. Available: https://ec.europa.eu/docsroom/documents/41863. (Accessed 1 September 2020).

CHAPTER EIGHT

Supply chain cybersecurity risk management, secure product development, secure manufacture, vulnerability management, and cybersecurity training

Introduction

Table 4.2 of Chapter 4 defines a set of capabilities that a Product Cybersecurity Organization for a Medical Device Manufacturer (MDM) should develop and maintain. In this chapter, the focus will be on five of those capabilities, as identified in Table 8.1.

Product supply chain risk management

The cybersecurity supply chain risk management capability [1] ensures that components procured from third-party suppliers do not have intentionally or unintentionally seeded vulnerabilities.

Why is supply chain cybersecurity risk management so critical for those in the healthcare industry? Here is a quote from the ICT Supply Chain Risk Management Fact Sheet published by the US Department of Homeland Security (DHS) [2].

> *Supply chain risk is amplified by adversaries' attempts to exploit ICT (Information and Communication) technologies and their related supply chains for purposes of espionage, sabotage, and foreign interference activity. Vulnerabilities in supply chains—either developed intentionally for malicious intent or unintentionally through poor security practices—can enable data and intellectual property theft, loss of confidence in the integrity of the system, or exploitation to cause system or network failure.*

Over the past few years, cyber warfare has become a new battlefront between competing nation states. Nation states that are using cyber warfare as

Cybersecurity for Connected Medical Devices
ISBN: 978-0-12-818262-8
https://doi.org/10.1016/B978-0-12-818262-8.00001-2

Table 8.1 Cybersecurity capabilities.

Capability	Definition	Procedural controls
Product supply chain cybersecurity risk management	• Supply chain risk modeling sourced from third-party suppliers as well of contract manufacturing (third-party manufacturing products on contract from the medical device company)	Product supply chain cybersecurity risk modeling
Secure product development	• Ensuring that the development environment for device software and hardware is secure • Securing the storage where cryptographic signing keys (e.g., Hardware security modules) are stored and of verifying the security technical controls that protect the storage	Secure development
Secure manufacture	• Ensuring that the manufacturing facilities are secure	Secure manufacture
Vulnerability management	• Continuous monitoring of external and internal signals for product vulnerabilities • Assessing risk of product vulnerability using Cybersecurity Risk Management for Medical Devices capability • Root cause analysis of vulnerabilities discovered on products which includes integration with a manufacturer's complaint handling and CAPA (Corrective and Preventive Action) quality processes • Cybersecurity patching • Communicating with external stakeholders regarding vulnerabilities	Vulnerability monitoring, cybersecurity patch management,
Cybersecurity training	• Training entire organization on cybersecurity concepts, as well as for training employees with respect to their roles and responsibilities	Cybersecurity training

part of their offensive arsenal have invested a lot of effort in compromising global supply chains—either by clandestine ownership of the companies that make critical components or by infiltrating established corporations and tampering with products during development and manufacture. The specific tactics used by nation states to compromise supply chains consist of implanting backdoors and surveillance elements in hardware [3] and by breaking into software delivery systems of component suppliers and then sending malicious software updates to their customers [4–7].

Global supply chains are intricate and complex. Third-party suppliers often source subcomponents from fourth-party suppliers and so on. MDMs are typically only aware of their own third-party suppliers, not the full chain. However, any compromise anywhere in the chain makes the MDM vulnerable. MDMs have historically had processes for ensuring quality of procured components, but these quality inspections are scoped on ensuring that the product complies with supplier specifications. A cybersecurity vulnerability inserted in a component is an off-specification feature, and is unlikely to be caught by traditional inspection methods.

The scope of supply chain cybersecurity risk management is not just limited to components that are part of the device build but also includes components that are part of the development infrastructure. For example software development and manufacturing environments, as well components used in servicing and maintenance environments, should all be assessed for supply chain cybersecurity risk.

An added source of supply chain cybersecurity risk is when services, as opposed to components, are procured from third parties. As an example, many MDMs do not manufacture their products themselves but contract out the manufacturing to outside contractors. The manufacturing infrastructure at the contractor facilities is not in their direct control, and there may be vulnerabilities that are being seeded into their products at the manufacturing site, that their end of line independent quality check is just not equipped to catch. As another example, cloud service companies are increasingly being used to host medical devices "in the cloud." Here, third parties provide standard tiered services (e.g., infrastructure-as-a-service, platform-as-a-service, or software-as-service) with defined cybersecurity responsibilities for the cloud vendor and the MDM, per service tier.

Product supply chain cybersecurity risk modeling (Fig. 8.1)

Create inventory of assets

The first step in modeling cybersecurity risk of the supply chain is to have a comprehensive inventory of third-party electromechanical systems,

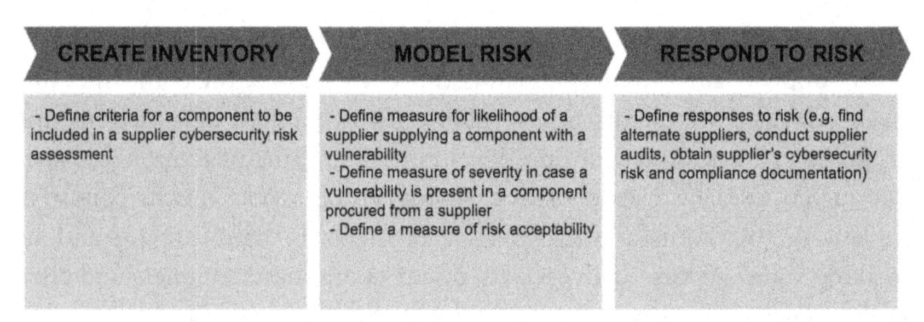

Figure 8.1 Product supply chain cybersecurity risk modeling.

software, and services that may be deemed to have potential impact to patient safety and privacy. The "potential impact" is important in order to scope the asset inventory—otherwise, pretty much all enterprise software and hardware assets would enter this list. While, in cybersecurity, there is never any harm in doing "more," since the focus of the book is workable solutions (i.e., solutions that can be implemented within realistic limits of cost and time), caution is urged in scoping the asset inventory for third-party cybersecurity risk management. If they are not careful, an organization may well bite off more than they can chew.

As an example, consider a design tool from a third-party vendor that is used as a Content Management System (CMS) for things like design requirements, risk assessments, design documents, verification reports, etc. Should this tool be added to the inventory of third-party assets for product supplier cybersecurity risk management? One may argue that this tool does have a potential link to patient safety. For instance, an attacker within the third-party vendor may have seeded a vulnerability such that the designs stored within the tool are changed by the tool itself in a malignant way. This is the problem with the word "potential." If any link, no matter how tenuous, exists, one can claim a "potential impact." In practice, it is highly unlikely that a change to a product design within a CMS would not be caught by the myriad design reviews and verification and validation that are conducted on the output of the CMS as part of the MDM's quality processes. Hence, it may reasonably be left out of this inventory of assets for product supplier cybersecurity risk management.

It is not that this CMS poses no or little cybersecurity risk to the MDM's business. It does. What is more likely than designs being "altered" silently within the CMS is that a vulnerability within the tool leads to exfiltration of proprietary designs to a nation state that has infiltrated the vendor from whom the design tool was procured. Thus, this tool needs to be under cybersecurity risk management, but *for risk in the domain of business risk.* This book is scoped on patient safety and privacy, which is the primary focus of regulatory authorities and device users, and hence, when we are doing an asset inventory for third-party cybersecurity risk management, tools like this may be kept out of scope.

Because of the often tenuous argumentation chains that are used to establish "potential" impact to patient safety, the focus should be on direct safety/privacy impact to the product. By direct, I mean that the third-party component should be one hop away from the medical device: either a component that is used for the development of the device's hardware/software, or for its manufacture, or an infrastructure component/service that is used during its operation. It's not that "indirect" impact should not be considered, but given that any realistic engineering effort requires establishment of priorities based on a conception of risk, the focus should be on the directness of impact. Specifically, the following criteria should be considered in creating this inventory of assets:

- Third-party components that are part of the device build (this list is obtained from the Cybersecurity Bill of Materials (CBOM))
- Third-party supplied development, build, and deployments tools for device hardware and software
- Third-party supplied hardware and software that are part of the manufacture of the medical device (i.e., hardware and software deployed on the manufacturing floor)
- Third-party supplied infrastructure services like cloud hosting
- Third-party network management and monitoring services for development and manufacturing networks and cybersecurity monitoring services for development and manufacturing networks

Model cybersecurity risk from third-party components

Wait, did not we already model cybersecurity risk to subsystems (software and hardware) in Chapters 5 and 6? Yes we did, but here we are assessing the risk of something else. Let us look at the difference. In subsystem risk modeling (Chapters 5 and 6), we are trying to assess the risk to patient safety/privacy from an actual vulnerability in the software and hardware subsystem. For product cybersecurity risk from third-party components, we are trying to assess the risk of an unknown vulnerability being present in a third-party component. We do not know, during the risk assessment of a supply chain component, what this vulnerability is. If we did, it would be assessed as a subsystem vulnerability—threat combination following the risk modeling approach outlined in Chapters 5 and 6. This is why CVSS scores cannot be used in the way it is used for subsystem risk modeling for modeling cybersecurity risk from third-party components.

A new metric of risk is thus needed for cybersecurity risk posed to the device by third-party supply chain components. Any such metric of cybersecurity risk should capture two things—(1) the severity of impact of a threat in case there is a vulnerability present in the component procured from a third party and (2) the likelihood of such a vulnerability being present in the component.

Since we do not know what exactly the vulnerability will be, the best we can do is to estimate severity of a potential vulnerability. One way of doing this is by characterizing the purpose the third-party component serves in terms of a metric, namely "criticality." Higher the criticality, higher the potential impact of a vulnerability present in the third-party component.

In Table 8.2, a simple bilevel scale is defined for Criticality. A component is likely to be critical for patient safety and privacy if it is on the medical device. This implies that all third-party components in the device CBOM, regardless of function, have a high criticality. Third-party components that perform security services should have a high criticality. This is because a vulnerability in the security posture of the device and its supporting infrastructure will likely have severe consequences. Examples of security services are authentication and authorization services (e.g., authentication libraries, domain controllers), access control services (e.g., firewall appliances and software implementing network-level controls like network isolation), secure

Table 8.2 Criticality of a third-party component.

Criticality	Criteria
High	Third-party component satisfies one of the following criteria: **1.** It is part of the medical device software build or is a hardware component of the device. **2.** It is responsible for implementing communication protocols (e.g., Bluetooth, wi-fi controller) or is responsible for security operations (e.g., authentication and authorization, secure key storage, log generation or monitoring, providing updates). **3.** It is part of the development, build, and deployment environment for the medical device. **4.** It is part of the device platform (i.e., operating system or the cloud platform). **5.** It is part of the manufacturing stations that manufacture the device.
Low	All other third-party components

key storage and signing services (Hardware Security Modules, Secure Key Storage software services, public key infrastructure [PKI]), secure data transfer (libraries that implement Transport Layer Security), and security monitoring of network and applications. By the same logic, high criticality should be considered for components that implement communication protocols like Bluetooth since communication security, cryptography, and key management are often inherent parts of these protocols. Similarly, operating systems and cloud platforms should be considered to be at the highest level of criticality since these platforms provide a number of security services (e.g., process isolation, key management, account management) to the device.

Several real supply chain exploits have been found in the development, build, and deployment environment with attackers focusing their attention on compromising trusted code update mechanisms by seeding vulnerabilities [4,7]. That is why these components should be considered to be at the highest level of criticality, along with components present on manufacturing stations that directly configure the product.

The likelihood of a vulnerability being presented in a component from a third-party is proportional to the manufacturer's confidence in the supplier, specifically confidence that the supplier's own cybersecurity processes and in-house expertise are robust enough to ensure that their products are free from vulnerabilities. This is represented by a metric called Trust (Table 8.3). Lower the Trust in a vendor, higher is the likelihood of a vulnerability being present in a product supplied by the vendor).

A risk acceptability matrix for cybersecurity risk from third-party components can be defined as in Table 8.4.

Formulate risk responses

For risks deemed "unacceptable" from a supplier cybersecurity risk perspective, risk mitigation activities shall need to be performed. These activities include one or more the following:

- *Change suppliers*: It is expensive to change suppliers or to reject a supplier who satisfies all other quality and cost requirements. However, sometimes the risk associated with maintaining a supplier relationship is deemed too high. In that case, taking your business to a supplier with better cybersecurity practices remains the only option for risk reduction.
- *Additional supplier controls*: While choosing a new supplier or renegotiating a contractor with an existing one, cybersecurity expectations can be contractually imposed to reduce the overall cybersecurity risk. These controls include the following:

Table 8.3 Vendor trust.

Vendor trust	Criteria
High	The supplier satisfies any one of the following criteria: 1. The supplier has a poor reputation for cybersecurity which may be because of one or more of the following: a. A record of cybersecurity incidents in its manufacturing facilities, deemed higher than normal b. A record of having not been forthcoming or imprecise in communicating cybersecurity incidents to its customers c. Have had significant issues identified in cybersecurity audits d. Have been assessed as non-compliant with supplier agreements with respect to cybersecurity expectations 2. The supplier has a very limited customer base for the component they supply, which means the component has not gone through extensive public scrutiny. 3. The supplier is a contract manufacturer for the medical device manufacturer
Low	All suppliers that meet none of the criteria of high.

Table 8.4 Risk acceptability matrix.

	Trust = Low	Trust = High
Criticality = High	Unacceptable	Acceptable*
Criticality = Low	Acceptable*	Acceptable

a. Asking the supplier to provide their own cybersecurity risk assessment, including a threat model, their cybersecurity controls, and ideally a cybersecurity risk assessment of their suppliers. In the case of a contract manufacturer, a full manufacturing cybersecurity risk assessment should be part of the set of expectations imposed on the contract manufacturer.

b. Asking the supplier to demonstrate self-attested compliance to Information Technology security industry standards like ISO 27001 [8] or SOC2 [9] or FEDRAMP [10] (if the supplier is a cloud service provider) or supplier cybersecurity risk standards like the US Department of Defense's Cybersecurity Maturity Model [11].

c. Fixing a regular cadence of supplier audits for cybersecurity, where the device manufacturer uses their security audit function to review not just cybersecurity policies and procedures of the supplier but the state of their execution and compliance in practice.

   d. Specifying requirements for reporting of vulnerabilities discovered on their products either by the device manufacturer or by third parties and timely remediation of vulnerabilities. This includes reporting requirements for cybersecurity incidents at supplier sites and a report of corrective and preventative actions taken in response to these incidents.

- *Additional component verification steps to search for backdoors and seeded vulnerabilities*: Supplier-focused risk mitigation controls like audits and compliance documents are indirect ways of assessing security risk of a third-party component. The most direct way is to do security quality inspections yourself. Evaluations for cybersecurity are costly at the individual component level, and one may argue that once components have been integrated into the product, they are subject to cybersecurity testing and penetration tests. So it's not as if supplier components are not being evaluated for vulnerabilities, they are just not being evaluated at the point of procurement. In theory, some vulnerabilities in supplier components may well be caught by using conventional security verification and validation procedures. However, many sophisticated vulnerabilities may likely slip past, like off-specification hardware appliances attached to supplier boards.

Since not all third-party components whose cybersecurity risk is considered unacceptable can realistically be made to pass higher levels of verification, a targeted risk-based approach should be taken to focus organizational resources. Additional verifications would be recommended if

1. The vendor is not trusted (i.e., Trust = Low) and Criticality = High and the component is on the medical device that is providing therapy/diagnostics and
2. The component is a software component supplied as an executable, i.e., no source code provided.

Since the component is provided as an executable, conventional static source-code—based analysis tools which otherwise are expected to be part of the product verification process will not work on it. This means if there are hardcoded credentials in the supplier executable, which might imply the existence of backdoors, these will not get caught. This is why it is recommended that such high-risk third-party components, provided as executables to the manufacturer, are subject to reverse engineering—based malware analysis tools, where hardcoded credentials and other forms of seeded vulnerabilities may be discovered.

For risks deemed "Acceptable*" from a supplier cybersecurity risk perspective, risk mitigation activities as detailed above should be considered (i.e., they are not mandatory). However, in case such risk mitigation activities are not being performed, a documented justification should be provided for the reason it is deemed infeasible.

Secure product development

The secure product development capability ensures that software and hardware of the medical device is protected from intentional, off-specification modification. In Fig. 8.2, a very simple high-level architecture

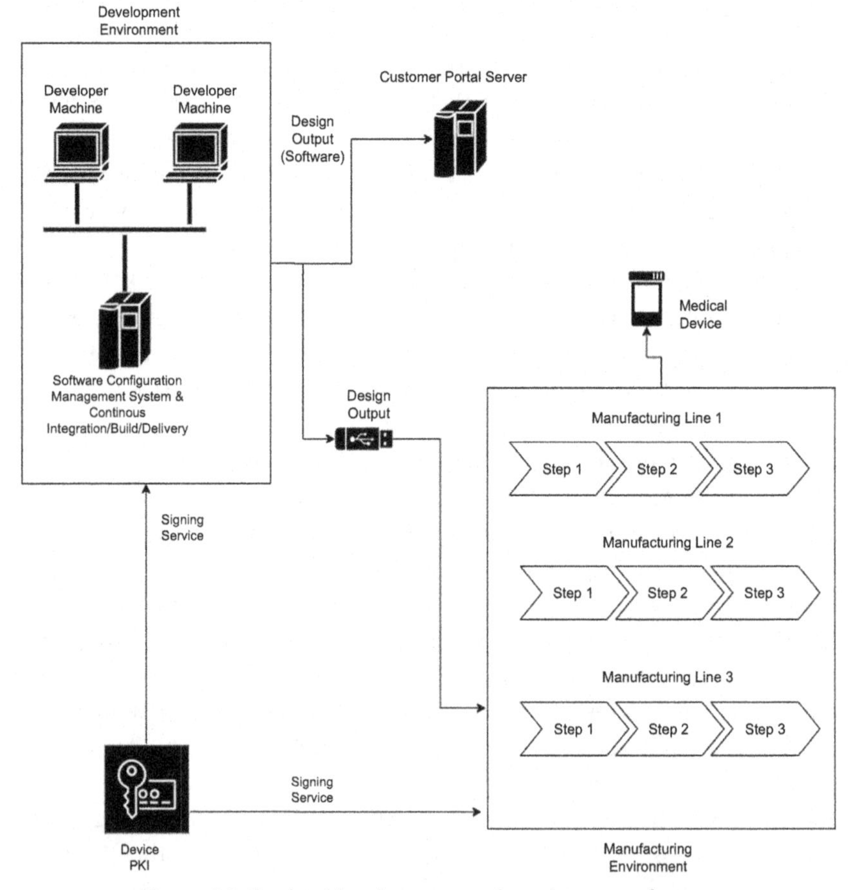

Figure 8.2 Product development and product manufacture.

is shown of the following components: the development environment, the device PKI, the manufacturing environment, and a customer portal for downloading software updates for the device.

The development environment is where the software code is developed and tested. It has a connection to the device PKI from which it requests signing services for code. The design output (device code, device configurations, etc.) is sent to the manufacturing environment (in the picture this flow is represented by a USB stick, but it can be sent over the network also), where the final device is assembled for shipping and deployment. The MDM may also have a customer portal for software updates. The manufacturing environment may also request signing services from the device PKI for device cryptographic identity.

Note that this architecture is highly simplified. An actual MDM will likely have more complex system architectures for their development and deployment environments, with separate environments for development, quality, and production. Further complications in the architecture are introduced if the MDM hosts the medical device (software as a medical device) on its own production servers or on a cloud service. The architecture in Fig. 8.2, rudimentary as it is, serves only to provide a layout for the discussion to follow.

Any procedural control for secure development should consider the following:

1. Access to development code should require user authentication at the development environment level. Authorization to access the code repository should be governed by the principle of least privilege. This access to the product code repository should be granted based on a documented process that verifies the "need to access" reason for the individual that is requesting access, and access should be rescinded once the need no longer exists.
2. During development, developer keys should be used to perform digital signatures. All production code needs to be signed through a different process, using production keys that are different from development keys. Only a very few privileged users and applications, who are authorized through a documented process, should be able to request signing with production keys. The reason for this is that typically a large group of developers need access to development keys to code and test the medical device. Access to these keys cannot be regulated effectively,

purely because of the number of people who have access to it, at which point of time there really is no guarantee that one is not making private copies of these keys.

3. All user activities on the code repositories should be logged and stored in a way that the integrity of the log file cannot be modified by anyone with access to the code repository. This is to prevent anyone from removing all records of their actions on the code repository.
4. All code during development should be cryptographically signed and the signature verified every time it is read from persistent storage. Malware detection tools should be run at a regular cadence on the code repository and on development machines.
5. Every cybersecurity incident within the development environment should be assessed for whether it meets the entry criteria of Corrective and Preventive Action (CAPA) processes for general quality management.
6. Any product software update portal provided by an MDM where customers can download code updates
   a. Should be accessed by a customer over a secure network connection (i.e., https)
   b. Should have customer accounts such that the record of downloads may be logged with the account which downloaded the update
   c. The downloaded package, which may include configuration files, should be protected with a cryptographic signature.
7. If code is delivered over a physical medium like an USB to manufacturing or to end users, the USB image should be analyzed for malware (to ensure that in addition to cryptographically protected code, malware has not been put on the USB). If the USB key is bootable, the booting process should be protected with cryptographic signatures (i.e., secure boot).
8. If the code is being delivered using a third-party software delivery network like Google Play or Apple Store, the manufacturer has to assess the risk of using infrastructure not within their direct control for software delivery. This is often the easiest and, in some cases, the only way to deliver software apps to mobile devices.
9. Since the cornerstone of code and data protection is cryptographic signing, the protection of the signing service or the device PKI is paramount for secure product development. The device PKI is the certificate authority that signs device certificates (these are used to establish

identity for communication), authorization tokens (these are used to establish membership of an authenticated identity to a role and its associated privileges), and code. Depending on whether the device PKI is an outsourced service, hosted on-premise or hosted in a public cloud in a device manufacturer-owned cloud subscription, the responsibilities and strategies for securing the device PKI will vary. The device PKI should have an interface that is able to cryptographically authenticate signing requests, such that an attacker cannot get their material signed by the device PKI. The keys to be used for signing should be protected by storing them in dedicated hardware whose functionality is to store secrets like Hardware Security Modules. It is worth reminding that the private signing keys are the true "crown jewels" of the entire device ecosystem. If these keys are stolen or replaced by an attacker, the entire device ecosystem stands compromised. This is why best-in-class physical, process, and technical controls should be used to secure the physical storage where private keys are stored.

10. Attackers may be present within the organization, and the last thing one would want is for such attackers to be able to get malware signed by the device manufacturer. In order to prevent this, the privilege of authorizing code-signing requests should be restricted to a very selective signing admin group. A ticketing-based system should be used by developers and engineers to make requests to get their code signed, all the signing requests should be reviewed by the signing admin group, and they should ensure that those requesting their code be signed have the proper authorization to make the request using a vetted process.

Secure manufacture

Secure manufacture [12] is the secure realization of the medical device's design at the time of production. The objective here is to ensure that a malicious attacker does not introduce off-specification elements into the final product during the act of realization of the design.

If you recall from the technical controls laid out in Chapter 7, the general protection for code integrity is cryptographic signing. But this technical control, by itself, will not protect the device during manufacturing. Remember, that when the code is being flashed onto the hardware during manufacturing for the very first time, there is nothing on the device that is checking the integrity of the code that is being deployed on it. Only once the public key of the root CA and the code that verifies signatures get onto the device, does the cryptographic signing control truly "kick in." Before that, other cybersecurity controls need to protect the device from being tampered with by an attacker.

Of course, an attacker may have intentions other than tampering the product. For example, an attacker may want to inflict damage to the business by stalling or shutting down the production line or exfiltrate intellectual property (e.g., product designs) off the manufacturing floor. But since the focus of this book is on patient safety/privacy, such threats are kept out of scope of this book.

Given this scope, there are three high-level threats that need to be protected against:

- Changing the code/public key of the root CA that is flashed onto the device hardware during manufacture
- Changing device parameters and critical security parameters that are set during manufacture
- Changing the behavior of the manufacturing process itself such that the device is not fabricated as per specification

Secure manufacture

A procedural control for secure manufacture should have the following components:

1. Risk-based prioritization of process steps: A process flow for manufacturing is a directed graph where the nodes represent manufacturing steps. A directed edge arrow between node A and node B signifies that process step A occurs before process step B, in the order imposed by the manufacturing process. As part of process risk modeling, MDMs construct, for each process flow, a PFMEA (Process Failure Mode Effects Analysis) [13]. A PFMEA defines, for every manufacturing step, the different ways that manufacturing step may fail and the effects on the product as a result. An attacker could use the PFMEA to understand which process steps to target and what failures to trigger, based on the effect of the failure at that process step. As defenders, we have to think similarly in order to prioritize our protection efforts. A three-level prioritization scheme may be used to annotate every process step in a process flow.
   - High Risk (Red Nodes): High-risk nodes are those steps in the process flow where (1) any fraudulent change to the device could cause patient harm and (2) the output of the process step is not

verified further downstream. Examples of such high-risk nodes are nodes where code is being installed on the device or where critical calibration parameters are being set, in that malicious values of these parameters can cause patient harm.
- Medium Risk (Yellow Nodes): Medium-risk nodes are those steps in the process flow where (1) any fraudulent change to the device is unlikely to cause patient harm but can compromise process integrity by producing nonconformant product and (2) the output of the process step is verified further downstream. Examples of such medium-risk nodes are changes during alignment of mechanical components, which would lead to product defect, but that defect would be caught by end of line testing.
- Low Risk (Green Nodes): Low-risk nodes are those steps in the process flow where any fraudulent change would not cause patient harm or a nonconformance. Visual inspection/testing may be conducted at such steps, and there may be a secondary intent of the attacker to change behavior at these steps so that their primary compromise, at a yellow node, is not caught.

2. Implementation of cybersecurity controls: A set of base cybersecurity controls should apply to every manufacturing step, regardless of its criticality. These are the following:
- The network on which the manufacturing stations which implement manufacturing steps are located should be isolated, as far as possible, from Internet-connected networks and other internal corporate networks.
- Anomaly detection appliances (hardware or software) should monitor all network traffic to and from manufacturing stations to ensure that only authorized devices are on manufacturing networks. Traffic within, from, and to manufacturing networks is usually very regular, which makes it feasible for baselining. Any anomaly from that traffic pattern may be an indicator of compromise (e.g., data being exfiltrated from a manufacturing station or a manufacturing station dialing out to a remote command and control center) and should be investigated. The anomaly detection appliances should ideally be agentless, so as to not affect performance of any manufacturing station.
- Any access to manufacturing stations from external vendors (i.e., remote access from noncorporate networks) should be disabled. If disabling access is not possible, remote access to stations should be

sandboxed at the application and at the network level. This helps mitigate the risk of external vendors accessing applications on the station they are not authorized to, or "jump" to other manufacturing stations over the network.

- Ensure that manufacturing stations are hardened sufficiently. Operators should not be given access to the underlying operating system (e.g., in Linux, this is accomplished by disabling OS user accounts, and in Windows, by enabling so-called "kiosk" modes).
- Ensure that manufacturing stations have secure boot enabled. This prevents an attacker from using a USB to boot to their own OS.
- Only default deny (i.e., application whitelisting) should be implemented on manufacturing stations to ensure that only "allowed" applications may be executed.
- Installation of code to manufacturing stations should be disallowed, unless through admin access. The admin access should be guarded by multifactor authentication for local and remote admin access.
- Every operator should have their own named account and their actions logged (which means no communal group account, with everyone knowing the password, with the password being written on a sticky note right next to the terminal).
- The credentials used by an individual to log into the manufacturing should be linked to the employee's corporate credentials. This ensures that with cessation of employment, access to all manufacturing stations is automatically removed.
- If feasible, every manufacturing station should have endpoint protection software installed and the software should run at bootup and at a regular cadence, ideally during downtime.
- Access to the manufacturing floor should be through badged access, with access to manufacturing floor be granted on the basis of the principle of least privilege (i.e., only those who have an explicit need to access the manufacturing floor should be allowed on the manufacturing floor and no one else). 24/7 monitoring of manufacturing stations using cameras should be considered as a means of dissuading prospective attackers that their activities are all being "caught on camera." There should be digital records of badge-in and badge-outs for physical access to the manufacturing floor.

A set of cybersecurity controls for red and yellow nodes, i.e., manufacturing stations with elevated risk that may be considered are as follows:

- Ensure that device code and device configurations and root CA public key that forms the root of trust are stored along with integrity measures (ideally with a cryptographic signature) in a centralized database. This database is then read by the manufacturing station to cryptographically verify the integrity of code, configurations, and keys before they are loaded onto the device. In other words, there is a last-mile-check before code, configuration, and root keys are flashed onto the hardware.
- Any manufacturing step that is responsible for provisioning device cryptographic identity has to communicate with the device PKI in order to get the device certificate signed by the PKI. This is an exception to the network isolation that is imposed for the baseline. This exception is needed since manufacturing stations have to initiate a connection outside the manufacturing network to a device PKI, which may be on the manufacturer's premise, or be hosted on a public cloud. The connection to the device PKI has to be guarded by mutual certificate-based authentication, such that the device PKI knows it is talking to a genuine manufacturing station, and the manufacturing station knows it is talking to the actual device PKI. The data path between the device PKI and the manufacturing station should be protected by transport-level security or a virtual private network, to ensure that data in transit are protected from modification. The manufacturing station that has to tunnel out of the network isolation to talk to the device PKI has to be configured that it takes no incoming connection initiated from outside, i.e., all connections outside the manufacturing network have to be initiated by the manufacturing station.

3. Vulnerability Monitoring and Risk Management: All software assets on manufacturing stations should be run against vulnerabilities in the National Vulnerability Database (NVD) and patches applied as soon as patches are released. If patches cannot be applied, (for manufacturing stations, applying a patch may have to be delayed for a maintenance

downtime in order to not disrupt manufacturing), the risk of not patching should be assessed. Malware detected on manufacturing stations should be flagged as cybersecurity incidents and investigated as part of internal processes. Every cybersecurity incident within the manufacturing environment should be assessed for whether it meets the entry criteria of CAPA processes for general quality management.

Vulnerability management

In order to ensure the quality of the products they manufacture, the MDM has to continuously monitor the performance of their devices for defects [14]. Once defects are detected, these defects need to be assessed for patient safety (i.e., does it cause harm to the patient?) and efficacy (i.e., does it still perform its stated clinical function risk?). If the risk of either is found to be outside the zone of acceptability, the defect is fixed through a product update in the field or by removal of product from the market. The root cause of the defect is then analyzed through the CAPA process of the quality management system (QMS), and based on the output of the CAPA process, the systemic issue that led to the defect being manifested in the field is sought to be remediated.

A subsystem (software and hardware) vulnerability is a cybersecurity defect. The same obligations for product performance monitoring apply for detection, risk assessment, and remediation of cybersecurity defects, and this responsibility is delegated to the vulnerability management capability.

Specifically, the vulnerability management capability consists of the following procedural controls:

- *Vulnerability Monitoring* for continuously monitoring vulnerability signal sources for potential product (hardware and software) vulnerabilities, and assessing which of these potential vulnerabilities and threats are actual vulnerabilities on the manufacturer's products.
- *Cybersecurity Patch Management* for assessing whether the risk to patient safety and privacy is uncontrolled (i.e., risk is unacceptable) using subsystem and system risk modeling procedural controls (see Chapters 5 and 6 for details of cybersecurity risk modeling). If the risk at the system level is deemed to be uncontrolled, then a cybersecurity patch should be developed and rolled out. If the risk at the system level is deemed to be uncontrolled, then developing and rolling out a cybersecurity patch.

In addition vulnerability management plugs into the following procedural controls that are maintained by other capabilities:

- Corporate communications: This capability is responsible for disclosing the vulnerability that leads to uncontrolled risk to stakeholders (customers, regulators, clinicians, patients) through the corporate communication processes. This communication that is crafted in a way that the disclosure itself does not compromise the security of the device, is unambiguous, is understandable by a wide spectrum of stakeholders, and is backed by evidence [15,16].
- The CAPA processes: This capability is responsible for determining the root cause of the vulnerability in terms of development practices, determining why it was not detected by quality processes, whether the root cause has led to defects in other products, and remediating the QMS itself to prevent further reoccurrences of the root cause.

Vulnerability monitoring

At any point of time, there are multiple signal sources that an MDM should monitor for potential vulnerabilities on their products. Vulnerabilities should be assessed for applicability for the MDM's products and records kept that capture the analysis performed. In other words, the process by which a "potential" product vulnerability is considered to be an "actual" product vulnerability should be documented. Signal sources that should be included in a manufacturer's vulnerability monitoring procedural control are as follows:

Product monitoring

Cybersecurity incidents can be identified from product monitoring, which ingests cybersecurity logs and operational logs to identify a successful compromise or an imminent compromise. In order for this kind of monitoring, the device needs to securely stream operational and cybersecurity logs to a monitoring service in real time or near real time. The monitoring service then correlates data from multiple streams, and then uses automated big data techniques to identify potential cybersecurity incidents. An analyst then needs to go through the flagged cybersecurity incidents and conduct further investigation to determine which of these are actual cybersecurity incidents.

For further reading on the topic of cybersecurity monitoring for vulnerability management, one should refer to American Association for Medical Instrumentation (AAMI TIR97) Appendix B [17] for monitoring of devices on hospital networks. While the focus of this book is MDMs, AAMI TIR97 concentrates on cybersecurity monitoring from a Healthcare Delivery Organization (HDO) perspective. The monitoring goals of MDMs and HDOs are aligned but not identical, and the types of events they "see" differ too.

The HDO will have visibility into network-level events (because they control the network) but not necessarily session- or application-level events. Application-level events (e.g., logins to the device) are part of the device design, and likely not to be available through an interface to external parties, even their customers. That is why HDO monitoring focuses on network activity, network addressing, open ports, and services available, while the device monitoring leans more on session-, application-, and platform-level events.

Internal product verification and validation

The Secure System Verification and Validation capability described in Chapter 7 is responsible for producing a list of subsystem (software and hardware) vulnerability—threat combination based on static and dynamic analysis techniques as part of product penetration testing, malware scanning, and vulnerability scanning. Such verification and validation activities are usually done during major product releases or at a periodic cadence (e.g., every year) as part of an MDM's commitment to continuous vulnerability vigilance.

Product returns and servicing

In devices that do not connect to a monitoring solution, product returns and product servicing should provide the opportunity to analyze operational and cybersecurity logs to detect cybersecurity incidents. These may be devices that lack connectivity or do not otherwise support a real-time or near-real-time monitoring solution.

As an example, let us consider a legacy device that was returned by the customer to the manufacturer because of in-field failure. The device does not have cryptographic code verification designed in. On analysis, an engineer finds that the code present on the returned device is not the code that is supposed to be on the device. Some bits have changed, but that the code still passes the same CRC integrity check as the original golden version of the code. Tampering then may be suspected, because it is unlikely that random bit flips in the device software would still maintain the exact same CRC. There is definite agency here, and hence, a cybersecurity incident should be flagged.

Customer complaints

Sometimes, customers and field technicians call into the MDM's call center in order to report what they believe to be cybersecurity incidents. These could be simply apprehensions ("the neighborhood kid threatened to hack my device and it started malfunctioning shortly thereafter") or suspicions based on specific observed events ("after I downloaded the medical device app, there seems to be malware on my phone, and I cannot connect to the Wi-Fi"). Either way, these are signals for product-specific vulnerabilities, and should undergo analysis and disposition. The MDM should monitor call center records, Email addresses provided as part of instructions of use and product manuals, and social media and online bulletin board discussions for such suspected cybersecurity incidents.

Supplier notifications

Suppliers/vendors of third-party components (software and hardware) that are part of the product may declare vulnerabilities based on their product validation processes. The following represent some of the supplier sources of product-specific vulnerabilities that should be tracked as part of vulnerability monitoring.

- Supplier communication: For suppliers with whom the manufacturer has a contractual relationship, communication of vulnerabilities may happen over a private communication channel, sometimes in advance of a public disclosure, to give the manufacturer time to come up with a strategy to mitigate the effect of the vulnerability.
- Supplier website or customer portal: Sometimes, a supplier may choose to do disclosures on their website or on a customer portal. The manufacturer should sign up for access to the portal or regularly monitor the supplier website for vulnerabilities and patches.
- Release notes: With open source software components and even with some contractual suppliers, vulnerability information may be present in release notes

Public sources of product-specific vulnerabilities

The MDM should monitor public sources of vulnerabilities to gauge which of them are relevant to their medical devices. The MDM should consider as "relevant" all publicly declared vulnerabilities for every component in the product's CBOM, as well as vulnerabilities publicly disclosed in competitor's devices.

The following represent some of the public sources of product-specific vulnerabilities that should be tracked:

- US-CERT advisories: The Cybersecurity and Infrastructure Security Agency (CISA) [18] is a US federal agency formed in 2018 that is responsible for protecting the critical national assets of the United States of America from cybersecurity threats. As part of the CISA's activities, it operates the Computer Emergency Readiness Team (CERT) program often referred to as US-CERT. US-CERT has an industrial control systems (ICS) focused suborganization, often referred to as ICS-CERT [19], whose advisories are particularly relevant for the medical device community. The CERTs, operating under the umbrella of CISA, take leadership in identifying national and sector-level threats and vulnerabilities, coordinating incident response activities between private entities and government agencies and disseminating cyber threat warning information. CERT publishes security advisories on specific products, which are a collection of one or more vulnerabilities discovered on products, with associated entries in the NVD.
- NVD [20]: This is the master directory for vulnerabilities on all software and hardware components and would be the primary recommended sources for pulling vulnerabilities for third-party software components. Each entry in the NVD is assigned an id called CVE (Common Vulnerability Enumeration) and is assigned typically a CVSS score.

Coordinated vulnerability disclosure

Sometimes the vulnerabilities on a medical device are reported directly to the manufacturer by an external agent like a security researcher before they are disclosed to the public. Disclosing vulnerabilities to the manufacturers first allows the manufacturer time to do their independent analysis, understand the severity of the vulnerability, and start developing/deploying a patch to remediate the vulnerability if the risk is unacceptable. This reduces the time available for an attacker to exploit a known but unpatched vulnerability. Getting informed before public disclosure also allows manufacturers to develop a communication strategy around the vulnerability.

Thus, it is in the best interests of MDMs to provide security researchers an easily accessible, well-documented process for communicating vulnerabilities to them in a coordinated fashion. This process is known as coordinated vulnerability disclosure [16].

One of the requirements of a coordinated vulnerability disclosure is that it should provide an interface for external parties to communicate vulnerabilities. This interface can be as simple as an email address displayed prominently on the MDM's website or something like a forms-based questionnaire which collects information from the researcher in a structured format. Some examples of information to collect from security researchers are the model number and product family on which the vulnerability is being claimed, steps to reproduce the threat, either in the form of a document or a video, and any assumptions the security researcher is making. Example references on the basis of templates for vulnerability disclosure which can be created are ISO 29147 Annex B [16] and Early Stage Coordinated Vulnerability Disclosure Template from NTIA [21].

The coordinated vulnerability disclosure process should have a clear delineation of roles and responsibilities in that, when an external researcher reports a vulnerability on a product, who within the MDM should be informed, and who determines how the engagement with the researcher should be conducted. An ill-advised strategy would be for the MDM to "lawyer up" and try to stifle the person(s) reporting the vulnerability with the threat of legal sanction or by imposing a gag order. Conversations with the external researcher should ideally be at the level of engineer to engineer. The MDM should avoid the purely human impulse to be defensive when someone outside the organization critiques their design, and listen to what the external researcher is saying, with an open mind. It is well within the rights of the MDM to not "accept" the vulnerability disclosure by a researcher, either fully or partially, or dispute the severity of the vulnerability. In case of such a technical disagreement between the external researcher and the MDM, a coordinated vulnerability disclosure process should provide avenue for third-party mediation. Depending on where the dispute is, this third party can be another security researcher or group of security researchers (if the technicalities of the vulnerability are being disputed), or a group of clinicians (if the clinical severity of the vulnerability is being disputed). Either way, the MDM should communicate clearly to the external researcher their stance within a reasonable period of time.

The inability to provide a clear, easy-to-find, easy-to-use, and most importantly, welcoming process for external researchers to communicate vulnerability information to the manufacturer can, in many times, force them to just go ahead and disclose the vulnerability to the world, which not only makes the manufacturer lose control over the narrative and have their call center get overrun with calls from concerned patients and hospitals but also might expose patients to actual threats being executed. Another reason why external security researchers sometimes go public is because they do not get an adequate response, or come to the conclusion, that the MDM is not treating their findings with the seriousness that they believe it deserves. The only solution is to have a timely and clear communication strategy that works of trust, and presumption of "good faith actions."

A controversial question among MDMs is whether they should incentivize security researchers to "have a go" at their products through security bug bounties (you break into the system, you get paid or recognized or both) and specific outreach activities to the "hacker" community. My opinion on this is simple and unambiguous—yes. In this day and age, backing away from engaging with the security community hoping that somehow they do not "notice" your products is an exercise in security by obscurity, where obscurity here means hoping that you are obscure enough not to get noticed. An MDM has to have confidence that a product that is shipped and made available to the public should be able to withstand intense cybersecurity scrutiny. That is why we see major medical manufacturers proactively partnering with some of the world's leading security conferences to hold exclusive "hack the device" contests, where participants walk into a room full of medical devices, and just start hacking, using their own techniques and methods.

Threat intelligence feeds

MDMs should be subscribed to general threat intelligence feeds like feeds from Information Sharing and Analysis Organizations (Health-ISAC for medical devices), DHS, Food and Drug Administration (FDA), and other regulatory authorities. They should also invest in staying abreast of latest developments in cybersecurity, and emerging cybersecurity threats, by attending conferences, both general cybersecurity ones as well as industry-specific ones. This kind of continuous "listening" keeps the MDM updated not just of product-specific vulnerabilities but also of general trends in cybersecurity and tactics and strategies being favored by adversaries.

Cybersecurity patch management

The cybersecurity patch management procedural control takes as its input actual vulnerabilities in the device's software and hardware. It then assesses the risk of these vulnerabilities using subsystem and system risk modeling procedural controls to determine if the vulnerability–threat combination leads to uncontrolled risk. Uncontrolled risk is a term used by the FDA postmarket cybersecurity guidance [22] which means the threat poses patient safety/privacy risk at a level that is not acceptable by the manufacturer's own risk acceptance criteria. If the threat leads to uncontrolled risk, then cybersecurity patch management procedural control is responsible for developing and deploying the patch to remediate the vulnerability, as per FDA's postmarket guidance.

Uncontrolled risk to patient safety/privacy is a necessary but not sufficient condition for developing and deploying a cybersecurity patch. In other words, if there is uncontrolled risk, a device should be patched, but that does not mean it is the only trigger for patching a device. Increasingly, HDOs are imposing requirements on MDMs to remediate all vulnerabilities, irrespective of risk, as soon as possible or at a regular cadence (e.g., once a year). While the "patch all vulnerabilities as soon as you can" sounds like a perfectly reasonable requirement (after all, do not we patch the operating system of our smart phones the moment an update becomes available?), in the domain of medical devices, this is easier said than done. Many devices are not connected to the Internet, requiring patients to be brought into the clinic, incurring costs to the healthcare system. Even if devices are connected to the Internet, rolling out patches has business challenges. A medical device product update has to meet a much higher standard of reverification and revalidation than an update to a consumer electronics device. Just because a Bluetooth vendor or an operating system vendor has created a patch for a vulnerable component does not mean the MDM can immediately deploy it to devices. Extensive testing of the device needs to be conducted with the updated third-party components before the patch can be applied. Hence, an aggressive "patch regardless of risk as soon as possible" policy is challenging for many MDMs to sustain.

A reasonable middle ground is to extend the risk-based criteria to encompass not just patient safety/privacy risk but also unacceptable risk to HDO infrastructure. An infusion pump on the HDO network may have a vulnerability that compromises the wireless password. While this technically does not lead to risk to patient safety/privacy, an HDO would reasonably insist that the MDM is obligated to remediate this vulnerability. There can, of course, be intermediate fixes or compensating controls to safely use the devices till a patch is deployed. For example, the infusion pumps could be isolated to their own wireless network with a password unique from the HDO network. However, the HDO would expect that these compensating controls should not be a permanent solution, and that the device patched within a reasonable timeframe.

The challenge with the "risk to HDO" approach is the definition of "acceptability." Since the risk is to HDO infrastructure, the onus of describing "acceptable risk" should be the HDOs. Different HDOs would likely have different appetites for risk, and different approaches for calculating risk. For the MDM, assessing risk of their device to HDO infrastructure, it would be difficult to come to a consensus that would be applicable to all their customers.

A more feasible approach would be to have a criteria-based approach. HDOs may want to consider putting language in their contracts and agreements that obligates MDMs to roll out, within a mutually acceptable time period, patches for vulnerabilities that may lead to attackers getting elevated access privileges to HDO infrastructure, even if the risk to patient safety/privacy is controlled. The example of the infusion pump leaking the Wi-Fi password would be caught under criteria-based approach. Since the infusion pump is allowing an attacker to elevate their privilege (they did not know the password before, now they know) on the HDO Wi-Fi network, the MDM should be obligated to patch the vulnerability. A yearly patch cadence of all vulnerabilities, irrespective of risk, may be expected from an MDM, only if their device does not pose any risk to the HDO infrastructure. Needless to say, regulator-imposed requirements for patching for uncontrolled patient safety/privacy risk will always remain applicable, regardless of negotiated agreements between HDOs and MDMs.

Cybersecurity patch management is also responsible for invoking two other organizational procedures:

External communication

The decision to issue a cybersecurity patch, or even the decision not to, must be carefully and unambiguously communicated to the outside world. When a critical vulnerability on a component being used by a medical device (e.g., a Bluetooth Low Energy stack or a TLS implementation) or the medical device itself becomes public knowledge, MDMs should expect increased stakeholder engagement. Regulators and security-conscious HDOs will likely reach out for an official response. If the vulnerability be picked up by the popular media, so will patients and clinicians. It is imperative for MDMs, as fast as possible, ideally within 24 h of an impactful public disclosure, to issue a response that is prominently displayed on their official website. The initial statement does not need to dispute or accept the findings, but should inform the community that the MDM is aware of the problem, and analyzing it. A time frame for resolution should be provided. Just saying "We are looking into it" without committing to when the community can expect an impact assessment is not particularly helpful. If the decision is taken not to patch the vulnerability based on subsystem and system risk modeling, the MDM should clearly explain the engineering argument as to why the risk of the vulnerability is acceptable. A simple declaration that there is "no patient safety impact" does not assure the extended community, in this day and age of heightened cybersecurity awareness, without some kind of engineering reason backing that up.

For regulators and HDOs, a more detailed engineering report should be prepared if the decision is taken not to patch a vulnerability that has garnered attention. This engineering test report should contain extracts from the risk assessment, including a full traceability to design input, and test artifacts to all controls that are being considered to be risk responses to the threat. If attack scripts exist for the vulnerability, the engineering report should contain the observed behavior of the device when the attack scripts are executed. Confidence in the risk assessment and the decision not to patch will increase with regulators and HDOs if it can be demonstrated, by the engineering report, that the risk of adverse outcomes is indeed low. Confidence can be further increased in the decision if the MDM hires an external and independent security company to validate their findings and test results.

In case the decision is taken to patch a medical device, either because the risk is uncontrolled or because of customer requirements or expectations, the risk of not applying the patch should clearly be explained to clinicians and users. In case patch adoption is slow, the MDM should craft further outreach activities to motivate clinicians and users to patch their devices. The MDM should actively try to find out why patch adoption rate is slow, whether the patch delivery mechanism (e.g., bringing a patient into the clinic just to apply a cybersecurity patch) is deemed too expensive by the HDO or whether there are fears from clinicians that an in-field update of the device might "brick it," leading to overall increased system risk. It then becomes contingent on the MDM, as part of their communication strategy, to address these concerns. For example, reliability metrics of patch updates should be provided to convince the user community that the patch process is reliable.

Corrective and preventive action

Any time uncontrolled risk results from a defect; best practices of quality management dictate that the QMS is revisited to find the root cause for the defect that led to the vulnerability. Once the root cause is discovered, the systemic problem needs to be remediated in the QMS to reduce the risk of the defect being manifested in the future in new products and in other fielded products. This process of discovering and remediating systemic problems as part of continuous quality improvement is known as the CAPA process.

When the Cybersecurity Patch Management procedural control finds a vulnerability that leads to uncontrolled risk, the CAPA process needs to be executed. The question that drives a cybersecurity CAPA is as follows: "How did this vulnerability that led to an uncontrolled risk not get caught by our quality management practices and how can we ensure that this does not happen again?" If the root cause is found to be weak processes, e.g., the quality processes do not properly impose compliance to cybersecurity standards and best practices, a quality plan needs to be formulated to bring the QMS to be compliant with standards and best practices. If the root cause is identified as not the processes per se, but adherent to them, then remediation strategies would include training and awareness and proper allocation of tasks to resources.

Cybersecurity training

Training is a requirement that flows from quality and risk management standards, with the requirement being phrased usually in the following way: "technical activities are performed by those that have the qualifications as well as the training required to perform the activities." This requires the MDM to align job responsibilities that require execution of cybersecurity tasks with requirements of appropriate training and qualifications. A cybersecurity task is any task that requires knowledge of cybersecurity concepts, be it for taking executive decisions, reviewing cybersecurity-related design documents or more core activities like conducting cybersecurity risk modeling, developing security architectures, or verification and validation. Not all cybersecurity tasks require the same level of cybersecurity expertise, and that is why training requirements should be calibrated based on specific roles and responsibilities. Table 8.5 contains a candidate set of criteria for allocation of cybersecurity training based on roles and responsibilities.

Since cybersecurity is a rapidly evolving discipline, cybersecurity training material should be regularly updated. As people move to newer roles, and the definitions of roles themselves change, the training requirements should be revisited to account for these changes. While it seems trivial to state this, often during a cybersecurity audit, one discovers misalignment between training records and job responsibilities, i.e., people executing processes they are not trained on, or assigned responsibilities for which they do not have qualification records on file.

Table 8.5 Cybersecurity training requirements.

Responsibilities	Requirements for training and qualifications
Executive management with responsibility of cybersecurity	*Executive training modules for cybersecurity:* • Basic cybersecurity concepts • Regulatory and quality expectations for cybersecurity
System, software, and quality engineers	*Basic engineering training modules for cybersecurity:* • Basic cybersecurity concepts • Training on all cybersecurity processes that are executed by the individual
Engineers who own, develop, and execute cybersecurity processes and do cybersecurity development and maintenance	*Subject Matter Expert training modules for cybersecurity* • Basic, intermediate, and advanced cybersecurity concepts including training on specific cybersecurity technologies relevant for job duties (e.g., secure web development, embedded systems security) • Training on all cybersecurity processes that are executed by the individual • minimum qualifications should be a Bachelors in Engineering and, optionally, cybersecurity certifications/advanced degree in cybersecurity
Engineers who review cybersecurity documents/artifacts that are produced by executing cybersecurity processes	*Reviewer training modules for cybersecurity:* • Basic cybersecurity concepts • Training on cybersecurity processes that produce the documents whose review is within the job duties of the individual

Summary and key takeaways

1. Supply chain risk management for cybersecurity consists of first identifying third-party components that can directly affect patient safety and privacy, then assessing risk based on the criticality of these components, and the trust that can be placed in the cybersecurity practices of the vendor from which the component is procured from. Based on whether the risk is acceptable or not, additional cybersecurity risk responses (e.g., changing supplier, additional controls on the supplier or on the component itself) are then formulated.

2. The medical device software development environment should be secured as well as the means of delivery of code updates to devices. The manufacturing of medical devices should be secured by implementation of a baseline of cybersecurity controls that protect the manufacturing environment in general, and then, by the implementation of additional cybersecurity controls for manufacturing stations that perform "cyber critical" tasks during the manufacturing process.
3. Vulnerability management consists of continuous monitoring of vulnerability signals, both external as well as internal, deciding which vulnerabilities apply to the manufacturer's own products, and then risk modeling to understand the impact of vulnerability to patient safety and privacy. Vulnerability management is also responsible of disposition of the vulnerabilities, be it through the development and delivery of a patch or through communication to external stakeholders, customers, and regulators, as to why a patch is not necessary.
4. Cybersecurity training should be administered in a way such that those who engage in cybersecurity activities have the appropriate qualifications and training required in order to discharge those duties.

References

[1] US Cybersecurity and Infrastructure Security Agency, Information and Communications Technology Supply Chain Risk Management (SCRM) in a Connected World, 2020.

[2] US Cybersecurity and Infrastructure Security Agency, ICT Supply Chain Risk Management, 2020.

[3] Bloomberg, The Big Hack: How China Used a Tiny Chip to Infiltrate U.S. Companies, October 4, 2018 [Online]. Available: https://www.bloomberg.com/news/features/2018-10-04/the-big-hack-how-china-used-a-tiny-chip-to-infiltrate-america-s-top-companies.

[4] Motherboard–Tech by Vice, Hackers Hijacked ASUS Software Updates to Install Backdoors on Thousands of Computers, March 25, 2019 [Online]. Available: https://www.vice.com/en_us/article/pan9wn/hackers-hijacked-asus-software-updates-to-install-backdoors-on-thousands-of-computers https://www.wired.com/story/asus-software-update-hack/.

[5] Motherboard–Tech by Vice, A Mysterious Hacker Group Is on a Supply Chain Hijacking Spree, 2019 [Online]. Available: https://www.wired.com/story/barium-supply-chain-hackers/.

[6] Wired, Inside the Unnerving Supply Chain Attack that Corrupted CCleaner, April 20, 2020 [Online].

[7] NPR, A 'Worst Nightmare' Cyberattack: The Untold Story of the SolarWinds Hack, April 16, 2021 [Online]. Available: https://www.npr.org/2021/04/16/985439655/a-worst-nightmare-cyberattack-the-untold-story-of-the-solarwinds-hack.

[8] ISO/IEC Information Technology Task Force (ITTF), ISO/IEC 27001 Information Technology — Security Techniques — Information Security Management Systems — Requirements, ISO, 2013.

[9] American Institute of Certified Public Accountants, Attestation Standards: Clarification and Recodification, 2016.
[10] The Federal Risk and Authorization Management Program, Program Basics, n.d. [Online]. Available: https://www.fedramp.gov/program-basics/.
[11] Office of the Under Secretary of Defense for Acquisition & Sustainment, Cybersecurity Maturity Model Certification, 2020.
[12] MEP National Network, Manufacturer's Guide to Cybersecurity for Small and Medium Sized Manufacturers, 2020.
[13] National Aeronautics and Space Administration JPL., PD-AP-1307 Failure Modes, Effects, and Criticality Analysis (FMECA), n.d.
[14] International Organization for Standardization, ISO/IEC 30111:2019 Information Technology — Security Techniques — Vulnerability Handling Processes, 2019.
[15] US Food and Drug Administration, Communicating Cybersecurity Vulnerabilities to Patients: Considerations for a Framework, 2020.
[16] International Organization for Standardization, ISO/IEC 29147:2018 Information Technology — Security Techniques — Vulnerability Disclosure, ISO, 2018.
[17] American Association for Medical Instrumentation, TIR97: Principles for Medical Device Security - Postmarket Risk Management for Device Manufacturers, 2019.
[18] Cybersecurity and Infrastructure Security Agency, CISA Factsheet, n.d. [Online]. Available: https://www.cisa.gov/sites/default/files/publications/CISA-Factsheet_14%20April_508C.pdf.
[19] Industrial Control Systems Cyber Emergency Readiness Team, n.d. [Online]. Available: https://us-cert.cisa.gov/ics.
[20] US National Institute of Standards and Technologies, National Vulnerability Database, n.d. [Online]. Available: https://nvd.nist.gov/vuln. (Accessed 25 September 2020).
[21] NTIA Safety Working Group, "Early Stage" Coordinated Vulnerability Disclosure Template v1.1., 2016 [Online]. Available: https://www.ntia.doc.gov/files/ntia/publications/ntia_vuln_disclosure_early_stage_template.pdf.
[22] US Food and Drug Administration, Postmarket Management of Cybersecurity in Medical Devices (Final Version), December 2016 [Online]. Available: https://www.fda.gov/regulatory-information/search-fda-guidance-documents/postmarket-management-cybersecurity-medical-devices (Accessed 1 September 2020).

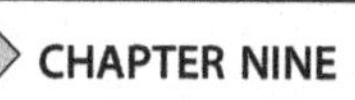

CHAPTER NINE

Product security governance and regulatory compliance

Introduction

Table 4.2 of Chapter 4 defines a set of capabilities (a capability consists of processes, tools, and people) that a Product Cybersecurity Organization (PCO) for a Medical Device Manufacturer (MDM) should develop and maintain. In this chapter, the focus will be on the two capabilities from Chapter 4, not touched upon thus far: Product Security Governance and Standards And Regulatory Compliance (Table 9.1).

Product security governance

The capability Product Security Governance is responsible for ensuring that the MDM has the proper people, process, and technology to support the design, execution, and maintenance of all other cybersecurity capabilities. Specifically, it is responsible for discharging the following responsibilities:

1. *Ensuring that requirements that follow from regulations, regulatory guidance, and cybersecurity standards are captured in the Quality Management System (QMS).* This activity consists of ingesting new cybersecurity regulations, guidance, and standards, distilling regulatory guidance down to a set of technical and procedural controls (examples of such procedural and technical control catalogs have been provided in Chapters 4 and 7, respectively), assessing gaps between regulatory requirements and the current state of the QMS, and creating a Quality Plan to bring the QMS in compliance with the new regulations, guidance, and standards.
2. *Oversight over developing capabilities:* This activity consists of managing the execution of cybersecurity capability development through a Quality Plan.
3. *Ensuring that capabilities are being executed and maintained properly*: This activity provides oversight over capability execution, i.e., to ensure that processes are being properly followed, resources are properly allocated with properly trained personnel executing processes they have the training and skills to execute, and that tools are available that facilitate process execution and productivity of personnel.

Cybersecurity for Connected Medical Devices
ISBN: 978-0-12-818262-8
https://doi.org/10.1016/B978-0-12-818262-8.00009-7

Table 9.1 Product security governance and standards and regulatory compliance.

Capability	Definition	Procedural controls
Product security governance	• Overall oversight of capability definition, maintenance, and execution	Cybersecurity strategy, cybersecurity management review
Standards and regulatory compliance	• Responsible for assembling regulatory submissions	Regulatory submissions

4. *Defining roles and responsibilities and information flows between organizational functions as well the external world*: This activity consists of defining roles and responsibilities for cross-functional cybersecurity activities. For instance, who needs to be informed when a cybersecurity incident on a medical device is detected? Between the functions Research and Development (R&D), Information Technology (IT), and Quality, how is responsibility for patching manufacturing and other nonproduct software divvied up? In many large MDMs, there is a corporate PCO with provides corporate-level oversight. This can either be an independent function by itself or be housed within corporate's Global Quality office. How then are roles and responsibilities for cybersecurity allocated between the corporate PCO and the PCO at the divisional level? These and similar questions need to be answered by the Product Security Governance capability.

The capability Product Security Governance itself is responsible for defining, executing, and maintaining the following procedural controls.

Cybersecurity strategy

The Cybersecurity Strategy procedural control defines processes for ensuring that the cybersecurity capabilities capture regulatory and standards guidance, that all cybersecurity capabilities are being developed, executed, and maintained properly, and that roles and responsibilities, especially in an organization where overall cybersecurity is a joint responsibility of multiple functions, are being properly discharged.

Procedural controls for cybersecurity strategy should define the following:

Criteria for identifying regulations, standards, and guidance that drive cybersecurity strategy

Which regulations, standards, and guidance should the MDM's QMS comply with? Who decides and based on what? Regulations and guidance issued by regulatory regimes in countries which the MDM does business in obviously have to be tracked through the QMS. But what about cybersecurity standards cited by regulators, such as NIST CCF [1] or NIST 800–53 [2] or the UL2900 series [3]? Does the MDM intend to comply with them too? One should remember that once a decision is taken to formally comply with a standard, one has to continuously monitor compliance else one runs the risk of being written up by an auditor. Unfortunately, decisions to comply with standards are sometimes taken without first considering the cost of maintaining compliance by personnel who are not authorized to approve the resultant financial load on the organization's resources. Besides standards cited by regulatory bodies, there are IT cybersecurity standards (e.g. ISO/IEC 27001 [4] for infrastructure, FedRAMP [5] for cloud deployments, and HITRUST [6] for data privacy) that MDMs need to comply with in order to satisfy customer requirements and corporate IT policies. Decisions should be made as to which of these standards are to be tracked through QMS compliance processes and which through IT governance processes that exist outside the QMS. Usually, regulations and regulatory guidance are tracked through the QMS because the QMS is what regulators audit, while general IT cybersecurity standards are tracked outside the QMS through the IT governance process.

Method for defining and maintaining mapping from regulations, standards, and guidance to set of technical and procedural controls that drive capability development

Once the set of regulations, standards, and guidance to be complied with are chosen, methods need to be defined to distill them down to a control catalog. A control catalog is a set of technical and procedural controls with traceability to clauses and sentences of regulations, guidance, and standards from which they originate.

Different standards sometimes refer to the same requirement using different language. At the other extreme, sometimes standards refer to requirements that on the surface look the same, but are not exactly the same (the devil they say is in the details). Finally, different standards are often at different levels of abstraction, some very high-level to some that are extremely prescriptive. Breaking them down to a manageable set of technical and procedural controls requires thought and effort, as does maintaining the control catalog as regulations, guidance, and standards evolve.

Method for gap and noncompliance assessment

When the decision is taken to comply with a new regulation or guidance or a standard, the QMS must be evaluated to assess the gap between the state of practice and the requirements of whatever regulation, guidance, or standard the QMS is endeavoring to comply with.

A realistic gap assessment should not just be about finding gaps in existing processes and policies—after all, people say the right thing in official documents all the time. It should also assess how those processes are currently being implemented, whether records of process execution are being kept, and whether the execution of the processes captures their regulatory and standards intent. Trying to add more compliance requirements to a system that is already noncompliant is a recipe for disaster.

One of the best ways of evaluating current practice is through cybersecurity audits. Before a major QMS update for cybersecurity, a cybersecurity audit should be performed, not just to evaluate *gaps* with the regulations, guidance, and standards to which compliance is being planned, but also *noncompliances* to the regulations, guidance, and standards that the QMS currently claims compliance with.

Method for gap and noncompliance remediation

Gaps between the QMS and the new regulation, guidance, or standard should be fixed through definition and execution of a Quality Plan. A Quality Plan is a set of tasks, set on a timeline and with resources allocated, that lays out activities that need to be performed in order to bring a QMS to comply with a new regulation, guidance, or standard. These activities could be related to defining new processes, procuring or developing new tools, or staffing up to be able to execute the updated QMS.

Noncompliances on the other hand should lead to cybersecurity Corrective and Preventive Actions (CAPAs). Noncompliances can be the following:

- *Process noncompliance*: This kind of noncompliance occurs when procedural controls imperfectly capture the intent of the regulations, guidance, and standards to which compliance is being claimed. For example, if compliance to FDA 2016 [7] postmarket cybersecurity guidance is being claimed, and yet, there is no requirement in the QMS to patch in case risk to patient safety is evaluated to be "Uncontrolled," that should be captured as a process noncompliance.
- *People noncompliance*: This kind of noncompliance occurs when processes are not being executed properly because of lack of training or lack of resources. For example, training records of individual engineers show that they were not trained on the cybersecurity processes they have executed.

- *Tool noncompliance*: This kind of noncompliance occurs when absence of proper tools leads to execution gaps. For example, consider the result of an audit in which cybersecurity requirements are being consistently traced to the wrong cybersecurity test cases. It's not that the processes stipulating such traceability do not exist, nor is it the case that the process execution is being done by people without sufficient training or background to execute the task. The root cause for the noncompliance is that requirements and test cases are being maintained as Excel documents. This makes difficult the maintenance of traceability across various artifacts, in that when someone changes something in one document the other document is not automatically updated.

Remediation plans for such noncompliance are a part of a CAPA investigation process, and progress and resource allocation is tracked through the CAPA process.

Defining and maintaining roles and responsibilities

How are roles and responsibilities for different cybersecurity activities defined and, even more importantly, how are they maintained? Delineating functional responsibilities for cybersecurity in a large MDM is frequently contentious, in that every function often ends up feeling they are underresourced for the responsibilities they have been signed onto. And that is just the easy part. Functions are reorganized, functional priorities are recalibrated, what could have been the role of one function may now have become another's. People leave the organization and the next person may not have been informed of their specific role for cybersecurity.

All of this organizational movement and evolution leads to the degeneration of the roles and responsibilities document. What is the result? The day a major cybersecurity incident happens, no one knows who to call, or bring into the war room. Decisions regarding project planning or product design are taken without involvement of all appropriate stakeholders. Overall, product security governance suffers.

It is thus important to capture as part of the strategy process, maintenance activities for the roles and responsibilities document. This includes periodic review of the roles and responsibility document with different stakeholders. Even more importantly, one should conduct table top exercises [8,9]. In such exercises, real situations are simulated (e.g., an external researcher makes a presentation at a security conference disclosing a critical cybersecurity vulnerability, someone calls into the call center claiming that they suspect someone hacked into the device and killed a patient) and organizational response observed. The purpose of regular tabletop exercises is to ensure that individuals within an organization remain aware of their roles and responsibilities at all time and have the proper resources at hand to discharge them.

Cybersecurity management review

Regular audits are not the only way for evaluating the health of a QMS. Management review is a QMS practice in which metrics of different types are collected and presented to executive management as a means of tracking how well a QMS is meeting its quality objectives. Procedural controls for cybersecurity management review should define the following:

Operational metrics

Example of operational metrics an MDM should track as part of management review for cybersecurity:

- Number of open cybersecurity CAPAs
- Number of cybersecurity Quality Plan activities whose deadlines have expired, but the output deliverables of the activity have not been incorporated into the QMS
- Number of medical devices in postmarket phase that have uncontrolled risk and have not been patched
- For cybersecurity patches for medical devices in the field, the patch adoption rate

Design metrics

Example of design metrics an MDM should track as part of management review for cybersecurity:

- For every medical device, number of cybersecurity system threats that are not mitigated by a primary control in the system cybersecurity risk model
- Number of medical devices that have uncontrolled risk items in its system risk model that have been resolved by a Risk Benefit Analysis
- Number of medical devices that fail to implement, totally or partially, a technical control from the master set of technical controls.

Standards and regulatory compliance

For medical devices, creating a secure design is not enough; one has to be able to explain to a third-party auditor as to why a design reduces patient safety and privacy risk to acceptable levels. Even with a device design that is best in class with regards to cybersecurity, an MDM runs the risk of going through seemingly endless rounds of regulatory clarifications, audits and reaudits, and even denial if the cybersecurity assurance argument is not solidly presented. The Standards and Regulatory Compliance capability is responsible for putting together the cybersecurity portion of the regulatory submission to different regulatory agencies. It is also responsible for answering regulatory questions on cybersecurity, and executing annual reporting requirements on cybersecurity. This capability is responsible for defining, maintaining, and executing the following procedural control:

Regulatory submissions

One of their principal complaints regulators across the world have is that they are often buried under a mass of documentation provided by the MDM as part of a regulatory submission, with no clear map of why these documents have been provided and what they establish. It is thus in the best interests of both regulators and MDMs to structure regulatory submissions in a standard semantic format that unambiguously articulates *how* the different components fit together to form the assurance argument.

An assurance case [10,11] is a semantic structure that has been used for decades to construct safety arguments for system of systems [12]. The fundamental principle [13] of an assurance case is that it establishes how a given claim is supported by evidence collected to assess the claim [14]. An assurance case has a tree-like structure, with claims labeling (internal) nodes and evidence labeling leaf nodes, with the top-level goal or claim as the root (see Fig. 9.1 to understand how an assurance case looks like). This root claim is typically decomposed into several subclaims, which may

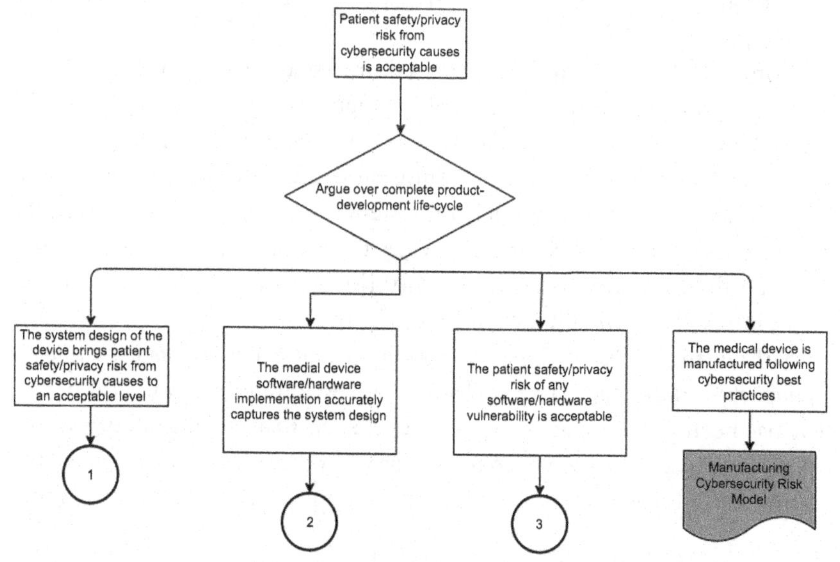

Figure 9.1 Top-level security assurance case.

themselves be decomposed until conclusive evidence is provided that establishes the leaves (i.e., the simplest and lowest level subclaims). Once that is accomplished, the root claim is automatically established [15].

As their name suggests, security assurance cases are intended to be assurance case arguments for the security of a system. Since assurance cases for safety have been recommended by the FDA through guidance documents for infusion pump safety [16], using assurance cases for cybersecurity is a natural next step.

For this book, claims/subclaims are graphically represented as rectangular boxes, and evidence nodes as gray polygons.

The root claim for the security assurance case is that Patient safety/privacy risk from cybersecurity causes is acceptable (as seen in Fig. 9.1). In order to establish this, we argue that over the entire development lifecycle of the device, patient safety/privacy risk from cybersecurity causes is acceptable. This leads to a decomposition of the root claim to the following four subclaims:

Subclaim 1: *The system design of the device brings patient safety/privacy risk from cybersecurity causes to an acceptable level:* Subclaim 1 ensures that system was designed in a way such that patient safety/privacy risk from system level threats is adequately controlled.

In order to establish this claim, the MDM needs to establish two lower-level subclaims (or more accurately sub-sub-claims) as seen in Fig. 9.2. These are the following:

1. Subclaim 1A: All system threats were identified
2. Subclaim 1B: Patient safety/privacy risk due to system threats is acceptable

Both Subclaim 1A and Subclaim 1B are established through evidence nodes, i.e., documents that are part of the regulatory submission, specifically the system threat model and the system cybersecurity risk model, respectively. Through this structure of claim—sub—claim—evidence, the reason why a system-level threat model and system level cybersecurity risk model are established and now the regulator has to be convinced of the evidence (i.e., the threat model and cybersecurity risk model are correct and complete) in order to formally establish Subclaim 1.

Subclaim 2: *The medical device software/hardware implementation accurately captures the system design:* In Subclaim 1, we established the medical device that has been designed at the system level such that patient safety/privacy risk is controlled. Now we need to establish that the design whose "veracity" we just established is implemented faithfully in device software/hardware.

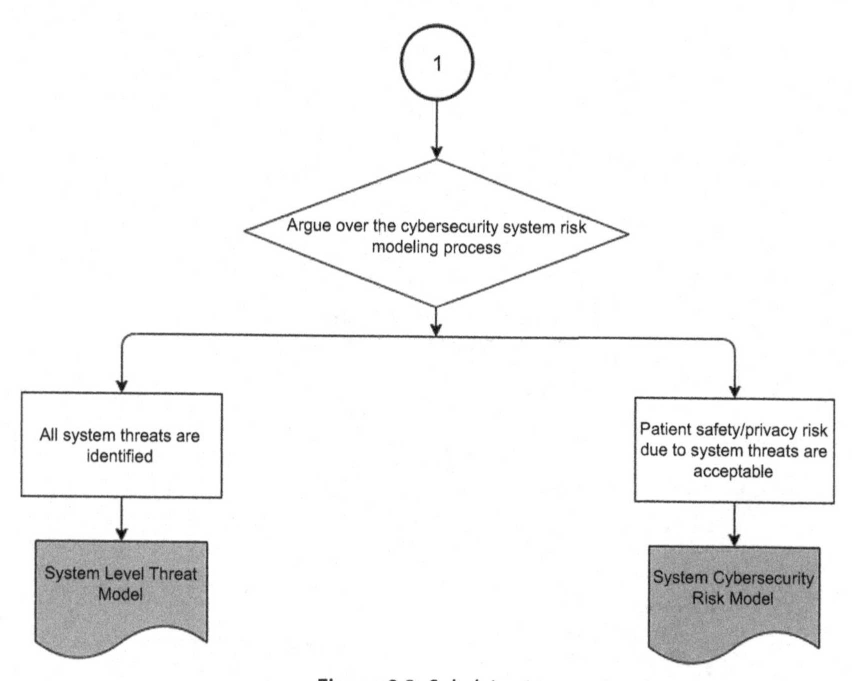

Figure 9.2 Subclaim 1.

Without this step, a critic can well point out "Okay, so you have established through Subclaim 1 that your design is secure, but how do we know that the device implements that design?"

In order to establish this, Subclaim 2 is broken into two further subclaims as shown in Fig. 9.3.

1. Subclaim 2A: All risk responses in the system cybersecurity risk model are mapped to design input
2. Subclaim 2B: All design input used as system cybersecurity risk responses are verified

Subclaim 2A is established through an evidence node which contains a traceability matrix between risk responses used as part of Subclaim 1B to design input, i.e., system and software/hardware requirements. This ensures that the requirements from which the implementation is built off are the ones that are used for risk responses for system threats. Subclaim 2B ensures that the final software and hardware implementation of the device satisfies the design input. The evidence of this is provided by requirements verification plans and results, where the requirements are the ones that were traced to as part of Subclaim 2A.

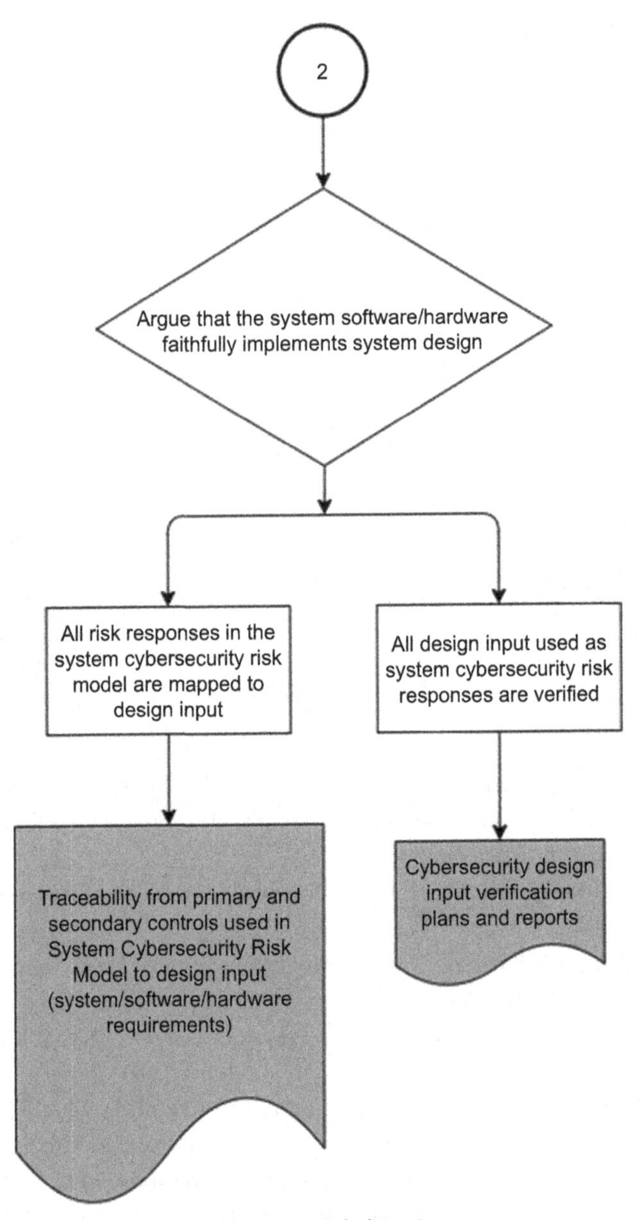

Figure 9.3 Subclaim 2.

Subclaim 3: *The patient safety/privacy risk of any software/hardware vulnerability is acceptable:* So far, we have established, through Subclaim 1, that the design is secure, and, then through Subclaim 2, that the design is faithfully implemented in the device. We still have to prove that no "off-requirements" insecure behavior has been introduced as a result of vulnerable software and hardware components. Subclaim 3 takes care of that.

It is split into two subclaims as shown in Fig. 9.4.

1. Subclaim 3A: All software/hardware vulnerabilities and threats are identified
2. Subclaim 3B: Patient safety/privacy risk due to subsystem (software/hardware) threats are acceptable

Subclaim 3A is established by providing as evidence as a Cybersecurity Bill of Materials with every third-party hardware and software component used, annotated with open vulnerabilities, as well as penetration test results. Subclaim 3B is established by providing as evidence the subsystem (software and hardware) risk model and the system risk model, in case system-level risk responses are used as mitigators for unpatched subsystem vulnerabilities.

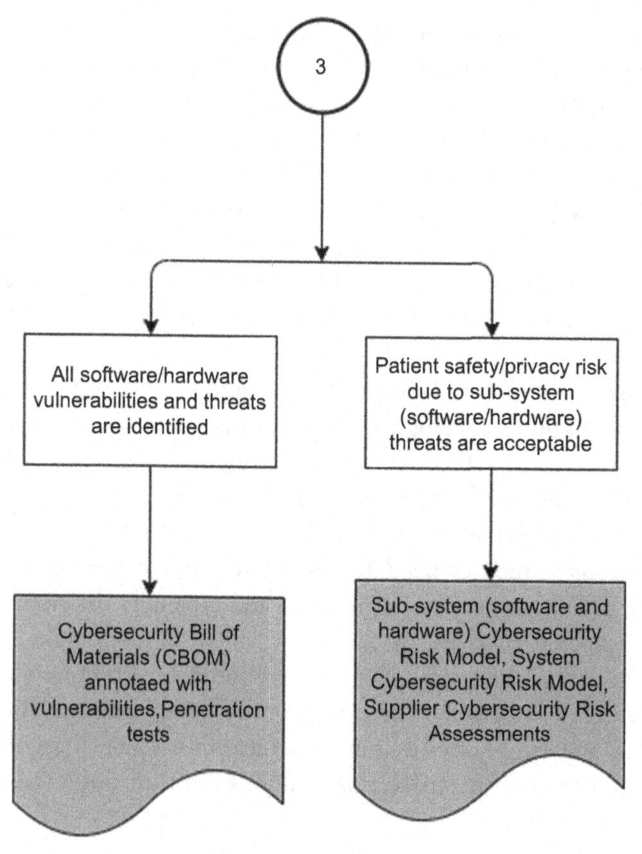

Figure 9.4 Subclaim 3.

Subclaim 4: *The medical device is manufactured following cybersecurity best practices.* This claim is established by providing as evidence the manufacturing cybersecurity risk model (as per Fig. 9.1).

In summary, by structuring out a submission through a security assurance case, the argument for assurance becomes more explicit, with both MDMs and regulators move from a document centric, checklist approach to one that is more semantically structured. Now, rather than the MDM providing documents to a regulator just because the regulator asked for it, they get to see why that document is needed, and how it supports the overall assurance argument. The structure of the assurance case also helps the regulator to "surf" through a cybersecurity submission and quickly focus on critical portions of the assurance argument.

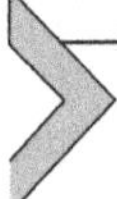

Summary and key takeaways

The key takeaways from this chapter are the following:

1. Governance for product cybersecurity should periodically assess cybersecurity regulations, customer requirements, and standards to evaluate which of these the business wants to comply with, this decision being taken considering the costs of compliance.
2. Before integrating the new regulation/requirements/standards, the QMS should be evaluated with an audit to ensure that the QMS, as it exists today, complies with all regulations/standards/requirements it claims to. Building on top of a noncompliant QMS is best avoided.
3. Organizational roles and responsibilities should be defined and signed-off on, with an understanding that organizational knowledge of roles and responsibilities atrophies over time. Specific maintenance activities like tabletop exercises need to be performed to ensure that incident response happens the way they are supposed to.
4. Cybersecurity metrics need to be defined and collected in order to ensure that the cybersecurity program and capability development/maintenance is effective.
5. Cybersecurity regulatory submissions should be structured to enable regulators to understand the cybersecurity design without the need for a to-and-fro of questions and clarifications between regulators and MDMs. One way of structuring a submission is through the use of assurance cases.

References

[1] National Institiure of Standards and Technologies, Framework for Improving for Critical Infrastructure Cybersecurity, 2018.

[2] US National Institute of Standards and Technologies, Security and Privacy Controls for Information Systems and Organizations SP 800-53, 2020.

[3] Underwriter Labs, Standard for Software Cybersecurity for Network-Connectable Products, Part 2-1: Particular Requirements for Network Connectable Components of Healthcare and Wellness Systems, 2017.

[4] ISO/IEC Information Technology Task Force (ITTF), ISO/IEC 27001 Information Technology — Security Techniques — Information Security Management Systems — Requirements, ISO, 2013.

[5] The Federal Risk and Authorization Management Program, Program Basics, n.d. [Online]. Available: https://www.fedramp.gov/program-basics/.

[6] HITRUST Alliance, HITRUST Cybersecurity Framework, n.d. [Online]. Available: https://hitrustalliance.net/product-tool/hitrust-csf/.

[7] US Food and Drug Administration, Postmarket Management of Cybersecurity in Medical Devices (Final Version), December 2016 [Online]. Available: https://www.fda.gov/regulatory-information/search-fda-guidance-documents/postmarket-management-cybersecurity-medical-devices. (Accessed 1 September 2020).

[8] The MITRE Corporation, CyberExercise PlayBook, November 2014 [Online]. Available: https://www.mitre.org/sites/default/files/publications/pr_14-3929-cyber-exercise-playbook.pdf.

[9] US National Institute of Standards and Technologies, Special Publication 800-84 Guide to Test, Training, and Exercise Programs for IT Plans and Capabilities, 2006.

[10] T. Kelly, Arguing Safety: A Systematic Approach to Managing Safety Cases, 1999.

[11] A. Ray, R. Cleaveland, Constructing safety assurance cases for medical devices, in: 1st International Workshop on Assurance Cases for Software-Intensive Systems (ASSURE), 2013.

[12] M. Bishop, P. Bloomfield, A methodology for safety case development, in: Sixth Safety Critical Systems Symposium: Industrial Perspectives on System Safety (Springer), 1998.

[13] C. Weinstock, J. Goodenough, Towards an assurance case practice for medical devices, in: Carnegie Mellon University, Pittsburgh, Pennsylvania, Technical Note CMU/SEI-2009-TN-018, 2009.

[14] A. Ray, Assurance cases: their use today and the challenges ahead, Biomed. Instrum. Technol. 46 (3) (2012) 195—200.

[15] A. Ray, A. Cleaveland, Security assurance cases for medical cyber—physical systems, IEEE Design & Test 32 (2015) 56—65.

[16] US Food and Drug Administration, Infusion Pumps Total Product Life Cycle Guidance for Industry and FDA Staff, 2014.

Afterword

Cybersecurity is a journey, not a destination. While this may be a well-worn cliché, that does not make it any the less true. As new technologies emerge and become standardized, so do new threats. As new countermeasures are designed, attackers react and adapt.

In this perpetual ebb and flow between attackers and defenses, what can you do today in order to prepare for the future cybersecurity landscape? While I don't claim to have a crystal ball, let me leave you with some closing thoughts:

1. Increased focus on the supply chain: Over the past few years, various industries have been subject to compromise through their supply chains. Here, it's not you that first got breached, but one of your suppliers. Since you have an implicit relationship of trust with your supplier, the attack now expands to your organization and its products.
   Supply chain attacks can be through device components with seeded vulnerabilities, or through malicious third-party software/hardware used in the development or operational environment, where the software/hardware was compromised at the vendor. Traditional methods of supply chain risk assessment usually do not factor in cybersecurity and, even when they do, as outlined in Chapter 8 of this book, there can never really be the kind of oversight that is possible on one's own products. One may have conducted a supplier cybersecurity risk assessment at the time of procurement, focusing on both the vendor as well as the component. However, how do you know subsequent changes to a vendor's system don't introduce vulnerabilities into your environment? One can of course mandate a cybersecurity-heavy validation process for any updated supplier component before it is deployed (e.g. executable-level analysis for any component that is updated). This becomes infeasible though when you are dealing with hundreds, maybe thousands of components continuously being provided functional and cybersecurity updates. With the direction laid out by US President Joe Biden's executive order in 2021, one can anticipate increased regulatory and customer scrutiny on this aspect of healthcare. Innovative strategies and technologies would have to be defined for a more robust and a more real-time supply chain cybersecurity risk assessment that is, at the same time, cost-effective to implement and maintain.

2. Operational resilience as an aspect of safety: The traditional focus of cybersecurity for medical devices has been on protecting the individual patient from clinical harm. This notion of safety, many in the industry now feel, needs to be expanded. Attackers are not motivated solely by motives of "let us try to harm a specific individual with a lethal shock or an overdose of a drug," or "let us sell patient records on the dark web," but also "let us harm the people of a nation by targeting the operations of its critical industries" and "let us try to extort money by taking control of some aspect of business operations." Since medical device manufacturers form a vital part of a nation's critical infrastructure, their operational integrity falls squarely in the cross-hairs of such threat actors. In response to these threats, cybersecurity activities which previously only concerned themselves with controlling risks related to patient safety must be expanded to encompass enterprise, manufacturing, and distribution infrastructure (see Chapters 5 and 6).
3. Cybersecurity for AI/ML systems: An industry trend that has truly taken off in the past few years is the use of artificial intelligence (AI) and machine learning (ML) to personalize therapies and extract clinical insights. However, the use of AI/ML opens up medical devices to new classes of threats. Attackers can now poison the learning process so that the system "learns wrong" (e.g., an attack may constitute providing an ML model an intentionally mislabeled data set), or outputs "something wrong" (e.g., introducing noise in a X-Ray image such that the modified X-Ray image is indistinguishable to the human eye, but when it is input to an AI/ML system, the system does not detect a tumor, where it would have, had it been shown the unaltered X-Ray image). There are also fundamental definitional challenges to cybersecurity when the behavior of a system is allowed to change dynamically (i.e., systems that use online learning). In such cases, how does one know whether a sequence of "puzzling" actions is an indicator of compromise or just legitimately learned behavior? How well medical device manufacturers implement defenses against adversarial ML will be critical in determining the confidence that regulators and clinical professionals will have in such medical AI/ML systems.

Finally, thank you for reading this book. I hope that I succeeded, to an extent at least, in achieving what I had set out to do—to provide a workable approach for defining and executing cybersecurity capabilities for a medical device manufacturer.

Index

Note: 'Page numbers followed by "f" indicate figures and "t" indicate tables.'

T

U

V

W

Z

Printed in the United States
by Baker & Taylor Publisher Services